ai - *a*pplied *i*ntelligence
New *Thinking* for Caribbean Prosperity in the 21st Century

ai

PERRY C. DOUGLAS

DouglasBlackwell Media Inc.
Writing Our Own Stories

ai

applied intelligence

To SaMaggie, Evadney, Sheila, & Petal–
the women who made me

Preface

Black history has been filled with trauma, which has confused and distracted our psyche. We have been dragged and left at the bottom of the universe, yet we still have the internal power to rise. We have choices in how we think and act, and no one can ever take that capacity away from us. Our time in the universe is infinitesimal. Our history is only approximately 400 years long, so we have far more upside than downside remaining to us. We must therefore look up instead of down and keep making progress; nothing is ever predetermined, and there is no such thing as "fate." Life is what you make of it, and the biggest challenge we face is overcoming ourselves. There must be no boundaries in the mind; but first, we must understand the true nature of the universe and how it works.

The world is about power, and although it is a large world, very few individuals and groups run it, and at the top of it lies a complex financial system dominated by people. The ecology of the universe has underlying systems of interactions in personal relationships that dominate—this is nature. Hierarchical structures and behavioural networks are the nature of humanity forming mutually beneficial relationships, including power networks and groups. The mutually beneficial objective now becomes the consolation of power, erecting barriers, but especially to protect and expand what they already possess, for the group's mutual security. This behaviour centers on self-preservation, which goes back to human hunter-gatherer days when humans joined together into tribes to claim territory in which they could hunt and gather for survival; this is fundamental in nature.

In the modern world, technology, finance, and globalization have added tremendously to the complexity of human nature; nevertheless, though times may have changed, human nature remains the same. Therefore, we should approach the universe by understanding its complexity first, with the understanding that nature will always stand as the common denominator in the universe. Nothing can be more powerful than nature! Therefore, finding and expanding on our intellectual selves and reducing our emotional selves would be very advantageous in our journey in nature. Also, we must clearly recognize that our survival and ability to thrive in the universe greatly depends on our ability to interact, cooperate, and simply get along with others. This is the human system—this is nature.

Although we tend to look to institutions to solve our problems or to shoulder the blame for those problems, institutions are merely where power plays out through real people operating in those institutions. Fundamentally, all systems are human-based, and both problems and solutions come down to human problem-solving. Therefore, access to institutions provides some access to power centres that influence our lives—power resides there. The nature of the universe revolves around small groups of individuals having a significant amount of power over other people and over systems that they themselves created and continue to support intergenerationally; this is how power flows. In this increasingly globalized world, these elite individuals, and groups—those who run large multinational corporations and multinational financial institutions such as large hedge funds—dominate the world. They influence wealth and inequality everywhere.

Therefore, understanding human relationships requires the application of intellect. It also requires emotional intelligence, because understanding networks and human systems quantitatively is key to successfully navigating your way through the universe.

Also, understanding your competitive advantages along with knowing the *winning playbook* is significant. It is imperative to know who the key players are and how the game is played! Understanding human interactions on the micro level while being hyper-conscious of the overriding macro environment; is essential to getting what you desire from life. This requires the application of intelligent thinking and not emotion or intuition. Understanding the complexity of human relationships, system architecture, and the way power flows is important for you to understand how to develop your own flow, your own power networks—to further your own ambitions successfully. The better you understand nature, the better will be your chances of succeeding within it; it is crucial to understand that power is intrinsic to the laws of nature. In other words, power *is* nature. Therefore, the quest for power is part of the human species' need for security, often achieved through wealth creation. Economic power then leads to political influence, privilege, power, and better justice outcomes for your group. As in ecology, organisms tend to expand by learning how first to survive and then to thrive in their ecosystem; human systems are very much the same.

Therefore, it is important for the survival of Caribbean peoples of African descent to seek power and align with powerful networks, because we cannot survive on our own. We need powerful links with other like-minded people who also understand how the universe works. We then need to interact and form mutually beneficial relationships with outer powerful groups in the universe—staying away from non-powerful groups. This is how we will achieve growth and power in the universe. Do not be deluded;

6

wealth is power, and good connections and relationships grow your power exponentially. The real power comes from the bottom up, through economics, not from the top down, through politics. Bottom-up growth is also how equity is created—through entrepreneurship. Wealth is the currency of power!

Those who have the currency spread the wealth, but only within their own groups. The laws of nature create a gravitational pull attracting others with wealth and like-mindedness. The levers of power in the world, at this time, remain largely in the hands of white male networks. Their domination of global capital flows determines what is important and what is invested in. They are *"the system."*

How the world works comes down to the laws of nature—the power of real, omnipresent networks, powered by human relationships that institutionalize power dynamics and outcomes. It superimposes informal structures around *capital, information, and opportunities*; that is what dominates our lives. Money is transformational, and profoundly influences any society; but the flipside of wealth is inequality and suffering. Therefore, by knowing how the universe works, you can decide how best to play it in your own best interest.

It is critical to understand the homogeneous character of nature, where people of shared backgrounds tend to coalesce, whether they be economic, social, or political groups, birds of a feather flock together. Historically, businesses have always formed via family and other networks within social classes, and the enterprise and its main shareholders become all-powerful. Their family, friends, and network associates benefit from that power, which in turn drives their privilege—there is always an inherent head start for those within this circle. The opportunities continue because wealth translates into attending the best schools and universities. Is it any wonder that so many financial leaders–the wealthiest individuals, investment firms, and banks–land directly on Wall Street? These individuals largely come from the Ivy League and other elite universities—Harvard,

Princeton, Yale, Stanford, and the Massachusetts Institute of Technology (MIT), as well as their elite business schools. They get there through wealth and privilege—the best schools, tutors, letters of recommendation, and corruption, of course. Have you ever heard Jared Kushner, Donald Trump's son-in-law, speak in public? He does not have a reputation for being the smartest person in the room; yet he got into Harvard nonetheless. Could it be that Jared's father pledged $2.5 million before Jared sent in his "application?" Well, essentially, that is the nature of power and privilege and how the universe really works. The world is not a meritocracy.

The reality is that nature rules the world, and those who can develop and expand on their self-interest and privilege will continue the concentration of their group's economic influence, which translates into political influence, which translates into POWER! So, you have a fundamental choice to make if you want to succeed in the real world. You must first accept the laws of nature as reigning supreme in the metaphysical world, then develop your playbook accordingly to get to where you want to go, in your infinitesimal time and place in the universe.

In the end, where Black people are concerned, progress is less about fighting racism and more about understanding the **Sophistication of Self-Preservation | SSP.**

applied intelligence

CONTENTS

Introduction   12

Prologue 1   22

Prologue 2   51

Chapter 1: The Nature of Economics   79

Chapter 2: Beyond Theories   107

Chapter 3: applied intelligence   130

Chapter 4: The Value of applied intelligence   153

Chapter 5: Individuals and Societies   174

Chapter 6: The Decade of Transition   196

Chapter 7: Quantitative Thinking &the Racism Disorder   220

Chapter 8: Real Truth Behind European Wealth Creation.   256

Chapter 9: Economics | Decision Making   285

Chapter 10: Food, Money & Power   299

Chapter 11: The Economics of Racism   329

Chapter 12: Do Not Blame China   352

Chapter 13: The Power Transition   365

Chapter 14: Caribentricity   379

Chapter 15: The Fierce Change of the Digital Now   393

Chapter 16: Emerging Markets Industrial Engineering   419

Chapter 17: Knowledge is the New Money   441

Chapter 18: In Long-Time   451

Chapter 19: Success is a Mindset   470

Chapter 20: You Simply Cannot Get Around It...   485

Chapter 21: Purpose & Wealth   505

Chapter 22: Talk & Ideology   514

Chapter 23: The Required Disruption Culture   537

Chapter 24: The Way Forward   550

Epilogue   563

PART I

Introduction

Thinking is what the mind does—all the time, even during sleep. Nonetheless, one of the great mysteries of the universe is to know how the mind actually thinks. Neuroscience has not figured out how the mind moves between consciousness and subconsciousness. So when it comes to thinking, we can only deduce through experience that our thinking can lead us down one of two paths, to either happiness or suffering; and that is what life comes down to in the end. Our journey in life then ranges between our experiences on these two paths, and all the events, trials, and tribulations we experience lead us to one or the other. Therefore, we exist only in nature, and nature does not know who we are, what we think, or how we might feel because nature is nature, and nature can only do what nature *is*. So it is up to us to understand the absolute certainty of nature and how we can best relate and manage ourselves successfully in our one time and place in nature. Nature is the truth, what we can rely on; it is the bedrock of reality. We humans are only some of the parts of matter that make up nature, its diverse particles and materials—like the soil and gravel that make up the bedrock.

Our challenge in life as a human species is to see nature for what it is and not for what we wish it to be. Navigating the world based on the reality of what it is is critical to our successful existence. Therefore, we must examine the use of our emotions and intelligence, sort out the usefulness of each, and carve the optimal path to the life we desire. Which one is better to live a happy life—emotion or intelligence? Is emotion good or bad? Are our emotions not really "emotional" at all, or can they be useful—but only when governed by our intelligence?

In the teachings of the Buddha, it is taught that what one ponders will become one's inclination. The teachings called for the training of the mind to be more in control of the desired outcomes because the untrained mind leads to troubles. The ancient Stoics, such as the Roman philosopher Seneca, also taught us that everything hinges on how we think. Both tell us that we are what we think, and our thoughts make the world. Therefore, our intelligence is our one true superpower, but we often allow ourselves to weaken our intelligence by becoming slaves to our emotions, which does not work. Poor, unsound thinking, overreliance on emotions and intuition, lack of logic, dramatic thinking, etc.—call it what you like, but the result usually leads to suffering.

In the globalized and technology-based world of the 21st century, the level and sophistication of our thinking and the flexing of our intelligence have never been so crucial for developing our prosperity curve, which is ultimately shaped by the degree of the efficient application of our intelligence. Therefore, an unfocused and distracted mind is dangerous to one's very existence. Happiness is not a given; it requires a foundation of sound thought and a clear understanding of the laws of nature and of how things function in an entangled and conflict-driven universe. Accordingly, mindfulness, awareness, and the practice of consciousness are all prerequisites for optimal thinking towards happiness. Knowing how to identify and avoid distractions requires the conscious application of intelligence. Relying on the subconscious mind is not the optimal use of human intelligence. Dependency on the subconscious is an experienced-based, emotional, and intuitive existence which is not optimal for success and happiness in the universe.

The Buddha, once again, tells us that before we can become wise, we must know how to control and manage our thinking, which is the true path to enlightenment. So our time must be spent on understanding the processes and dynamics of good thinking, and how our environments and experiences can shape our thinking patterns. Awareness of that fact is key to good thinking, actions, and outcomes. And how you optimize your mind to get the outcomes you want is the most fundamental and natural function of human progress, yet we are often not even consciously aware of that. We become lazy and rely on our emotionally driven and experience-based subconscious minds. However, you can only bend your prosperity curve through the conscious, intelligent mind. And so it is for Caribbean people of African descent. A good thinking system is paramount for our progress towards economic success and ultimate happiness—to release ourselves from the suffering we have endured for far too long now. Therefore, the beginning of the end of suffering starts with the application of *applied intelligence* in our lives, an intelligent framework for decision-making and critical thinking, which is critical for our prosperity in the 21st century.

So regardless of the changing times, self-interest remains steadfastly embedded in our human condition. This is the nature of things; but without the sophisticated application of our intelligence function, we will simply carry the burden of those who are applying intelligence. Because those who apply intelligence have a significant advantage over those who lead with emotion, the application of intelligence achieves things and emotion usual frets about things. Self-interest, individual gain, is the bedrock force of our human progression. It plays a core, functional role in harnessing our efficiency and productivity; it is how we create our value. Critical understanding of the laws of nature, both the physical and the cognitive, is the core imperative that has driven successful civilizations over time. Therefore, a good understanding of the laws of nature—of the universe—is central to any individual or group navigating their way through the rough seas of life. If, however, we fail to understand the workings of the universe and its innate natural functionality, then how can we find our footing and pathways through it?

And so, in our metaphysical existence as a species, as Caribbean people of African descent, the shaping of our real-world success must come down to pursuing what we want most and finding those useful utilities and functions that can help us get things done. Therefore, *applied intelligence* must lead our new thinking in the 21st century—to a Renaissance in Caribbean Thinking, which is the first step to a future by design.

This book seeks to be honest; it stays away from distracting, emotional, lazy, and convenient storytelling explanations about the workings of the universe. It focuses instead on what is true and what is real in the universe. It also builds towards a culture of intelligence and high performance, putting self-interest and self-preservation as primary and value creation as the underlying driver of our need for security, through the very necessary pursuit of wealth and power in the universe. So what this book is doing is nothing new; frankly, it is ancient, and it concerns the age-old question about the fulfillment of life. Much of that thought has been attributed to the ancient philosophy of Stoicism coming out of ancient Greece; however, much of that same thought can be found in Eastern and African philosophy too. Unfortunately, in the Western world, dominated by Eurocentric ideas, people have come to believe wrongly that "the West" is responsible for all that is civilized, and for setting standards for civilization. The reality is that most have not read beyond Western thought and literature to understand the truth.

Nevertheless, this book's purpose is to turn thinking into action effectively. It is about forming a reliable system of thought that can inform actions through the realities of the universe: physics and a system of logical thought, because to think is the very nature of our being. Moreover, doing it better than most will get us results better than most, and this is the nature of *applied intelligence*. So the applied intelligence system is one of discipline that forces us to ask ourselves

15

difficult questions about our existence, our place in the universe, and how we can find our happiness.

Therefore, if the ultimate goal of human existence is to find happiness, then it is only logical that we must understand the universe, how it works, and how to relate to it, in order to plot our path to that happiness. There is no magic-bullet answer that we need to seek, because none exists; so we are not going to waste time on something that does not exist. This book is not about philosophy; it is more about practicality. It is simply about knowing ourselves and our place in the universe—about your own values, not those of the herd, in fulfilling your life and happiness. So a major part of thinking is how to stay away from distractions that can negatively affect your life, and this is why the book works to draw a clearly-thought-out distinction between the optimal, intelligence-based, thinking path instead of the suboptimal, emotional path in life.

As the ancient Roman emperor and Stoic philosopher Marcus Aurelius wrote: "The happiness of your life depends upon the quality of your thoughts." Therefore, it is only sensible that the best-quality thoughts come from our intelligence. None of what Aurelius wrote was philosophy; it was practical and addressed nature. However, thinkers like Aurelius are often quoted out of context and misunderstood by those looking for quick, easy answers.

In an article about Marcus Aurelius, writer Steven Gambardella, PhD, listed many of his quotes and sought to explain their meaning. However, from my perspective, all of the quotes listed were not "philosophy;" they were his simple explanation of nature and those laws in nature that cannot be anything other than what they are. And this goes to the crux of this book: that we exist in nature and
we cannot defy or fool nature, and not accepting the laws of nature is highly emotional and foolish which will lead to non-success and unfulfilled life.

Here are a few of Marcus Aurelius' quotes from Gambardella's article:

"All things are linked with one another, and this oneness is sacred."

"Everything that happens happens as it should, and if you observe carefully, you will find this to be so."

"You have power over your mind — not outside events. Realize this, and you will find strength."

"The impediment to action advances action. What stands in the way becomes the way."

"Everything we hear is an opinion, not a fact. Everything we see is a perspective, not the truth."

"…the infallible man does not exist."

As you can see, he is simply explaining nature, how to relate to it, and how to make it work for you.

Applying intelligence to decision-making and the long-term impact that those decisions can have has been the focus of my writing. Additionally, the book seeks to provide insight as to how long-term quantitative thinking can be most optimally beneficial in those pursuits, as intelligence is a core embedded functionality in quantitative thinking. In fact, we are essentially useless without the proper application of our human intelligence. Our thinking must also be inclusive and make room for the broader implications of our decisions, because every decision—or indecision—matters.

If you conduct yourself in a manner that does not benefit you in the future, you are building towards a future of nothingness, living in delusion. We must think of ourselves as individuals with the understanding that we are a dynamic part of a whole, and our actions always matter to our community. Decisions have a frequency in the universe, and when that frequency develops strength from within, it can send powerful signals out into an entangled world. It is of paramount importance, therefore, that we build strong frequencies and entanglements, remaining highly focused on what is being done and what we must do next.

Therefore, as Black people of African descent, we have a moral obligation and responsibility to think and behave intelligently, enterprisingly, resiliently, and powerfully, because so many of our ancestors have suffered enormously and paid an unimaginable price. We owe it to them and to our future generations to do our absolute best in our relative time and place in this universe—to build prosperous existences and shape desirable intergenerational opportunities.

However, to be effective means strengthening oneself with a view to also strengthening the whole. So the pursuit of self-interest cannot be narrow-minded, because when each part of the group engages in self-preservation, their frequencies go out to the whole, strengthening it and pushing it forward. This broader understanding of individualism and community is essential and symbiotic.

Accordingly, to understand the complexities in this world, we must rely on our intellect, on scientific approaches, using mathematics and physics as underlying guides to reality. And we must get a firm grip on the relative first principles that apply to the problems we are trying to solve. We must separate objective truths from philosophy and focus on math and physics because the **universe is math,** and so logic must prevail. We must focus our minds, looking for what is true and what is not true about the universe. This is the underlying approach taken by *applied intelligence.* Readers must leave their intuition and feelings at the door, keep open minds, and rely on intellectualism while seeking objective truths.

The central problem we confront here is how Black populations of the Caribbean can break out from the bottom rungs of the global economy and society and from our irrelevancy in the global community. We must examine how not to be fragile, and not continue to fall for incoherent and ineffective thinking that others place in our minds. We also need a keen understanding of probability as it relates to our existence and our potential extinction as a species. We often focus on reactionary solutions that are emotional and romanticized—that feel good at the moment, but end up hurting us in the longer term. The emotional tendency is to focus on symptoms rather than causes, but the causes usually go to the heart of problem-solving. Do we understand the critical difference between causation and correlation? The root of a problem? How to get to the real or the original questions? Not knowing or not applying intelligence to problem-solving often leads to the creation of more problems—vicious circles—and emotionally developed errors in judgement.

Mathematics can be helpful to us because it gets to the root of problems, breaks down their complexity into basic natural elements and parts, and then looks for solutions from the bottom up. Socio-economic problems are complex, but superficial symptom-focused approaches will not solve them; they only cause more and more errors.

So, *applied intelligence* establishes science as the most reliable utility for problem-solving. It does not follow distracting theories, ideologies, stories, or random assumptions down rabbit holes. We cannot afford to rely solely or primarily on philosophy. As in calculus, life is about understanding the differential, and the differential is simply a function or way of differentiating certain values, basically figuring out how to get us from *here to there*. This is fundamentally what life is about, and inputting the integral variables of the situation that can provide us with clarity and usefulness in our understanding

19

of how to plot our journey. This math-type approach leads us to do things by a process of logic, not emotion.

The first principles of thinking require us to boil things down to the most fundamental truths because it is better to know only a few fundamental truths than to have many vague understandings. Therefore, *applied intelligence* is concerned more with looking at the building blocks of truth and knowledge. We must become the opposite of fragile, i.e., resilient, if we want to compete and win in today's technology-driven, globalized economy. Emotional thinking will not get us there; only adherence to knowledge and intelligent thinking will. We must understand the laws of nature and come to terms with its entanglements, with a disciplined approach to connecting the dots and building on first principles. The process of relying on our gut is unreliable, primitive, and harmful to our aspirations for success in a complex and sophisticated universe. Reliance on emotion must be overcome; intuition and ego limit our quantitative capacity to think effectively, which then limits our potential. In the end, we must seek truth as the main underlying principle of our existence. In order to find it, there are a few rules of thumb to keep in mind:

- Challenge conventional wisdom, the status quo, and seek to know what is true or false.
- Always look for the evidence for ideas presented to you.
- Keep an open mind and consider alternative views; no one has yet cornered the market on good ideas.
- Consider the consequences and implications of every decision you make.
- Be willing to take risks, and if you do not have any skin in the game, understand that your commitment and sincerity will be questioned.

- Always question the original questions, and if you do not know those original questions, seek them out. Questions often have answers embedded in them.
- Maintain a healthy skepticism. There is no original thought; everything in this vast universe has been put out there or done before at some point in history. The more you read, the more you will realize this—and you will also come to understand that history is your most powerful learning resource. Usually, all the original questions can be found in history, but it may take some work to find the answers. However, many questions cannot be answered, so be wary of searching Bible stories for those answers—that path will lead to suffering. Therefore, this book does not have any *new* questions and is certainly not looking to build new theories or philosophy; it is primarily focused on what is true about the universe, and how we can navigate it to succeed in it.

What I am saying here is nothing new; many good thinking practices can be traced back to ancient times, whether it be Western, Eastern, or African philosophies. In the end, they all ask the same questions that revolve around nature: Is human nature inherently bad or good? Can it be cultivated, and can there be continuous self-improvement? Moreover, since the laws of nature are supreme in the universe, the universal questions discussed going forward are based on nature: How should we live our lives in order to experience happiness and avoid suffering?

Prologue 1

THE RELEASE OF FEAR is essential to success, but it is also essential in order to live a life without self-imposed suffering. The human need for security drives us to live in a constant state of fear, and we experience fear through our imagination which manifests our suffering, as if we cannot live without it, as though suffering is necessary to live. Fear digs its way into your subconscious and avoids the light of consciousness; therefore, the only way to relieve and eventually free yourself from fear is through the insight of conciseness and a focus on reality. Therefore, unless you can understand how fear works, you risk living a life where fear becomes part of your identity.

However—unfortunately—fear is a significant and embedded part of religion. Religion thrives on fear to thrive, and the vast majority of Black people rely on the dogma of the Christian religion to guide their lives. They rely on Christianity, which creates a culture of fear and suffering. So instead of taking concrete actions to guide our lives, we exercise the fantasy of praying instead, never to face challenges with intellect and logic. Prayer is a fundamental operating function of the Christian culture of suffering, and we have trained ourselves in the infliction of suffering upon ourselves.

Religion instills a cowering character in its practitioners that denies them the courage to take action to thrive and succeed in the universe. The reality is that living requires courage—the full exercise of self-preservation! Praying to God to solve your problems or hoping for your problems to end on their own is not an existence; in reality, it is a controlled delusion. So if you do still want to pray, hopefully, it creates spiritual energy for you—but it would still be more useful to pray for the courage to live in reality than to be guided by the fantasy of religious doctrines. Pray instead for the will to escape the culture of fear and suffering, for the courage to step into an actions-driven life, with an intelligent and logical mindset.

Therefore, we are faced with simple choices in life. One of the core ones is either to agonize and hope that our problems will go away (they will not) or to face reality and face our challenges with the weaponized courage of a controlled mind. We may have little choice in the systemic environment or circumstances that surround us, but we do have a choice as to how we respond to them. "It does not matter what you bear," Seneca once said, "but how you bear it" is what matters most. And when we confidently know that we can control our responses, it is then that we find our strength and move with the courage to navigate life.

The French philosopher Michel de Montaigne once wrote about philosophy as being the study of learning how to die. "A man who has learned to die has unlearned how to be a slave," he wrote. But this is simply wrong! His writings are based on fear and the suffering culture. Philosophy, from my perspective, is based on how to live; however, philosophy cannot do it for you. You must take the ideas and put them into action yourself. Mindfulness creates clarity, allowing you to see the objective reality and rationality instead of imagining your existence in fear and anxiety.

We must stop existing in the culture of fear. Fear, however, is one of the main ingredients embedded in Christianity; so ceasing to believe in Christianity could be the beginning of the end of our suffering. Our physical slavery ended a long time ago, but mental slavery is a choice we make because we control our minds, on one else does. Believing in your free will is what will make all the difference. You must be fully aware of your surroundings and the universe around you, and make conscious decisions based on reality and not on the *imagination of fear*. A non-fearful mind is a clear mind—a mind that is open to better learning, that makes better decisions, that is creative and that adopts the growth mindset, which is better for achieving goals. At a minimum, mastering yourself leads to a less stressful life. The only thing you have power over is your mind. Use it effectively in the present, because you cannot change the past and the future is determined by actions in the here and now.

We must build foundations of reason and intellect to identify what we want, without any fear of actually obtaining it. Life is abstract, and figuring it out can inspire fear, so we tend to shy away from our big dreams and aspirations out of the imagination of fear. Therefore, it is difficult for us to align with the things that we must do in order to achieve what we want to achieve. We become confused about everything, and our thinking becomes counterproductive. Confusion leads to misalignment with reality, and one develops a hallucination about one's existence—and for African descendants, it transforms into a lack of self-confidence, self-love, and self-acceptance. It is exceedingly difficult to achieve anything meaningful in life without those ingredients.

This damages our self-esteem; as a result, we tend to look to others or to society for approval. We tend to stay in our lane, the very slow one, while others confidently speed ahead of us. This existence, of course, is an unconscious one, which is how we end up living the vast majority of our lives. We begin to tell ourselves that this is living, this is a good life—but in truth, this is suffering!

Confusion generates fear, which is not conducive to self-preservation. The purpose of self-preservation is to advance in order to create security for oneself, to satisfy the needs of the human condition—to *preserve* yourself so as to live well in the universe. Without the switch to conscious clarity about the universe it is unlikely you can win in it; and suffering will be your hallucinated outcome; you will never be able to thrive. This self-constructed hallucinatory mindset will prevent you from being bold, from going after things, for fear of being judged. The intrinsic fear of failure will ultimately manifest and reinforce a subconscious failure of your existence.

THERE IS NOTHING SIGNIFICANT about *statistical significance,* so be aware of how statistics can lie to you as there is usually no significance to the statistics presented to you. Cassie Kozyrkov, the Chief Decision Scientist at Google, points out in her article *Fooled by statistical significance: do not let poets lie to you* that contrary to popular belief, the term "statistically significant" does not automatically mean *important, momentous,* or *convincing.* She observes that it does not necessarily mean that anything significant happened, or that the results are noteworthy or interesting. All it means is that someone is claiming *it is or might be.* Usually, it does not tell us anything useful, because those being fed this information often do not even know anything about the original question, or whether there is a coherent question in the first place. So *significance* is a matter of opinion, and Kozyrkov points out that results are rarely important, and they only occasionally raise interesting questions, "but often they are irrelevant."

So be aware of the deliverer of statistics as a reliable source of good explanations; it is often an exercise in nothingness. Therefore, *applied intelligence* is in no way based on statistics. Rather, it involves learning and updating your mind with the most relevant knowledge—the objective truths that give us a more balanced view of the landscape. It is still difficult for us as humans not to make assumptions; however, *applied intelligence* protects us from being driven by our emotional and biased assumptions, which often leads to errors in judgement and poor decision making.

Moreover, as author Stanislas Dehaene says in his best-selling book, Neuronal Man (1985), "Learning, in man and machine, always starts from a set of a priori hypotheses, which are projected onto the incoming data, and from which the system selects those that are best suited to the current environment." So, *applied intelligence* is a selected *system* to vet the incoming information, to see if it could be usefully applied to the problem one is trying to solve. It looks to capture

25

knowledge, sort it, and apply it accordingly and purposefully, and in a disciplined way—*applied intelligence* elevates one's thinking by constructing coherent logical models that can produce practically useful and effective solutions in the real world.

In the end, statistics or data are simply another set of tools. How you use them is up to you, and their use in gathering information does not mean in any way that you are right or even effective. It will be as individual as any other thing, says Kozyrkov. And as we know, two different decision-makers can use the same data or statistics and arrive at completely different conclusions. So statistics can be highly personal.

The point to be made here is one of awareness, and that finding answers is not easy, but difficult. This is where methodology and process can be very helpful: in the augmentation of thinking and decision making. As Kozyrkov writes, knowledge sharing—the acquisition of knowledge and the development of knowledge ecosystems—is one of the things that make human beings and societies successful. So if you are not dedicated to the pursuit of knowledge, it is unlikely that you can be a consistent winner in the universe.

ADAM SMITH'S WORK, *The Wealth of Nations*, published in 1776, remains the most comprehensive treatment of the nature of economics and political economy ever written. *The Wealth of Nations* is not a book about "capitalism," as many have come to believe. Instead, it explains the true nature of human behaviour and decision making, and how economic self-interest is central to our existence.

It is human nature to seek personal gain; self-preservation is embedded and underscores our primal instincts, our resilience, growth, and adaptability to an ever-changing universe. Since Smith's seminal work, many economists and philosophers have come and gone, but no one has ever written a better explanation of the true *nature* of economics. Today, economists often put morality at the forefront of economics, but economics is not a morality play; it is a power play. It is not based on benevolence by any means. Adam Smith pointed out that "it is not from the benevolence of the baker that we get our daily bread, but from the baker's self-interest in organizing the factors of production in order to bake and sell it.

Smith's views are as relevant today as they were in the 18th century. He was not an "economist" by training (*The Wealth of Nations*, Introduction section); his purpose was simply to explain how societies function. *The Wealth of Nations* is an argument against "moral philosophy." Smith explains how the individual quest for personal gain, profit, and growth is critical to an economy's future. The wealth of any given nation is formed by individual pursuits for personal gain, which manifests itself in the form of benefits for the entire society.

Smith seeks the truth and then uses it to explain the path to prosperity for people and nations. For Caribbean people, Smith's first principle is extraordinarily helpful in explaining the nature of the universe and how to go about winning in it. Through quantitative analysis as opposed to philosophy, we can find the truth in our world and harness it for our self-interest. Truth helps us to identify reality and steers us toward logic.

Perhaps the fact that Smith was not an economist is precisely what enabled him to understand the true nature of economics so well. He focused on human behaviour, not on theoretically driven mathematical models that cannot capture the real nature of the human condition. Smith focused on "natural economics," while explaining the nature of real-world human decision making. Primal instinct is central to human survival, yet complex sophistication is necessary for one to thrive in the universe. Scientists still know relatively little about the transition from unconscious to conscious decision-making. So if we know so little about consciousness in general, how can we claim to predict economic decisions and outcomes accurately? That is why economists are always wrong! Their models and thought processes are fundamentally flawed. Their equations cannot ever fully capture real life, so they distort reality with theoretical constructs that create constructive delusions of reality to explain their theories.

From my reading of Smith, he understood that both the physical and the cognitive universe are linked, and our actions are predicated on the very nature of those interactions. One's basic natural state and motivation are to improve one's own life, family, and tribe constantly and to spread their culture. One must move beyond survival and toward intellectual sophistication in order to thrive in the universe—and to do that, one has to seek power through knowledge acquisition for the purpose of personal gain.

Economics has become an oversimplification of the complexity of the real world. Nevertheless, all these models and theories are not completely useless; at the very least, they can help us to understand what not to do, or how not to think. Useless predictions are generated through faulty analysis, so we must be cautious and skeptical of economic pontificators. Economics today has also become an academic pursuit for the elites in society so they can feel morally better about themselves. Of course, they are given Nobel Prizes by their elite peers to keep up their philosophical morality discipline.

The Wealth of Nations is "resolute about human beings—their capacities and incentives to be productive, their overall well-being" (Wealth of Nations, Intro pg. XVii). So the connection between well-being and productivity is central to prosperity and power in society. To Smith, it was morally justified to have self-interest, and self-love — "private interests and passions" (Wealth of Nations pg. XVii). Putting oneself first works in the holistic best interest of the whole society.

For the people of the Caribbean, it is time to make a serious effort to understand the first principles of our economic existence, the nature of things as they pertain to us, the truth about us, and what is necessary for the survival of our species. Self-interest is good and necessary, not only for the survival of the species but in order to thrive in the 21st century, the digital era – for adaptation and change.

This book puts forward a disciplined, science-based, strategic approach to building a transformative mindset, towards the intrinsic understanding of power for the pursuit of a prosperous and happy Caribbean society.

Socrates advised us over 2000 years ago that our escape routes from ignorance and suffering are found through our internal search for knowledge. So the search for knowledge holds the key to disentangling ourselves from the mental slavery from which the Caribbean psyche continues to suffer. What we are willing to learn is enormously more important than what we already know, or what we think we know. The world is a hyper-intense, a knowledge-based place where technology continues to change our very existence daily. If you are not inside that knowledge-pursuit loop, then you are on the outside. Everything we do matters—everything!

So it is time to stop with the excuses, stop *liming* and stop asking others to do what we must do for ourselves. It is time to stop with the veranda complaining, the lamenting and the romanticization of suffering. Your past suffering must only be taken as lessons for your future prosperity and happiness. The future is now; prepare yourself to face it. What is your plan? Your strategy? How are you going to execute it? What knowledge acquisition targets do you have in mind? Determine the real priorities: education, math and science, technology, and wealth creation. Those are all things in the natural universe that must be mastered. Otherwise, know that the unprepared are set to languish on the earth like disturbed people; only the well-prepared will survive.

It is time for the people of the region to understand the difference between consciousness and subconsciousness. Effective thinking is a skill that must be developed, and anyone committed to it can become good at it. Subconscious thinking is effortless, but it can be dangerous and debilitating, because it makes you unaware of your surroundings. Conscious thought, however, is difficult but rewarding because you remain aware of your surrounding reality.

Once you sort out your mind and the thinking process, you become better aware of the real world. You step out of the darkness of self-doubt and anxiety and into the bright light of confidence and opportunity.

Therefore, rational thought, embedded in and within the existence of nature, is central to a good life. Applying logic and intelligence is also central to dealing with the universe, and to do that successfully, we must accept nature as the one truth! The physical universe is what is real, and what cannot be altered. Therefore, reason can be the only rationale applied in successfully navigating the universe. It does not matter how you feel; the universe isn't aware of you, nor does it care about you, so emotions and intuition matter less in the effective navigation of the real world.

Morality, therefore, is neither relevant nor helpful in the real world because morality is defined by others trying to also compete and succeed in the universe. Hence, morality is often used against you, and the less informed among us will fall for morality. In a conflict-driven world, morality must be determined by you, so do not fall prey to the morality that others have defined and want you to adhere to. What is a good person anyway? And who has the divine right to decide that? It depends on perspective, and on what you are trying to achieve, so let your individualism determine who you are or want to be. Religion is essentially ideology and dogma, institutionalized by others rather than by you, so morality is relative. do not be a sucker for dogmatic religious morality. We all have the innate ability to determine right from wrong ourselves—without religion.

Once we free our minds from the religious trap and its supportive suffering culture, we will realize the power of our independent individual minds. Humans are imperfect beings, so why would you depend on them for your moral governance?

For philosophers like Kant and Nietzsche, the biggest obstacle for us is overcoming ourselves. Therefore, adherence to the very nature of things is critical to not living a delusional life, to not misunderstanding the universe and not over-relying on feelings and wishful thinking, which only leads to suffering. "Not only are we a confused muddle of emotions, passions, desires, and inclinations," explains Karen Stohr PhD, philosopher, Senior Research Scholar, Ryan Family Professor of Metaphysics and Moral Philosophy. She goes on to say "but we're also prone to misusing our reason in ways that make things worse." So in a nutshell, emotions are not helpful; adherence to reality is—and for Black Caribbean people of African descent, living in reality is imperative!

Improving ourselves does not mean listening to the ideologies of others. Listening to the intrinsic nature of our universe is far more reliable. So every decision matters, but if we are making decisions in *non-reality*, how can we possibly succeed? Accordingly, if you do not want to be a fragile person, always suffering instead of living, then reason supported by *applied intelligence* is the path forward!

ADAM SMITH talks about individualism—conscious thinking about oneself. Successful people, wealthy people, and great leaders usually have one thing in common: they think for themselves and have the courage of their convictions. They are resilient freethinkers with the ability to separate themselves from the crowd. Wealth is created by entrepreneurship, which in turn is based on leadership and vision, both of which require individual courage. Blindly following the herd always leads to mediocrity, but individualism gives you the chance to be exceptional. In the end, life and happiness overcoming oneself, not conforming to the herd, and finding one's own identity, is what it comes down to in the end. And in the wise words of Bertrand Russell, renowned British mathematician, philosopher, and social critic, thinking for ourselves first is "the most important rule of all." So this must also be the mindset that Caribbean people must adopt.

Black populations of the Caribbean must change their collective mindset, from accepting every story told to them and always waiting for others on the outside to do things for them. They must
recognize from a historical perspective, that their belief systems are not of their design, and they were constructed to serve the economic interest of the colonialists.

Further, the blind acceptance of Christianity is one of the biggest underlying causes of the lack of progress in Caribbean societies. The cultural belief system that promotes the acceptance of *fate* and *hope* over reality and logic means surrendering your individual free will. Separating oneself from the addictive, corrupt application of Christianity is central to self-determination. The nonsense of a god in heaven, the immaculate conception, and a child who happens to be white with blonde hair and blue eyes, whom the dark-skinned people must worship as their lord and saviour, is one of the most consequential tales ever told. Adherence to Christianity is adherence to a white supremacy culture that portrays us as subhuman beings. This has been the basis for trickery and manipulation for the benefit and dominance of one group over another. The doctrine of Christianity and the institution of the church have provided the false hierarchical underpinnings of white supremacy and black inferiority for hundreds of years.

Therefore, a more quantitative understanding of how the universe works will allow us to see Christianity for what it is: **a clever**

system of control for the economic domination of one group by another. Black Caribbean populations must commit to existing in consciousness, self-awareness, personal responsibility, and accountability both for actions and inactions. We must take responsibility for what happens to us and come to terms with the hard truths about us, about our selected belief systems, and how they have held us back. If we do not confront ourselves, then we will always be lying to ourselves.

Adherence to Christian doctrines as a core part of our cultural belief system is highly counterproductive to Black societies. It causes its believers to abdicate from logic and common sense and instils in them a subconscious preference for being domesticated and dominated. Christianity has turned Black culture into one of delusion and fragility, believing in Bible stories and the fallacy of hope instead of relying on logic and evidence, on intellect and actions. Blacks have bought into the Christian narrative about suffering being virtuous, which is false. Whether we want to hear it or not, the *noise and nonsense* of Christianity have led us to accept suffering as part of our identity. "Human suffering is often caused by belief in fiction, but the suffering itself is real" (Harari, 21 Lessons, pg. 250). So unless there is an intellectual detachment from the cult of racist Christian doctrines, the region will never fulfil its potential nor take its rightful place in the universe.

So we must make a seminal effort to understand and learn from history. But we must read all history skeptically as well, with the understanding that history has all too often been primarily written by those in power: white men.

Therefore, our *applied intelligence* is the pursuit of intellectualism, so that we do not engross ourselves in emotion and find millions of ways to suffer. The American theologian Reinhold Niebuhr highlighted the wisdom of knowing the difference between nature and self, the mind, of what he can control and cannot control when he wrote "…grant me the serenity to accept the things I cannot change, courage to change the things I can, and wisdom to know the difference." This quote of course is taken from a famous modern prayer; however, it is not self-contradictory to my views on religion. That is because I apply intelligence to words and extract intellectual value from them. If the words make sense to you intellectually, you do not need to accept the religion along with it. Just leave the emotion and dogma out, the intellect of the words provides the real value. Marcus Aurelius wrote, "become indifferent to what makes no difference." In short, life requires no great philosophical thought, merely the simplicity of intellectual understanding.

Pursuing an intelligent existence brings clarity to your life because you see things as they are, not through the stories of others. Intelligence is intrinsic to happiness because it does not rely on emotion, which restricts your mind. Intrinsic intelligence disentangles the complexity of life and expands your mind through the simplicity of awareness; consciousness is the highest state of mind, the lucidity to see the universe. Therefore, if you learn to disentangle your mind from the trap of emotional and religious belief systems, only then can the adherence to stories that de-intellectualize your mind move you towards your ultimate human nature: your individualism.

The Black mindset must move to another dimension in thinking, a discerning one with awareness of how the universe actually works. In this dimension, truth exists, and this is where your intrinsic intelligence becomes productive and powerful, reaching your free will—your sophistication of self-preservation state.

DISCIPLINE IS YOUR SALVATION. "Salvation" does not mean deliverance from sin and its consequences, as told to us by Christian doctrine. Salvation is about preservation and perseverance, deliverance to a better existence, one of choice. Salvation means the end of suffering and the beginning of enduring and authentic happiness. However, getting there requires discipline, not merely talking the talk but walking the walk—the conscious practice of self-awareness and training of the mind. But honesty is number one, because there can be no progress without practicing honesty first.

Making the best of this life requires an intelligent and focused system, however. Regardless of the system or methodology involved, discipline is always required. Discipline is the bedrock of achievement—developing good habits. Ultimately, everyone has the freedom to choose one of two paths: the path of discipline and achievement or the path of excuses and suffering.

In a recent article titled "5 Surprising Habits Of Extremely Disciplined People," author Moreno Zugaro highlights the disciplined behaviour of people who can achieve whatever they put their minds to. One of my favourites is what he lists as "They Embrace the Suck." Succeeding at the most meaningful things in life requires doing the hard things first, but most people never do so; therefore, they never get what they desire most out of life.

Most people resist or avoid uncomfortable situations, always running away from the fire; sidestepping challenges through well-fermented habits of making excuses. They always find the escape hatch. However, disciplined people do the opposite: they embrace adversity and endure the grind. Adopting this attitude is the beginning of the end of suffering, and when it is over, you realize that instead of killing you, the ordeal actually made you stronger.

Discipline means playing the long game and requires self-care:

- Creating healthy diets, lifestyles, and healthy relationships, and avoiding nonsense-infused negative people;
- Developing a schedule and doing the things you need to and the things you enjoy;
- Relaxing, resting, and recharging; getting enough sleep is critical;

- Celebrating your achievements every step of the way, because doubt fear and worry will only slow you down; and
- Engaging your natural energy in spirituality and freeing yourself from the restrictive ideology of religion, and its culture of suffering.

You must go the extra mile and do the things that others will not, separating yourself from the herd. This is how success happens. And "when you've reached the end of your comfort zone, pushing further becomes that much harder. But that is what disciplined people do," says Moreno Zugaro. Every action you take each day defines more of who you are. It defines your identity.

Discipline requires focused thinking and helps avoid the crippling, self-inflicted condition of constant avoidance and excuses, never taking responsibility and accountability for your decisions or behaviour. So resist the need for instant gratification and think long-term instead, because negative situations usually develop over time. Accordingly, positive outcomes develop over the long term, too. Remember, a crisis is temporary, but you can also use it as a wake-up call, a life lesson, so as to do better the next time.

Reading is essential to a good life. Being well-read requires focus, discipline, and always paying attention to the necessity of life-long learning. It provides you with knowledge, perseverance, empathy, humble confidence, and fair-mindedness. Reading slows things down, allowing for reflection, less emotional thought, precise thinking, and imagination. It uplifts your consciousness, your sharpness, your thinking and perspective, and gives you better contemplation of virtue. It intensely drives your curiosity to ask more inquisitive and insightful questions and to explore more ways to acquire more knowledge. It breaks you away from the conformity with which society stifles you. As you are learning new things, you are also building new foundations of growth in understanding the universe, its basic concepts, and the laws of nature. These concepts provide for better footing in the universe, which allows for more efficient and effective thinking. Logic and intelligence now begin to prevail over emotion and intuition; self-reliance enters your existence.

"Everything hangs on one's thinking," said Seneca.

Knowledge acquisition helps with objectivity and clarity and builds your courage to become an independent thinker with intellectual humility. When you do not read, you degrade yourself to denseness—to various forms of willful ignorance, such as relying on social media as your main source of information. Not managed properly, social media simply makes you foolish.

Thus, the more you read, the more you realize how little you do know, but the more you want to learn. In the end, life is Game Theory, the interactions between people and their agents—only the game is played in the real world, not the classroom. Your points are accumulated from what you value, relative to what is valued in society; that is the game. So winning is defined relative to what you authentically want out of life versus what society tells you should be.

Focus on the process instead of the results. Life is discovery work; it must be led by evidence, not intuition or feelings, and the insights that you discover along the journey create you. Your value then creates confidence and inner freedom. Fear and anxiety begin to evaporate, and your trajectory toward fearlessness and leadership begins to take a directional shape. Your circumstances are neutral; it is how you deal with them that matters most—do you choose fear or courage?

So when you employ discipline as your salvation, your fears—fear of losing money on an investment or an entrepreneurial venture, or fear of embracing individuality, or in my case, fear of plunging into writing a future best-selling book—those fears and anxieties can no longer exist in a focused and disciplined environment. Achievement and goals now become a matter of taking action. Nevertheless, thinking and reading will not make an ounce of difference by themselves. The difference will only come when one finds the courage to take a disciplined approach to life. In the end, it is actions, not talk, that make all the difference in the world.

MOVING TOWARDS SCIENCE: THE END OF STORIES

This section is heavily influenced and referenced from the best-selling book *Guns, Germs, and Steel,* by author Jarad Diamond, it is one of those books everyone needs to read at one point in his or her life. I use a lot of his work as a biologist and apply it to help us move from emotional explanations to more of applying science to our thinking process, and explanations.

The abundance of fossil evidence confirms that human life began in East Africa. The earliest stages of human evolution we can find come from Africa. From what we know, human life began some 7 million years ago, and within that time frame, a general population of African apes broke off into several other populations, which proceeded to evolve into the modern gorilla, then a second line into two modern chimps, and a third, humans. I do not mean to attempt to be an evolutionary biologist here, merely to establish science and evidence as reality. Science, not Bible stories, is what accurately explains human existence. Again, we are focused on finding out what is true and distinguishing our analysis from what is not true, or the constructive delusions that currently exist about the universe.

Fossil evidence leads us to believe that the evolutionary line evolved to achieve an upright posture about 4 million years ago, evolving to an increased body and brain size about 2.5 million years ago. If we fast forward a bit, we get to *Homo erectus,* standing upright; this stage of evolution came around 1.7 million years ago and was close to the modern human in body size—but its brain size was

38

barely half that of the modern human. "*Homo erectus* was more than an ape, but still much less than a modern human" (Guns, Germs, and Steel, pg. 36). The first finding of *Homo erectus* outside of Africa attested to by fossil evidence was found in the Southeast Asia Island of Java — conventionally known as "Java man." The earliest unquestioned evidence of human life in Europe appeared about half a million years ago. See the map below for the migration and colonization patterns from Africa to the landmass of Eurasia.

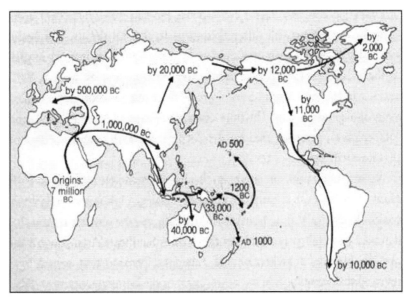

'Guns, Germs and Steel': The spread of humans around the world.

African and European skulls of half a million years ago were "sufficiently similar to the skulls of us modern humans that they are classified in our species, *Homo sapiens*, instead of in *Homo erectus*" (*Id.*, pg. 37). The distinction is arbitrary at best, so the main point is that the evolution of apes into modern humans explains how we got here.

Human history took off only about 50,000 years ago, and the earliest sign of that take-off comes from East African sites, where the first standardized stone tools and preserved art and jewellery appeared. If you do not do well with accepting scientific evidence over Bible stories, you may have a hard time reading the rest of this book. This book is about the application of exercising intelligence and free will to the reality of the natural world or the metaphysical universe.

THEREFORE, in moving towards science and logic in our thinking, we must not get sidetracked from the core tenants of our existence and our capacity to thrive, like any other group of people. However, we are often caught up in our emotions about racism, and we come to define ourselves in *racism* itself. However, this is wrong! It is also very distracting, tricking us into holding our own selves back.

Back in 1975, author Toni Morrison, in an interview at Portland State University *'Nobody really thought that Black people were inferior,'* told us that the racism fight is a masterful distraction. The Black human condition—like that of any other population—exhibits a need for security; but our experience with slavery, colonialism, and racial injustice has led us to believe that the Black identity is all about fighting racism. Of course, you must speak up about racism and protest where it is both necessary and effective to do so. However, we cannot let that struggle dominate our emotions and take over our identity. Moreover, there is no such thing as a completely fair and just society. Even in a racially homogeneous society, perfect fairness is a fantasy that does not exist in the real world. Furthermore, the false narrative of White superiority and Black inferiority has distracted and misguided us so much that we cannot even see our own potential for prosperity. We get trapped in trying to prove that our ancestors built great ancient cultures and civilizations in Africa to rival those of

Europe. We become so preoccupied with proving that African societies made their own great achievements in commerce, science, mathematics, medicine, and other fields that we end up wasting time and energy instead of focusing on actually making it ourselves in the real world. We keep losing, because we keep letting ourselves get distracted.

So we end up in a place of frustration and humiliation, and all we can do is scream "Black Lives Matter!" But what really matters, what will really make the difference, is our understanding and acceptance of the laws of nature and of the reality that the basis of our universe is self-interest. Therefore, unless we focus on economics first, our Black lives will continue *not* to matter. Unless we
create value, we will have no value with which to transact, to influence others and our surroundings. Politics and justice flow directly from the economics we can create. That is how the world turns, and
without understanding that reality, we will continue to suffer from the "fraud of racism" as Morrison characterizes it.

> The very serious function of racism is a distraction. It keeps you from doing your work. It keeps you explaining over and over again, your reason for being.

> —Toni Morrison, Portland State University, 1975

Morrison talks about having to stop fighting the symptoms and fight the disease, and the disease is about power she says. However, power is not a disease; power is a necessity that we all seek in order to thrive in the universe. Therefore, Black people must acquire power too, for the sake of self-preservation—like everyone else in the world. The game is no different for us, and the more we fail to play the real game, the less likely we are to win. So as long as we remain distracted or stuck on this useless *racism-based identity*, we will not be able to create value and wield influence in the world, and so we will remain powerless.

> If I take your race away, and there you are, all strung out. And all you got is your little self, and what is that? What are you without racism? Are you any good? Are you still strong? Are you still smart? Do you still like yourself? I mean, these are the questions. Part of it is, "yes, the victim. How terrible it has been for black people." I am not a victim. I refuse to be one… if you can only be tall because somebody is on their knees, then you have a serious problem.
>
> —Toni Morrison

Racism is a construct—a social construct created to benefit those who know how to use it effectively. It has a strong and dynamic social function in white supremacy culture. And Black people who hate themselves and use racism as an excuse can feed off of the racism narrative in order to feel better about themselves.

Yes, we know that racism is real; but white supremacy culture is not going to change anytime soon, nor take away its own power nor share it with anyone else, so get over the emotion of racism and move toward using our minds and *applied intelligence* to find our power. Our thoughts dictate our reality, so we must apply our intelligence strategically. Distractions only divert us from what we all really want in life: POWER!

KNOWLEDGE, CAPITAL, and TECHNOLOGY are the core components in the pursuit of prosperity and happiness. They are the formula for making things happen. Throughout the evolution of

42

civilizations, those three factors have been consistently determined. History shows, through evidence and analysis, that those groups of people, societies, and nations that have focused on developing knowledge ecosystems, facilitated by the underpinnings of technology, and fueled by capital, have been able to thrive exponentially over the very long term. It was precisely this enlightenment about science and capitalism that allowed Eurasia to become the driving force in the world.

> So it is hardly coincidental that science and capitalism form the most important legacy that European imperialism has bequeathed the post-European world of the twenty-first century.
>
> —Yuval Noah Harari

This book is about living in consciousness and understanding the circumstances in which we live, playing the cards we have been dealt, and not developing constructive delusions of the mind. We ask hard questions throughout these chapters—questions about why Black people have seemed not to grasp the reality of nature, or how we must understand nature to survive. Are we satisfied being at the bottom rungs of the universe as Caribbean people of African descent, irrelevant and devoid of influence over the directional forces of the universe?

Why is it that the Caribbean region, for example, has the most ideal naturally competitive advantages in land and environment for the business of agriculture, food production; and as history tells us, this natural asset has been an enormous source of wealth creation over many centuries, for many civilizations and societies. Yet the Caribbean remains essentially non-producers and non-competitive in the exportation of value-added food products, left to the irrelevant and unprofitable production of commoditized export. Others in the world with much less hospitable environments continue to outperform us dramatically in the global agriculture sector, through innovation and the development of knowledge ecosystems. So in the end, everyone's history matters, but what matters most is your mindset today, about what you are going to do next. Getting ahead or getting what you want is a function of adherence to consciousness, thinking quantitatively, intelligently applying knowledge, and acting on that information and knowledge building.

TODAY, THE WORLD is at another transitional point in its evolutionary history—a critical juncture at which many societies around the world are faced with similar and fundamental economic decisions, whereby new, robust, and transcendent technology is increasingly determinant of successful economic outcomes. For the Black populations of the Caribbean, success in the 21st century means quick and precise adaptation to the digital world. In the history of civilizations everywhere, *Homo sapiens* have been able to learn and adapt to changing environments; that trait is in our nature. So the question is, do we want to make the effort or not because it's in our nature to succeed? Or would we rather sit on our verandas, enjoying the warm and gentle Caribbean Sea breeze, complaining about how unfair the world is? About how the government is not doing enough for us, consciously ignoring the reality that it is always up to us to change our situation?

If we do not extract ourselves from the victimhood mindset, the abyss is where we will stay. Scientific discovery, trial, and error, risk-taking, experience, natural selection, and large-scale cooperation and collaboration within communities are how success happens—not through constant complaining.

We are all connected in the universe, and we must stand, find, and deliver our value in it. Climate change, for example, is an

44

existential threat to the small island states of the Caribbean, but it also represents one of the biggest growth opportunities in the history of the region. It represents the opportunity to transform Caribbean economic structures and mindset, to use our natural competitive advantages in order to rise as a sophisticated economy and culture. We must view the climate crisis for what it truly represents: an economic transformation opportunity. We must not foolishly fall for "global climate action," in which we end up working for the climate actions that benefit the Western developed world most, and not us. We must focus on our own problems and seek our own economic interests. This is the essence of self-preservation—the pursuit of gain, using crisis as opportunity.

The zero-emissions-technology-based economy is here and moving rapidly; it represents the single biggest economic growth opportunity the Caribbean has ever seen. But if we do not pay attention, we will miss out on it, and a new level of acute suffering will come upon the region. In the coming decade, if the region does not capitalize on these types of generational economic opportunities, it will surely set itself back for a hundred years or so. History teaches us that long-term success or failure, prosperity or poverty, stems directly from what societies do in those periods of transition. Opportunities for advancement appear in many forms—but if we are not aware and sophisticated enough, we will miss them, and our fate will remain in the hands of those who are consciously aware, or not on "island time."

Urgency is a key word when seeking to make things happen and building the human capacity to enable future dynamic growth. "After four billion years of organic life evolving by natural selection, science is ushering in the era of inorganic life shaped by intelligent design" (Harari, 21 Lessons pg. 124). Your intellect is paramount in shaping your existence! The nature of our primal cognitive existence remains the same, but the world is tremendously more complex today. In this era, the forward journey requires more knowledge than ever before, and the utility and leveraging of data science and artificial intelligence becomes ever more important to our existence.

I believe that it was Einstein who once said something to the effect that we cannot solve our problems with the same level and dimension of thinking with which the problem was created, in the first place; so we must step into a higher dimensional framework in order to succeed. Therefore, what Einstein is saying is primarily what this book endeavours to achieve: to show Caribbean people of African descent that our very existence as a species depends on a higher level or dimension of thinking—that our current dimension of thinking is not conducive to the long-term survival of the *Caribbean-species*. As times change, the fundamentals of life and self-preservation remain the same; however, the application of information and actions must be consistent with the conditions of the time and place in which one lives. Accordingly, creating a higher-level dimensional framework in which the Caribbean-species people can succeed requires a higher-dimensional framework of thinking toward relative action. So *applied intelligence* becomes the relevant underlying function for the advancement of Afro-Caribbean peoples in the twenty-first century.

THE AFRO-CARIBBEAN PEOPLE, descendants of enslaved Africans, have endured a tremendous amount of suffering over the last 400+ years, to say the least. We have survived journeys in slave ships, subjugation, brutality; and yet we are still standing! We are inherently resilient people. However, we must learn to *harness* that resilience and become sophisticated towards our self-preservation. We must become quantitative thinkers in order to maximize our underlying resilience. We need to take core primal instincts and apply strategic intelligence to them, focusing on building resilient and

prosperous Caribbean societies. We must understand relativity, how to adapt to the times
and how to strive in new environments; that is what long-term survival is all about. We may as well embrace volatility, because volatility creates disruptive opportunities that can be the catalysts for real change.

The Caribbean remains stuck in the mindset of its colonial past, whether people like to hear it or not; but of course, it is the objective truth that this book seeks, not emotional feelings. People remain confused, timid, and unable to find their purpose and create the necessary empowerment ecosystem to drive prosperity and power for themselves. We are afraid to stand up straight and be confrontational about the things that stand in our way. Timidness and pushing hope rather than self-reliance will not be helpful to us.

Do we expect the same people and the same systems of white supremacy that have spent centuries systematically relegating Black people to the bottom rungs of the global socioeconomic ladder to have a sudden change of heart and begin acting in our best interests? Do we truly believe that anyone will give up the power and privilege that they have worked for centuries to obtain? Wishful thinking is extraordinarily self-destructive; what we think or believe about the way the world *should* work is irrelevant. The world can only be what it is, and the sooner we take the rose-coloured glasses off, the better off we will all be.

> […][R]acism is not simply a function of individual attitudes, and it cannot be eradicated by changing hearts and minds. Racism is the social, legal, political and economic distinctions that mark and maintain unequal access and entry points to privacy, property, protection, prosperity, and personhood. It is embedded in structures, institutions and ideas, especially those about work, deservedness,

representation, redistribution, and even the proper role of government.

—Dr. Debra Thompson

Time is running out! This is the transformation decade. We must put aside fear and find courage. We cannot afford to wait for leaders; we must lead ourselves and be entrepreneurial in everything we do. We must put aside the constant complaining and break free of Christian doctrine. Suffering is not a virtue. We need to change our attitudes and seek to build power ecosystems of opportunity throughout the global economy through technology-led entrepreneurship. We must learn how to think mathematically, be strategic and scientific in approach, and learn how to bend the curve in our favour. Borrowing a few principles from the field of physics, quantum entanglement explains the intertwined nature of the universe. Unless we become active and energetic in our lives and begin to think consciously about our functioning in the universe, it will be practically impossible for us to succeed in the universe.

Time and time again, some in the Black community continue to lament the past, about Africa, when we were "kings and queens," as they say. However, in the real world, kings and queens have lots of castles, gold, cash, property, armies, and taxes that pay for their upkeep; we do not! So this romanticization of the past is dangerous to our future. We are better off staying in the here and now and keeping it real, keeping our distance from distracting fantasies. Reality is something we create; it is not absolute, predetermined, immovable, or God-created. Rather, reality is created through the values that one holds and the actions one takes. The real world has always been created and run by entrepreneurs; enterprises and industries underpinned by technology that has allowed civilizations to grow by leaps and bounds. The human experience has been driven by globalization, and globalization will only continue to intensify.

Knowledge is power, so we must first seek to acquire knowledge if we want power. Free thinking takes courage in a confirmative world, but perseverance, vision, leadership, and purpose fuel courage. Self-awareness helps one take responsibility for one's own life, and a conscious mindset is vital to self-preservation. A person's ability to understand and differentiate is what separates him or her from the herd.

Conscious living tests *will-to-power* to find our true nature. What are we made of? What can we withstand? Do we have or can we develop the capacity to create real economic value ourselves? Who we are or what we have become is determined by the decisions we make, so it is from a place of intelligence that we must seek the mechanisms to apply intelligence to make things work in our favour. The universe is what it is; its primal nature cannot ever be changed. So if we continue to stand idly by, engaging in wishful thinking, we will be run over by those who live in reality. Again, Adam Smith tells us that gain is good, and economics is not a morality play; if we pursue individual economic gain, it will impact our broader community as well. So do not believe the Christian dogma nonsense, money is not the root of all evil, it is necessary.

Success, then, can only be measured based on the way we live our lives versus the way we *desire* to live our lives. Remember, it is not the universe's fault that we are where we are in life; in the end, it is always up to us to change our condition. We are not helpless, and most importantly, we are intelligent. We must shed the illusion of economic equality as an automatic human right, because ultimately, the ability to exercise our "rights" is determined by our economics. Societies are inherently unequal, and wealth and power are a function of the inherent value we create—nothing else. In the digital era, wealth and power will increasingly be more concentrated in the hands of those who create power and privileged ecosystems, those who can be entrepreneurially disruptive to the status quo. First, we must find our footing by determining how to acquire the knowledge necessary to compete in the 21ˢᵗ century. We must ascertain how to apply knowledge and match it to the necessary technology.

Therefore, when it comes to the common pursuit of happiness, we must remember that happiness is not free. No one is simply going to hand us happiness; we must work hard and intelligently in order to achieve stainable and authentic happiness. For Caribbean people, keeping a firm grip on reality is critical to achieving basic happiness. Equally critical is the intellectual understanding that happiness is not the absence of adversity, but knowing how to overcome it. Just as important is the understanding that the injustices that we as a people have suffered do not make us special to the universe. The universe does not know you. Problems do not go away; they merely evolve.

Taking personal responsibility is the key to happiness because taking responsibility for our problems empowers us by prompting us to take control of our lives. Yes, there have been terrible injustices inflicted on Black people—but changing the past is impossible. The only thing that is possible is to take responsibility for our lives in the here and now. Victimhood or feeling that the world owes us something will only lead us to suffer.

If we live life moment-by-moment and in a state of emotion, then we will live in continual fear and despair, over-sensitive in a destructive victimhood mindset, and susceptible to all the distractions of the universe. Happiness is best achieved by decoupling one's emotional self from one's intellectual self, allowing the intellect to take the lead in determining one's behavior. The brain has more capacity and stamina than the heart; one's intellectual self is more powerful than one's emotional self. We must figure out our core values and purpose in our lives, set the intellectual framework for decision making, and then commit to it!

Prologue 2

Christianity – the Barrier to Black Progress and Prosperity

> When you give up all the fictional stories, only then can you observe reality about yourself and about the world.

> —Yuval Noah Harari

Before we engage in the Christianity discussion, it would help us to position ourselves to better understand the ideas and doctrines behind morality, more deeply, and how it plays into our decision-making matrix. For this, we must turn to Friedrich Nietzsche, one of the most important but misunderstood philosophers in history. Nietzsche's works should be required reading for Black people because his thinking was honest and practical. Friedrich Nietzsche essentially said that we must move beyond governing our lives via tradition and past social experiences; he called for breaking everything down and creating new pathways. He is most famous for declaring "God is Dead," but most people do not understand the context of his declaration. He was declaring that whatever truth Christianity may hold, its traditions are no longer legitimate or relevant to the pursuit of morality. Christianity in itself is the problem—and so Christian morality is corrupt, and we cannot continue based on this tradition in the modern world.

Nietzsche believed that the European Christian moral system was both harmful to humanity and destined to collapse; of course, that did not happen. Yet Nietzsche correctly understood that our decision-making is primarily based on our conception of morality, which flows from religion. Therefore, as Black people, if we adhere to the European version of morality that is based on self-serving

51

European Christianity, our belief system will work against us. In his book *Beyond Good and Evil (1886)*, Nietzsche argues that the prevailing morality law is based on an artificial creation and not natural laws; this is fundamentally correct, for men wrote these laws to serve their own interests. These morality laws were effectively meant to control the masses.

In short, laws are written to constrain us through the use of morality. The upper classes wrote the laws and established power over the lower classes, creating a new social order underpinned by the morality of Christianity. So over time, those in the upper classes came to believe that they were superior to the working classes and that they therefore deserved to be privileged over the latter. They distinguished themselves with an air of supremacy, associating positive character traits such as virtue and intelligence with themselves and attributing negative traits such as inferiority to the lower class, both physically and intellectually. This, of course, was the prelude to the justification for slavery and the use of the church to reinforce it.

The upper classes become all-powerful and exert their power over the lower classes. In the experience of Africans, being classified as inferior and at the very bottom of humanity, it was only *normal* to be used as slaves for the economic advancement of Europe. Nietzsche identifies Christianity as the suppressor of the lower classes; he talks about how Christian doctrines taught us to "turn the other cheek" and that "the meek shall inherit the earth." This reinforced Christian dogma and the narratives of the hierarchical structures in society.

Nietzsche says in his book *Will to Power* that "[F]rom a moral standpoint the world is false. But in as much as morality itself is a part of this world, morality also is false." Therefore, for Nietzsche, we all have our willpower and must exercise our individual agency, for nothing is ever predetermined; everything is a function of actions taken. Nietzsche argues that it is within our power to believe in ourselves and to engage in self-preservation; we must be responsible for ourselves. Our basic drive in life is to overcome challenges and find happiness by finding the truth. Morality is subjective, and we do not need a Bible to tell us the difference between "good and evil." Christianity is false and uses "morality" and the institution of the church to drive the self-interests of the upper classes over the lower classes, of the master over the slave, and of white supremacy over Black inferiority. However, in the final analysis, we can master ourselves, Nietzsche says.

Nietzsche did not hate religion; he simply believed in each individual's willpower, for example, he even said that one should *do what Jesus did* and blaze one's own trail. Again, Nietzsche exhibited his intellectualism by using the Bible's many contradictions to make his point about individualism versus
following the herd. He saw the dogmas of Christianity as no longer useful in a modern and enlightened world. He wanted to tear down everything and start new—but that is not sensible where Black folks are concerned. It is not sensible to tear things down and start new. What is necessary is to apply intelligence to nature, your surroundings, and environment and let your individualism, intelligence and logic find your path to prosperity in the 21st century.

THEREFORE, our passive and trusting nature and our tendency to believe in things without evidence has left many Black people believing in Christianity, a religion that was purposefully designed to dominate us. Christianity is a religion formed to serve the purposes of white males, and it is inherent in white supremacist culture. In the experience of Caribbean people of African descent, Christianity is not a religion of our own making. It was forced upon us to underpin white supremacy's agenda of economic and cultural domination. Christianity, therefore, has been enormously powerful, purposeful, and extraordinarily effective in engineering barriers against the natural state of intellectual progress, prosperity, and power of people of African descent.

The Church as an institution has been a blunt instrument of the white supremacist agenda; it has been extremely effective in distracting Black people from the reality of their existence. Christian dogma has contributed greatly to many modern Blacks' embrace of a non-realist existence, instead hinging our lives on Bible stories. Therefore, one cannot even merely perceive, much less experience, progress, prosperity, and power if one doesn't even understand how things in the real world are formed. The fantasy of religion means non-adherence to the natural world. So if you are not conscious of the reality of what is necessary for your self-preservation and advancement, then you do not exist in consciousness, and success will be elusive to you.

It is important to understand that even though we may not be conscious of our lives, we do indeed spend our lives creating who we are. Our lives come from our choices. So to live life as a free individual, the most important thing is to live authentically, in harmony with the nature of things, and not to conform to man-made stories that are inherently self-serving to those writing the stories.

Being authentic means taking responsibility for our own lives, responsibility for our own decisions and behaviour, and not blaming others. Living an authentic life and expressing individuality is the natural state of human existence. Therefore, wasting our freedoms by allowing ourselves to be overtaken by the tyranny of the perverse Christian herd, is the opposite of living responsibly and authentically. And it is certainly not living free. Bending or surrendering to the conformity of the herd is a forsaking of one's free will, intellectual capacity, individualism, logic, and basic reason.

There is no set essence to being oneself, so an authentic, responsible, and fulfilling life requires lifelong learning and adherence to reality, always in the pursuit of truth. Because *nothing is or exists in reality except Truth,* said Mohandas Gandhi. However,

54

"Sometimes people do not want to hear the truth because they do not want their illusions destroyed," said Friedrich Nietzsche.

And these are among the fundamental challenges that we Blacks face in the modern world. Many of us do not want to face our real-world challenges, so clinging to the illusions provided by religious belief systems is convenient for avoiding reality.

Since the Catholic Church came into existence as an institution, leading Christianity, it has been the cornerstone of white supremacist cultural expansion for the express purpose of wealth creation by Europeans, and Europeans only. We must not be under any illusions; Christianity is about money and power, and Black people have been used as an economic resource over many centuries for the enrichment of white populations. The trans-Atlantic slave trade was all about economics, first and foremost; labour and raw materials are the ultimate creators of massive wealth and power. Slavery was the greatest wealth-creating engine in the history of the world. The slave plantation economy contributed significantly to the wealth and privilege that the United States, Britain, and other Western countries enjoy today. It is the slave economy that paid for those castles, estates, and aristocratic lifestyles that still endure today.

Thus, the superior-inferior/black-white complex emerged through the Christian wealth creation agenda. Therefore, the narrative of racism was purposefully created to support European economic expansion and power. The justification for enslavement and brutalization of Black bodies needed a false moral underpinning on which to build. White society needed to accept racism, and be convinced of its necessity, for the sake of their own self-preservation. The church played the role of the "moral" authority, using "God" to fortify the entire corrupt ecosystem—both for Blacks and Whites. Therefore, racism was developed as a rationalizing concept in support of the emerging socioeconomic white supremacist expansive push around the world. Again, economics is a power play!

The result of all that has created a Caribbean culture built on the enduring legacy of the slave plantation hierarchical system. Today, for example, *colourism* still endures in the region and even in its diaspora as well. Consequently, we have a Caribbean psyche that is fragile and trauma-based, resulting in a confused Caribbean identity.

In the 21st century, whites have become less and less religious while Blacks are more reliant on religion, with a tendency to remain stuck in past trauma, whether real or perceived. A Pew Research survey found that on the whole, Blacks utilize religion in fighting racial injustice and economic inequality—even though it has proven widely ineffective in garnering real results. Pew goes on to say that today, most Black adults say they rely on prayer to help make major decisions. This is intellectually unsound, naive, lazy, and overly reliant on the unreliability of emotional decision-making. Therefore, when we make decisions in the context of a world that does not exist, the real world will continue to kick our collective rear end.

Nevertheless, there is some hope. Pew's research highlights that Black Millennials and members of Generation Z are less likely to rely on prayer, less likely to have grown up in Black churches, and less likely to report that religion is an important part of their lives. This is very encouraging for the future survival of Black society, because only through intellectualism, adherence to reality, and the rules of nature can we survive in the universe.

The image of a white, blonde, blue-eyed Jesus Christ has been the foundational story embedded in the Black psyche through religious indoctrination, and it has created an enduring mental picture of what is beautiful and good and what is not. This fictional white male, Jesus, is also said to be our "Lord and Saviour," and acceptance of him is mandatory to be a good Christian and to live a proper life—to be saved, they say. This idea of Jesus creates a subconscious adherence to white supremacy through the images and words in the Bible. It gives white supremacy moral authority and governance over Black people who follow its teachings. This virus of thought is deeply embedded in the Black psyche, controlling subconscious minds—worshipping a religion designed to subjugate us.

The major underpinning of Christianity is about *suffering* being a virtue, and Blacks have built an entire culture of suffering through the church, embracing the struggle as if it were fundamental to our existence and identity. This is nonsensical, and it is what happens when we accept fantasy instead of reality. To break free of this suffering culture, we must first learn to be skeptical and to seek objective truths. We must not accept things simply because they have always worked a certain way. Let us exercise our free will and individualism and resist the pressure to conform to the irrational herd. We should never deny ourselves real information, learning, and knowledge acquisition in the pursuit of free thinking.

In the final analysis, the idea of "God" is a primitive construct created by men. God is a functional creation based on emotionally driven, supernatural explanations of the universe. White men created the idea of God and developed and codified it through the doctrines of the Catholic Church, bolstering and enforcing it through tradition, rules, and Christian codes. Doctrines became like statutes that laid down the common laws for each given society. That is how "God" was created—by power-seeking white men in Rome, and in their own image, too, of course. Why did they not create a brown-skinned, Middle Eastern-looking Jesus? After all, "Christ" was born in Bethlehem, so geography and science should dictate that he would have had Middle Eastern features, should they not?

The "One God" Christian narrative was not achieved through any graceful or intellectual appeal, nor through any peaceful convincing or preaching to convert people away from the polytheist (belief in more than one god) world at the time. Instead, the emergence of Christian monotheism was built on fear, lies, superstition, cohesion, rape, perversion, and violence. In the end, the Christian religion and its doctrines were created through force, storytelling, thievery, deceit, treachery, and misinformation, supportive of advancing the bogus "one true faith."

The Greek philosopher Lucretius over 2000 years ago explained the universe to us: *"An infinite number of atoms move randomly through space and time, colliding, intertwining, and forming complex formations and structures known as matter."* Therefore, the universe consists of matter, energy, and emptiness, and only the scientific method can define and explain nature. There are no other measures available to explain the universe, except mathematics, physics, and the other sciences; matter can only be quantified mathematically and explained scientifically. Lucretius also explained that there is no master plan, no intelligent design; and those species that exist today, and the ones that have effectively managed to thrive in the universe, are those that have best been able to adapt to changing environments.

The scientific evidence tells us that all human life began in East Africa approximately seven million years ago. From *Homo erectus* (an upright-walking human) to *Homo sapiens,* our species walked right out of Africa to populate the entire world. That is how it happened—not through the fable of Adam and Eve. So we ought to put down the storybook of the Bible and pick up some science and math books, fortifying our children to be resilient rather than fragile.

Africa is the mother of all civilization!

Think for a moment! How incredible is it that white supremacist Christianity has managed to convince Black people to believe that white people accomplished all of this, that they are at the centre of the universe? How amazing is it that they have successfully convinced us to disregard the scientific fossil evidence about Africa and the true history of the origins of humanity? Instead, they have led us to believe in stories and lies about a virgin giving birth to a blonde, blue-eyed baby in the heart of the middle-east. So without reliance on our intellectual capacity and critical thinking skills, as Black people, we are vulnerable to being easily fooled, and our survival in an advancing hyper-competitive world will be highly suspect.

Therefore, the time for us to move beyond religion is long overdue. Only atoms are real, and atoms form to create matter. Lucretius wrote that we should not engage in superstition, storytelling, and fiction; that we should conquer our fears and accept the fact that we are only transitory in the universe; that we are nothing special, merely a part of nature. The human race came into being through unpredictability and randomness. Nothing is ever predetermined for anyone.

CHRISTIANITY began its rise approximately 2,000 years ago, by challenging, discrediting, and ridiculing the intellectual and tolerant culture of classical Mediterranean reasoning. Here we see the formation of Christianity through the storytelling and weaving of absurd supernatural narratives.

The path to the one Christian God was littered with violence — attacking and burning polytheist texts — ushering in the emergence of heretics. Humans are not by any means special in the universe, nor is there a grand plan for us, for any individual or group of people. All of it was nonsense, made up by a group of perverted white men in Rome. The Catholic Church moved its part of the world from one of reason and tolerance to one of dogma, corruption, lies, and violence.

In the end, what we think or what we believe, or what we think we know, is of little consequence; the only thing of consequence is what is real! The universe does not care about anyone because the universe is made up of matter. We must liberate ourselves from the mental entrapment of superstition, fear, and suffering in order to be effective in the pursuit of our relevance in the universe. If we do not adhere to science and intellectualism, we will remain slaves to emotion and storytelling, generating acute poverty and powerlessness as our identity into the future.

WE SIMPLY cannot thrive as a species in a state of fragility; extinction will become increasingly likely. Suffering is not a virtue but a made-up narrative, one that was engineered for us to suffer while white supremacy prospers. In reality, Christianity is nothing more than a white Christian nationalist movement around the world, based on sexism, misogyny, and hatred against Black and non-white populations as well as Jews. That is what the storming of the U.S. Capitol on January 6, 2021 represented: an effort to establish America as a white, Christian, non-democratic country. The white mob of January 6th is similar to the many other white Christian mobs over the last 2,000 or so years, all of which had violence at their core. The dimwitted but dangerous white Christian nationalists believe that the U.S. was founded as a Christian country, and white evangelicals use Christianity as politics, believing that "God" has chosen them to lead the world.

The general historical records (depending, of course, on who is writing it and their perspective and motivation, so we must generalize here) tells us that before Christianity began to take shape, there were centuries of religious pluralism in the Greco-Roman world. This was called *paganism*, which is a derogatory term attached to religious pluralism by Christians. "Pagan" essentially means "peasant" in Greek. For a while, pagans, Jews, and future Christian converts all existed in a relatively intellectually sound pluralistic community, with religious and cultural tolerance, reason, logic, and knowledge-seeking, which formed the identity of society at the time. However, Christianity took civilization backwards. The society of intellectualism and reason that existed would soon come to an end in the early fourth century AD as the Roman emperor Constantine began the process of making Christianity the official religion of the Roman empire. Next, Constantine's zealous successor, Theodosius the Great, began to issue edicts embarking on the official state-led

60

destruction of paganism. So the formalized process of establishing Christianity by force, violence, and terror officially began. Theophilus released his mob of Christian zealots to roam the streets insulting, mocking, and demonizing pagans. The violent cult of Christianity was now coming into full stride.

Much of the coming section is highly influenced by and generally referenced from the Pulitzer Prize-winning and National Book Award-winning work *The Swerve: How The World Became Modern* by Harvard Professor Stephen Greenblatt. This is another must-read book for anyone who believes in lifelong learning and seeking the objective truth. The book is brilliant in how it explains how the fiction, lies, and sheer brutal manipulation of Christianity came into being—how it penetrated and became culture. It reads like a thriller at times, as you learn what you did not know nor could ever imagine. It goes to the core about the random nature of the universe, how, and not intended, but how white supremacy came into being.

Christian monks moved into pagan precincts and temples with a "holy" mission against the "infidels" and began burning and destroying pagan symbols and practices to the ground. "Headless, limbless trunks were dragged to the theater and publicly burned." Monks moved into the beautiful pagan temples and converted them to churches. Christians would now erect Christian statues to stand in triumph. At the time, the pagan poet Palladas expressed the devastation this way:

> *Is it not true that we are dead, and living only in appearance,*
> *We Hellenes, fallen on disaster,*
> *Likening life to a dream, since we remain alive while*
> *Our way of life is dead and gone.*

The significance of the violent destruction went far beyond the physical. Christians were the original terrorists, destroying other belief systems and ways of life. Libraries were destroyed, along with schools, museums, and other institutions, none of which could withstand the onslaught of the violent assaults of the Christian mob.

Cyril, the successor to Theophilus, intensified and expanded the reign of Christian terrorism, now directing its wrath against the Jews. "Violent skirmishes broke out in the theater, in the streets, and in front of churches and synagogues." Jewish homes and shops were plundered. Hundreds of monks joined the mob as Cyril demanded the expulsion of the city of Rome's large Jewish population. The flames of Christian fanaticism were now ablaze, and it would henceforth drive the "one-God" Christian doctrine to take over societies by violent means.

The demonizing of women and violence against them also have their origins in Christianity. Those women who spoke out—who men felt should play no leadership role in society—were marginalized and branded as witches. Women were pulled out of their homes, stripped naked, raped, and burned at the stake, beginning the long Christian tradition of subjugation of women. This made possible the transformation from a pluralist, tolerant world to a world characterized by the big lie of the "one true faith" happened.

IN THE CARIBBEAN today, consider the example of Jamaica. LGBTQ people are subjected to widespread violence in a country that claims to be a "Christian" society. However, Jamaica's national profile, according to United Nations, World Bank, and various human watch-dog agency findings, is one of violence, having the second-highest murder rate in the world, per capita, after El Salvador.

Jamaica is wrapped in the hypocrisy and lies of Christian cultural belief systems, including the use of the Bible to justify violence against our LGBTQ brothers and sisters. How can Jamaica consider itself civilized if, even in the 21st century, it is still defending a colonial-era Offences Against the Person Act dating back to 1864, which punishes the "abominable crime of buggery" and acts of "gross indecency"?

Time Magazine once dubbed Jamaica "the most homophobic place on earth." Forbes has ranked Jamaica as the place to which you do not want to travel if you are gay. How can Jamaica be part of the modern world while clinging to backward colonial-era laws? According to *Human Rights Watch*, "Many [LGBT Jamaicans] live in constant fear. They are taunted; threatened; fired from their jobs; thrown out of their homes; beaten, stoned, [set on fire, chopped up,] and killed." So what is the difference between Christianity 2,000 years ago and Jamaica today? Once again, the Bible and the one-God narrative leave Jamaica as a primitive, backwards society, medieval in character—very much in the tradition of the lies, corruption, and brutality of Christianity. Therefore, regardless of the adoption of Christianity by many cultures and the creation of enduring institutions, Christianity was built and maintains itself on a monumental lie.

A lie does not become truth, wrong does not become right, and evil does not become good just because it is accepted by a majority. — Booker T. Washington

In *The Swerve*, author Stephen Greenblatt describes the violent transformation of Christianity this way:

> *The murder of Hypatia (an intellectual woman) signified more than the end of a remarkable person; it effectively marked the downfall of Alexandrian intellectual life and the death knell for the whole intellectual tradition. Museums, all schools, and all ideas were no longer at the protected centre of civil society, virtually all the sum of classical culture had vanished without a trace.*

ai

*Their hero Emperor Cyril was eventually made a Christian
saint.*

The one-God Christian religion was built on evil and lies, which
continued over many centuries—causing injustices and atrocities such
as the Crusades, the Holocaust, the transatlantic slave trade, the
plantation economy, various Inquisitions, imperialism, colonialism,
Canada's residential schools' system, the Rwandas genocide and the
role that the Catholic Church played in it, and so on.

The continued protection of perverted priests by the Catholic
Church and other Christian denominations might seem difficult to
understand. However, again, Christianity is about the maintenance of
power and domination above all by white supremacy culture and
white male hierarchical leadership. This is what happens when we put
God above humanity.

The church developed through hierarchical structures
whereby noble and aristocratic men and their families paid Latin
scribes to write religious doctrines. So this societal structure
translated into the hierarchical structuring of the church, with
bishops and cardinals now running the corrupt curia courts, where
the Pope was the absolute authoritarian head of this corrupt universe.
The office of the Pope was about power, nothing more; the church
financed wars and the theft of gold and other treasure to support this
powerful institution of lies. Thievery, force, and brutality were
normalized in Christian culture. The church developed as a tool of
power and access to wealth. Under the curia, lies and laws were
manufactured through the one-God narrative. Fantasy stories were
now written as religious doctrines; this became the Bible.

The Catholic Church in particular was a massive bureaucracy,
and one's relative proximity to it determined what levels of wealth
and power one could attain. Religion became a business, and the
institution of the church and its lies permeated everywhere.

Greenblatt describes that a scribe writing at the time described the corrupt curia this way:

> *The papal court — witty gossip, along with fantastic food and drink served by beautiful, young, hairless boys. And for those whose tastes do not run in the direction of Ganymede, there are the abundant pleasures of Venus. Mistresses, adulterous matrons, and courtesans of all descriptions occupy a central place in the curia, and appropriately so since the delights they offer have such a central place in human happiness. Lewd songs, naked breasts, kissing, fondling, with small white lap dogs trained to lick around your groin to excite desire.*

In the end, the universe is *nature*, and nature consists of atoms, energy, and emptiness, as written by Lucretius over 2,000 years ago. There is no divine plan, and Providence is fantasy. There is no intelligent design inherent in matter. There is no world of fate, daemons, celestial messengers, or spirits of the dead. Human existence is random, our life after birth is unpredictable, and when we die, we return to the *matter* of the soil. According to Lucretius, all the other claims, the "glorification of the gods or the ruler, the arduous pursuit of virtue through self-sacrifice—are secondary, misguided, or fraudulent." The overriding message here for Black Caribbean people is—Christianity is a fraud!

Religion stifles intellect and leads to reliance on emotion. It traps us in what is our greatest challenge as humans — overcoming ourselves, which requires exercising our free will, intellectual capacity, and individualism. But Christianity takes all those essential things away from us, through lies and pressure to conform to those lies. We must not succumb to dependency on emotion and fantastical explanations; look to math and science, not superstition, Bible stories, or ancient speculation.

Lucretius's great work *On the Nature of Things* provides us with the objective truth about the universe. If we are not diligent in the pursuit of real information and knowledge, i.e., *the truth*, we will simply end up overwhelmed by the narrative of Christian suffering while the rest of the world prospers around us. Willful ignorance is a choice! Adherence to suffering is not innate to the human condition; it is a learned behaviour, so it can be unlearned.

If we wish to progress individually and as a people, we must remove those mind-blinders that have been cleverly placed within our subconscious. Focus on the nature of things instead. Move to logic, reason, exercising free will, individualism, and the intellectual capacity we all have inside of us. Walk the enlightened path. Nothing is ever predetermined; life is inherently unpredictable and filled with randomness. Humans are inherently free, but we all too often compromise our freedom through willful ignorance and laziness. We are all responsible for ourselves in the end, so it is up to us to give meaning to our own lives. No reliance on Christian dogma is necessary. We ought to look to the *realness* of spirituality instead, because our spiritual energy in the universe is real; our human body consists of electrical currents to function, and requires fueling through nourishment. This is how energy is created, and the mind and body form a single energy force with real frequencies. That energy powers our bodies and minds and those forces are generated in the mind; where our spirituality comes from. Religion is not natural, so not conducive to spirituality, and if you use religion as a source for spirituality, then it is only artificial, not sustainable as part of your nature.

Apply intelligence, because religion makes you a slave to an unnatural existence. Ultimately, your progress, prosperity, and power depend on what you do next. Therefore, we must first distinguish ourselves from the conformity of the herd. We are now in the 21st century, after all.

Towards A Required Renaissance in Black Thinking

> Only 0.35% of the Universe is observable; the rest is invisible to the naked eye. All modalities, in this case, Science and Religion use beliefs to interpret reality.

> –Unknown

Nature is truth, religion is storytelling, and as Mohandas Gandhi once expressed, nothing is or exists in reality except truth; and to find the truth, one must first seek knowledge. Science and math are the languages of nature; they explain the metaphysical world and show us the truth about the universe. Only through the science of nature can we get the truth about the universe. Therefore, devotion to truth and not religion must be our primary purpose in life, and all our activities should be centered around seeking knowledge in order to know the truth. Without truth, it is impossible to observe any principles or rules in life, again according to wisdom from Mohandas Gandhi.

During the period of the European Enlightenment—its Renaissance era—French philosopher René Descartes in his Discourse on Method (1637) said *"I think, therefore, I am"* as a first step in demonstrating the attainability of certain knowledge. Our existence in the universe is confirmed because we can think for ourselves in nature, confirming reality through our knowledge and understanding of our existence. There can be no doubt about that!

We are not the creation of fantastical, man-made Bible stories. Only nature is pure; man is corrupt, and fantasy is the antithesis of reality, counterintuitive and counterproductive to our real-world existence. So if you rely on emotionally-led fantastical belief systems—such as religious doctrines—then you will not function well in the real world. Therefore, for the Black populations of the Caribbean, there can be no doubt about our existence in reality. How we think determines how we act, and our behavioural habits, so if we continue to think and act with emotional habits, we will always be susceptible to being misled by entertaining stories. Therefore, we will remain at the bottom rungs of the universe, never catching up, always behind the prosperity curve.

So our mindset must be about understanding the universe, distinguishing what is real from what is not real and knowing the difference between causation and correlation. According to the philosopher Soren Kierkegaard (1813–1855), life is not a problem to be solved, but a reality to be experienced. Decisions are the most important things that shape the experiences of our lives. Over time, knowledge-seeking and entrepreneurship have enabled many enterprising individuals to engage in quantitative thinking, enabling them to identify and interpret their physical environment, to innovate and to gain from it. Innovation enhances the efficiency and dynamic characteristics of production outputs, leading to profits and higher living standards for any given society.

Nature is ascertainable through mathematics, and those who exercise mathematical thinking will thrive over those who engage in emotional thinking. The intellectualization of the mind, thinking quantitatively, always doing the math and adhering to the laws of nature, is how prosperity is created. Therefore, adherence to reality is a fundamental prerequisite for happiness. Only through the intellectual process can we compete and win in the universe. As Caribbean people of African descent,
we must always adhere to reality, not continue to be massively side-tracked by religious narratives that do not exist in reality.

Aristotle once said that it is always up to you. And Bob Marley said Emancipate yourselves from mental slavery; none but ourselves can free our minds. Although over 2,000 years have elapsed between the two, their insights are timeless. This simply confirms that nature never can change fundamentally; it cannot ever be anything other than what it is. So the objective truth about our humanity never changes, it is only the times and the relative technology that becomes contemporary to us.

Blind adherence to Christianity continues to be among the most significant factors holding back Black societies of the Caribbean—self-suppression via attachment to Bible stories. This tendency also continues to deny us our true potential to create a great Caribbean civilization. We continue to live our present lives orchestrated by the past, based on blueprints written by corrupt white men and relayed through ancient Christian doctrines.

The legacy of the trans-Atlantic slave trade, the plantation economy, colonialism, and neocolonialism has been supported by White Supremacist Christianity (WSC) throughout the many centuries. The Black psyche has been dominated by WSC, and it has become a defining feature of the Black Caribbean community and its diaspora. WSC has brilliantly managed to maintain the lion's share of the wealth curve in the universe by intellectually and economically understanding that the control of minds makes chains unnecessary. WSC has convinced Black populations that suffering is a virtue, that the sufferer goes to heaven. There can be no virtue in suffering. Not striving for personal gain is non-nonsensical, because the pursuit of gain is the very genesis of the socioeconomic security that the human condition requires. Without productivity and wealth creation, we can have no political power and no privilege. If we believe that hope and prayer can bring us security, then we are not living in reality; we are living in delusion, a controlled hallucination of sorts. WSC is about the purposeful control of the factors of production for the primary purpose of long-term wealth creation, and security for the ones who control it.

While modern Black communities continue to embrace Christianity and suffering, whites continue to move within reality, intellectually exercising their quantitative and mathematical mastery of the universe for their benefit. And they have worked brilliantly to maintain the economic status quo over the centuries.

For example, the British aristocracy's defining feature was not any noble, virtuous aspiration to serve the common good; rather, it was a desperate singular desire for wealth through stolen riches. They stole land under the pretense of religious reverence. They seized it through conquest, and they expropriated and enclosed everything for their private use under the guise of efficiency and society. They then corruptly carved out industry, commerce, and trade on a global basis for further self-enrichment and the linear bequest of privilege to be leveraged further by future generations.

So behind the beauty of the British aristocracy's stately homes and the sometimes romantic and eventful lives they led, lies a darker story: a legacy of theft, violence, and unrepentant greed.

—Chris Bryant, The Guardian

Do we continue to bury our collective heads in the sand, choosing to be willfully ignorant about the reality of the universe—to settle for existence in the comfort of our self-delusion—or do we seek the objective truth? Shall we choose victimhood and suffering over intergenerational wealth and opportunity for us?

STILL, the human condition does require emotional support; we are emotional beings, after all. However, we are also intellectual beings, which allows us to manage our own emotions. So our intellectual capacity must remain at the forefront of our thinking and behaviour. Over-reliance on religion only exacerbates this delusional existence and conformity to WSC. The human condition requires many things—economic security and survival being at the very top—and achieving that requires more intellect, not more emotion. Our intellect is responsible for our survival and our success, and it is also our emotions, more often than not, that are responsible for our failures.

So while modern Blacks stick with the emotionally driven ideology of Christianity, whites utilize their intellectual capacity towards the goal of self-preservation through entrepreneurship, controlling the factors of production, profit, wealth, and political power in the world. WSC has stealthily weaponized religion to secure and maintain its wealth and power intergenerationally. Blacks have fallen for the classic ruse, "Do as I say, not as I do!"

To address and serve the emotional side of our human condition, we must turn to spirituality, not religion. Spirituality is internal, with real energy frequencies. Spirituality is scientific; it is about biology and neuroscience. Our internal energy forces can be harnessed for our spiritual and mental well-being. Religion, on the other hand, is simply heavy, always weighing us down. Religion does not help the human spirit; it burdens it with conformity and dogma. Spirituality is embedded in us, like our very humanity; we merely have to find it. Spirituality enables our individualism to flourish while religion stifles it, therefore, spirituality is the precious seeking of our individualistic selves in nature, non-alignment with the Christian herd. Hence, spirituality is individualism, and we must strive for being our intellectual and spiritual selves.

Our self-worth and self-esteem, courage, resilience; our passion, creativity, empathy, and purpose—all come from our minds and are driven by our human spirit as real energy forces. Happiness requires having the intellectual capacity to make decisions as an individual, based on what is real—not falling prey to Bible stories that suspend our intellect and suppress good judgment. One's own naturally occurring spirituality belongs only to oneself, not to the herd; it is deeply individual, and it strengthens each individual person. With WSC, however, we exist within the fragility of the herd because everything is made up, with a set direction for the herd to follow, nothing is authentic, and energy and time are squandered. Spirituality builds natural, energy-based confidence; religion builds delusions of reality. Spirituality generates the energy to soar; religion only mires us in suffering!

So what is the most critical decision we make in life? It is to understand oneself, and the true nature of the universe—to find truth through spirituality rather than religion, to find the natural means by which one can live the truth. Discerning one's path in life is difficult, and unpredictable as life itself, however, the one true thing always remains the truth.

Kierkegaard writes, "Truth always rests with the minority, and the minority is always stronger than the majority, because the minority is generally formed by those who have an opinion, while the strength of a majority is illusory, formed by the gangs who have no opinion—and who, therefore, in the next instant (when it is evident that the minority is the stronger) assume its opinion...while truth again reverts to a new minority."

Therefore, attaching oneself to the herd of WSC and detaching from the individualism and free will of your spirituality has been a very costly mistake for Black populations of the Caribbean. Seneca, the stoics, stresses that it is dangerous to attach oneself to the crowd and that we are often more willing to trust others than ourselves. And as Friedrich Nietzsche put it, "sometimes people do not want to hear the truth because they do not want their illusions destroyed." So Black people must wake up and escape WSC and move towards science and truth-seeking — knowledge acquisition so as to understand how to win in the universe. Spirituality helps us; it makes us robust and anti-fragile. A free mind frees the spirit, liberates the soul, and dismantles the barriers of restrictive thinking. A renaissance in Black thinking must occur now! We need a new, free, and truth-seeking Black mind, driven by the enlightenment of science and technology towards an intellectual existence.

Through the clever utilization of Christianity, white supremacy has positioned European and European-descended populations as the top of the socioeconomic ladder in the world. Meanwhile, Black people, with our over-reliance on emotion and religious storytelling, have not been able to extricate ourselves from the bottom rungs of that ladder. Therefore, remaining willfully ignorant of

the reality of the universe makes us complicit in our own demise. For Black people to find wealth, power, and privilege, a 21st-century renaissance in thinking must be at the top of the agenda.

Therefore, the most important thing for Black populations of the Caribbean to do in the modern era is to enter into the 21st century fully. This begins by moving away from both WSC and the suffering/victim-based, "woke" mentality and by moving toward the bright light of intellect and logic. A renaissance in Black thinking is required because suffering is not the natural state of any human or race of people. Nothing is ever predetermined. Seeking personal gain is essential to life, security, and happiness. Therefore, mastering self-preservation is absolutely critical to our existence, and to our very survival as a species.

The immense forces of the human spirit, coupled with the awe-inspiring power of the mind, is the only superpower you have. Let reality be your common denominator in life, the most powerful guiding principle. Nature is math, the truth, so to find wealth and prosperity, you must always be doing your math, so to speak. Happiness is the meaning and purpose of life, and freeing the Black mind from mental slavery is the way forward, according to Bob Marley. Then the whole aim and end of human existence can only be to seek the truth about finding happiness.

Authentic Happiness – Meditations in *applied intelligence*

"Happiness is the meaning and the purpose of life, the whole aim and end of human existence," said Aristotle; and Einstein followed with, "if you want to live a happy life, tie it to a goal, not to people or things."

Bob Marley put the cherry on top, saying "Love the Life you Live. Live the Life You Love."

If the meaning of life is to find happiness, then one must find a purpose in order to live a happy existence—as opposed to living a mere outer existence, which means conformity, living for the approval of others. Hence, individualism is the path to a happy life. Material things are fleeting. The outer existence will fail you; friends can fail you, and society will fail you. Your underlying anchor must be responsible, which can apply to all areas of your life—careers, relationships, health, and lifestyle. Living a purposeful life with long-term goals can drive authentic happiness. Goals trigger passion and the zest for living, which can be among the most powerful drivers of human happiness. To change one's life, however, one must apply intelligence and adopt life-changing pursuits, because change can only happen when one decides to change oneself first.

So if we want to live happy lives, we must set goals for ourselves. No one is entitled to happiness; happiness must be worked for. Authentic happiness is not about enjoying oneself; it is significantly more immense than that. Happiness is the aggregate output of what we invest in life and the strategy that underlies that investment. In the modern era, one example might be investing in relative technology, for example, to augment our existence (whether it be for work or play), or the use of mental health or wellness apps or working virtually so that we have more time to spend with family. Technology is highly useful for living!

Therefore, technology is not only advantageous to businesses to make them more efficient in creating value. Technology is also very useful and effective in maximizing the value of time. Our time here on Earth and the space we occupy in the universe is minuscule, so we would do well to augment them through the usefulness of relative technology to create space and time for us to live well. Logically, if technology makes our lives more efficient—and it does—then it can make us more productive in seeking our goals and aspirations as well. Hence, technology is a major player in human-life-value creation.

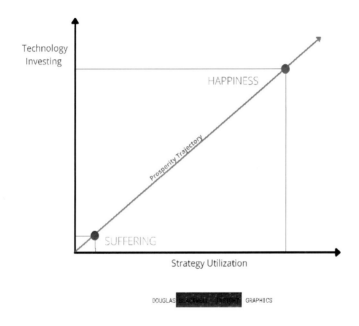

So we must not wait for life to happen; we must make life happen ourselves, which requires investment in life and a strategy for living and achievement. If not, we will only bring about our own misery, blaming others for your suffering instead of taking responsibility for your own. Design your happiness through your defined purpose and individual values, setting your priorities and doing the necessary work in pursuit of that authentic happiness.

Working for happiness requires living in consciousness more than subconsciousness, being mindful and intentional about what we do, and the tasks and activities that we take on. If we do not prioritize these activities, we will waste a great deal of valuable time. Not everything can be a priority, so unfocused activities act as distractions, and it then becomes more difficult to define the important and impactful tasks in your life. We become rudderless in our navigation. The investments we make in life must always be attached to a strategy; otherwise, there can be no good execution, no return on investment, and no measurement or accountability, and thus no value can be created. If your focus is

simply on healthy living and spirituality, focus your time investment there, and create a realistic strategy that can facilitate it.

If you are searching for meaning in your life, then put meaning into your activities. You are in search of deeper knowledge and wisdom, you say? Then are you reading the classic philosophers—the ancient Stoics, for example? Are you reading one of the greatest Black thinkers, Franz Fanon? Fanon was a psychiatrist who explained the confused Black human condition in his outstanding analysis of colonialism and decolonization in his classic book *The Wretched of the Earth*. That work addressed how both of those historical processes distorted Black minds and left our psyches damaged. Or are you spending all of your spare time on Facebook or other social media platforms, making yourself stupider, chasing after Likes? Life is straightforward; it is about what you do, not about what you say you want to do. You cannot fake it; you are only fooling yourself in the end.

It is always up to you; this is the main theme of stoicism. Marcus Aurelius, in his night-time meditations, emphasized that we need very little to create a happy life; happiness is within us, our inner selves, determined by how we choose to think. You get out what you put into life. So the biggest investment you must make is the investment in yourself.

The most critical questions are how to live our lives and what we should do to bring meaning to life. Therefore, it would make good sense to have a disciplined framework of analysis and strategy to help us through this important process. After all, we only have one life; we should be living it well!

Life often becomes complicated because we cannot distinguish what is really important from distraction, yet avoiding distractions is critical for success. Simply steering clear of things that can put us in negative territory becomes a critical skill for success and happiness. Consider the guidance of Epictetus, the influential and profound Stoic, over two thousand years ago, on his continued discourse on happiness which is interpreted widely in Stoic philosophy, talking about happiness as an internal process of focusing on what you have control of—your mind. His main point, and that of the Stoics, is that one should not be concerned with things one cannot control; rather, one should focus on the things that one can control. Epictetus was not a theoretical philosopher; he was a thoughtful and practical man, and his advice could always be applied to the real world, which is the purpose of *applied intelligence*. Application is key, because what is the usefulness or value of something if it cannot be applied to help you? Good theories that lack any practical application are useless theories.

On the whole, the Stoics taught that the world is random, and there is no divine intervention or celestial hand; the universe does not know who you are. We must learn to accept the reality of human existence. Confronting reality is essential to achieving good outcomes, and to do so, a disciplined quantitative system of thinking and analytical framework is indispensable. And this, essentially, is the value of *applied intelligence*. Epictetus believed that all humans are in search of happiness, but we can become distracted from the path to happiness, or we can go about pursuing it the wrong way. Whether you think and act in a disciplined manner will ultimately determine your level of happiness or suffering.

For it is within you, that both your destruction and deliverance lie. — Epictetus

Therefore, we must work with a higher-dimensional level of analysis; applying intelligence to dismantle the old legacy systems and barriers of the past. The general goal is to awaken ourselves to a higher state of consciousness, to the objective truths, applying logic and intellectualism, innovation, and entrepreneurship—putting science, mathematics, and technology at the forefront in order to drive us to prosperity.

Today, the world is in transformation, and this decade may represent unsettling change for many. However, the history of civilization has taught us that embracing change relative to your time and place in the universe is a positive and productive thing. Remember, disorder and uncertainty create opportunities for growth. Put aside all morality-driven philosophies and fantasies and stick to the laws of nature! That is the most reliable approach.

Societies have always organized themselves in hierarchical ways based on the value that members of society are perceived to be able to create. This is how the world works, and our willingness or refusal to accept that reality does not change the hard bedrock reality of life. So spending time in the depths of morality thinking, trying to change the hearts and minds of others about fairness and equality, is futile. People cannot be guilted or shamed into sharing their wealth. One of the most critical teachings of the Stoics concerns not wasting time and energy fretting about things we cannot control. We must focus our energy on what we can control—our ***thinking!***

However, also be cautious of overthinking, or analysis by paralysis. Start doing the calculus and begin with step-by-step problem solving and move along. Just get cracking!

CHAPTER 1

The Nature of Economics

In October 2021, the new Nobel Prize in economics was awarded to three men, David Card, Joshua Angrist, and Guido Imbens. The prize was awarded for their work done regarding labour and growth—but I, for one, honestly did not see its practical real-world application. The average person on the street, I imagine, might say, "Tell me something I do not already know." Nevertheless, the Prize shone a bright light on a major problem in economic development theory: the disconnect between classroom economics and real-world economics. Much of the work is obvious from where I sit in the practical world, with no time to waste on philosophy; but like most things in classroom economics, it is made complex, so it can no longer be useful to the person on the street. From a theoretical perspective, the study was great for academic discourse on a philosophical level, but not of any usable value in real people's lives, which is what I believe economic work number one priority must be. To go deeper into it you can look it up online under David Card, Nobel Prize in Economics.

Therefore, over-academicization when explaining the nature of economics distorts *real-world economics*. In reality, economics becomes philosophy: a series of artificial constructs and theoretical models that end up being used mainly for teaching purposes in the classroom. Academic quests to develop neat equations to explain things only end up distorting things in the end; they are not helpful to real people.

THERE ARE laws and limits in ecology that always emerge and work themselves out organically. Economic ecosystems are similar; they regulate and sustain themselves organically over time. As in ecology, real-world economics—the dynamics of which involve growth, death, periods of bounty and drought, adaptation, thriving, extinction, etc.—simply creates an ecosystem that works *in nature*. And so, this upcoming section relies on a great book, a quick and easy read, by Jane Jacobs, *The Nature of Economics*. Jacobs simply uses ecology to explain real world economics because class-room economics is practically useless in explaining the real world, as I read her work. Here, we apply *applied intelligence* to the analysis for the purpose of understanding or living in the real world versus the class-room world.

We would save a great deal of time and money if we could spend less time studying things that offer no value to the universe and spend more time instead on solving real problems in the real world for real people. Consider climate change mitigation, for example. How can small island states (SIS) of the Caribbean use climate change mitigation as an economic opportunity to build prosperity? Can the pursuit of a zero-emission economy not create economic growth organically while mitigating climate change? "Development" discourse does not align with nature, its processes, and its limits. Studying how different ecosystems develop in nature can be helpful to the organic economic development of Caribbean SIS, instead of the ideological or theoretical, top-down approaches that continue to be presented. Unfortunately, the field is dominated by academics and "development" experts instead of local entrepreneurs, even though it is well known that it is entrepreneurship that drives economies. But instead, Caribbean economic development continues to be driven primarily by academics who know nothing about the real world and never were or can be entrepreneurs themselves.

Differentiation flows from generalities. For example, it is illogical to assume that one type of plant that thrives in one environment can automatically do the same in another. You cannot simply plant a certain species of plant in another location, in a different type of soil, and expect it to thrive. There are multiple scientific environmental variables at play in different ecosystems that are all unique to each environment, the soil in particular. The artificial, top-down nature of development discourse has characteristics of the latter example—the belief that one size fits all and that abstract theories can be easily replicated in different real-world environments. In reality, introducing a new species into a foreign environment can be hostile and even detrimental to the local ecology. These top-down implementations inherently fail because they are not a natural fit for local environments, since they do not consider the uniqueness of the local ecology.

Additionally, the hierarchical structures at play in "development" discourse have underlying white supremacist elements attached, carrying paternalistic views that are designed to overwhelm local knowledge systems and entrepreneurship. This prevents organic socio-economic ecosystems from taking root. Such ingrained white supremacy domination creates dysfunctional local systems, preventing them from organically connecting their local economies to the global economy; leaving them as economic basket cases. In reality, however, they never had a chance. They are casualties of a vicious circle that merely creates more work and justifications for Western-led academic and development advisors to fix a problem they help create. But of course, the arrogance of white supremacy does not allow them to see their errors.

Once again, as Adam Smith observed, personal gain and entrepreneurship are the natural bottom-up paths of development—and these are the paths that Caribbean people must pursue. It has worked for thousands of years for many other civilizations and groups, so why would it not work for Caribbean societies? Where in the world has academia alone ever created thriving, sustainable economies?

THE THREE MAIN EUROPEAN COLONIAL POWERS, Spain, France, and Britain, were all developed by state-sponsored capitalism, using colonialism as their economic expansion model. This process included the use of military conquest and even genocide to build their wealth. Slavery was one of the biggest historical contributors to European socioeconomic wealth ever. It provided a massive head start as there was no cost base, so the ROI was phenomenal. Slavery was fundamentally about economics; but we have become too preoccupied with the injustices of slavery, diverting our attention from the economics of it all and the enduring socioeconomic impact it continues to have on the entire world. This emotional response then leads us to lament racism subconsciously and to focus more on the romanticization of the struggle against racism, instead of focusing on how we can create greater economic value in the universe.

We fail to examine it from an economic perspective and wrongly believe we can change systems by changing hearts and minds—never! We simply become overwhelmed by past trauma and fail to focus on the present and the future, on what we must do next in order to thrive in the universe. An excessive focus on the emotions of racism and a lesser focus on the key to self-preservation—especially entrepreneurship—has not been helpful to the economics of Black people. The application of your feelings will not change anything, but the intellectual process will lead you in the right direction.

We need to examine the first principles of what motivated Europeans to develop and institutionalize slavery. It is also critical to understand that the American Civil War was fought over the economics and geopolitics of the slave plantation system and that it was not about morality. Readings on Abraham Lincoln and the Civil War in general, and particularly a read of the book *Team Of Rivals: The Political Genius of Abraham Lincoln,* by Pulitzer Prize winner Doris Karns Goodwin, reveal that for Lincoln, the war was necessary because the American South was holding the North back from future industrialization and modernization. Lincoln feared that the industrialization that was happening in Europe and elsewhere in the world would push these economies past the United States if the South was allowed to maintain the manual labour-intensive method of production that was inherent in the slave economy. Therefore, while much of the rest of the world engaged in innovation and invention, the South remained manual and backward due to the plantation system. Lincoln recognized that and concluded that war was the only way to an industrial and profitable growth future for America.

As MENTIONED earlier, generalities help to frame perspectives and ideas, so differentiation is the main factor in how value is created. Nature and development are both complex with a great many different variables at play. It therefore stands to reason that artificialized classroom explanations and top-down theories of development can get around the hard laws of nature.

For example, oranges are a staple fruit around the world, and Florida dominates the global market for both oranges and juice. Would it make sense for Caribbean countries to try and plant the same species of Florida orange trees, take decades for them to grow, and then try to enter the market to compete against Florida? This, of course, would be ridiculous. The Caribbean has many species of citrus fruit, a different soil construct, and from my vantage point, has incredibly better-tasting citrus and a variety of fruit in general. Growing up in Grenada as a very young boy, I can still taste the spectacular flavours of several of my grandmother's citrus trees in the back of the house, which she often sent me to pick for her to use to make juice. She blended her oranges with another citrus, a unique Caribbean species of lime, and add in raw cane sugar; the result was beautiful and delicious.

Therefore, the intelligent move would be to work with the local growers of this better-tasting citrus to try and carve out a new market space based on the quality and uniqueness of the Caribbean product, utilizing innovation and technology to our advantage, instead of trying to copy another system that cannot be replicated in the region. It would be better to innovate and create a "Pure Caribbean" juice brand for export—a pesticide-free, clean, organic food product and create new demand and develop new markets. The differentiation factor is a value creator. Why can it not be done? More importantly, why has it not been done already?

It hasn't been done because the Caribbean people often hold themselves back. We have bought into a culture of white supremacy that tells us that we must adhere to white supremacist economics, which means not thinking for ourselves and trying to replicate what the supposedly superior white man does. This, however, is counterintuitive and counterproductive and works against us. It propagates a vicious circle of dependence. So what we end up with in the Caribbean is a culture of trepidation and fear of entrepreneurship—never wanting to be the first, sitting back and watching foreign investors come in and turn Black Caribbean populations into low-wage workers. The result is that these local economies cannot become middle-class-driven economies, which is necessary for sustainable growth and a prosperous economy.

Agriculture in the Caribbean is a massive wealth-creating opportunity; however, it continues to be wasted by poor leadership and thoughtlessness, timidity, and by the failure to build scalable knowledge-based ecosystems that can capitalize on the region's natural competitive advantages. Accordingly, in development, time must never be wasted on top-down academic exercises. Time must be spent instead fostering the organic socio-economic growth environments that can be leveraged in favour of sustainable Caribbean economies, from the bottom up. We must focus on those material variables of growth, seek differentiation through creativity and innovation, and drive towards an export-orientated, zero-emissions-based economy. This is the only way we can create economic value for ourselves, our families, and our societies.

THE REASON WHY top-down development economics amounts to nothing is that it is artificial, self-serving, and not aligned with the real economics of the region and its people. The Caribbean would do better to move away from "development" discourse and focus on self-reliance, which will spur entrepreneurship and growth organically. Enough sitting and waiting for others to do things that we must do ourselves. Real sustainable growth can only come from within, organically; it cannot be directed from above by bureaucrats and institutions that unfortunately continue to dominate the Caribbean region.

Differentiation spurs individualism, innovation, and entrepreneurship, which is essential for civilizations to prosper; this was the central theme of Adam Smith's *The Wealth of Nations*. Differentiation drives innovation for the survival of the species and uses the sophistication of self-preservation to find ways to adapt to changing environments.

You cannot stop time, but you must be aware of your time and place in the universe. Therefore, the selection of strategy in approaching growth is critical to good outcomes. The selection of applications selected is critical, all variables matter, and some more than others. So top-down generalities and assumptions usually fail because they operate on models based on the past, with no relevance to the new variables in the present. Textbooks simply cannot keep up with the pace of the modern world. A bottom-up approach, however, builds on the present, and of course, still uses history as a guide, with the understanding that accounting for current variables is critical to first understanding and defining the problem. Then we must find the right methodology and processes to try and solve these real-world problems. Value creation through the entrepreneurial culture, leveraging the Caribbean's natural resources as a comparative advantage, is the only path to prosperity for the region. So engaging in bureaucratic development is simply continuing to be willfully ignorant of reality.

COMMUNISM, the most notorious of all the top-down approaches, was also a miserable failure. China today falsely uses the "People's Revolution" only as narrative propaganda to engage in "command" capitalism. Communism, the Soviet Union's ideology, has created more problems for the world than any good it might have done. The ideology of conformity and the removal of individuality is always dangerous. Autocratic rule limits free will and democratic systems, which is what is necessary for differentiation and entrepreneurship.

Similarly, organizations like the World Bank have created autocratic, ideology-driven institutions that are incompatible with real-world value creation. They only create more problems. It is an unstoppable destructive monster that has to eat, and regions like the Caribbean are prime feeding grounds. World development agencies and development banks are harmful and unnatural in the context of real-world economics. Often corruption seeps in one way or another, and only the elites, academics, and cronies in the society benefit from dealing with these organizations—never the people or the real economy. Development agencies and banks become dividers, creating imbalances, inequalities, and more socioeconomic problems. They are top-heavy bureaucracies filled with technocrats who know absolutely nothing about organic entrepreneurship and long-term growth. Yet they continue to have a stranglehold on Caribbean economies, stifling any hope of future prosperity and self-determination.

These agencies have turned real life into the "Things Theory" of development, addressing how they believe the factors of production work rather than the true nature of things. Excessive theorizing and the arrogance of white supremacist domination of the economist "profession" over the region has dragged the Caribbean into the abyss. Deeply entangled in the destructive noise and nonsense (nn^2) of development discourse, a never-ending, looping vicious circle of harm and frustration.

Again, economics has strayed far from observation and explanation of human behaviour to grinding people down to be identified through the fallacy of math equations. But the "proofs" do not work. The tragedy is that these academics and development institutions have become the theoretical authorities on "development," wholly discouraging natural real-world entrepreneurship and growth in developing economies. Subconsciously, the discourse only reinforces in people's minds the idea that they are incapable of leading themselves and plays into the hands of white supremacist narratives and ideals. The hierarchical, communist-command bureaucratic tint of top-down development suppresses local creativity and innovation and crushes the human spirit and its primal instincts. "The eight million employees in the bureaucracies that were the Soviet Union's economic planning were believers in the
Thing Theory of development—but then, so are our policymakers, politicians, and civil servants, for the most part" (Jacobs 34).

The only pathway to a dynamic and prosperous regional economy is for everyone to get on board with moving the agriculture sector forward, driven by technology and automation. And pushing an export-led economy supported by a zero-emissions development profile is central to all that.   Export-led growth under a zero-emissions profile creates higher value-added exports produced at lower or zero energy costs, and lower operating costs due to technology, innovation, and automation. All of this ultimately amounts to higher profitability. Hard foreign payments flow right back into local economies, boosting economic activities in those economies—precipitating expansion.

The Caribbean simply cannot expand to a state of sustained prosperity without a strong export economy. Internal consumption spending cannot create wealth for businesses and cannot lead to income growth and the rise of the middle class. The past import-substitution or development projects have been tried in the past and have failed. Common sense alone tells us that if a local company expands its sales via export, there are simply more people to sell to. Common sense math tells us that Grenada, with a population of around one hundred thousand, versus the United States, with a 330 million population and higher per capita income…in which market do you think there is a greater probability of success?

Export economies earn more, create more local jobs, and those jobs pay more, so incomes rise; this is natural, bottom-up economics. So when export cash flows back, local economies get "liquefied" and growth begins to flourish. Increased consumer demand leads to more supply ramping up—new household goods, auto sales, clothes, food, more teachers, doctors, lawyers, diversified service providers, housing, construction, skill trades, financing needs, and so on. So once again, back to Adam Smith: individual gain through entrepreneurship results in societal gains from increased economic activity.

AGRICULTURE — LAND & SUN are two key natural comparative advantages available to the Caribbean to be used effectively towards building a zero-emissions, export-led growth economy. First, the prime objective is to move up the high-value supply chain with more high-value agriculture-based food products. The second step is to transition and combine renewable energy production in all farm and food processing operations. By coupling the two, you create a high-performing, high-value, enhanced earning export economy—not to mention the climate change mitigation effect.

Think clearly and quantitatively for a moment: If we could eliminate high energy costs in our business operations, those savings would go right into the bottom line, back into people's pockets. Further, morally, why use dirty energy or fossil fuel sources when we can use clean and renewable sources, such as the sun? Intelligent use of natural, non-polluting assets like the sun can create a competitive cost advantage for regional producers. A well-cultivated economic ecosystem creates profit, profit creates value, and value creates wealth, which enables us to amass greater power in the universe.

Many centuries ago, Venice's initial main resource that helped it rise in Eurasian trade and commerce was the mining of sea salt, which they began by trading heavily with Constantinople. The salt resource was a natural gift of geography to Venice based on the luck of location. Sea salt was a natural resource, but the quantitative knowledge Venetians were able to apply to it helped Venice evolve into a successful mercantile city-state. The salt itself had no intelligence; the intelligence was exhibited by entrepreneurial merchants who were enterprising, creative, and innovative with their resources. Venetians utilized their salt resource cleverly, directing the salt to concentrated areas of evaporating ponds in their lagoons. This brought the salt closer to land for efficient harvesting, and nearer to the ports for efficient loading onto ships.

Enterprise, innovation, and engineering made things happen; nothing happens on its own. Whatever the true details and processes were, the point here is that we must think quantitatively, and mathematically, and apply knowledge to generate economic value. So as the salt trade came into being, foreign payments were earned, capital began to flow into the Venetian economy, new merchants emerged, state currency value was created, and tax revenue was generated. History today often classifies Venice as the *birthplace of modern capitalism,* in Western culture but from the perspective of understanding enterprise and intelligence, this early mercantile state began with a simple natural resource and used a bottom-up growth process and intelligence to monetize production.

Let us now look at the academically inspired but short-lived import substitution experiments, which provides a really good example of the constant failures of the artificial nature of top-down economic tinkering. Import substitution was tried in many Latin American countries in the latter half of the 20th century. In brief, Import Substitution Industrialization (ISI) is a top-down trade and economic policy that advocates replacing imports with domestic production for supply. It is based on the premise that a country should attempt to reduce its foreign dependency through local industrialization and the production of products. However, common sense would tell you that such a policy goes against the natural ecology of real-world economics, and the basic principles of supply and demand. We will go into ISI analysis later, but for now, the point is that ISI was one of those artificial bureaucratic top-down approaches that are neither based on reality nor conducive to organic growth.

ISI theory is a perfect example of how academia can hinder or even ruin developing economies. Artificial systems introduced into natural ecosystems or new environments become like invasive species, threatening the natural ecology of ecosystems. Artificial top-down applications lead to imbalances, more problems, and the creation of a vicious circle of constant errors, often setting local economies back or preventing them from hitching onto and riding the global wealth curve, driving them to the lower realms of the global economy.

Import substitution advocates—mainly economists, policymakers, and the bureaucratic intelligentsia—continue to theorize and install nonsense applications that obstruct the natural flows of developing economies, like the ones in the Caribbean and Latin America.

> *Economic history is stuffed with expensive duds undertaken by people who thought they could predict the future by shaping it. The foreign-aid import-substitution fiasco is an example: big, quick fixes for big problems"* (Jacobs, pg. 139).

"Technocrats will never understand…natural processes put limits on what we can do and how we can do it" (Jacobs, pg. 82). Differentiated and diverse ecosystem economies sustain and regulate themselves naturally; if we tinker too much with them, they fall apart. So we must know how to be a productive part of the "nature of economics," instead of trying to artificialize it through top-down development discourse. Everything in ecology naturally connects and forms a strong and resistant web that supports its growth and expansion in the universe, which is impossible to replicate artificially. Therefore, we must understand how we can fit in and enhance things naturally to create the wealth we need, and on a basic level, the sophistication of self-preservation is entrepreneurship, which is fundamental to growth.

We in the Caribbean must face up to the reality of our natural world. There is no alternative universe, no new brilliant other theory that will provide a shortcut to prosperity. So we must stop being deceived all the time, fooled by "development" discourse, and stop making excuses for the negative position that we occupy.

Therefore, embrace globalization, see the world, and seek opportunities in it. Take what the natural world gives you, and work with it because "opportunity, not necessity, is the mother of invention" (Jacobs pg. 90). A change in thinking and an attitude shift are first required—self-reliance, resilience, knowledge acquisition, and opportunity seeking. Most importantly, stop sitting around waiting for others to do for you what you must do for yourself.

Economics has not advanced all that much since the days of Adam Smith; it still "dwell[s] on arid arguments about whether supply generates demand or demand generates supply—arguments that continue to this day" (Jacobs pg. 106). However, embedded in Smith's explanations was the fundamental understanding that human behaviour is inherent in economics, so economics may often fit better into the discipline of psychology. As a first principle, survival is the first objective of self-preservation, so the region must first learn how to survive before it can think about thriving in the universe.

The poet Goethe said, "Life belongs to the living, and he who lives must be prepared for changes." Similarly, the philosopher Lao Tzu observed, "Life is a series of natural and spontaneous changes, do not resist them; that only creates sorrow." LET REALITY BE REALITY.

Therefore, if you do not understand how the world works, you are likely to make mistakes, sometimes fatal ones. A virtuous life connects to living with nature, but thriving in nature requires applying a defined, 21st-century system of thinking and decision-making, augmented with data science applications and methods—in other words, *applied intelligence*.

IN THE END, we must learn from nature, for it holds all the answers to the questions we have and the questions that we do not yet know but need to ask. Ecology and economics are similar in nature, but the artificialization of economics has turned it into philosophy, shifting it away from an effective focus on solving problems in the real world. And many Caribbean economies have become economic theoretical experiments for World Bank-type advisors who only create more problems so they can get more work and earn higher salaries.

Adherence to the intellectual and scientific understanding of ecosystems, in their primal, regenerative, and adaptable states, the natural environment of living systems, is how the real world effectively looks and works. We would be better served being guided by the laws of nature rather than trying to get around them. To avoid extinction and to ensure longevity is a choice; the people of the Caribbean must understand our unique ecological ecosystem and situation and how to survive in the *global ecology*. We must not fall victim to artificial and delusional constructs of socioeconomic reality; we must find and keep our footing in nature. Primal instincts are fundamental, but the pursuit of self-preservation is necessary for development, and intellectualization of those instincts helps you navigate successfully in the universe. Your value-creation power rests directly on the strength and integrity of your internal will to survive and thrive as an individual in any ecosystem. Therefore, it is futile to try and circumvent universal principles, laws, and natural systems. We must "beware of the drift into ideology. Economic ideologies are a curse" (Jacobs pg. 147). The human ego takes over, philosophy starts to dominate, and theories act as blinders to reality.

We often bury our heads in the sand, blinding ourselves to the real-world meaning and application of rational decision-making. To assume that people make decisions primarily based on broadly defined supply and demand assumptions is a gross oversimplification. In the information age, simple supply and demand characteristics are no longer of the utmost relevance to economic outcomes. Culture and belief systems, social media, technology applications, and transaction systems are evolving and shaping outcomes more and more. Relevance to time and place has never been as important as it is now in the digital era. Evolving trends and dominant demographics are highly influenceable in the supply and demand matrix. One's perceived moral value systems shape one's economic decisions: media influence, climate issues, corporate responsibility, and cultural values, all have a significant impact on consumer decision making.

The rationality principles of the discipline of economics only work if people make their choices inside the straitjacket of the theories themselves; classroom economics fails in real-world application. Theoretical models do not come close enough to empirical reality for them to be useful when the time comes to apply them in the real world. Hence, economics confines itself to creating a discipline of philosophy, more than a practical understanding of the universe. There is no more time for theories for Caribbean people of African descent—only executing real-world applications that can change lives.

THE "CREDIBILITY REVOLUTION" has transformed economics somewhat, but as usual, that transformation has not yet found its way to the Caribbean. The entrenched old-guard institutions of the development discourse universe dominate the region through bogus development theories, often using their capital to bend each country's political leadership to go along with their convoluted projects. This development monster has so overwhelmed the region since the post-World War Two era that it remains in a neo-colonial type of state of existence. This development monstrosity has become an abnormal, "too big to fail" type of situation, and the more things fail, the more work these development institutions create for themselves.

The stark reality is that these institutions care more about maintaining these sham jobs than about getting effective results.

Moreover, there are no performance metrics for these institutions that can measure success or failure. More problems to solve means more job security for bureaucrats. The Credibility Revolution exposes classroom economics to the complexities of real-world economics. As touched on earlier, David Card, the winner of the 2021 Nobel prize in economics for his work on how a rise in the minimum wage affects employment—how employment decisions are more complicated than the straightforward economic textbook explanations would have us believe. Card looks at how so many other more relevant variables influence economic outcomes. The independent variables contain the unpredictability factor, so although it is a variable, it is hard to say how it will behave or react under a given scenario. To keep things brief, Card's main point is that it all comes down to using real data instead of theoretical models to get to the answers and to avoid going around in circles of nothingness, propagating non-credible explanations.

Professor Card and the other prize winners used "natural experiments" and empirical research to reach their conclusions; this winning work sheds light on the many challenges to the usefulness of economic theories and models in helping society. Of course, these "natural experiments" are not "natural" at all; they are artificial and can never come close to the natural complexities and self-regulation of the ecology of real world economics. More reliance on empirical data rather than theories is certainly a good thing, nevertheless, these experiments and observations still took place in a relatively controlled environment, or with selected and defined data sets. So some important things that we cannot anticipate at the time will always be missing.

This now raises the question of the usefulness of the observation or models to real people's lives. For the peoples of the Caribbean, solving real-world problems must be the priority—and that is the critical question to be answered before application. Card's work is still useful enough, however; it does help to advance our understanding and separation of real-world economics from its classroom counterpart. Therefore, the point to be made here is that you should not limit your thinking to classroom thinking, and we must be highly conscious of what we are doing—the purpose and objective of it all.

Also, simply applying more data does not put one in a better position to solve the problems either, for improper use and analysis of data can lead to poor insights drawn. Mere possession of data is not a magic bullet; one must also be familiar with the proper analysis and interpretation of data. Careless top-down applications, when using data analysis, still often lead to the morphing of new unintended errors: distortions, disconnections, and the wrong applications to problems. David Card was honest in saying that his profession is too focused on theories instead of realities:

> *"I think partly it is that most economists were from rich families, and never worked as teenagers, and haven't had experience in real jobs in the market. A huge number of economists have never actually done anything. They do not have much contact with real-world situations."*

Lived experiences will always shape how one sees the universe. Textbooks can be fine, even necessary to build some form of a base for learning. However, relevance and *realness* must be brought into the forefront of learning; otherwise, it can degenerate into miseducation. Identifying and distinguishing classroom philosophy of economics from real-world economics is important for learning what is *real* and what is *not real* about the universe. And what is the purpose of learning if it cannot be applied practically for the purpose of helping others? The academic process can be a setback to learning and real-world application. The better the real-world critical thinking is, the more useful it will be for real-world optimization. In the end, we do live in the real world and not in classrooms, after all.

The emphasis on the "usefulness" of education in the real world should be paramount! Education is no longer something for aristocratic elites, or for the privileged to treat as philosophy. In an interview after receiving the prize, Professor Card also said "I think that is very depressing; I think that is why I am much less optimistic that scientific knowledge and research will change anything. They certainly will not change anything in the near future."

What is also amazing is how people can still be surprised by the system, says Robin Kaiser-Schatzlein, in the September 30, 2019, article "The Tyranny of Economists," asking, *"How can they be so wrong, so often, and yet still exert so much influence on government policy?"* Kaiser-Schatzlien nails the point that the science of economics is ***"politics for the technocrats and the well-off."*** Economics reveals itself, for those who are paying attention, as ***"a moral and political science all to itself,"*** and its doctrines simply are not coherent enough; it needs constant explanations of its philosophy. Kaiser-Schatzlien further points out that economists have a creepy secret: that they do not know how the real world works, so they turn it into a philosophical discipline where real answers are no longer required, and mere good-sounding theories will do.

The Tetlock case study

The Tetlock study, conducted by psychologist Philip Tetlock, is about the business of political and economic "experts" wreaking havoc in people's lives and calling it "development" (Talib, The Black Swan pg. 151). Development is not supposed to be destructive. Tetlock's study had various specialists judge the likelihood of a number of political, economic, and military events occurring within a specific time frame (approximately five years). It consisted of about twenty-seven predictions, involving three hundred specialists; economists represented about twenty-five per cent of the sample. The study ultimately revealed that the experts' error rates were significant, far higher than was predicted. Tetlock's study showed that there was no difference between the specialists, the ones holding PhDs, undergraduate degrees, or journalists. The only regularity his study found was that "those who had a big reputation were worse predictors than those who had none" (Talib, Black Swan pg.151).

You can look the study up yourself if interested; but it should suffice to say that the study reveals the fragility of so-called expertise. Even after numerous studies that show experts can essentially be no better than the average cab driver in making predictions, their philosophical predictions continue.

> *"Instead [economists-statisticians] have concentrated their efforts in building more sophisticated models without regard to the ability of such models to more accurately predict real-life data"* (Makridakis and Hidon).

So since we know these "experts" are no better predictors than we are, let us rely on doing our research, data analysis, fact-based discoveries, critical thinking, and the application of science and technology to solve our economic problems. Let us lead ourselves. *Applied Intelligence* as a strategy is about effort and processes, to help us apply that knowledge to the real world. Quantitative thinking and actions backed by scientific approaches and rigour constitute the most optimal pathway to solving complex socio-economic problems.

In his book ***Range: Why Generalists Triumph In A Specialized World,*** author David Epstein demonstrates that the most efficient path to success in any domain is often away from reliance on specialists. He dispels the notion that only people who have accumulated thousands of hours of study are the best qualified and are the ones that we must listen to. Often, he says, economists only muddy the waters, further complicating things and creating unnecessary problems that did not exist before.

Range reveals that specialization is the exception, not the rule. Epstein's research also shows that in most fields, especially those that are complex and unpredictable, generalists, not specialists, are the prime problem solvers. And often, they come in the form of entrepreneurs. Generalists are not restricted in their thinking or restricted by their academic discipline; they are not intellectually constricted and can juggle many interests and concepts at once. They are more open to new ideas and can think outside the box. Generalists are lifelong learners; creative, agile, fearless thinkers. The academic specialists' training often restricts them inside a box of thinking not necessarily in line with real-world activity. *Range* shows that being proactive, rigorous, and all-engrossing can cultivate growth even where massive inefficiency once dominated.

Those who can cross domains rather than being restricted to one domain become the most effective problem solvers. They are exposed to more information and accepting of more real-world variables. They usually do not have pre-set opinions and methodologies, which can block you from practical thinking. For example, Epstein shows how "experts" operate within silos and predefined models of thinking, while generalists tend to accept and rely more on technology, data science, and artificial intelligence (AI) to augment their thinking and application. Generalists are more concerned with getting the job done effectively than with their theories and models. And entrepreneurs in particular are more interested in value creation, so they do not waste much time on superfluous things that do not create any value. For Generalists, using data and AI tools is simply seen as necessary, practical, useful, and effective in getting things done quickly. Therefore, the region needs an ecosystem to process information and optimize it for better decision-making—and this is where data science becomes critical to successful outcomes.

FOR SOME TIME, neuroscience has been telling us that emotion is a purely chemical occurrence in the brain, and those chemical reactions dictate emotional responses. However, more recently, another scientist seems to have discovered better explanations as to how the brain works. Dr. Lisa Feldman Barret has a theory about how emotions happen, the *Theory of Constructed Emotions.*

Barret's research tells us that our thoughts and emotions are developed or based on past experiences that control our present emotional reactions; past experiences can influence our present lives. Therefore, emotions are constructed in the brain by drawing quickly upon those past experiences to formulate emotional responses. This is very much in line with Nobel Prize-winning behavioural economist Daniel Kahneman's work on decision-making. In his book *Thinking, Fast & Slow,* Kahneman talks about two systems of thought; the first is System 1 (SI) which is quick and spontaneous, but often inaccurate, and System 2 (S2) is slow and methodical and looks for facts when engaging memory. Therefore, System 1 is emotional and based on drawing conclusions quickly. In short, both Feldman Barrett and Kahneman are saying that emotional decision-making is not about brain chemistry alone; it is about how one thinks and utilizes past experiences that count more towards outcomes. Accordingly, quick, emotional decision-making associated with S1 is sub-optimal, so it is S2 that is more effective for good decision-making. Therefore, *applied intelligence* would lie in the S2 thinking and application domain.

When confronted with various scenarios, humans quickly trigger S1 thinking first, and the brain constructs past instances of emotion to construct and frame their present experiences. Others have classified it as constructed conscious delusion, but we know that emotions are more than mere hardwired reflexes that trigger sensory inputs. Yet we still know very little about human consciousness. And this lack of understanding has driven human beings to create storybook explanations to explain what we do not know. This is where our troubles start, for these stories are not reality.

"Experience" is so important to our human existence, critical to decision-making whether its done through the S1 or S2 framework. It is similar to the way we drive from memory: we do not need a GPS every time, our subconscious mind simply takes the wheel, so to speak. And as one's life develops; one's subconscious mind updates one's experiences—so the way one might react at age 21 will be very different from how one would react at age 40.

In any case, we need not overcomplicate the nature of our human existence. Following a better framework for critical thinking would be optimal, and this is where *applied intelligence* comes in for Caribbean people of African descent. Because we need a higher dimension of conscious thinking, a framework to contain our past traumas as it pertains to the negative effects they may have on our future existence.

OUR socioeconomic environment and our past experiences contribute greatly to our emotional responses and decisions. Therefore, things must be managed with the highest level of intellect and analysis; otherwise, we fall vulnerable to the trap of storytelling. A constructive delusional state of reality forms through cultural belief systems, because those belief systems are not primarily based on science but on Christian-inspired stories that are unnatural to our very human existence. And since Bible stories are pure fantasy, with the lure to attract the willfully uninformed, we can easily build our entire lives around these stories that separate us from the reality of our existence. In altered mental states, governing our lives becomes difficult, stifling free will and individual thought.

Anti-intellectualism can begin to dominate our thinking, which can drive our lives into ineffective thinking, fear, and inaction. Our psychological lens reigns supreme over us. Errors and miscalculations in our judgements are intrinsic to the human condition. Perfection cannot ever be achieved, and humans are not machines; although we are capable of being highly intellectual, we often allow poor thinking and adherence to stories or easy explanations to diminish our intellectual capacity. The mission of *applied intelligence* is to create the intellectual framework for effective quantitative thinking and analysis that can meaningfully boost the quality of decision-making in order to improve people's lives.

MATH has always been a mandatory class to be taken throughout the education system, and whether we like it or not, math is critical for effective human existence. In this universe, math cannot be avoided; it is an inescapable natural part of our universe. I am not asking anyone to take math courses or the like. I simply mean that more mathematically conscious thinking will benefit us. Therefore, we must bring math to the forefront of our lives. For people of the Caribbean, the further we stray from always *doing the math,* the more we allow others to do it for us. Math is always math; it is universal. 2 + 2 equals 4 in any place and at any time, so once you know the math, you will be on a firm foundation in any of your dealings. Therefore, when things simply do not add up, you can immediately identify problems and not be fooled by others, because your focus or navigator in life is math. Mathematical thinking elevates the mind away from lazy thinking and adherence to storytelling and directs it toward logic and reason.

Black populations in the region have come to rely on religion and ideologies, rather than facts and science—this is an S1 existence. Which leads to altered states of reality, the avoidance of objective truths, and reliance on wishful thinking. The laws of nature...the physics of the universe, is all math.

So if the world is math, then why do we keep creating a non-mathematical cognitive existence for ourselves? This is going against nature. In the universe, connections are made, and responses are generated, there is friction in space and friction among people. Friction generates energy, collisions, new formations, and outcomes, this is what happens with particles of matter in space and what happens with human interaction in the metaphysical world. And the world keeps spinning, stopping for no one. So if you want to achieve something in your infinitesimal time here on this earth, it makes sense to seek a good understanding of nature before you interact and entangle yourself in the universe.

The key to learning is not to corrupt yourself with the laziness of falling for easy soothing explanations or stories, going with the easy or the most convenient explanations is usually the worst way to go. Stories are not real so they cannot ever be reality. Simplified stories can miseducate and create distortions of reality instead, and new sets of problems keep developing for you. However, taking a mathematical thinking approach inherently leads you to ask more questions, and seek more logical and better fact-based explanations—S2.

Calculus can tell us how properties behave in the natural world, and it can be useful in figuring out ways to solve big problems. Understanding the principle of the differential equation, for example, helps us understand how we get from point A to point B most efficiently and effectively. In brief, calculus is about simplification not complexity, so you divide your problem into subproblems and keep dividing them until the problem is solved. It is the divide-and-conquer approach to problem-solving. So once you know the answer to your first subproblem, the answer to your second subproblem is in your first answer; and so you move on down the subproblem line towards solving the original problem. No stress is necessary; it is simply your internal math. Everything is a series of small calculations, and this is how life goes; a good life does not mean creating an absence of problems, it is about solving or at least managing those problems. So these small calculations in the short term keep you moving in the right direction, avoiding errors, it keeps identifying and reinforcing the correct steps to take to get you to where you want to go. It also helps you understand limits—since the laws of nature are embedded in math, the process of mathematical thinking will be highly useful to the successful outcomes you seek.

With clarity of thinking, you will have a better chance at identifying and acting upon the best exponential growth opportunities that the universe presents to you or doing the math can help you to quantify opportunities and execute effectively, and profitably. Doing the math gives you the confidence to act decisively, and that is how winning happens.

Math is the language of the universe, so it can always be applied in our navigating the universe; as Galileo put it, "The laws of Nature are written in the language of mathematics." S, it is of the utmost importance for one's successful navigation of the universe to be able to see things differently. The ability to change your perspectives and to have a better understanding. To help yourself and change your situation for the better, math can be extremely helpful in that regard. Because only when you can change your perspective can you discover new opportunities that can change your life.

So it is intelligent to think mathematically and to try and change your perspective, become more mentally agile, efficient, and effective in your life pursuits. Math when applied is beneficial to your self-interest. Math speeds up your analysis but with precision and confidence as opposed to slowing it down with the clutter and unreliability of emotional thinking. It makes you open to new ideas and new things as the world evolves around you. Therefore, understanding is the first step to succeeding because if you do not understand or take too long to *get it,* then you will miss opportunities. Further, if you do not have an efficient and disciplined way to process information for understanding, you will remain behind the prosperity curve.

IN the book **INFINITE POWERS, How CALCULUS Reveals the Secrets of the Universe,** Professor Steven Strogatz says that in analyzing complex things, one should apply the *Infinity Principle*, which essentially means when analyzing something complicated, you should first break it down into an infinity of simpler parts and analyze those. Putting those infinitely many analyzed parts back together into an analyzed whole can be difficult, but it can be easier than analyzing the complicated whole directly. Therefore, you should first break down the big problems into several simpler parts to be solved and analyzed in order. Problem-solving is continuous and you cannot usually solve a big problem through any single grand theory. So the *doing-the-math* approach is optimal in solving real human problems in the real world, effectively!

In the academic domain of economics, as we have been seeing, science can often become like 'faith,' concocting narratives and belief systems, and regression into ideology. The *Infinity Principle* helps us to understand better that nothing can be so simple that you can merely create a grand theory and believe it can be a solution. Accordingly, when economists use statistics to justify conclusions as "good answers," be very skeptical of this. Statistics can often create illusions of reality, distortions leading to faulty reasoning and bad decision-making.

In the 21st century, the main Caribbean Problem remains how to free the region out from the bottom rungs of the global economy. To create relevance for the territory. However, without the right and effective mindset in place first, nothing will change, fantasy is not compatible with reality Acute poverty and disrespect will continue to be suffered in the region, and the new economy's digital divide will only widen. The task of digital transformation and getting it right and not falling even further behind is paramount for the survival of the Caribbean species, a mere fifty to one hundred years from now, and when you compound the problem with the reality of climate change, if the region does not get its act together the region faces a coming disaster, natural and human.

CHAPTER 2

Beyond Theories

Theories primarily act as thinking frameworks for ideas to develop, and good ideas come from constructive thoughts, accompanied by logic. However, the challenge is how to effectively engage in theories for their usefulness to society but learn to jump off when they begin moving toward philosophy. So we must not look to generate good ideas based on the laws of nature for practical application to help humanity – usefulness must be the main objective. Striving for philosophy can be distracting from achieving goals. We must look for authentic solutions, and if theoretical modelling happens to be useful and necessary to the greater societal good, then we would be foolish not to apply it.

Having said all that, theories are an emotionally led pursuit that seeks to find understanding of problems and things which we do not understand. However, we must go beyond developing theories to finding practical and useful applications to solving real problems in real people's lives.

If I can use the ancient Indian parable here, where four blind men came upon an elephant in the jungle. They have never before experienced such a massive creature and being blind made things even more challenging for them. So upon meeting this massive creature they each reached out and touched it in different areas. One man said it "feels like a snake," that is because he felt the elephant's long trunk. The other one said it feels like a "column," while feeling the muscular leg. Another heard the animal cry out loudly and pronounced only that it sounded like a "trumpet." Finally, the elephant began to move, so, the fourth felt the ground begin to shake and he said we were experiencing an "earthquake."

The moral of the story is that we often approach problems by relying on our own past experiences and taking partial experiences to represent the full truth about a situation. However, different people forge different perspectives based on their experiences, so "truth" is subjective and based on the unreliability of experience.

However, nature is the only thing that is true, we must then do our best to get beyond theories to understand the system in which the problems rest. And if we can apply more system-based thinking, intelligently, as a methodology approach to problems we have a better chance of solving problems. If you can now apply thinking in a systematic way to life or business problems, you will become more efficient in dealing with problems and succeeding. If we can take our instinctive emotion and experience approach out of things, then that is a good way to begin applying intelligence to problem-solving. In the case of a business problem, whether it is about product sales, operations, or human resources—everything is a system problem at the core. Therefore, if you can understand that fundamental reality, you can then apply systematic intelligence thinking by understanding each part and begin to connect them back to identify the elephant. Once you see the elephant (the full picture view) you can engage in a more intelligent way to solve problems.

Therefore, the natural question becomes how we can improve system thinking to be more useful—and for this we use intelligence; combined human and machine, which is optimal, and this is where *applied intelligence* is going. Usefulness to real people in real life and business situations is what applied intelligence concerns itself with most. Therefore, applied intelligence is fundamentally a bottom-up process that applies to internal processes. In an enterprise, for example, if we cannot get our internal process right our outputs will be problematic, this is why Legendary investor Warren Buffet says that management is the most important thing for business. This is because management is an exercise in systematic thinking and the application of intelligence—human and machine, i.e., AI to optimize decision-making in order to maximize enterprise profitability. Hence, everything involves the application of systematic intelligence thinking; so, a framework that can capture system thinking that can be usefully applied is what applied intelligence is about.

The process of applying intelligence can add tremendous value to an enterprise—first helping you to simply understand the landscape then it gives you feedback that can be useful to the enterprise—to the specific business objective you are working towards. It can tell you what to add or what to cut or slow down with or increase. It is useful by supplying you with evidence-based analysis to make confident decisions. It is effective in solving problems by identifying patterns that can tell you things based on facts, relevant to time and place. Relying on personal past experiences is very problematic because no two situations are exactly the same, and as time passes, there are new variables involved, so relevancy (time and place) becomes key. Therefore, pattern recognition and the utilization of data science are important tools for good decision-making.

Inherently, systematic intelligence thinking is about learning through the application of applied intelligence, moreover, as you learn you can apply your newly acquired knowledge to your problem agenda. It also frees you from human bias and assumptions, the emotions involved in decision-making which often can block discovery and innovation—ultimately blocking your progress. You can now work faster and with more precision, with confidence, raising the probability of great success.

SO, THE QUESTION BECOMES: what is the best way to get the most out of life? After all, life is what you make it. But there is no straight life trajectory in the path of fulfillment. This is why all of the truly inspiring stories about successful people, such as in the fields of business or politics, include pathways filled with peaks and valleys. The climb is never a non-emotional, non-eventful, straight line upward, regardless of the application of intelligence. Therefore, emotion is part of the bedrock composite materials in nature, the soil and the gravel that form its bedrock. We can compare human nature to a composite material, and the combination of the two materials with different metaphysical make-ups. Emotional chemistry creates certain forms of thinking and behaviour, and similarly, intelligence thinking creates other forms of behaviour. When we juxtapose the two forms of thinking, the result is the manifestation of different forms of behaviour, often in an effort to solve the same problems.

However, as promised, we are not going to become philosophers wasting time discussing which one is *better*, emotion or intelligence, obviously intelligence is better. Its intelligence, thinking and innovation make the world; emotion usually causes problems that require intelligence to solve. So we will not waste time here. What we can say is that emotions are a core part of the human condition, part of your human nature, and it cannot be anything other than what it is, so our task in life is to manage our emotions in consciousness to ensure it does not take the best of us and detract and derail our being.

Right about now, the usual thing for writers, especially academics, is to try to explain and shape "their" ideas by trying to label them, so they can get credit for creating a "new" social science *theory*. This is how we get to useless philosophy, and truth be told, in one way or another—particularly in the Western world—those new ideas can all be traced back to ancient times, ancient Greece and the stoics. If you read the ancients, you will realize that most of the work over the many centuries by philosophers or academics stems from the ancients. It is merely that as our knowledge of science and mathematics, technology, and innovation build, we can apply our knowledge, and our intelligence more, to flesh out and explain nature more scientifically. But in the end, this "philosophy" is not anything fundamentally new; it consists of the same original questions about life, merely upgraded and applied relative to the relevancy of the writer's time and place in the universe.

Science and access to more and more information have allowed us to become more knowledgeable, and enlightened, otherwise, we will still be thinking that the earth revolved around the sun.

Therefore, through the application of quantitative thinking we are essentially flexing our intelligence, and our egos, of course, are always developing new social science clarifications. In modern times, classifications like emotional intelligence, fragility, antifragility, emotional agility, and cognitive behavioural theory, can easily be found by reading the meditations of Marcus Aurelius, Aristotle, Seneca, and Epictetus. So that is where the credit belongs. In the end, we are merely applying our intelligence to explain nature and how to get along in it.

To return to the main point, no matter how much knowledge we have and intelligence we can apply, we are emotional beings. However, the beauty of nature is that we can harness our emotions productively and fuel our creativity and innovation talents and underly with intelligence to thrive in the universe. Therefore, there is no need to be a slave to our emotions if we can manage them with our intelligence. All the thoughts and feelings we have is part of our nature, our inner selves, but before it is released outwardly to form critical actions, it is wise to put them through our self-governing, due diligence and editing process, our *applied intelligence* discipline.

How we respond to our inner emotions, and our internal experiences drive us in the outer world, in our other relationships, and so, our happiness or suffering trajectories are very much dependent on how we manage back and forth between the subconscious (emotion) mind and the conscious (intelligence) mind.

Therefore, resilience, antifragility, and emotional elasticity, adaptability, are core attributes of the power to move toward success and happiness and away from suffering. Fear, anxiety, stress…all the usual suspects are always there in your subconscious but recognizing it and bringing it to the consciousness surface allows you to confront and manage it. This is what being is about—life is not about the elimination of stresses, we cannot ever eliminate our humanity, life is knowing that stresses will always exist and overcoming adversity is part of making yourself uncomfortable to move forward. And so, the utility of applied intelligence allows you to intelligently, courageously, and effectively manage life to find happiness in it.

NASSIM TALEB in his best-selling book *The Black Swan* said that the awareness of a problem does not mean very much, especially when you have special interests and self-serving institutions involved. Those special interest institutions are prone to creating more complex explanations and methods to justify their existence. The main function of these institutions then becomes the perpetuation of their interests – the institution becomes one of self-preservation itself—protecting the jobs of the academics and bureaucrats inside the institution.

Finding the right solutions are never easy, but fabricating helping people is a terrible thing to do, according to Talib, and it does not matter if you feel you are doing the right thing as an institution, feelings do not create wealth. Effective actions do. We must be interested in results, not nice theories.

So do not fear randomness, it is a phenomenon of life and so are unpredictability and volatility. do not shy away from any of them. Look for the opportunity when randomness and unpredictability appear, history happens in leaps so missing those big deviation moments in life can be costly. Being opportunistic and capitalizing on a single event can set you and your family's life up for generations. Identify opportunities, and how to apply knowledge to them to extract value.

In the 17th century, Isaac Newton helped accelerate the enlightenment period. Newton advanced calculus and discovered a small set of equations that helped explain the universe's nature through his laws of gravity and motion. In brief, "Newton's science" confirmed that the universe abided by a set of laws and that these laws are always true, and everywhere. Newton showed us that nature is always living, sophisticated, complex, logical, and cognitive, with its own set of rules that no one can get around. Fact flows from one form or context to another, and by a process and factor of logic, from event to event, cycle to cycle. All laws are omnipresent and inescapable. Therefore, the stage has already been set by science in the physical world, and we are mere matter, actors, trying to understand our roles and how to play them. This is what life is about, figuring things out! Therefore, we are constantly engaged in figuring out the differentials that can help us navigate this universe successfully. It is only logical and practical to have strong but flexible "learning" tools, to help us build a decision-making system in support of our desire to successfully navigate the universe. So for this purpose, *applied intelligence* is the framework thinking structure that can help us first understand the universe before we make meaningful moves in it.

GALILEO came up with the explanation of inertia: that in the absence of any outside force, a body at rest stays at rest, and a body in motion stays in motion. Galileo was important and contributed significantly to the enlightenment period, but it was Newton's work that shined a bright insightful light on Galileo's brilliance. Galileo provided us with one of the most consequential equations in history:

113

$F = ma$

Force (F) acting on an object is equal to the mass (m) of the object times its acceleration (a)

A simple enough equation that illuminates way beyond its mathematical usefulness, the equation describes life itself, the consciousness of actions and outcomes. It tells us that life is about continuous movement, static is not good, and you must keep moving—standing still achieves nothing. You can never get any momentum towards achieving anything if you do not move, movement and curiosity create friction in the universe, which makes things happen. So you either stay at rest or stay in motion, both cannot be true at the same time.

Now, relative to solving the *Caribbean Problem?* The pursuit of a *Caribbean Renaissance* in thinking and application? The answers will rest in our examination of the questions themselves, so you will simply have to keep reading. But for now, we merely want to make the point that all things centre around the forces and actions that moves critical mass, metaphysically. Therefore, flowing and system of intellectually driven dynamic logic, acting in relevance to time and place, and the careful selection of precise systems to execute through, is how winning happens. It is about how to apply force and energy to navigate in one's favour, so it is critical to understand how to get momentum, how to stay in motion and how to get things done for personal gain. The simplification of the complex is most critical for the human mind to begin to act with confidence and to begin breaking things down to *first principles*.

Logic dictates that the law of inertia applies to our whole and only universe. We cannot apply logic to what we do not know. Doing things logically and limiting the noise and distractions will keep you in full productive motion…accelerating at an exponential rate of change. Knowledge acquisition and clarity of purpose are what the

114

Caribbean needs most in this decade of critical transformation. A strong and flexible framework to work through can be helpful to the purpose of building resilience. We need to know where we are going by having a defined road map and applying *the calculus* to our navigation, we must find the quickest, most effective, and most precise way to get onto, and ride the global wealth curve. Time is massively against us, and as other nations are rapidly advancing in highly strategic ways, the Caribbean continues to be distracted and unfocused, going backwards, because if others are moving forward while we stand still then we are effectively going backwards.

By having disciplined and strategic blueprints in place, backed up by data science, AI, and ML, we can enormously augment our human intelligence which increases our intellectual capacity, leading us to push forward successfully. There are no smooth paths in the universe, no straight-line trajectories upward but history has demonstrated repeatedly, that winning usually happens when disciplined preparation meets opportunity.

VALUE IS ALL SUPREME, the universe rewards those who can create real value. Therefore, if you are not creating value, you are simply not valued in the universe—a harsh reality, but the objective truth. And this is within the laws of nature—survival of the fittest, natural selection. Get your collective heads around this because this is how it is. Reality is civilization.

The Mongol Empire understood value creation and was the most successful and longest reigning empire in history—the Mongols ushered in the modern world through its expansion and dominance of Eurasia between about 1206 to 1368. The Mongols were sophisticated pragmatists at the core and profit trumped conflict for them. For example, to be a part of the Mongol empire, each person had to prove their worth, their value to society, and the empire.

Whether it was through being a warrior, merchant, craftsman, farmer, priest, medicine person, taxpayer, tribute, etc., whatever it was, you had to contribute value to the Mongol empire in one way or the other to be useful to it.

Value creation was a matter of survival for the Mongols, particularly being nomadic, they still needed stable and sedentary systems in place throughout the vast territory to grow and manage all they conquered. They needed supportive environments for trade and commerce because self-preservation depended on having well-functioning systems. "Once the incorporated enemies and bo'ol proved their value, they received a share of war spoils" (The Horde, pg. 39). Society did not owe you anything, you owed society instead, and to integrate into the regime, proving your value, your worth to it was central to Mongol communities throughout the vast empire. The regime would reciprocate by providing members of society with security, with pathways to social and economic advancement. As the Franciscan Friar Iohanca put it in 1320, the Mongols always took the pragmatic option, and "could care less to what religion someone was as long as he performs the required services, pays tributes and taxes and satisfies his military obligations according to the law" (The Horde pg. 14). Therefore, many centuries might have passed but the nature of self-preservation for groups, still requires building sophisticated systems to survive and thrive.

Therefore, to change one's circumstance, one must first see the world for what it is, and how it functions, and stay away from making moral judgements about it. The focus must be on reality and practicality, develop a working strategy to compete successfully within the natural universe, focusing on what is real! Learn to thrive in the one universe, the one reality in which we exist, and do not seek fantastical stories to explain what you do not understand; rely on scientific and quantitative approaches, not emotion.

As Historian Yuval Noah Harari points out, *Homo Sapiens* are built as they are, ruled by their nature, and at the core, you cannot change *human nature*. Your time in this universe is minuscule, do not waste it fiddling in ignorance and wishful thinking. Britain and America have been in decline for a while now, China is rising and seeking a geopolitical empire, India is becoming an economic powerhouse, and Africa with its mass population is figuring things out and gathering momentum. No one is concerned about the Caribbean, the Caribbean must be concerned about itself, and what it does next. This is the nature of things as it happens, civilization stays in motion, dynamic species around the world are flexing, and the power and ecology of the universe are changing once again, like spring. Transforming, and taking shape to forge a new 21st century, but the Caribbean people and its leadership are still on Caribbean time, and a body at rest stays at rest.

NATURAL SELECTION always prevails, that is the way things are; that is nature! Life requires effort and the ones who put in the effort usually win more than they lose and advance themselves in society. The frequencies of those applying intelligence and efforts will connect, mutually beneficial alliances will form, and new alliances and economic and political ecosystems will emerge. So without action or staying in motion, nothing of any value can ever be achieved, and for the Caribbean people of African descent, the extinction of the species becomes more realistic each day we remain at rest.

$E = mc^2$ *(Energy equals mass times the speed of light squared)* must be the master equation Caribbean people need to adhere to, and on a most basic level. Once again, life, the universe…nature is math, and this equation tells us that we must always be doing something productive because a *body in motion stays in motion.* And that energy and mass (matter) are interchangeable, they are different forms of the same thing. Therefore, interpreting this equation for everyday life is

117

simply about activity and effort, and if you do not keep moving life falls apart. So you cannot simply sit idly by, complaining and expect things to happen.

Life has less suffering when you are active and your mind is fully engaged in life itself, non-activity means you are not in motion, and you are only creating fertile ground for stress and anxiety to thrive within you. Self-inflict suffering. However, we can overcome suffering by changing our behaviour, taking action, engaging in *applied intelligence*, and embracing lifelong learning. When you are metaphysically inactive your negative imagination runs wild, you become consumed with negativity, and your life becomes filled with worry and stress about things you cannot control. You live in past traumas, and your life becomes unhealthy, and chaotic, without order and spirituality—this is the *negative zone* of life, where everything is negative. Negativity overwhelms, and anxiety becomes the norm, your identity.

THE VERY CARIBBEAN tradition of sitting on the *veranda complaining* about how the world is unfair, the government is not helping us, and God is the answer for everything—this nonsense keeps us trapped in our willful ignorance. It is your choice to sit on the veranda and complain as opposed to getting in motion. It is your choice to watch others seek knowledge and become creative and innovative, entrepreneurial, and it is also your choice to sit envious of others. But the universe does not care, and the universe does not know who you are. However, you then turn and *ask* others to share their wealth with you, but the universe owes you NOTHING! Like Mongol society, you need to create value to exist in society. You are entitled to nothing! The wealth of others, ill-gotten or not, owes nothing—understand the saying 'who has the gold rules.'

Therefore, forget about your fantastical thoughts of "changing the world;" the world is perfectly fine! This is nature. You are the one that needs change, focus on changing yourself and creating your value in your time and place in the universe first and foremost. Understanding the metaphysical world is paramount to survival in it—applying knowledge strategically, and intelligently is the optimal path to succeeding in the universe.

In the end, our economic value is created by how we navigate the laws of nature. For the Caribbean people, it is most critical to grasp this reality of the universe or continue to suffer from it! Stop wasting time on the veranda complaining, get in motion, and stay in motion, change your damn situation. And the first step is to get off the veranda!

The $E = mc^2$ example is simply telling us that the universe is math, and science, not emotion and intuition, and you have to always be in motion and doing the math.

The universe is unforgiving, so being trapped in your mental inactions, and allowing yourself to stay marginalized in a darkened corner of the universe is not rational. Despair and bewilderment, once set in, are extremely difficult to escape from. You must create value to prosper, it is as simple as that! do not be distracted by all the noise and nonsense (nn^2,) and the bogus philosophies which are embedded in stupidity—the Facebook-type stupidity. Exercise your intellectualism with adherence to the natural laws of the universe.

Recalibrating thinking, quantitatively, to the quantum entanglements and frequencies of the universe, to the functional physics and utility of it all, for the effective navigation in the universe is the only way to succeed in it. Your activities will resonate, impacting other activities occurring simultaneously and everywhere, your frequency will attract other like-minded people, and forces connect creating positive energy for real change. In short, prosperity is ultimately a function of proper calculation and effective execution. Leave emotion on the veranda.

Decisions based on knowledge, intelligence gathering, and deliberate actions, are holistically central to realizing rewarding future outcomes. Focused thinking will be the underpinning of a true **Caribbean Renaissance** movement. We must adapt to the new digital and transformational decade currently in motion, and think and behave to what is relevant, do not get caught up in the distractive drama of race and morality because that cannot change hearts and minds. do not seek to be loved by others, seek to be respected through the power you bring through the value created. Seek power with your value, that is what works in the universe. Winning creates wealth, and wealth creates power, and influence, which are the most valuable things to have in a competitive and conflict-driven world. Work with the sophistication of *applied intelligence* to dismantle the enduring legacy systems of the past, those negative cognitive influences that remain embedded in our subconscious minds. Create new structures of support that can set new winning conditions, and awaken with the fierce urgency of now, to a higher state of consciousness with a relentless adherence to winning.

Fundamentally, we are not products of our circumstances, but products of the decisions we make, so, in the end, we must clearly understand that our future is not determined by our past experiences or traumas, instead, it is determined by the decisions we make in the now.

So when approaching writing a strategy for future success, focus on a series of fundamental first principles. Make the questions relatable to the factors critical to the success of your plan – relationships, or new ventures, and make sure the plan has a purpose. It is critical to understand the context and structures that could be supportive or harmful to your plans, risk assessment is also critical, so do not avoid those critical questions. You must spend time learning as much as you can about the operational environment that you want to develop the opportunity through and have a framework in place to respond to inevitable changes which will surely occur along the way.

In the end, success comes down to all the questions you are willing to ask. Curiosity is essential. Success awaits those that engage in more scientific approaches and processes.

BIG PROBLEMS take a long time to happen, accordingly, they can take a long-time to solve, or not. That depends on your decision-making. So to drive real change, a new, disciplined methodology that is driven by scientific decision-making processes is the optimal way to approach complex problems. If of course, they are complex, to begin with? So it is wise to focus on what is real, taking small steps to find firm footing first, and that begins by understanding how the game is played first—the laws of nature and the math of the universe.

Approaching problems quantitatively instead of reactionary is the better way. If you do not fundamentally understand your systemic environment, how systems work, and how influence and power happen, then it will be very difficult to see how you can problem-solve successfully.

At this critical juncture of digital transformation, we are presented with an opportunity to flex our imaginations through the utility of technology and innovation. Real change, the one that delivers true sustainable growth and happiness for people, is derived from the *motions* of economic activity. If you are not in motion, you are out of the economics of prosperity. In the end, life comes down to successfully navigating the world of socioeconomic conflicts, armed with the awareness of self-preservation tactics first. Value creation or lack of it will ultimately be the determinant of your prosperity, or poverty.

Life is never predetermined; it is what you make of it. Therefore, all decisions matter and the most fundamental and critical decision facing the Caribbean people today, is whether or not to get moving, and adopt the intellectual mindset, or stick with the current motionless, unproductivity, emotional existence.

Historically, the future wealth of any nation is directly correlated to its innovation and productivity gains, derived through technology investments which drive efficiencies to enhance profitability. The Caribbean now stands at a critical juncture in time, whether to be self-transformative or not. Whether to drive responsible and relevant economic policy and position its nations with a vision of the future that can bend its wealth curve to an accelerated upward trajectory. Do we want to thrive for a more efficient and inclusive economic existence, where all citizens can participate in the pursuit of prosperity and happiness, or not?

Our ability to design our future depends on if we know the tools and applications to do it with, how we first see and adapt to it, and how we innovate and respond to challenges. Human existence is always evolving, all species must adapt to the ever-changing environments, or they perish. This is nature. The survival of any species is by no means guaranteed. Survival requires constant effort and motion. Only when we understand this primal nature of things, that the universe cannot ever be anything other than what it is, will we begin to behave following reality. Only with a true existence, in reality, can you have a realistic opportunity to achieve prosperity.

ACCORDINGLY, if we do not know the reality of who runs the world, our ignorance about the world will work against us. Therefore, it is worth spending some time discussing some insights from the best-selling book, *SUPERHUBS How the Financial Elite & Their Networks Rule Our World;* by author Sandra Navidi. There are some reviews about the book that criticizes the author for not condemning *the system,* those readers feel that she sits on the fence a lot and reports like an observer. However, these people are missing the point, her main objective is to show that the world is run by the most powerful, those elite few in global finance. Therefore, spending time criticizing "the system" would only serve to distract from the pure observation and insight about the elite-run system. Therefore, things are what they are so let us leave emotion out of it and learn from the observations and think about what you are going to do next about exercising your self-interest to allow you to carve out your place in the universe. So criticizing the elite *Superhub* system is fine, but it generates no value for you in doing so, it will not change nor will your life change. This is as we have been discussing the nature of things and things cannot be anything other than what it is. And as long as you exist in nature your best bet is to figure out how to navigate it in your best interest. So energy and time would be better spent on carving out your success and optimizing your happiness in the universe. Again, as Aristotle reminds us, the universe cannot be anything other than what it is. And that is the nature of the laws of nature.

As discussed previously, for the species to thrive it must first learn how to survive, so adaptation to the metaphysical world is key. Navidi tells us, like in ecology, we must understand the systems and network formations of groups of people to first survive before they begin to thrive and take environments. Like attracts like and their ecosystem strengthens through natural selection. Relationships broaden in support of each other and begin to compound and grow exponentially, major financial forces form and then dominate. Power becomes concentrated and becomes homogeneous, keeping others that do not look like them out, and they work in their own interest to make their culture and all-dominating, the standard, supreme in the universe. A homogeneous power ecosystem controlled by old white men. This is how power, and privilege happen; this is the reality of the systemic socioeconomic system we live in.

And so, it gains momentum, the financial elites decide what technologies to invest in, and what social issues politicians and policymakers should prioritize. So whether you know it or not, investments in technology and related enterprise are what moves the world and the big financiers like Larry Fink, of BlackRock, Jamie Dimon of Chase, and the likes of George Soros, and the closed circle of billionaire hedge fund managers and major law firms enabling them, control global markets. Therefore, they are the deciders of investment and growth in the universe, and naturally, they begin to control politics with their money, and society and culture come along under that power ecosystem. So the woke themes of achieving racial equality through the political process or appealing to the hearts and minds of those in power are neither, intelligent nor rational thinking. It is more uninformed thinking, not understanding what power is or how power flows and influences. They do not understand the inherent laws of nature.

Superhubs give us a good view into the reality of 21st-century finance—these hyper-networks comprise three forces according to Navidi: *technologisation, financialisation and globalisation,* that propel the forces and power in the universe. Therefore, if you somehow believe that you can have any influence in the world without wealth, you are delusional. If Caribbean nations are not putting everything into digitally transforming their economies during this decade of global transformation, then they exist in madness! Linear thinking is bad thinking, naive about nature and it becomes highly counterproductive. Without an understanding of the ecology of systems, webs of alliances and the power of networks; it is only in the darkness one will remain, never to see the guiding light to their prosperity.

Right now, for example, in November 2022, at COP27; Bloomberg News reports that there's a breakdown between north and south. The relationship between developed and developing countries is breaking down at the global climate summit in Egypt. United Nations Secretary-General Antonio Guterres said, "the blame game is a recipe for mutually assured destruction." However, this is really about money and power, and the north not wanting to give it up or share it with the south, even when it comes to saving the earth. This is fundamentally human nature and self-preservation at its *finest!* Some southern countries are demanding an agreement to establish a new finance mechanism, a fund or some sort that can be accessed to compensate those nations who are unable to pay to rectify the damage caused by "cyclones, floods, droughts and rising seas." In other words, the north, with all the money does not want to give share any of their wealth and give up any of the power they currently enjoy. Only the white guys can have power!

This behaviour by the north is how it goes in nature; people, or groups, especially those with power only look out for their own best interests and seek to maintain their power and influence in the world. It is the preservation of the existing hierarchical power structure; morality is nowhere to be found. This homogeneous force of white men effectively rule the world, "shape history, transform the world we live in, and determine the future of our financial system, economy, and society" Navidi says.

This influential network in finance over time takes on certain excluding dynamics against others, forging a system based on familiarity—race and culture. Navidi shows us that we need connections and relationships to thrive, therefore, the longer Black folk take to come together and invest in each other, within the region, and form networks and power ecosystems. The longer the suffering will last, only get much worse as the divide between the north and south gathers increasing momentum in this decade of transformation.

The Jews have come to understand that the world is about power, they have suffered for two thousand years and have had enough of it. So they do not sit and beg to get into power systems, and they do not engage in fantasy, instead, they create their own enabling ecology systems to generate wealth—and soon enough influence and power happen.

125

The Jewish people returned to their land, the State of Israel (a matter of debate, of course, and one in which I take no side; I am merely using Israel and the Jewish people as an example of people who understand reality and have used it to their advantage) and build prosperity out of a barren desert. Israel has grown into an innovative nation driven by technology, and entrepreneurship, so, Israel fundamentally understood that self-preservation would come down to economics, and the value it could create for itself. Moving from survival to thriving would take wealth and power, so they went out and got the job done. It is just that straightforward. Israel had a practical plan, a strategy for them to survive and thrive in the universe.

The state of Israel did not waste time arguing the moral case; they knew that the critical factor was to identify their interest—the sophistication of self-preservation—and move forward with their purpose to pursue and preserve the security, prosperity, and permanence of the Jewish state and its people. To do that, Israel needed power! So making Israel very powerful and productive was a matter of survival in a harsh, conflict-driven world. I refer to economic power, not military power; however, it costs money to provide military power to ensure national security. Fighter jets, weapon defense systems, drones, and cyber security all cost money. Therefore, without economic might and power to pay for its own security, Israel could not even exist, much less survive. Israel today is one of the most thriving free market advanced economies in the world, having risen in per capita income to become wealthier than Japan, France, Britain, and Germany. Israel boasts only one-tenth of one percent of the global population, with a minuscule territory; yet it is one of the mightiest and most influential countries in the world. They understand power, how to create it, and how to use it effectively to survive and thrive!

All power flows from economics! The Jewish people have long understood this; indeed, they have been persecuted for thousands of years partly because of it. They have also decided that they will not be victims and have built an influencing political power structure based on economics to ensure their longevity. This is what you must do in nature—put self-preservation first.

We do not want to live our lives angry at the system, being constantly disturbed and distracted; that is only a waste of time. Instead, we should take the advice of Epictetus:

You are not disturbed by things in themselves but by the principles and notions which they form concerning things. When, therefore, we are hindered, disturbed, or grieved, let us never attribute it to others but to ourselves—that is, to our own principles.

[And so,] the unwise person blames other people for what are, in the end, her own judgments about things; the person who is making progress does not blame others, but only herself; the wise person does not blame ever herself.

Therefore, Epictetus is reminding us that to achieve happiness in life, we need to focus on the things that we can control, our minds and behaviour. Moreover, as Aristotle tells us, the universe cannot be anything other than what it is; the nature of ecological networks is nature in action. So finding your place in nature is best. Freedom is about fulfilling your desires and not wasting time being envious of others, which never serves you well. So we must go beyond the theory and focus on real life. As Seneca said to Lucilius, "The happy life is to have a free, lofty, fearless and steadfast mind—a mind that is placed beyond the reach of fear."

So your objective and energy should not be spent trying to join the *Suberhub* but growing your own *Financial Elite & Network to establish your place and influence in the ecology of the universe.* Success is not about trying to be someone else or like others, trying to get into exclusive clubs and networks. Life must be about exercising your free will, painting your own canvas, doing so and the universe will notice

127

the authentic and real value you create, and your influence will sprout in nature's ecology, where you will no longer be an endangered species—how you survive. And this goes to the core of the sophistication of self-preservation—how you thrive in the universe.

Therefore, it does not help to be reactionary or emotional about things, again this is only the nature of the universe playing itself out. The optimal thing to do is not to be reactive, emotions ignite thoughts and actions that are not usually effective in solving problems or getting the outcome you desire. Being reactive gives away your power, it is better to activate your self-interest and self-preservation, and figure out how best to play the cards you have been dealt. And play them for the cards that you want, which can help win. You didn't create the system, environment, socioeconomic circumstances, etc., however, while things might not be of your making, your fault, you must still deal with them if they affect your life. So figure out what you can learn, what is in your control, how you can improve your situation, and what truly matters and what does not, that is where your thinking must be focused in the 21st century.

MOVING BEYOND nice theories is when you actually start experiencing real life. Author, Desiree Peralta points out some "Uncomfortable Truths About Life" and if you can make yourself uncomfortable you can get ahead of 95% of the people who cannot do it. Here are some of her thoughts highlighted below:

You will never be presented with challenges you cannot overcome. You either want solutions too fast or are too lazy to fight. People often have the wrong ideas about success and most times they talk a good game but are unwilling to acquire the knowledge it takes to walk the talk. *No matter how many advantages you have in life, it is not the only thing you need to be successful.* In short, dreaming is great but hard and smart work underpinned by the common denominator of a correct strategy is most important to successful outcomes. However, even the best strategy cannot happen on its own, it has to be applied to be successful. ***You cannot be generous with others without being selfish with yourself; Think about which one is more worth it.*** In a nutshell, this simply goes back to self-interest/self-preservation. You cannot be helpful to anyone unless you have first helped yourself into a strong value position to be useful to the universe and others.

Complaining leads to misery. This one is easy…do not be a veranda complainer!

Everyone is doing everything they can with their current state of being. *To have more, you have to do more. To do more, you have to be more. If you want to change your life, you have to start focusing on what things you need to improve in your daily tasks to achieve it because you will not grow to do the same things over and over again.* Additionally, you must embrace change and must be prepared to do what 95% of the population will not do: be a part of the 5% of successful preaddressing what is true but uncomfortable is to have an objective, quantitative mind, and this mind helps you understand the laws of nature and how to come to terms with your own existence in it. Focusing on objective truths helps us focus on what really matters for our defined success and happiness. Therefore, by grasping clearly what can impact your life you have more conscious control of your life, effectively, you do not let anything that does not add value to your life, into your life.

CHAPTER 3

applied Intelligence

Who Owns the Data Owns the Future — Yuval Noah Harari

The pursuit of a *Caribbean Renaissance* movement is a movement to advance the level of thinking to a higher dimension. So constructing an end-to-end, fit-for-purpose solution that can integrate into our consciousness requires building a framework methodology for that higher level of thinking, which is what *applied intelligence* is about.

Still, to move forward, we must confront some hard objective truths about ourselves. Our future depends on being honest with "Us." Continuing to lie to ourselves is nothing more than fooling ourselves. Which may provide comfort in the short term but will only intensify long-term suffering more. To improve our situation, we must take personal responsibility, with no excuses and rationalizations, so we must apply intelligence over emotional decision-making.

At a certain point, the region must realize that the solutions they need cannot be provided by anyone else other than themselves. No development agencies, academia, etc.; dependency is a vicious circle, continuous loops of despair. In the final analysis, if others have dominion over you, then you are not truly free. Happiness does not come easy, there is always a price to be paid, there are no free lunches in the universe, and everything must be earned. Accordingly, in the end, your level of happiness is relative to the value and satisfaction that you can create for yourself.

As the centuries have gone by, technology has consistently improved the quality of our lives. Global productive capacity has increased exponentially through technology utilization and industrialization.

The universe has also gotten more complex, and we are now at the beginning of the *5th Industrial Revolution* — information, knowledge, and capital, hyper-dominates our existence.

To understand where *applied intelligence* is coming from and where this book is taking us, we must understand more about data science. So from any viewpoint, all data is from the past, so the actions that arise from that data are about things that have already happened. But data has become all the rage these days, like a magic bullet it seems. But data and AI are overrated. There can be no data about the future, no predictability about the future good enough to justify the hype about big data/AI. So as we gently come back to earth, we come to understand that data is best served and utilized as an optimization tool that can assist humans with tasks and decisions.

Below is what the progression from data science to AI looks like.

data science

Progression towards AI and ML

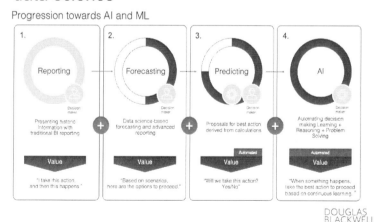

As we can see data science begins as a reporting tool and on pure information, then it moves to stage two and the information begins to be analyzed, the analysis then moves to stage three when it takes on prediction scenarios and guidance on best actions based on the analysis of the information. Stage four is where AI happens, the decisions become automated and learning and reasoning take place and

ultimately move to problem-solving, which is fundamentally what we do as humans. Therefore, AI can be seen as an ultra-powerful extension of the human mind. And remember, AI is still under the control of humans as AI is nothing without programming and we humans do the programming. So again, do not believe the hype around AI.

The above chart tells is good because it tells us the true story of data science, the top left quadrant informs us that AI is essentially a **very useful** tool, the highest level of data processing because of its usefulness as an extension of the human mind. Therefore, the visual below tells us how about the usefulness of data science as a business intelligence tool, for example.

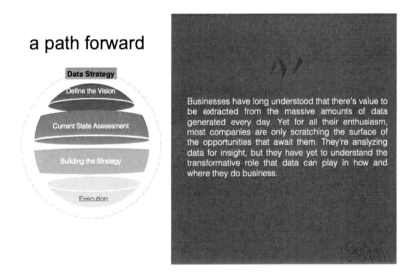

So the optimal use for data science is strategy formation and you are understanding that it is not a magic bullet but good enough processed information that can be effective in developing a strategy to execute upon. The data strategy begins with the data helping you form a more realistic vision of your objective because your vision of the future is now augmented by real information or evidence. You can move confidently now, and Define a Vision based on the Current State of Assessment, to **Build a Strategy** for Execution.

Therefore, businesses have long understood that there is value, and competitive advantage in information and the more you can get massive amounts of information, and process it with speed and accuracy the greater your business advantage will be. So there is nothing really new here about the universe, the only thing really *new* is the advance intelligent technology applications that can process and provide insight into decision-making for humans. So we can break down data into six dimensions to generate accurate data analysis and predictions bringing data science down to earth for our understanding of it for its usefulness to society.

the six dimensions of data

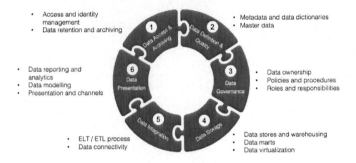

- Access and identity management
- Data retention and archiving

- Metadata and data dictionaries
- Master data

- Data reporting and analytics
- Data modelling
- Presentation and channels

- Data ownership
- Policies and procedures
- Roles and responsibilities

- ELT / ETL process
- Data connectivity

- Data stores and warehousing
- Data marts
- Data virtualization

1 Data Access & Archiving
2 Data Definition & Quality
3 Data Governance
4 Data Storage
5 Data Integration
6 Data Presentation

DOUGLAS BLACKWELL

Measuring data quality dimensions helps you identify opportunities to improve and enhance your outcomes based on the application of your gathered data, and to ensure that the data represents the real-world analysis we must be vigilant to be accurate, complete, and consistent when handling data.

THEREFORE, *applied intelligence* seeks to be a practical *good-enough* strategy tool to provide a useful strategy formation framework for people and "good-enough" is all we can get. With all the great mathematical models' theorems and theories out there, it is only an embodiment of some general principle, but these math proofs still can get us to any level of useful predictions about the future. For example, if we examine two of the main schools of thought about

134

probability—Bayesian and the frequentist approaches, even those cannot come close to predicting outcomes. Bayesian thinking is an idea based on the subjectivity of probability, where the probability of an event happening is based on an individual's beliefs in the end, regardless of all the math employed in the Bayesian approach. Frequentist, in contrast, probability is objective and based solely on the frequency of an event occurring. I make no pretence to be an expert in any way on these two approaches, only to say that although they are two very well-accepted theories in analysis, they are not necessarily useful in predicting outcomes in any meaningful way.

Bayesian thinking allows for the incorporation of acquired knowledge or one's beliefs to be inputted into the analysis equation, however, the complexity of the Bayesian process makes it more confusing and uncertain than useful. Frequentist thinking on the other hand, although more uncomplicated and straightforward than Bayesian, it still does not allow for prior knowledge, so it does not give for developing a framework for analysis. Both simply add to the uncertainty in fancy and complex ways giving people the falseness that this is "smart" and useful. In contrast, applied intelligence offers a practical and good-enough, disciplined, non-pretence-based overly complex and mathematical framework for optimal decision-making—applied intelligence simply wants to make itself useful to people.

So, FOR EXAMPLE, in today's climate, the top-down "development" institutions that have become the arbiters of other people's lives often point out that they use "data" in their approach to justify their actions. However, we have no visibility or analysis of how they use data, to examine if it is even good and accurate information and if the methods are relevant and useful and free from Western white supremacist bias. And with no objective third-party measure of performance, their claims of the use of data analysis is good for nothing.

For Black populations of the Caribbean, the 'development' discourse industry continues to promote spurious top-down bureaucratically led development, without having any *skin in the game*. And they have no risk, so they have no concern as to whether things working or not. The Caribbean has been turned into one big theoretical and experimental basket case, run by academics and their local indoctrinated and unsophisticated wingmen. Everything becomes disconnected from real people and good results are the exception and not the norm.

Nevertheless, notwithstanding the above information, data can be very useful to us when utilized properly and ethically. It can provide enormous value, but the handling of it is most critical to good outcomes in our favour. We must be highly conscious of the many problems with data, there are good and bad, depending on how it is applied, and how it is collected. Has it been *cleaned* properly and who are the ones "cleaning it"? Do we know if it has been manipulated to align with the researcher's pre-drawn conclusions? And what about the algorithms used overall? Who wrote them? Algorithms like everything else in society are created by humans and humans are inherently biased, so algorithms can be racially biased too.

When it comes to development organization types like the World Bank and related institutions, it is highly unlikely that these bureaucrats and advisors use data properly, if they use it at all. What this means is that these bureaucrats are making decisions about people more on paternalistic assumptions and colonial legacy systems rather than on solid research and evidence. This also means that they are essentially using their embedded white supremacist cultural biases, and arrogance, to be the arbiters of Black people's lives.

The structure, and how data is gathered, organized, analyzed, and applied. All those processes are important factors because data must be properly interpreted to be effective in decision-making. So. if the process of processing, and analyzing is flawed or influenced by bias, that data is tainted and not reliable for answering questions or framing policy.

In the 21st century, technology is everywhere, therefore, data strategy as described above is a critical process for leveraging its utility. Data strategy is highly useful for entrepreneurial pursuits, as good research can create good insights towards developing good business ideas or solving social problems. In today's world, the utility of data science is useful for insight and engineering opportunities from discoveries made. Industrial engineering of those found opportunities is the most optimal way to efficiently pursue entrepreneurial ventures. There are no guarantees of course but at a minimum, the analytical approach is more reliable than going on instinct and emotion, when seeking to create value.

The ancient philosophers were the original data scientists, amazingly, without computers, they were able to analyze the universe with great precision. Explaining how the universe functions, and giving us the hard objective truths, the truth about nature and ourselves. So data has always been useful for intelligence, knowledge building, and quantitative thinking, and in the digital era, speed and precision in processing information are critical to competing successfully in the digital age. Nothing has changed; it is simply happening a lot faster now. Therefore, the proper utilization of data will increasingly become critical to winning, and winning requires preparation, applying rigour and intelligence for achieving good outcomes.

A shift to the economic value creation mindset is paramount, shifting to being the aggressor versus the victim is essential for a 21st-century existence. Speed, ingenuity, creativity, innovation, power-seeking, winning, antifragility. Those must all be in the new characteristics of the people of African descent in the Caribbean.

Therefore, it is only intelligent to utilize data and processes in any of those respective pursuits.

COURAGE AND STRATEGY are a must to break free of this vicious circle of inaction and trepidation which currently plagues Caribbean leadership, which also trickles down to its people. We must break free and build our superpowers and become fearless in necessary pursuits, so the more information you have and methods to process it and make effective decisions, the more confident you become. So applying data analysis is the intelligent path and must be accompanied by the most rigorous, practical, logical, and common-sense real-world growth applications for achieving optimal results.

We must also apply industrial engineering and utilize analytical methods and combine it with our imagination. Investment is necessary for technology infrastructure, software, and applications, which are the basic things that must be done merely to stay within the range of the wealth curve. The purposeful application of data and industrial engineering and AI will naturally accelerate problem-solving and spur entrepreneurship and enterprise. Without intelligence-based tools and systems in place, there is no chance of a new economy for the Caribbean. The evolutionary and sophisticated nature of growth today simply needs a new level of thinking and analysis, and intelligence is at the centre of it all.

Case Study Analysis
Nature Always Prevails – The Curious Case of Long-Term Capital Management (LTCM)

"Risk is based on the assumptions of the existence of a well-defined and constant objective probability distribution which is known and quite

possible. Uncertainty has no scientific basis on which to form any calculable probability."

—John M. Keynes

Long-Term Capital Management is the ideal failure to help us illustrate the reasons why you cannot change the 'nature-of-things,' and how the wrong, self-serving, ego-driven application of 'data' can lead to major blow-ups. LTCM illustrates how normally smart people can engage in *constructive delusion* or hallucination, drawing on arrogant thinking which can lead to disastrous outcomes. LTCM was a hedge fund founded in 1994 and led by two Nobel Prize Laureates and other leading economists, who were titled "geniuses." LTCM used complex mathematical models to drive huge returns, and investors had to "qualify" as wealthy and sophisticated to get into the fund, which of course was part of the allure of it all. The more exclusive things appear, the more people want in, losing their good minds in the process.

LTCM operated at a high leveraged position of 25:1; meaning $25 of debt for every $1 of capital. Without any formal financial training, common sense alone should tell you that this was not tenable. So as with the nature of gravity, in August of 1998, the fund lost 44% of its value overnight. So much money was lost, and so quickly, that it led to the Federal Reserve intervening and gathering 11 other banks to bail out LTCM at the sum of US$3.65 billion.

The fall of LTCM was set off by a major and unpredictable event — the Russian-led liquidity crisis in 1998, and an immediate flight to liquidity in global markets began. The liquidity crisis pushed LTCM's leveraged positions to reach astonishing levels: 250:1. The fund's investment strategy was inherently fragile, and vulnerable to unpredictable shocks because of its extremely leveraged positions. It was a powder keg situation in which any small spark could set the whole thing off, and that is exactly what happened—the Russian liquidity crisis lit the fuse that blew LTCM up. For all the "genius" accolades and Nobel Prize winners in economics at LTCM, these "geniuses" still made elementary math mistakes, and basic errors in thinking and judgment, because they were inherently driven by ego and the belief in their self-created artificial methods, that they thought could override the laws of nature.

In brief, LTCM's strategy was designed around a predictive, mathematical, computer-driven investment model which imputed infinitesimal amounts of variables/data, and the received outputs were automatically taken to execute the trades. Essentially, these people assumed that they were smarter than everyone else, even smarter than the market—and most fatally, they believed that they could outsmart nature. So arrogance led to non-adherence to the intrinsic math that is embedded and entangled in the universe. They failed, however, to understand that nature's math is supreme and cannot ever be defied. The use of artificial math to circumvent the laws of nature can be perilous for your finances, as LTCM's clients discovered.

Not factoring in the always looming and mighty independent variable also became detrimental to LTCM. In short, it does not matter how many dependent variables you throw at any given model; the mighty independent variable can always crash the party and change the outcome in an instant. The liquidity crisis was all about unpredictability and the mighty independent variable, the latter of which superseded all the infinitesimal amounts of dependent variables that LTCM factored into their trading equation. The model, therefore, was inherently fragile and susceptible to shocks, and the independent Russian liquidity crisis event blew up LTCM.

In the final analysis, LTCM's investment strategy was bogus and ego-driven and created monumental risk due to the *artificiality* of investment methods, which were not grounded in nature's math. As a result, there was no place for the shocks to be absorbed or neutralized by this faulty and fragile model. The model could not solve for uncertainty, unpredictability, and randomness, so in the end, LTCM engaged in constructive delusion, a controlled hallucination of their own making. Fooling themselves first and then others by waving their PhDs and Nobel Prizes in front of peoples' faces to gain credibility. People bought into the philosophy, and elegant theories, and not adhering to nature's fundamental math—that there is nowhere in the universe where 1 + 1 does not still equal 2.

LTCM, made up of Nobel Prize Laureates and other leading economists, was all hype; in the end, it was simply a feel-good story that fooled a great many people. It was so complex that people could not understand the trading algorithms or how LTCM essentially made money. So everyone made up the nicest stories to explain it all; however, since everyone was making money, no one cared to ask or didn't want to, for fear of looking stupid in front of the managers or the wall street herd. Things worked for a while of course, but because the model was fragile it was not sustainable. LTCM got away with defying nature for a bit because humans are susceptible to great storytelling. Choosing to focus on a good story instead of applying logic was harmful to their investors.

THEREFORE, events like LTCM will happen over and over again because beautiful suckers are born every day, there's always someone in search of the next herd. Hubris also leads to decoupling from reality, allowing even the smartest of people to de-intellectualize their minds in the presence of great storytelling.

So what was ultimately the real difference between Bernie Madoff and LTCM? Nothing! Constructed delusional storytelling and egos gone wild existed in both situations. And the real result in both cases was that everyone lost money! And today, in early 2023, there is a new and curious case of FTX, a cryptocurrency exchange; but to be honest, I have no idea about how this business worked. Nevertheless, FTX was a success story almost from the very beginning. In three short years, it went from nothing to a $32-billion company and the madness of the crowd took over. Everyone, including journalists, investors (the "smart" money), and politicians—all of the usual suspects—jumped on the bandwagon, even though most had no real idea about the operations and the balance sheet of the company. Even government regulators dropped the ball!

In short, FTX developed a "proprietary trading strategy," a.k.a. nonsensical philosophy that sounded so good that the so-called "smartest" of investors rose like fish to a bright, active bait. And again, when the herd moves, no one wants to look stupid by making intelligent observations such as "I do not understand how this business makes money." And of course, they made the twenty-something-year-old youth look like a genius. What else is new? And to be honest, I cannot explain how this structure worked; but it should suffice to say that it was all smoke and mirrors. And it was the same thing as LTGM—borrowing/leveraging to trade, which can be enormously profitable, but equally devastating when things go the other way.

Nevertheless, as always, there are red flags and some sounding the alarms; but the herd again drowns them out. Orthogonal Credit, in performing its due diligence on the company, pointed out that the company had declining asset quality, unclear capital policy, less than robust operational and business practices, and an increasingly byzantine corporate structure. And Marc Cohodes, the perennial short seller known for pointing out market frauds, put it this way: "In my view...nothing ever added up...I think [FTX] will make Bernie Madoff look like Jesus Christ."

So like FTX, LTCM cleverly turned artificial math into a working theory to sell investments. LTCM in their delusional trance, somewhere between reality and non-reality made their math match their preconceived investment conclusions. And of course, to make a lot of money for themselves; naturally! Hence, LTCM's strategy was a pseudo-scientific philosophy. And data, as it stands alone, is "ignorant" and can be easily manipulated by those in delusional states.

Not being skeptical or always accepting of what others in "authority" have to say is a mistake. Question everything! If the dots do not add up, then go back to the original question, the main problem, which usually provides focused logic to the problem and our understanding of reality. Further, do not engage in listening to elegant theories when making important decisions, that only leads to errors in judgement. Instead, exercise your intellectualism and individual free will, acquiescing to conformity leads you into the abyss.

Do not be fooled by specialists; often, their thinking is limited by their training. They operate in mental silos, in classroom economics with a delusional philosophical understanding of reality. But of course, the universe does not care about your philosophy, because the universe cannot be anything other than what it is. Your range or scope, your domain of influence, competence, vision, understanding, and cognizance, is always limited by reality. Once you begin to believe otherwise, or you have no limits, you are bound to encounter trouble.

The main lesson about LTCM is that despite its star traders and Nobel laureates, the ship still went down and in flames. LTCM tried to augment nature, artificialized things and created spurious math, disobeying first principles and the cardinal rules of investing. You must always know the rules of gravity.

Remember that all data is from the past, and past events or occurrences are not necessarily indicative of future events or outcomes. In other words, economists cannot predict a damn thing! As mathematician Sofia Kovalevskaya tells us, "Nonlinearity places limits on human hubris." The natural world is impossible to predict, and there isn't any math for that.

143

EINSTEIN ONCE SAID that his work fell into two parts: the first consisted of discovering primary principles by which to proceed, and the second was to draw on them to help form conclusions that followed from those first principles—*applied intelligence* follows Einstein's logic by first establishing scientific principles and a framework for problem-solving. This process of logic is optimal because it avoids theorizing, personal bias, emotion and intuition, and the pull towards conformity.

In his book *Fear of a Black Universe*, Black Physicist Dr. Stephon Alexander talks about thinking big and creatively, which often requires stepping out of your domain, your comfort zone, to find the solutions to complex problems. Einstein discusses the importance of regulating your work by evaluating it through rigorous application—the application of scientific values which rests on cognitive rationality. This simply means as Alexander explains that the processes involved must be highly disciplined, a flawed process leads to ineffective or wrong solution outputs that can lead to the creation of more complications and problems. The process must, therefore, be underpinned with logic and coherence and be "empirically warrantable," according to Alexander.

Decision-making Process

Here we use an example taken from an article in the medium.com titled *The Ultimate Superpower is the Ability to Simplify*

For illustrative purposes let us look at when a patient is suffering from a heart attack and enters the hospital. Doctors need to make quick and accurate decisions about whether the patient should be treated as low-risk or high-risk. Such decisions can save lives. In 1993, Leo Breiman, a statistician, and a pioneer in the field of Machine Learning developed a *decision tree* to classify patients according to risk. The decision-making process moves through a series of cues and depending on those combined cues, classifications on the level of risk for the patient are provided—from high risk to low risk. And a patient who has a systolic blood pressure of less than 91 is immediately classified as very high risk—no further risk cues are needed. The decision moves to the next cue of analysis: age—a patient under 62.5 years is low risk; if he is older, then the medical team checks the final cue: sinus tachycardia—and so on. I've simplified things here to make the main point, which is that having a disciplined system or process of decision-making in place helps one make better decisions. Therefore, systems and frameworks can be very helpful and necessary for optimal outcomes, and this is an important objective of *applied intelligence.*

The disciplined simplicity of the ***applied intelligence*** decision-making framework is intrinsically supported by the robustness of data collection and analysis, and it lends to speed and accuracy, which leads to confident decision-making. So *applied intelligence* is a tool that performs three main and critical tasks. ***Firstly,*** it focuses on the most relevant details or the ones important enough to count the most in the decision-making process. ***Secondly,*** it lays an intellectual foundation to build upon, by adhering to the first principles and *original questions.* And the ***third,*** it is a "stepwise" process that moves along based on evidence and a verified process of connecting the dots. It does not build on nice theories. The complex simplicity of *applied intelligence* constantly questions its process and performance, for reliability and accuracy, functionality, and utility. Most importantly, it constantly questions its usefulness.

So *applied intelligence* is similar, from a fundamental methodology, similar to the Leo Breiman method; both uses simplified yet inherently complex decision-making systems. Bringing disciplined and practical processes and methodology to the table to stay focused and to keep it simple for effective problem-solving. We simply seek to find what is true.

"Truth is ever to be found in simplicity, and not in multiplicity and confusion of things"

— Isaac Newton

In-process and systems of analysis, the primary responsibility is to connect the dots and stay away from making theoretical judgments. Dr Alexander makes a very good point about the "blurred line spin" on how science can crossover into theory, so we must always be conscious of our human tendencies, because *"facts are statements about phenomena, but they do not exist on their own; they are always conceptualized, which means that they are if only implicitly, constructed theoretically,"* he says. So from an application perspective, *applied intelligence* allows us to answer questions through the construct of logic, within the reality of the real world, not the classroom or theoretical world – *applied intelligence* is about efficient and intelligent leadership, and vision, bottom-up processes that are led by quantitative thinking and approaches—*applied intelligence* utilizes the awesome utility of technology and knowledge ecosystems, industrial engineering, functionality, lifelong learning, inclusiveness, self-improvement, and value creation, to drive its performance. Above all, it adheres to real-world activities. To solve the most pressing complex economic development and social problems facing the Caribbean today, the application of *applied intelligence,* as a highly disciplined intelligence-led process can be highly useful to Caribbean society.

So **applied intelligence** identifies and determines the correct problems to solve...defines solutions based on evidence and selects the right technology application or methodology to solve them. It

146

identifies the white spaces for the defined technology applications that can drive innovation and growth. Filtering ideas down to the optimal potential of success, using computational, quantitative, and qualitative measures to evaluate opportunities through rigorous testing across different analyses. The end objective is an effective strategy useful for **winning!**

applied intelligence simplified: ap^3

ap^3 is **VSP** + **DS** over **TU**

$$\frac{\text{Vision, Strategies, Performance (VSP) + Data Science (DS)}}{\text{Technology Utilisation (TU)}}$$

$$ap^3 = \frac{VSP + DS}{TU}$$

ap3 takes a discovery approach, harnessing the power of human intellect through a process of logic, organizing, and leveraging analysis with imagination. For example, in enterprise development and growth, ap^3 flows along the development curve with a step-by-step process to optimize decision-making for enterprise growth.

six step approach to data intelligence

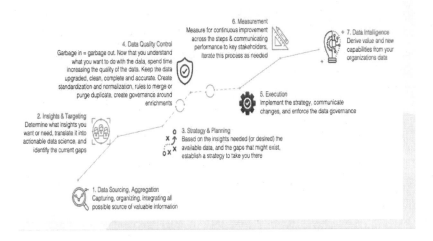

So applied intelligence is all about data and intelligence and as you can see the ap^3 framework equation is an evolving process: **1. Data Sourcing, Aggregation** capturing, organizing, and the integration of all possible sources of valuable information; and that information is, of course, represented as **V**ision, **S**trategy, **P**erformance **(VPS)** values and **D**ata **S**cience **(DS)**—the common denominator being **Technology Utilization (TU).**

We move next to **2. Insights and Targeting** to determine what insights we want or need, and to translate them into actional data science to identify the current gaps and how best to fill them or what additional information might be needed. **3. Strategy and Planning**, based on the insights needed to formulate a sound strategy to take us there. **4. Data Quality Control**, this part is so crucial because it is about what you put in, so if you put in irrelevant inputs, you will get the same coming out, or simply, Garbage in Garbage out. Therefore, because you understand where you want to go from the previous stage, you must spend time ensuring or increasing the quality and relevance of your data. The data must be cleaned, upgrade quality, and as complete and accurate as possible—data governance is critical.

    Stage 5. Execution: implement the strategy and communicate it and make changes as information and analysis guide you to do so and continue to enforce data governance. **6. Measurement:** measuring for continued improvement across all steps along the way, performance measurement is key to good results, and it is important for all stakeholders because we are trying to achieve something, so we need to continuously get better so monitoring helps with that. And finally, **7.** we reach the highly useful domain of ***applied intelligence***, where we can derive value and new capabilities from data science. Here, we can apply it to whatever problem that we are dealing with—business, social, environmental etc., it does not matter. The application of intelligence is agnostic and non-judgmental. It cares only about the inputs and the disciplined process. As long as ap^3 can be highly useful to real people in helping to solve real problems or build good strategies it will be *good-enough*. And of course, as discussed earlier, there is no math that can predict the future.

WE ALREADY HAVE learned, from the likes of LTCM that it is impossible to capture everything in any process or model, and of course, ap^3 respects the awesome power of the all-mighty independent variable. Nevertheless, *applied intelligence* is fundamentally based on scientific realities, science has proven to be the most reliable path to solving the most pressing problems humanity faces. So it is most intelligent to apply a scientifically practical approach to the problems and challenges facing the Caribbean today. Therefore, applied intelligence *is* inherently a bottom-up process that tests ideas and seizes upon any relative opportunity that is discovered through the process, that can be useful to us.

In sum, *applied intelligence* gives us an optimal decision-making platform, with elasticity to drive our rate of change, to leapfrog into to global economy. It is, at the very least an enabling tool and an opportunity to help us compete in an increasingly technology-driven, globalized world. The new economy is a new reality, so you either figure out how to compete in it, or you will be crushed by it.

We've often heard the fear-driven narrative saying that humans will be replaced by AI. However, AI only augments human experiences. AI helps to maximize the operating processes by introducing high efficiency and intelligence into tasks. Advanced analytics in the workplace, for example, only helps good leaders make better, more informed decisions. The more efficient we can become the better the quality of our lives, and AI is only the newest and most efficient technology that can improve our lives. Data science and AI can help us to consider facts and processes we cannot normally perceive and anticipate with our human minds, so...

- AI is not about replacing humans, instead, AI fills the big gap in human decision-making and efficient tasking, where uncertainties have always existed.
- AI takes away the mundane, repetitive tasks that consume time and human resources. Once those low-productivity tasks are automated it saves the enterprise time and money; efficiency increases profitability. The removal of the mundane provides a runway for the creative class, it opens our minds to curiosity, imagination, innovation, and the fundamentals of discovery which are necessary to create the next generation of things. Therefore, users of technology create increased hyper value through its utilization. The recent pandemic has brought in new remote working cultures, and innovative cloud platforms are the applications powering change today.

- Increased task efficiencies will create a more creative and innovative workforce, providing the opportunity for less developed societies to empower themselves through technology utilization to compete in the new global economy, more quickly. We simply need to ask ourselves a few basic questions first:
- Which AI technologies have the greatest potential benefit to your organization or society?
- How might those technologies enable new strategies, business models, business process designs, and social impacts?
- What data resources do you have—or might you need to obtain?
- How do you anticipate AI will impact your workforce, and how can you begin to prepare staff/people to augment AI capabilities?

Overall, the people or narratives that say machines will replace humans are based on a lack of understanding of AI. The reality is, that AI/ML augment human activities, adding efficiency and value to enterprise and societies, and increasing the quality of our lives. So to succeed in the emerging digital era is about having an open mind, creating a solid strategy, learning, risk-taking, executing with precision and minimizing error. Therefore, *applied intelligence* helps with the processes involved and the utilization of intelligent technologies within the processes. So over this decade of digital transformation, investment and alignment with intelligent technology ecosystems becomes increasingly critical. So ap^3 can be viewed as an augmentation of the human mind for creating the right disciplined framework that can assist in growth acceleration. It is essentially a framework for better thinking, examination, and iteration, for the expansion of entrepreneurship and economic activity throughout the Caribbean region.

The strategy then flows from engaging *applied intelligence* | ap^3 effectively in the process of identifying, quantifying, and mitigating risks inherent to the strategic objective. For example, in an agriculture enterprise pursuit, Caribbean nations will want to use a strategy of differentiation, to intelligently maximize our natural competitive advantages in agriculture. Differentiation must be utilized in creating value by maximizing operational efficiencies for productivity and enhanced profitability, which can translate into long-term sustainable growth and intergenerational wealth creation for the Caribbean people.

CHAPTER 4

The Value of *applied intelligence*

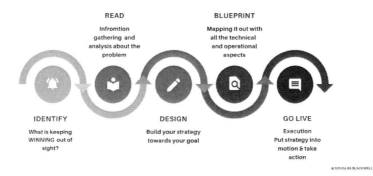

With everything that you are hearing these days about data, artificial intelligence (AI,) analytics, automation, robotics, etc., it might seem that these technologies can do it all. Knowledge remains central to growth, and knowledge and application of technology, of course, can assist in doing it at a much faster and more precise rate. The processing of information and executing tasks efficiently and effectively is at the forefront of creating competitive edges and creating value for societies. Still, AI is no magic bullet, by far, it still

153

comes down to functionality in executive human decision-making. AI can be dramatically helpful to growth objectives as a tool; it keeps you competitive in a hyper-competitive globalized world. So using intelligence-based technology tools is no longer an option, it is a necessity.

AI is most optimal for your desired outcomes when it is given proper instructions to execute your vision, AI requires leadership so it can assist you in producing your desired outcomes. However, it can be counterproductive and even dangerous in the hands of those without realistic expectations, and a clear understanding of data science in general. Human intelligence, therefore, remains the main thing in value creation with AI because human intelligence makes the ultimate executive and creative decisions. But data science can give you a significant information and efficiency edge, improving your odds of success and outperformance, versus not utilizing it at all, which wouldn't be the intelligent or rational thing to do. To win you must use every helpful tool or asset at your disposal; so, you must lead AI.

HARVARD BUSINESS SCHOOL Professor John P. Kotter writes on the topic of leadership and change, in his book, *Leading Change;* he shows that in any era, and by any objective measure, *"the engine that drives change is leadership...and always found in successful transformations, none is more important than a sensible vision."* Moreover, he points out that vision must also be driven by a *strong strategy*. Therefore, regardless of the technologies, having a strategy, underpinned by leadership remains the common denominator in successful outcomes. Therefore, leadership and vision coupled together are critical to the effective utilization and guidance of intelligent technologies.

It is important to pause and point out that the programming outputs therefore often reflect the majority view which can often reinforce all the same dynamics and stereotypes in society, so algorithms often reflect the majority or more powerful societies. So algorithms play on socioeconomic systems and dynamics, power, privilege, and inequality. Therefore, from the Caribbean perspective, if you are not consciously aware of technology it may work against you in many situations. AI can reinforce the many inequalities and restrictive economic progress in less advantaged societies. Nevertheless, innovation creates opportunity and brings along progress with it, so, normally, new technologies can have some negative traits and create vulnerabilities. Nevertheless, this is no reason not to use it; simply be aware and utilize it accordingly.

Further, "clean is not the same thing as accurate, and accuracy is not the same thing as actionable. Problems on any one of these vectors could impede an A.I. model's development or interfere with the quality of its results." Marianne Belloti, (A.I. Is Solving the Wrong Problem). Belloti goes on to explain that data can be problematic because it can be factually incorrect to begin with, corrupted, or not properly formatted. That the message can often be distorted, asking the wrong questions, receiving the wrong outputs, badly misinterpreting and providing wrong solutions. Causing more problems and unnecessary complexities to deal with. Compounding errors and setting back people. Again, be aware, so you can avoid misuse and going down rabbit holes with data.

Therefore, in the end, it is still up to human intelligence to make good decisions, so the usefulness of strategy is of central importance to good outcomes when utilizing data. Hence, a strategy-leadership framework aligned to the necessary intelligent technology ecosystems, geared to the stated mission objectives is central to succeeding in the 21st century. And this is the effective utility of *applied intelligence*. No matter how much data we get, and how fast and powerful the machines become, perfection or total reliance on AI for success remains out of reach at this time. Human intelligence is always required.

Therefore, we must strip away the uselessness of things and get down to the first principles of effective utilization. In the business environment, having embedded business intelligence assets in our enterprises and societies can be an effective tool if implemented with purpose and strategy. We must drive for maximum efficiency without fear of change, and we must be consciously aware of how the utility of technology can change our lives for the better. Therefore, creating an operational strategy framework to leverage in helping the region reach its prosperity objectives requires a strategic framework approach. Hence, we must build a road map using *applied intelligence* towards what we want to achieve.

In the medical space, pattern recognition is utilizing AI increasingly, it can give clinicians firm views, eliminating the "educated guessing" that essentially diagnosing. When clinicians have accurate information, their human intelligence picks up and they become better clinicians due to more factual information to draw insight. Helping them to execute their medical practice better, and with more time for empathy. AI also allows medical teams to look at all possibilities quicker, ruling out certain diagnose right away, removing the inefficient and possibly dangerous cycle of making assumptions, ordering more unnecessary tests, and simply narrowing the possibilities. AI becomes valuable to humanity because it has the utility of removing uncertainty, and giving precious time back to people, which can improve their quality of life. Time is the most precious thing in the universe, and since our time here is minuscule, the most efficient and productive use of time is critical to making the best of our own time in the universe. So we must sensibly use the resources and technologies at our disposal to improve our lives by managing our time. AI is not about replacing humans; it is about leveraging machines to be supportive of human intelligence. Data science/AI, like it or not, is now a big and growing part of the reality of the universe, and it is a part of your daily lives whether you know it or not.

INVESTING INTELLIGENTLY

The investment world is saturated with good investment opportunities in the Western world, and those are what we call efficient markets, which makes it difficult to score big in these markets. However, history does show that the best-oversized investment opportunities usually come from identifying value-creation opportunities in unexpected places. Caribbean markets are typically overlooked because they are often considered too small, unsophisticated, and inefficient. This is based mainly on biases and misperceptions coming out of colonialism, relative to white supremacy culture, but these misperceptions endure nevertheless, unfortunately. Therefore, it is difficult to lure investors to the region, however, we cannot dwell on the challenges; instead, we must create an overriding strategy to change things. The reality is that the future survival of the Caribbean species as an economic going concern depends on getting investment capital to build out its economy, and foreign capital is at the top of that requirement. There can be no doubt about that!

Nevertheless, the white supremacy investment 'establishment' perspective is rooted in the enduring legacy of slavery and colonialism—racism. However, we cannot be distracted or put off by the realities in the universe, and so, it is the very examination of our colonial past that provides us with insight into how we must go forward. Because there is no chance of riding the global wealth curve without investment in our regional economy and making it a force in the world—tiny Singapore did it, why cannot we?

Hence, value can only be created by first changing the mindset and dialing up the aggressiveness of local populations. A change in thinking will generate a behavioural change which will, in turn, resonate and connect with other like-minded frequencies, regionally and throughout the world. This is how change happens. If we can set the frequencies right, investors will gravitate to the region because they see a path to making money, and money is all that interests them. And that is the way it should be and necessary for capitalism to work. Therefore, we must understand these first basic principles of how venture capital investing works to build a successful strategy for getting it.

Therefore, understanding the nature of investing is critical to good decision-making in furthering our growth objectives. For example, when one looks to invest from the perspective of picking individual winners; investing often results in highly skewed power-law distributions where the non-linear relationships amplify results. In short, this simply means that only a small handful of opportunities ever become hyper-performers, and most opportunities become low performers or non-performers. So the probability of finding many high performers is extremely low. Therefore, an approach to looking to identify the major long-term transcending investment trends first, in the extant macro environment is the more intelligent approach to investing. And particularly, in the current rapidly evolving technological and knowledge-based investment universe, it is also highly intelligent to seek out opportunities in markets where most do not look—the Caribbean territory. The region, similar to past emerging markets around the world, represents a massive tech-based infrastructure play. Everything from 5G to the basic efficiency digitization of the broader economy. What that means is significant derivative investment opportunities will come to light organically for local entrepreneurs to jump on and foreign capital to fund. This is the natural bottom-up growth formula that has worked elsewhere in the world for centuries, so why does Caribbean leadership continue to push top-down, agency, and academic-led development when the evidence continues to tell you that it does not work? In plain speak, this paternalistic, unintelligent nn^2 must stop, or our march to extinction will only intensify.

The most logical or common-sense path to building a successful, tech-based, export-driven vibrant Caribbean economy, is the proven path of bottom-up growth approach, supported by *applied intelligence*. In short, we need big transcending, technology-first growth opportunities to populate our regional landscape.

So what can that teach us about investing in the Caribbean or the strategy for convincing foreign investors to come to our shores? It tells us that we must show them the better probability of success in investing in markets that are set to emerge...and that the holistic opportunity will give them better money-making investment opportunities. Versus their chances in more efficient markets at home. You can also look at it, as a rising tide can lift all boats, so these investors just need to get their boats in the Caribbean Sea. Conventional investing wisdom would tell us that supposedly "intelligent" VCs should pass on most deals they see. However, research indicates otherwise, and at the seed stage at least, investors would increase their expected return by broadly indexing into every credible deal they can. Therefore, VCs need to put egos aside (not likely of course) and look at the science of investing. The VC industry is ego-driven, privileged, and white-male dominated, highly biased to their networks and investing in things and people that look like them. It is inward-looking, these white males are given way too much credit for their success when the data tells us how the *success* really happens. Here, investing is primarily based on personal preferences and past experiences, and it has nothing to do with *careful analysis* or any of the bullshit they spew to the public on social media. Therefore, the purpose of the latter explanation is not to discourage, but to understand the game, and to build intelligent strategies to overcome challenges. And, of course, if you do not know you know!

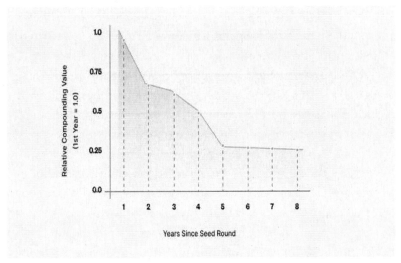

@Abe Othman, Head of Data Science, AngelList Venture

ANGELLIST VENTURE research (see the previous chart) found that when they analyzed the thousands of deals syndicated over the past seven years, to test assumptions about the nature of venture capital returns, they found that missing the best-performing early deal can cause you a theoretically infinite amount of regret. So how can you avoid missing the best deals? The simplest way according to the research is to put money into the most credible deals that you come across relative to available capital. Therefore, the Caribbean's pre-emerging market offers a big opportunity to the intelligent investor, as a ground-level infrastructure play, where probability tells you that there are significant opportunities at the foot for long-term value and wealth creation.

Research simulations on 10-year investing windows for seed-stage deals suggest fewer than 10% of investors ever beat the index, but the reality is that it is well below 5%. Even though the venture guys are plastering their websites with all the "successful deals" in which they have, the vast majority of those "businesses" will not be around three years from now, according to the information. Similar to what the Vanguard Funds have taught us about stock market investing, individual venture investors could benefit more by viewing deals like index investing. And applied to Caribbean investing, it is about first identifying and verifying the big picture play, and applying capital scientifically, based on math, probability, and logic. Instead of bias and ego, which can result in better long-term sustainable investment returns. Furthermore, your capital will have more impact, as profitable economic activity lifts the socioeconomic situations of the broader local economies and populations, it is a—win-win outcome.

SEED-STAGE returns tend to be more extreme than later rounds for two reasons: start-ups tend to grow faster earlier, and seed investments have longer to compound these higher growth rates. So. by the time these companies go public, their growth rate has tailed off (consider Uber, but this time at its IPO). We used AngelList data to compare the relative value of each year of a start-up's life on its compounded returns. We found that growth drops off in a start-up's second year of funding and continues to decrease from there:

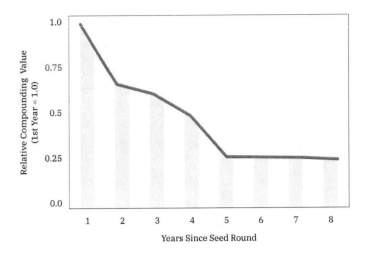

Years Since Seed Round

Therefore, if we can create meaningful full capital markets activities in the Caribbean, there, companies will not be pushed to go IPO so fast and the business remaining private longer will produce rising returns. Again, win-win! Venture investing in North American markets, for example, has become a game of hype, with the sole purpose of raising valuations so investors can cash out with future fragile monetization or IPO existing strategies. This is why in rising markets, the tech hype—you see investment in bogus deals because it is not about real value identification or creation, it is about the hype, phone valuations as the money-making mechanism—nn^2. So as Newton thought us about the laws of nature, gravity always brings us back to normal.

As briefly mentioned earlier in this chapter, we can "learn" from our colonizers, (and remember that slavery was about economics.) They saw the ground-level economic opportunity and created a strategy to win—this slave plantation economy created massive wealth for themselves, changed the course of history, producing massive wealth transfers to their future generations, a

162

linear line based on racism—the enduring white superiority and Black inferiority narrative. This is the embedded narrative that has allowed for their maintenance of wealth, power, and privilege in the universe. So you can look at the colonizers as early investors, who invested in the holistic big picture play, and each who had access carved out their start-up enterprises, which evolved into massive wealth-creating machines—the British sugar and tobacco barons, banking…Barclays Bank, which emerged out of Jamaica by financing slave and cargo merchandise ships to-and-from the colonies. Once again, this is not to discourage but to enlighten—if you do not understand the history and take lessons from it then how do you expect to win in the future?

In a recent report titled *"SEC Concept Release,"* the report called for broad-based early-stage venture capital indexing to the 90+% of unaccredited retail investors, while maintaining appropriate investor protections. In short, this just means trying to take the power out of the VCs and institutions' hands, which can benefit pre-emerging markets like the Caribbean, because investment bias and networks are currently held in the hands of privileged white men, and they are shaping the direction of the world. When one biased group controls the market it also controls the investment themes that dominate capital flows. This is why all the new tech founders look the same, white, and this is why a blonde, white woman, Elizabeth Holmes, former Theranos founder was able to perpetuate a 9-billion-dollar fraud on the Silicon Valley investor community. Because that community and networks are inward-looking and invest not intellectually, but with their intuition, and emotion.

Therefore, and according to where the Caribbean is concerned, the optimal investment strategy is to move towards digital transformation and show the big long-term infrastructure play that exists, and how there is big money to be made—white folks understand green. So we understand the many challenges and the engrained human biases of others, but we cannot let that stop us, our long-term survival as a species depends on finding investments for economic growth and sustained prosperity. We must focus on that! There is no reason whatsoever why the Caribbean cannot transform itself into a sophisticated knowledge-based, technology-driven economy in the 21st century. The only question to be asked is whether or not we are willing to do the hard work and apply intelligence to the tasks ahead.

IT MAKES SENSE, from a development perspective that the regional leadership should also make the iconic business strategy called **Blue Ocean Strategy (BOS)** part of its *applied intelligence* development model. BOS is based on a study of 150 strategic moves (spanning more than 100 years and 30 industries), BOS development models show that lasting success comes not from battling competitors but from creating "blue oceans"– untapped new market spaces ripe for growth. The irrationality of Caribbean leadership falling for the same old top-down 'development' theories of the institutions like the World Bank is not logical and not even based on evidence of it being effective. Therefore, if something continues to fail, over and over again, you might think it is time to try something new. Success in economic development has proven to be a bottom-up entrepreneurial pursuit and to expect to be led by top-down academics to deliver growth is nothing more than an exercise in delusion.

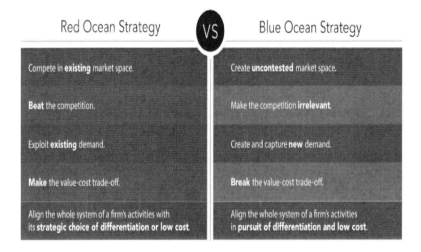

Red Ocean Strategy	VS	Blue Ocean Strategy
Compete in **existing** market space.		Create **uncontested** market space.
Beat the competition.		Make the competition **irrelevant**.
Exploit **existing** demand.		Create and capture **new** demand.
Make the value-cost trade-off.		**Break** the value-cost trade-off.
Align the whole system of a firm's activities with its **strategic choice of differentiation or low cost**.		Align the whole system of a firm's activities in **pursuit of differentiation and low cost**.

© Chan Kim & Renee Mauborgne

Find the mega-trending opportunities first, then support the entrepreneurs who know how to make things happen, by applying intelligence. Nothing has changed, relative to growth in the history of civilization, so stop the foolish ignorance of believing in the grand theories of others to save you, because only you can rescue "you." Accordingly, the business growth objective of applying BOS is to carve out new uncontested market space by creating and capturing new demand and pursuing differentiation at low costs.

At the end of the day, we live in a globalized world and digitally geared businesses can sell to the entire world. The entire Caribbean is a transformation and digital infrastructure opportunity, so put all the short-sighted, backward, white supremacy colonial legacy views aside, and focus on reality! Moving away from emotion and towards intellectualism and execution is how we make things happen for us—emotion is not conducive towards good sustainable growth outcomes.

An integrated BOS enterprise development strategy must be driven by digital technology. The business strategy needs to be well defined, not just towards digital tech, but on how to operate to drive value and maximize financial performance too. The approach to defining strategy needs to be applied practically. Digitization of the core operating model — for successful digital transformation. Businesses need to digitize their core capabilities — i.e., all along the value chain. When speaking of digitization of the operating model, it does not solely refer to the automation of organizational processes, but rather to the end-to-end customer experience design.

Developing and aligning the enablers of digital transformation: **1)** ***People and organization*** — which is about structure, recruiting, training, scaling operations, culture, governance, adopting new ways of working, etc. **2)** ***Data and analytics*** — despite the penetration of big data and advanced analytics jargon into organizations, we need to overcome misconceptions to foster its core value offerings — **3)** ***Technology*** — utilizing digitally ready functionalities of current technologies while addressing internal tensions within the legacy system — and **4)** ***The business ecosystem*** — finding the right partnership frameworks to manage the new and complex building blocks of digital transformation—in more open business architecture.

In the science of winning: A digitally ready technology team is required to keep up with new customer expectations and fast production cycles of digital innovators or disruptors. For incumbents to stay relevant in the 21st century and to thrive in it also, a second gear is required to drive digital transformation execution until a "full" transition to the new global economy is achieved. The ultimate goal is to converge execution speeds in the technology function together with the business side into a single, unified operating model, aiming for agility at scale in the mid to longer time frames. The role of business leaders is to recognize which combination of environments they are operating in and orchestrate different approaches simultaneously. This ecosystem-type approach whereby ideas are sourced externally is the pragmatic approach for businesses that are unable to manage ambidexterity with internal resources. In practice, this can result in acquisitions, partnerships, incubation, or other more informal exchanges of ideas. For example, today, many banks are running their open innovation Fintech incubators, acquiring, and making large investments into start-ups to build an ecosystem. This is how Caribbean incumbent businesses must think and help to foster an innovative and prosperous environment.

Caribbean governments can create similar entrepreneurial and digital transformation facilitation in support of the new-economy growth. Creating this ecosystem and culture is how the regional economy can enterprisingly leverage its core competitive resources to create maximum economic value. It can engage in horizontal, vertical, and cross-industry partnerships that have functional utility benefiting the predefined growth ambitions of the region. Also, cooperation and collaboration domestically, regionally, and globally, within the industry and outside of respective industries is a requirement for sustained dynamic growth and prosperity in the 21st century. Becoming digitally ready requires a massive change in how the region thinks and operates, requiring a whole new set of capabilities and culture. Ambidextrous leadership, fast execution, experimental and design thinking mindsets.

The methodology application approach puts ego aside and looks to a more time-tested, scientific approach, and seeks to identify investment opportunities that can produce not only extraordinary returns but can also contribute to great societal change. Investing is not for wishful thinkers; investing is a long-term affair that can change the reality of any given society—from poverty to prosperity. Therefore, digital transformation for growth must be taken deadly seriously, and understanding that without a credible investment strategy, and application for execution, the extinction of the

Caribbean species creeps more and more into the long-term picture. Without a reality-based vision, an intelligent strategy, constant attention to detail and design thinking in developing an underlying knowledge-based ecosystem. There simply can be no chance for future prosperity for the region.

TRANSITIONING TO THE DIGITAL AGE through the application of *applied intelligence* will make it increasingly possible to identify the undercurrents of the evolving megatrends that will be needed to propel growth. And so, the application of technology ecosystems will be needed to be applied to extract value from those trends. Agriculture is the primary growth prospect for the future economic viability of the Caribbean, **NOT** tourism—tourism never was and never will be ***the one***!

Therefore, real sustainable opportunities for the Caribbean rest within combining agriculture and technology—***Agritech***! Opportunities exist for advanced technology investments to become the main catalyst for the disruptive transformation of the region. To transform Caribbean economies from manual, low-income producers, to high-value, high-income export producers—significant technology and knowledge-based investments are required to get there. The *applied intelligence* process is based on spotting the developing undercurrents of the advancing waves of economic disruption, by navigating us to the mega-trending opportunities in the universe. Good investing occurs through innovation, historical examination of trends in wealth creation, fact-based analysis, and spotting and evaluating genuine society-changing opportunities that can multiply exponentially.

For successful investing the investment process itself is imperative. To recognize technologies' extraordinary enterprise worth and apply it to the right value advancing tasks, and processes is the way forward. Science over intuition. So simply, the scientific

168

processes must be applied through ap^3 using its scientific methods to build fact-based investment solutions, that can be highly useful in solving complex business and societal problems. Solving problems has always been the path to creating tremendous value for societies through entrepreneurship.

From developing new Intellectual Property (IP) to generating new business, the *applied intelligence* industrial engineering process funnels opportunities by using data science to help separate the real market opportunities from the noise. The real opportunities must be targeted to create extraordinary long-term value for investors, entrepreneurs, communities, and countries. With such a holistic approach...everyone wins—foreign investors and the Caribbean people.

The approach also provides for broad strategic value goals and *applied intelligence* underwrites those strategic plans with operational vigour, to achieve that value. It addresses enterprise value creation and challenges the norms and the status quo. By clearly understanding what an enterprise's future objectives are, processes can be useful in developing roadmaps to achieve them.

- Uses data science and advanced techniques to discover new insights by focusing on the core competitive advantages of an economy, the business, and supportive organizations; applying data science in helping projects create value effectively.

- *applied intelligence* | ap^3 provides a clear playbook for how to integrate and capitalize on advanced technologies—across an entire company, and in any industry. With a strong dedication to helping real people, the ap^3 system is scientifically intuitive and brings an owner's mindset approach to exist on the precipice of business and technology.

- Using artificial intelligence, ap^3 is a constructed series of processes to identify the white space of evolving megatrends, and industries, that can offer opportunities, for example, to generate $100M+ market opportunities. It builds full-picture views of the target market or industry by establishing signals of early opportunities detection and potential risk. It relies on operational improvements, innovation, and tailored growth strategies to develop and build companies of lasting value, that can move societies forward.

With the power of intelligent technologies, there has never been a better time to develop and launch new products and services in the global marketplace. So a systematic and disciplined methodology to optimize transcending investment themes, that involve looking at the big picture and then breaking it down into smaller parts, is the quantitative thinking approach to economic growth. Always using the history of civilization and entrepreneurship as a guide to identifying the best opportunities, but also to be aware of the patterns of risk formation. Leveraging innovation and collaborating with multiple stakeholders is very necessary too, which represents the human side of *applied intelligence*. This ecosystem must include participation from a facilitation perspective, local governments, and organizations towards beneficial socio-economic impacts on local communities.

HERE ARE THE TOP FIVE ROARING WAVES OF

opportunity, spaces of the future, which will help the Caribbean achieve exponential and transcending growth outcomes:

1. Agriculture Technology | AgTech

Rapid population growth is projected to reach 9 billion by 2050, accompanied by increasing urbanization, and an expanding global middle class will continue to drive demand for specialized and high-value food. Regional agriculture is at a critical juncture as Caribbean nations seek to balance the achievement of food and nutrition security, and the pursuit and development of profitable high-value agriculture will be vital to that realization.

Artificial intelligence & data science is helping to create significant value in farming all over the world. Intelligence can help in building transformative, smart farming ecosystems, digital marketing, and sales platforms to accelerate localized agriculture, and industry, leveraging land as a competitive natural resource advantage.

2. Towards a Zero-Emissions-Based Economy

Land, water, energy, materials, interior, landscape integration, clean, vision, innovation, living, transportation—full ecosystem approach based on the latest innovations. From sustainable eco-friendly architecture, including energy-efficient equipment and technics, to Electric Vehicle (EV) transportation economy, and lifestyle. Moving towards a zero-emissions-based economy is the natural evolution of human existence. A green socioeconomic existence will incorporate itself into every part of Caribbean economies. Therefore, significant infrastructure investment opportunities, driven by entrepreneurship and innovation will create a more robust universe of enterprise development and start-up growth, over the long term.

3. Virtual and Telehealth Care

Institutions, especially in healthcare, used virtually to lower their exposure to COVID among patients and workers. However, in the post-COVID era, many of these practices will continue as it makes sense, is efficient and saves time and money for both sides. So there is no doubt that many private and public practices have started implementing many telehealth offerings. Traditional in-person primary care will become more augmented via virtual and as other technologies develop.

Studies show that 80% of primary care services can be delivered virtually. Telehealth visits have surged by 50% over pre-pandemic levels. IHS Technology predicted a few years ago that 70 million Americans would use telehealth by 2020. Forrester Research also predicted that this number would surge to close to a billion globally in the coming years, and logic would tell you that the pandemic has helped accelerate this.

Beyond the virtual health focus, there are many other focuses on healthcare that we will see exponential growth from going forward, and advancements in biotech, artificial intelligence, and machine learning continue to create opportunities to help support diagnosis as well as admin work.

4. Online Education

Education and highly skilled workforces have underpinned successful economies and societies throughout the history of civilization. So it is obvious why online education has had a huge growth spurt since the pandemic began. The history of civilization has been one of adaptation and innovation. The awareness that societies must continue to retrain and upskill simply to remain relevant is nothing new. Governments and institutions too will have to spend significantly to adjust to the future of learning, the future of work, and to remain competitive in the new economy era.

Therefore, there is a huge opportunity in the market with schools, colleges, specialized learning or skills training, and even coaching centres conducting classes via video conferencing. The model for how knowledge and learning will be delivered in the future is being redefined, representing multiple and significant long-term investment opportunities to look out for.

5. Using 5G – "Smart Islands"

There is no doubt that the demand for higher-speed internet and a shift for well-connected homes and businesses have pushed the advancement of 5G. This is because, for better connectivity, we need better networks and increased efficiencies. Many Telcos worldwide are on track to deliver 5G. There are over 380 operators currently investing in 5G; 35+ countries have already launched commercial 5G services. This has proved a fertile ground for start-ups, M&A activity, and retooling mature enterprises for future growth that can utilize 5G within its services.

One key area, for example, is how 5G is impacting smart cities across the world, helping municipalities manage their public lighting network and smart city data through sensors. Connecting entire islands, therefore, should be a priority for Caribbean leadership. Setting policy towards that and encouraging investment throughout the entire region—a *Connected Caribbean* should be a priority in this build-back better world. Greater connectivity can efficiently and effectively create greater and more efficient productivity and output for any society; besides, the region will need this infrastructure in place if it is going to connect and compete in the new global economy. If the world is digital, how can you do anything if you remain manual?

Chapter 5

Individuals and Societies

Our minuscule abilities as humans to process mass amounts of information relative to what a machine can do is another reality. So we must quiet the ego and let AI work for us where it can, and to our competitive advantage. With our limited processing power, we as humans tend to make up stories to explain the things we do not understand or what we think we understand but aren't so. This leads us to an existence where emotion, intuition, and ego often prevail over science and logic, where poor and emotional decision-making become the norm, even part of our identity. We have to flip the script on this.

This is precisely why we need math and science, data science and AI in our lives, it helps our human intelligence accelerate information processing and knowledge acquisition. The sociological limitations of human problem-solving are compounded by the amount of time it takes to learn and generate useful utility knowledge. So in the digital age, if we are not maximizing machines to help us think and make judgements then we are simply underutilizing our human intelligence. In a hyper-competitive and globalized world, where digital is the norm, how can we survive as a species if we are not utilizing intelligent technology to compete? That would be nonsensical, and such ignorance would only push us further into irrelevance, and right to the bottom rungs of the global society.

The use of AI, and ML, and within the applied intelligence framework, allows us to learn, develop strategies, and apply them effectively. The *applied intelligence* process leverages data science for scientific discovery processes and applies to stated objectives. It also allows for immediate feedback so we can adjust and do better the next time. It seeks to move the Caribbean mind away from under the spell of top-down development discourse, academic pontification, generalizations, and ineffective and irrelevant development applications. It seeks to disrupt the antiquated hierarchical, and racist status quo, and dismantle the embedded white supremacy culture that still lingers in the region's collective heads.

Again, we are not trying to build a "machine" that will replace human intelligence, instead, we're building a practical scientific process, highly relevant to the unique challenges the region has. We are capable of thinking for ourselves and solving our own problems. The region is so far behind the global wealth curve that there is no more room to "play the fool" as my dear grandmother used to say; and/or be played the fool by others. We must become surgically aggressive, and ambitious in our growth pursuits. We cannot exist in randomness as we have been doing this for far too long now, always accepting unproven development theories from foreign advisors and academics who know nothing about us.

These so-called "advisors" have no skin in the game and cannot be helpful to us; they have nothing to lose, and it is essentially a working vacation for most of them. We must find our primal instincts and motivate ourselves through self-preservation and develop a broad level of sophistication and intellectual processes, strategy, and clever execution in engineering our way to prosperity and power. Power above all must be the main thing! Because without power, you do not stand a snowball's chance in hell; *applied intelligence* provides us with that defined path to power!

The universe is entangled, so your reality is always affected by what is happening elsewhere in the universe. Therefore, the survival of the fittest is through natural selection, as it requires individuals and societies to make good and relevant choices to further themselves. The universe does not know who you are, nor does it care about you,

175

so only what you do counts. If you are asking others for help towards your advancement, that is a weakness, and weakness is not a common character trait for success.

THE AGE OF BIG DATA is changing how we live, work, and play. Technology efficiency allows for precision, cutting off the fat and getting on with whatever we must get on with. The use of machine learning (ML) in ap^3 gives us a tremendous advantage with speed and accuracy, and if you do not have them, you simply cannot compete effectively.

Traditional statistical models are useless unless they are part of a broader more robust intelligent decision-making agenda and process, and even then, you must remain skeptical about the usefulness of statistics. Statistics on their own can often be misleading through the misuse of numerical data, either intentionally or by constant inherent errors, found in the statistics themselves. Stats' results are often very unreliable and do not provide any real insights, so people end up constructing whatever they *read* into it, and it becomes more harmful than useful. Often contributing to delusional constructs of reality that often lead to false narratives around a given topic.

This decade will be the defining transcending decade for the Caribbean—or not; it all depends on what we do next. So the transformation from acute poverty to one of prosperity will be challenging, and the climb, a steep one. So everything matters, and you do not get to choose outcomes if you do not engage in action—outcomes depend on what you do. So errors in judgement and random thinking and behaviour will be detrimental to outcomes. Therefore, a disciplined scientific process reinforced by robust intelligence applications will keep errors to a minimum. Good decision-making is paramount, so, the process of making decisions must be based on a framework of intelligence, sophistication, and resilience.

ap³|*applied intelligence* pushes us right past the distracting and destructive carnage of "the noise" …conventional wisdom, pontification, the conformity and confinement of normalized thinking. With a keen understanding that it is more important to study what we do not know instead of what we already do know. No one is interested in the trivialities of theories; we are interested instead in ***"what is in it for me!"*** What can be done to better 'my' life? that is the question that can only be answered through real actions. Economic self-preservation is the most natural primal state of our existence and one of those things in the universe that cannot be anything other than what it is. Therefore, entrepreneurship is simply the extension and sophistication of self-preservation, in its most elegant form. It is the organic driving force of individuality and differentiation in achieving personal gain, securing the necessities of survival, to thrive in the creation of your value in the universe.

Accordingly, in the new economy, we must build an entrepreneurial culture through knowledge acquisition and self-determination, developing innovative Caribbean entrepreneurs by providing them with the essential underpinnings of knowledge ecosystems, to engineer bottom-up enterprise growth. From idea generation to commercialization, real support systems are needed.

THE COVID-19 PANDEMIC is one of the most extraordinary events we have ever seen in our lifetime, although a crisis, it has ushered in opportunity in a changing world, offering societies everywhere the opportunity to change the trajectory of their existence via technology. Crisis usually creates opportunity, but you must know how and where to look for it. As the world continues to evolve it gets more complicated, but the complexity is not something to worry about, it is simply the evolutionary nature of the universe.

The AI revolution is only another evolutionary stage of continued industrial revolution advancement. All societies have the opportunity to take advantage of change and change themselves for the better. Change and transition in industrial revolutions are based on the natural selection of those things, and the selection of those things that can produce prosperity has value. So the continuation of long-term global industrial trends, revolutions, or whatever you wish to call it is not new to civilization—this industrial revolution is the 5th Industrial Revolution (5IR). Caribbean people of African descent have to open their eyes to see the universe and become mindful of an unfolding world.

> "Why are we blind concerning randomness, particularly to those large deviations [that change the trajectory of our lives,] why do we tend to think in pennies instead of dollars?"
> —Nassim Taleb

So for Caribbean leadership, it is time to start thinking in dollars and not in cents. Leaders must escape the mediocrity of their thinking, think more transformative, stop focusing on the normality of their society, the mundane, and think differently and bigger and bolder. Therefore, when it comes to the utilization and application of *applied intelligence* towards the latter, it does not seek to develop complex mathematical models or explanations, rather it focuses on the practical in aiding to getting things done. It simply serves the processing of useful information to solve Caribbean problems.

Keeping one's collective head buried in the warm Caribbean sand, because of the exhaustion of dealing with our problems, is understandable, but we cannot let emotion and stress hold us back, prosperous outcomes are a function of the application of intelligent strategic actions. Also, disruptive thinking is the first step to change. We must engage aggressively and do away with negative things that may subconsciously hold us back, like our identification with "island time." We may see this concept as humorous, but it is embedded in our subconscious mind, and it controls part of our behaviour and our acceptance of things that have negative impacts on our existence.

For any chance of real prosperity, a realistic understanding of how we get along in the systemic environment is important. So facing up to the things that identify us is critical to seeing the challenges in front of us more objectively. Therefore, if we do not seek to change and control our own identity…write our own story, others will continue to write it for us. We must also be mentally strong and of clear minds to detach from the holds of our subconscious mind and become savvy in bringing our conscious mind to the forefront of our lives. If we are practicing awareness of ourselves and our surroundings, then how are we going to identify the opportunities to advance to prosperity? We need to develop opportunistic optimism to fuel and encourage our minds, to build the courage to fight for our place in the universe, our slice of the prosperity pie. To capitalize on those life-altering big deviations Taleb described above. You must know how and what to do to win, this is how you gain your footing and position yourself to take advantage of opportunities—you must train your brain to think as a winner and not a whiner sitting on the veranda complaining all day and night.

Never fear the volatility or uncertainty that comes along with trying to create something, if it were easy then everyone would be rich, and that is impossible, everyone cannot win, the world needs losers. Therefore, you must decide what you want to be; however, simply wishing for that outcome certainly will not make it so; strategy, process, and intelligent actions are required—for the individual and the society. As pointed out concerning Adam Smith earlier. Volatility provides opportunity so if you cannot stand the heat then you must exit the kitchen.

Entrepreneurial disruption must become the prime cultural trend, a habit, coupled with analysis and imagination to drive forward in the universe. And have no illusions about how prosperity happens; we have to make it happen, organically and from the bottom up! There is no way around that reality. The future evolves relative to what we design it to be, we are the architects, and we must engineer our lives—build from the bottom up. Applied intelligence is the firm cornerstone for building good strategies, blueprints, and our prosperity.

AN ARTICLE WRITTEN by author and businessman, Levi Borba, the article discusses *antifragility*, and how being resilient is central to succeeding. Antifragility originally emerged as part of a dialogue of authors, Stephen Dubner, author of *Freakonomics*, and Lebanese author of numerous books such as *The Black Swan*, Nicholas Nassim Taleb.

Borba makes the point that resilience and entrepreneurship are the most proven survival method, and he uses the Lebanese people's experience to articulate his point. I found the article highly useful, so instead of trying to interpret it for you, I will simply summarize the author's words instead:

> If you look at ten or twenty or thirty of the richest countries around the world, among the richest people in those countries are someone from Lebanon. He points out that Lebanese are over-represented in multiple countries, in multiple positions of power — from business to academia and politics. Taleb was not bragging about his own country. The Forbes list confirms that what he said is true.

Brazilians—as well as Argentinians, Mexicans, Caribbean, or people from a myriad of other places, are familiar with the multiple Lebanese surnames in the highest spheres of power. In nearly every place with a significant Lebanese diaspora, they outperform the rest in terms of business or financial achievements.

To put it into perspective: In the '60s, Brazil had a population of three hundred thousand Lebanese—first or second-generation—meaning 0.4% of the total population. But a study made by Bresser-Pereira, from this period showed they owned roughly 10% of all Brazilian industries. They also influenced the political arena in Brazil. Despite being just 4% of the São Paulo inhabitants, over 1/3 of the mayors had Lebanese origins between 1982 and 2017.

Lebanese diasporas continue to outperform various groups that arrived at the same time and with similar conditions.

So what makes for this success if you take in Borba's and Taleb's research?

The following is the answer according to them:

The idea is that in a natural setting, anything natural, anything organic, anything biological, up to a point, reacts a lot better to stressors than without… a few adversity results in a little bit more performance in anything.

Adversities are natural in the Levant, the region where Lebanon is located; it is a land that over the many centuries has been threatened by wars, natural disasters, economic meltdowns, and various other catastrophes. It forced residents to build up themselves to thrive under stress. In a rudimentary comparison, Black Caribbean people of African descent, have also faced unimaginable adversity, but have not been able to use that adversity to their own advantage in the way that the Lebanese diaspora has. Of course, every population's experience is different, and the enslavement of Africans was especially unique in the history of civilization. However, the main point is how people can use their suffering, adversity, and trauma to fuel their future prosperity and power. While many of us Black people continue to be controlled by past trauma, the Lebanese people, as well as the Jewish people (through the Holocaust) as well, have learned about the realities of the universe and have behaved thoughtfully, strategically, and proactively to advance themselves and prosper accordingly in the world. Through thinking and actions, they have made themselves resilient; they have executed under the first principle of self-preservation, which is to first survive before you can thrive. So regardless of how different each people's experiences might be, it still comes down to what you do in the end.

So what does *"antifragile"* mean exactly? According to Taleb, "Some things benefit from shocks; they thrive and grow when exposed to volatility, randomness, disorder, and stressors and love adventure, risk, and uncertainty. Yet, despite the ubiquity of the phenomenon, there is no word for the exact opposite of fragile. Let us call it antifragile."

Taleb explains that "[antifragility is beyond resilience or robustness. The resilient resists shocks and stays the same; so, the antifragile gets better. This property is behind everything that has changed with time: evolution, culture, ideas, revolutions, political systems, technological innovation, cultural and economic success, corporate survival, good recipes (say, chicken soup or steak tartare with a drop of cognac), the rise of cities, cultures, legal systems, equatorial forests, bacterial resistance ... even our existence as a species on this planet.]"

Learning from the Lebanese about how to become antifragile would be useful to Caribbean people. Nobody wishes for civil wars, invasions, economical collapses, or natural disasters. But these constant tragedies in Lebanese history drove adaptations, innovation, and creativity that defined the path for the next generation's resilience to succeed. Similarly, Caribbean people today must get over their inherited trauma and focus instead on understanding the universe, applying strategic intelligence to their lives and moving forward. Enough with the emotion, it only holds you back.

Here are some examples of characteristics that made the Lebanese antifragile according to Borba:

> Lebanese emigrés are often trilingual, being educated in English, French, and Arabic. All these languages came through foreign occupying forces (Britain, France, and the Egyptian Mamluks).

> Civil wars and unstable politics often put the Lebanese in situations where they need to improvise to make an income. They cannot rely on public support because it rarely exists. If you are familiar with the Impact vs likelihood matrix, think that what we know as rare catastrophes, in Lebanon may be regular disasters or even casual accidents.

ai

The uncertainties tuned their social skills. Years of sectarian strife made local allies necessary for citizens, families, and societies to exist.

The mercantile nature of Lebanon (and their Phoenician ancestors) flourished for millennia. The trading activity inspired the residents to master skills such as scarcity management, risk assessment, and negotiation. This explains the outstanding performance of Lebanese immigrants in finance and politics.

A risk-taking posture and constant scarcity lead to greenfield projects. Lebanon is a country with chronic natural and social risks, so the inhabitants learned how to minimize their downside during a crisis. One example is the idea of a permanent liquid reserve. Something that, for example, the billionaire Slim Helu used in 1990, when the Mexican government privatized the telecom company Telmex for a reduced price after financial losses. Slim was one of the few investors with the resources to buy it. This company later became the multinational Claro.

Now, as always, there will be the chronic excuse makers among us that will say that the Lebanese experience is very different from the Black Caribbean experience; but these people simply do not get it, so do not listen to them. They are stuck in the emotional abyss of their inherited trauma. The central point here is that adversity and challenges exist everywhere in the universe, and for many people. So Black people should not feel special and lament their past traumas, regardless of how disproportional they may feel their traumas are. Because, regardless, you still must deal with it because it is yours to deal with, and no one else is going to deal with it for you. It is always up to you in the end. Overcoming challenges is universal and so is building resilience as a core characteristic of survival. Therefore, if you remain fragile then you will have trouble dealing with uncertainty, and volatility and such a state of existence are not conducive to finding opportunities for prosperity. In that case, you may as well stay on the veranda. Caribbean people must make deliberate and conscious efforts to shed fragility and build towards antifragile.

> The antifragile loves randomness and uncertainty, which also means—crucially—a love of errors, a certain class of errors. Antifragility has a singular property of allowing us to deal with the unknown, to do things without understanding them—and do them well. Let me be more aggressive: we are largely better at doing than we are at thinking, thanks to antifragility. I'd rather be dumb and antifragile than extremely smart and fragile, any time.

> —Nassim Nicholas Taleb

By adapting to invasions, war, and turmoil, the Lebanese became antifragile and utilized that into becoming resourceful, entrepreneurial, successful. The Lebanese diaspora, with those inbuilt qualities from their native culture, prospered in multiple countries, particularly in the Americas. Nowadays, their success reflects how they are disproportionately represented in the business and political spheres of power.

Using the same concept of antifragility, the Caribbean people must turn current challenges into opportunity—go from fragile to antifragile, trauma into power, experiences into wisdom that can be utilized effectively to make those crucial decisions that can usher in new business and industry, creating wealth and prosperity for themselves and future generations.

TRANSITIONING TO THE PLATFORM ECONOMY

The first step toward transformation is to recognize that the world is a complex place, with many different moving parts that must be treated as active variables. Every decision matters, and each one has a value-creation functionality.

In my past experience with capital markets, I have found that a good trader could execute perhaps 5 to 10 complex, well-thought-out trades on any given day. Today, however, with high-frequency algorithms at traders' fingertips, over 10,000 trades can be completed every second. It is futile to resist this kind of change; instead, capitalize on the utility of technology and make it work in your economic favour. Put your ego aside, elevate your intelligence, and adapt to using the technology tools of the day. Enormous value has been created over the last 2,000 years or so; let history be your guide to future prosperity.

The top-performing economies in the world are no longer the ones dominated by certain physical assets—property, land, plant and equipment, and capital-intensive heavy industry. Today, the linchpins of prosperity are things such as IP, platform technology, and knowledge-based ecosystems and networks. Driven by AI, technological innovations and increased online connectivity have transformed everything; the past norms for assessing or measuring value have been altered to keep pace with the changing times. Increasingly, platform enterprise architecture attributes more worth and value to enterprises than the intuition of entrepreneurs and managers. As the platform economy evolves, Caribbean commerce and enterprise must evolve along with it. If not, then—as nature tells us—through the process of natural selection, the region will be on its way to becoming effectively extinct. Therefore, the accelerated progression of and adaptation to the platform economy are paramount for the future relevance and very survival of Caribbean peoples in the 21st century.

The old economy was linear, characterized by businesses dealing directly with customers and products and services, primarily in a physical and structured environment. The new platform/cloud-based business models are now the main thing! It creates value by connecting users in an online marketplace—giving people what they want when they want it. The sales process is now interconnected and more informative; the consumer has a significant amount of information at hand with which to make good decisions.

The strength of the platform does not stem from "ownership" of the factors of production; rather, it stems from the use of those factors at maximum efficiency, connecting people with the unique goods and services they seek. Airbnb, for example, has become the biggest and most impactful hotel-hospitality company in the world, even though it owns not a single piece of real estate. Airbnb's success demonstrates the power of the platform/cloud economy! The platform's strength lies in its ability to execute transactions effectively and to deliver products and services optimally, with satisfactory customer experiences that keep them coming back. Airbnb is a splendid representation of the new industrial world.

THE INEQUALITY OF TECHNOLOGY and The Danger of a Subconscious Existence

Sociologist Dr. Alondra Nelson points out that one of the main blind spots in the fight against racial inequality is a lack of cognitive awareness and knowledge of the surrounding reality, relative to the impact of technology on the lives of Black people. Nelson says, "I think that if we want to understand anything about science and technology, we need to begin with the people who have been the most damaged, the most subjugated by it." Black people have always been users of technology and its mediums, but not developers or owners of it.

The intersection of technology and social inequalities is undeniable. Dr Nelson's work explores science, technology, and medicine in the context of what drives social inequality. Nelson has contributed to national policy discussions in the United States on inequality and the social implications of new technologies, including artificial intelligence, Big Data, and human gene editing. What is becoming increasingly clear for Black people is that we have failed to recognize what role technology in general and data science in particular play in furthering inequality; this lack of recognition has become problematic to our existence. As a result, when employing data science in business and social environments, it often reinforces the existing structures of power and inequality. Therefore, if you are not thinking in a state of awareness, you are living a subconscious existence; accordingly, critical thinking is important, because the challenges we face are often attractive opportunities in disguise. And we seldom approach it with a critical and intellectual eye, letting emotion dominate our thinking instead. Therefore, it is up to us to think clearly and quantitatively, to understand our systemic environment and how to think and act to win in it.

Once we learn how to leave emotion and fear at the door, begin to think more calculatedly, and take responsibility for our own lives, we begin to see the silver lining in the challenges we face.

Another brilliant Black woman and thinker, Dr. Timnit Gebru, researcher and co-founder of Black-in-AI, an organization that increases the presence and inclusion of Black people in the field of AI by creating space for sharing ideas, fostering collaborations, mentorship and advocacy. Dr Gebru has raised concerns about technology and inequality in AI. Gebru is widely known for miring Google in a scandal after she was dismissed as head of Google's

Responsible A.I. and Ethics research program after she criticized Google language models as discriminatory against Black people. And more recently, the New York Times published a story titled "Google Sidelines Engineer Who Claims Its A.I. Is Sentient"—the main accusation being that "Google and its technology engaged in religious discrimination."

Dr. Gebru is one of the highest-profile people in her field, and a powerful voice in the new field of "ethical AI," which seeks to identify issues of bias, fairness, equality, and social responsibility in the AI domain. Dr. Gebru points out that AI is increasingly influencing our lives to a greater degree than we know, and without diversity in our set of researchers, programmers, executives, policymakers, and most importantly, entrepreneurs! Others will continue to control and suppress our socioeconomic trajectory.

To counter this, we need to apply more robust quantitative thinking and intelligent framing of problems through a developed, conscious decision-making ecosystem. Most importantly, we must fully recognize that—as Dr. Gebru points out—if we do not seek to play a meaningful role in building new technologies in the world, our relevance and existence in it as a people will begin to fade more rapidly, relative to technology acceleration. We have had an inverse relationship between global growth and prosperity, and other groups have understood how to leverage knowledge and technology to their economic benefit. We have not! Afro-Caribbean populations will continue to marginalize themselves and be relegated to the bottom rungs of the global socioeconomic ladder—a place of powerlessness, irrelevancy, and despair.

The explosion of the non-profit organizations that came onto the scene after George Floyd is nothing more than a misguided distraction; this is what is not necessary for the climb to prosperity and power for Black folk everywhere. The very idea of a non-profit organization leading economic change in a world ruled by profit is a prime example of Black people's misunderstanding of how the world works and how prosperity and power are generated. Again, if you are fragile and afraid of volatility, you will not stand a chance. To make things happen in the real world, you must disabuse yourself of the emotional delusions of trying to advance Black people's fortunes by attempting to change the hearts and minds of the oppressor. That has never worked! Once again, economics is not a morality play but a power play. Furthermore, if these non-profit organizations do not even understand or exist in reality, how can they be helpful to us? The world is what it is, and the nature of the universe can never be changed.

Our strategy for Black uplift must be aligned with the real world and the truth about human nature, intrinsically coupled with time and place in the universe. You cannot live in the past or the future, only the present; but present actions will determine your future outcomes. The push must be strategic and utilize intelligence systems that are based on data science for business, social, and institutional environments in order to advance a prosperity agenda.

In addressing the Plenary Session at the World Economic Forum, Indian Prime Minister Narendra Modi predicted that in the future, whoever controls data will control the world. He went on to say that data is the ultimate form of wealth, which is true, because everything starts with information and knowledge building. The global flow of data is creating major opportunities as it helps to illuminate—often hidden in plain sight—those trending demand opportunities for entrepreneurs to act upon. So if you are not aware of the process of wealth creation, then wealth itself will remain elusive to us.

Data science is a man-made extension of our natural environment, an extension of our consciousness. Technology did not come with nature; humans created technology to enable us to be more effective in nature. Technology, then, as an artificial extension of nature, can be used for advantages against rivals. Technology is a competitive tool in nature—a hyperextension of the sophistication of self-preservation. Therefore, the undercurrents of inequality exist everywhere; you cannot get around the metaphysical existence of nature, so stop wasting time and get back in touch with reality.

Therefore, Black people need to acquire *ownership* of technology, its infrastructure, architecture, algorithms, ecosystems, etc.; without that, we will continue to have absolutely no influence or power in the 21st century.

Accordingly, Black people need to think long-term, because change will not happen overnight; change must be invested in, and it also requires a cultural mind shift. And real change begins at home, by pushing our children and culture into the 21st century, embracing math and science, and encouraging entrepreneurship, creativity, innovation, and leadership. We will not achieve real change by adhering to the status quo, the "safe" or traditional professions. These careers are no longer safe in an AI world anyway. Moreover, it is important to recognize that the education system, particularly our universities, is at least 20 years behind the new economy curve. Playing it safe, staying in your comfort zone, and staying subconsciously harnessed to the past will only serve to keep you in the past, far behind the wealth curve.

We must be highly conscious of how we think, what we think about, and what we think we know—and focus more on what we do not know. We must also be highly conscious of the subconscious religious influence that dominates our lives and cultural belief systems. Rigorously seeking knowledge, a better understanding of how the world works, and developing intelligence-based ecosystems to leverage that acquired knowledge in seeking personal gain is the name of the game!

Diversity and representation matter! AI has the potential to solve an incredible spectrum of problems for humanity. Where Black people are concerned, there is a widening disconnect between the people who are introducing and deploying AI-based solutions and those who craft the policies that govern when and how these solutions are applied. Without diversity along the supply chain—relative to developing algorithms and applications as well as entrepreneurship—the human bias and domination of the systemic environment by the majority will continue to control Black people's lives.

The racially marginalized groups will have an inverse relationship to technological advancement, and its benefits, mainly global prosperity. Our condition will only deteriorate as we become dramatically less relevant in the future. Your value determines your power and influence; no value means no power. If Black people continue not to make a real effort to understand the laws of nature, continue to be lackadaisical, settling, non-disruptive of self and systems, and always acquiescing to the delusional comfort of "woke" culture, then nothing will change; the whining and complaining will only intensify, and so will be the loss. Moreover, according to Gebru, algorithmic bias in AI systems, in which machine-learning algorithms train on data, will continue to be dominated by those funding the writing of the algorithms. Just as it works in nature, natural selection will continue, and the historical discrimination that Black people have experienced will simply be replicated and magnified in the technology of the day.

So wokeness will not change a thing. Only strategic thinking followed up by real actions will. Here, honesty and courage are required to advance our people entrepreneurially to prosperity in the 21st century; there is no other way.

Software developers, engineers, tech entrepreneurs and innovators alike, similar to our broader society, bring their human biases, experiences, and traumas directly to the keyboard. So no one should be surprised by the adverse impact that intelligent technology has on marginalized communities, pushing them further back into the shadows of irrelevance and suffering—far from the wonderful wealth opportunities constantly arising in the 21st-century's knowledge-based economy.

Data scientists often say that generating a model is a way to predict the future. This is a common and dangerous misunderstanding of what a model does. Rather than predicting the future, a model projects the past into the future (Aisulu Omar, *The Inequality in the Data Science Industry*).

Therefore, exactly like everything else, algorithm development is influenced by each developer's past experiences and the effects of those experiences on his or her psyche; as a result, stereotypes become embedded in the structure of technology applications. In other words, your view of the world is not yours; it is the technologist's and the corporations'. Big Data is running your life; for example, Facebook's cognitive algorithms influence your thinking and behaviour, influencing your perspective and your feelings and orienting you toward a herd mentality. The data shows that proportionately, Black people are among the biggest users of Facebook, and are thus the major group adversely affected by those embedded algorithms. This dramatically influences what we think and post, shaping how we view issues, themselves, and the universe. Therefore, Facebook acts as a shaper of the Black identity—nn^2.

So whether these Black Facebook users—especially heavy users—know it or not, they are practically *products* of Facebook algorithms. It is also important to note that Black people are heavy Facebook users and are generally more unhappy than those who use it infrequently, minimally, or not at all!

Consciousness matters, and it matters a great deal. It fills our interior and exterior existence; so our conscious connection to how we experience nature through technology will only increase exponentially in the future. Consequently, if we do not play a role in designing that future, we will simply become zombies watching the world go by.

The danger comes into play when those in control of the technology say they are building toward a level playing field, but instead build extension bridges that benefit the majority populations, those in control. White supremacist dominance simply continues. Those who are in the know, the ones designing the systems, look after their self-interest first, always—that is simply nature.

The German Enlightenment philosopher Immanuel Kant recognized how perception depends on the process of "judgment and inference," since we seldom have direct unfiltered access to objective reality—i.e., to the truth. Our sensory data inputs are influenced heavily by the systems and structures around us. We are very much programmed by and dependent on the systemic environment, and therefore, those in control of the environment are in control of us. Nurture, not nature, shapes our outputs. Our lives are dominated by intelligent technologies everywhere, influencing our subconscious existence tremendously. If we are not conscious of the power of the subconscious world in influencing and directing our lives, then we will always fail to identify the asymmetries in our midst. Our existence will remain dominated by others unless we make a conscious effort to change it.

UNDERSTANDING THE BLACK SWAN THEORY is critical, because it is what we do not know that impacts our lives most. And if we could *see* what we are missing—see what we do not know—then our self-preservation instincts should kick in. We would aggressively seek access to an information, technology, and knowledge ecosystem to propel ourselves and our economies forward exponentially. So what we think or believe is of little consequence; in the end, the only thing of consequence is what is real. Therefore, if Caribbean people of African ancestry do not integrate themselves smartly into the new global economy of the 21st century by embracing rapidly evolving intelligent technologies, we will continue to suffer and not profit from it. We will have no one but ourselves to blame. We'll simply continue to be taken, willingly, as useful suckers. While we continue to fear volatility, satisfied with remaining employees rather than owners, others will continue to build their wealth, power, and privilege. Missed opportunities in tech entrepreneurship, for example, are missed opportunities for future prosperity. Intergenerational wealth creation cannot happen if you do not even understand the game. Wins or losses always reverberate over many generations, so figure things out, and fast! Take the necessary actions now, in order to make prosperity happen!

*(**Note**: For the record, at the turn of the 20th century there was no way for the Caribbean region to have participated in the Industrial Revolution. The region was a set of colonies, and the colonizers purposefully prevented industrialization in those colonies. So the Caribbean did not have a chance at modern industrialization due to colonial rule. The colonies had to serve the supply needs of European and American industrialization and could never go beyond being mere suppliers of raw materials to be sent to Europe for manufacturing. And this is where trade and commerce took place, which created profit and wealth for European society. The cost of missing out on industrialization at a critical turning point in human history is incredibly difficult to quantify, but there is no doubt that it set the Caribbean region back more than 100 years relative to those societies that experienced industrialization.)*

Chapter 6

The Decade of Transition

"It is not the strongest of the species that survives, nor the most intelligent that survives. It is the one that is the most adaptable to change."

— Charles Darwin

Change can only happen when people first change the way they think and behave. The rationality of critical thinking and challenging the status quo is fundamental to our humanity. Disruption is critical to change, so adapting your mind to the necessity of disruption of self is critical to change overall. All thoughts and applications must be relevant to the time, place, and context, to be useful to our growth objective.

When the COVID-19 pandemic struck in March 2020, many businesses were suddenly forced to close their doors and transition to the "new normal" of working virtually from home. Little did most realize that this change would seal the fate of the old economy and that we would see the advent of a new economy. This transformation, however, was already in the cards—the natural evolutionary transition driven by the advancing digital world. The pandemic simply sped things up. Decades of behaviour relating to work changed virtually overnight because of the need to adapt. The disruption of daily life and the rapid adaptation that ensued are only the latest example of humans' adaptation to changing circumstances over thousands of years. We naturally select the people, places, and things that provide the greatest benefit to us, forming those networks that best help us survive and to thrive. In the end, self-preservation and natural selection are the combined foundational factors that serve as springboards to success for people and civilizations.

Many have been able to be opportunistic and innovative and take advantage of the COVID period for financial gain; they parlay disruption and volatility in their favour, and treat such crises as opportunities. Disruption has always been a constant feature of human life; it is only happening more quickly and intensely due to artificial intelligence-based technologies. As a result, the best future business opportunities often present themselves in times of economic downturn and heightened volatility, even widespread fear. However, only those who are aware of how the universe unfolds can seize upon these transcendent opportunities. Most people are mere spectators, watching from the sidelines and offering countless reasons why any given venture will not work. This is why we have a proverbial "1%"—those who can embrace volatility jump in at the bottom, when everyone else is running scared. They identify opportunities, execute innovations, and ride the wave of volatility back to the top. Uncertainty brings us opportunities, but only the courageous among us capitalize on them.

The objective truth about the Caribbean today is that we are not trying to win. Worse, we would rather watch others win and hope that we can pick up some scraps, rather than get into the game and try to lead ourselves. In the competitive universe in which we all live, not winning means losing. We cannot afford any more excuses or rationalizations for losing. This is why it is so critical not to miss periods of economic transition and change; doing so sets us back greatly, whether we realize it or not. However, we are now in 2022, and we cannot afford to dwell on our past trauma—so what we do now will determine our fate for the next 100 years and beyond.

No ONE is coming to save us. We must strategize and fight intelligently for what we want—and sometimes be ruthless, as that is what is required. The universe is driven by conflict—economic and otherwise—in which fighting for scarce resources is part of the laws of nature. So let the sophistication of self-preservation naturally kick in and underpin your pursuits. And if you do not fight, then you are only proving white supremacy right—vindicating the stereotype that Black people do not have the mental capacity to achieve, compete, and win. This is precisely how white supremacy spins the narrative that Blacks *deserve* their position at the lower rungs of the global wealth curve.

This decade of the 2020s is shaping up to be the greatest period of industrial transformation in history. Digitization and transformation are happening extraordinarily faster in this 5th Industrial Revolution (5IR). With the extraordinary utility of AI, the entire planet is transforming at a pace and precision never before seen in human history. This decade will make or break the Caribbean, depending on what the region does or does not do. History happens in leaps and bounds; those very few unpredictable events in a lifetime are what drive civilizations forward exponentially. If we fail in these transcending times, we will only saddle future generations with even greater challenges and built-in suffering.

Not holding our leaders accountable and engaging in political tribalism on tiny island states is pure self-destruction. Are there any meaningful identifiable ideological differences between Black populations in Caribbean countries and territories? Of course not! So why should we continue to buy into the things that divide us?

If you are not conscious of your existence, then you will not be able to recognize your own participation in your demise. Consider Grenada for example. After about 30 years in power, all that Prime Minister Keith Mitchell has accomplished is to push Grenada closer to an acute and persistent state of poverty, not unlike Haiti's situation. That is Mitchell's true legacy. Yet the Grenadian people continue to listen to the same "old talk" and continue to elect leaders like Mitchell repeatedly! At some point, we can no longer blame the politicians and other elites; blame must also be taken by those that elect them.

Another example of citizens needing to be honest and take responsibility relates to the COVID pandemic period. When Grenada's Carnival was prohibited for COVID reasons, some people in Grenada—those with no sense—still went out to play "Jab Jab" – (dressing up as a devil-like character, tared body, in carnival, carrying whips used for hitting other devils.) It appears that health and safety were less important to that crowd than a virus that spread like wildfire and could have wiped out the entire tiny population of Grenada. These are the irrational actions that people take when they let emotion rule over intellect. If we do not understand risk and remain willfully ignorant, not taking ourselves seriously, then how can we expect others—especially foreign investors—to take us seriously? If we continue to behave impetuously, driven by emotion rather than logic, we are simply proving the white supremacists right about us. In the end, our behaviour, not our talk, determines our outcomes.

Another example of the suspension of intellect is the anti-COVID vaccine sentiment in the Caribbean. What is intriguing about these people is that most of them seem to have no idea how they became anti-vaxxers in the first place. Facebook and its many algorithms control their thinking—finding them through their "Like" patterns and feeding them nonsensical anti-vaccine propaganda; and because they do not read, they become susceptible to believing that nonsense. Anti-vaxx ideas first caught on widely in the Trump-supporter crowd, i.e. right-wing nationalists. Yet somehow, thoughtless, anti-intellectual Caribbean people find themselves on the same side as these people!

Algorithms have found you, and you do not even recognize that your thinking is being influenced by emotional algorithms; and the more you like, the more they influence you. Facebook makes a great deal of money by instigating conflict among the willfully ignorant—those susceptible to misinformation, and conspiracy theories. Facebook requires herds of "useful idiots" to pump out profits, and it seems there are many of them in the Caribbean for Facebook to deceive and exploit.

We cannot afford to waste valuable time any longer on these people. As my mother used to tell me, people like that will only drain you, and you cannot save the unsavable. It makes no sense to drown yourself trying to rescue someone who dove into the deep end knowing that he could not swim. Therefore, we must learn to make hard choices in the interest of our self-preservation, and those hard choices begin with fine-tuning our thinking.

And if people are not willing to read, to learn, to help themselves, then that is their choice; we are all grown adults with free will and agency. Getting involved in the nonsense of the willfully ignorant makes you more of a fool yourself, you are essentially engaging in destructive delusion. Nevertheless, everybody cannot win in the universe—that would be unnatural—so you must decide if you are going to pursue winning or simply sit on the veranda complaining.

DIGITIZATION is the highest form of productive efficiency for business and society. It improves value, creates wealth, and improves living standards. However, digitization can easily be underestimated because it might seem innocuous, and some might feel that it poses no real threat to existing systems and incumbents. Nonetheless, digitization is transforming the physical world at breakneck speed. Working and shopping from home may not seem very significant, but the entire global economy is moving more and more to online platforms, which is a major development. The new normal has been that way for a while now. Not recognizing the change or living it only means that you are behind the times, and behind the profit curve as well.

For the Caribbean to transition properly to prosperity over the next decade, there must be a firm growth framework in which that development can happen. In other words, how the world works, the nature of evolving civilizations, and having a firm transcending economic strategy to execute. This is what will shape future prosperity. We must evaluate the best ideas and use disciplined methods of research discovery, and implementation.

GIVEN the number of variables at play in the *applied intelligence* process, it makes sense to produce a limited set of possible worlds against which to assess the quality of those ideas being brought forward. This approach can only improve the success potential of those selected and analyzed ideas.

In order to represent a possible world of select opportunities, the characteristics of that world must first be defined. A characteristic is composed of values that are tied to a particular world that one envisions, and those values all have functions which inherently evaluate any derivative exponential functions generated—serving to interpret each other to form a vision of this future world. In short, it asserts that a property has a specific value in that world, industry, society, etc. Given a set of worlds, each one will differ by at least one characteristic from every other world, so the world you choose must contain functional variables most conducive to your country's natural competitive advantages from a business perspective. All in all, this simply optimizes or improves your chances of success.

Nevertheless, what is important to understand here is that regardless of how good an idea is, the conditions and systemic environment can be more consequential to outcomes than anything else. How those multiple variables react and function under those conditions and environments is critical to successful outcomes. With a scientific understanding of this, we are set on a firm foundation to represent a set of properties more reliably, extracted from general categories as useful in the pursuit of successful bottom-up enterprise development.

The next step is to determine the requirements of the idea. These requirements will be a set of world characteristics that maximize the idea's chance of success. Again, a country's natural competitive advantages and industries relative to global demand trends are optimal.

The idea's requirement will be divided into two parts:

1. The characteristic's numerical value, and
2. The characteristic's importance to the idea.

Finally, in the ap^3 process, we need a method to measure the variables' ability to bring the idea(s) to fruition. To do this, we use an artificial construct from mathematics called a *utility*. A utility is a numerical value used to represent the amount of benefit that is achieved through the implementation of an idea. A world better suited to a particular idea will allow that idea to yield a higher utility than that of a world that does not meet the idea's requirements. The utility is used to allow the evaluator to measure the likelihood that the idea will reach its objective. However, all ideas have a corresponding world where their implementation is best suited; the probabilities of those worlds existing are independent of the idea.

Very simply, the goal is to select ideas and processes that have the highest utility across your selected world for the most probable desirable outcomes. For example, it would not make practical sense to build a fine rug-making business on a Caribbean Island, as we do not possess the necessary competitive advantages for that industry to succeed, and the past negative connotations of using small children with small hands to craft "hand-made rugs" would also be a natural ethical killer to a foolish business idea in any case. Nevertheless, multiple variables must always be considered, including the cognitive environment as a significant contributing factor.

Again, it is more logical to align natural competitive advantages with confirmed global demand trends and respective cognitive environments before you pursue the idea. The mere fact that an idea sounds great does not change one key fact: the conditions necessary for that idea's success are based on how the future is unfolding and its relevance, which may be independent of the idea itself. Maximum Utility is expressed below:

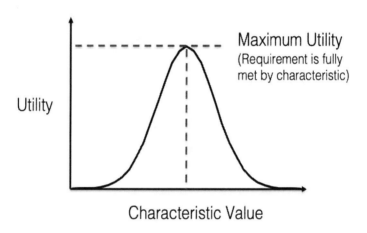

In order to evaluate the maximum utility of an idea, we compute the probability of each possible world occurring for you based on the likelihood of its characteristics being true. Given that we do not know what the future will be, we establish a set of possible worlds and determine the associated probabilities of those worlds being realized. For illustrative purposes, we can use the following equation to calculate the chance of each of the world's characteristics occurring to the variables defined lower down as the "Definition."

$$p(W_n) = p,(C_{1m}) * p_2(C_{2m}) * \cdots * p_n(C_{nm}) = \sum_{i=1}^{n} p_i C_{im}$$

To calculate the probability of each character's being realized, we will have to make predictions based on the available data or use predictions from trusted sources to help us better quantify things.

We then compute the utility of an idea in a particular world as a function of the requirement and its associated world characteristic, weighted to the probability of that world occurring.

$$U_{Wm}^A = p(W_m) \sum_{i=1}^{|n|} w_n f(C_{nm}, \Omega_n^A)$$

To determine the utility of the idea within a particular world, we will have to create a function that can compare the requirements to the characteristics of the world and return a numerical value based on how well the world satisfies the requirements. Each requirement is weighted by importance, such that the utility reflects the idea's hierarchy of needs.

Based on the information from Step #1, there is a higher likelihood that each requirement of idea "A" will be met in the most probable world. This yields a higher utility than idea "B," given that the world necessary for idea B to be successful has a lower probability of being true. The utility will be described by a numerical value. The higher the utility, the higher the value will be. We find the expected value of the idea's utility by summarizing all the utilities from each possible world:

$$E[U^A] = \sum_{m=1}^{|m|} U_{Wm}^A$$

After calculating the utility of each idea in each possible world, we will determine the idea's expected utility, which will give us the expected performance of the idea based on the possible worlds that may occur. This is an important step, because we do not know which word will be realized. By calculating the expected utility, we will determine the best idea to select based on the range of possible futures most likely to occur.

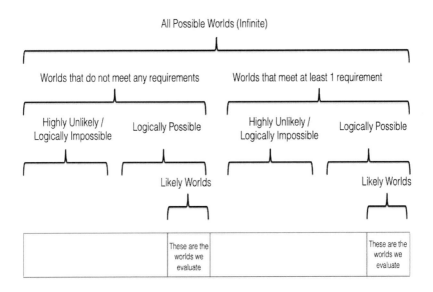

Variable	Definition
U^A	Utility of idea A across all possible worlds A
U^A_{Wm}	Utility of idea A in World $_m$
Ω^A_n	Requirement $_n$ for idea A
W_m	Possible World $_m$
$U^{\Omega^A_n}_{Wm}$	The Specific Utility set by the nth Requirement of idea A in World $_m$
C_{nm}	World characteristic $_n$ in world $_m$
w_n	Requirement weight; $0 \leq w_n \leq 1$

All of this explanation is simply to say that the universe consists of math and that decision-making as a process essentially consists of applied mathematics. However, my main objective is to demonstrate that the application of mathematical thinking to problem-solving is highly detailed, calculative, and complex. And in the 21st century, the use of intelligence-based technologies, particularly artificial intelligence and machine learning, is simply the smart thing to use if you want to win. Therefore, if you are not using data science, AI, or ML as a tool in your decision-making, your chances of success in this hyper technology and AI-driven world will be slim to none! Speed and precision are the names of the game! And the ***applied intelligence | ap³*** equation simply provides a simplified method, discipline to make practical decisions in an intelligence-based framework for *decision-making-to-success.*

In less mathematical terms, for example, here is how the enterprise development process would look under the applied intelligence methodology:

Blueprint

Articulate the strategy characteristics relative to future platform ...identify growth opportunities

Output
• Vision
• Prospectus Documentation
• Product/Services & Offering Dimension

Design & Architecture

Build a conceptual design aligning strategy to platform

Output
• Conceptual Strategy Design
• Technology & Architecture Diagram
• Process Flows Diagrams

Implementation Planning

Utilize Blueprint and Design to build out commercialization strategy.

Output
• Platform Development Plan Roadmap
• Strategy for Development

Again, quantitative thinking—all thinking–is of course based on nature and math, since only math can properly explain nature. So the point is, if we can consciously respect the mathematical thinking process, we just might succeed more frequently.

Emotion can control our psyche and distract us from the critical thinking we must do, and we may miss the best ideas, because we do not have an S2-type method of evaluation. Emotion can trap us in the abyss of ideology and religious dogma, fighting against the natural flow of our intelligence. In an increasingly complex and globalized world, competing without the utility of intelligent technology to augment your human intelligence puts you at a significant disadvantage, making it more difficult to win in the 21st century.

If one cannot put aside ego and use the awesome power of machines to help process, think, make judgements, and assist in delivering better outcomes then one stands no chance at winning in the 21st century!

Further, mathematics goes into everyday decision-making; we are all mathematicians in our subconscious and conscious minds.

Algorithms, for example, are extensions of ourselves, helpful for us to function efficiently in the systemic environment. So it is only natural to rely on algorithms in our world to help us achieve our objectives, as efficiently and effectively as possible. Artificial intelligence must be looked at as the height of machine intelligence that can effectively augment human intelligence so as to get things done. After all, what is the purpose of learning science if we do not maximize it to create value and happiness for ourselves? This is the **utility** of *applied intelligence*; when effectively utilized, it can assist the Caribbean people, entrepreneurs, leaders and policymakers, and stakeholders, all of whom are interested in the advancement toward sustainable prosperity.

Demonstrating an understanding of the quantitative process of decision-making is most important for success to occur. Randomness always has a lot to do with success, and randomness is an accounted-for variable under ap^3. Nevertheless, the evidence stands that disciplined and strategic approaches to decision-making are more effective and reliable. The level of technology and information flow and the sheer complexity of an ever-evolving universe make the probability of Caribbean extinction something that is more real than not.

THERE MUST always be a defined framework and rigour through which to make decisions. Otherwise, we will only exist as illogical emotional vessels, unenlightened wonders—nothing more than sad complainers at the bottom rungs of the universe, where our lives become trivial, the stuff of academic experimentation. We will be mere charity cases in the crevasses of the universe. In short, math must always add up and align with nature. Our job, then, is to figure out the optimal applications that work for us under the laws of nature. We have a moral responsibility to lay the groundwork in our lifetime for future generations.

The modern world is still extraordinarily young; as a civilization, we are still learning. Therefore, we must move beyond the superstition, emotion, and ideology of religion, exist in a conscious state of intellectual pragmatism, and build our capacity to compete effectively with our underlying drive for security through prosperity. Our over-reliance on emotion, intuition and religious faith is only holding us back. Faith is antithetical to nature, making us believe in things that do not exist, so it is impossible for your prayers to be answered. Therefore, it is simply more logical to create a belief system based on efficient thinking and real actions, for such a cultural belief system is aligned with the metaphysical world. Our survival as humans has always owed to our ability to think, create, and innovate. That is an intellectual process, and adaptation to new or harsh environments has been the mark of successful human civilizations. Accordingly, in an increasingly intensified knowledge-based world, history is not on the side of overly emotional beings. It is human intelligence that created technologies for and utilized science in agriculture so we can feed ourselves and exist as stable societies. So to win in the 21st century, we must understand how to apply ourselves intellectually to our environment and use the tools, processes, and technologies around us to our competitive advantage. Again, as Adam Smith explained way back in the 18th century, long-term economic gains and prosperity form the optimal path to productive and sustainable societies.

UNDERSTANDING HOW ALGORITHMS WORK and how they are essentially an extension of the human mind might be helpful at this point, so we will touch on it. The rudimentary visual below shows the basics of the decision-making pattern and flows of an algorithm. An algorithm, therefore, is a set of instructions that perform certain tasks. It emits actionable outputs based on inputs and programming. This is very much the same how the human brain works–we take instructions to emit actions and we are essentially programmed by our very existence in society, by nurture, belief systems and religion, societal norms, and past experiences, particularly traumas.

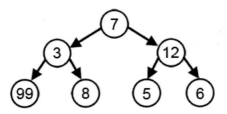

Visual of how algorithm decision-making works

To derive change, focused and advanced-thinking methodologies are required. This scientific approach creates rational ecosystems, and human and artificial intelligence is used, combining to strengthen and optimize the decision-making process. Our scientific *applied intelligence* method capitalizes on AI-powered research capabilities combined with computational engines that identify emerging innovations, trends, and risks. How we adapt and thrive requires sensible and balanced frameworks to make decisions and build real strategies. Effectively, *applied intelligence* is a practical decision-making algorithm that applies to real life.

The goal is to create a new intelligence-based ecosystem through rigour and relentless iteration. Human intelligence remains central to everything, but human intelligence is more productive when powered by artificial intelligence. Data and quantitative analysis fuel imagination, which becomes more effective when it is based on reality. When you understand the nature of things, you can think more boldly and dynamically, freer, because science is the great optimizer of imagination.

Adopting new technologies requires information, investment, entrepreneurship, and an understanding of dynamic global markets through the analysis of data. We should not strive merely to exist, but to jump in, participate, design, and lead our future. We must strive to be at the forefront of the business and technology frontiers, offering comprehensive, holistic, science-based approaches to growth and development. In order to have an impact on the world, we must not accept irrelevance, and we must not think of ourselves as victims. We must engage in controlled aggression to get what we want and where we want.

THE COVID PANDEMIC has struck a major, unprecedented blow to the Caribbean, a region already lacking any meaningful exports and industries. Tourism, a leisure service, represents an average of 40% of the GDP of many of these islands. Dependency on tourism over the decades has left many nations ill-prepared for transformation and the new economic road ahead. While many nations are engaged in significant and innovative planning and execution, on the whole, the evidence shows that Caribbean leadership haven't even realized the significance of the digital era for their future socio-economic survival. The simple-minded have no clue and are stuck in the mud on the side of the road while the world passes them by. There is no thoughtful road map or blueprint, no strategy formulation or methodology in place. They continue to rely on foreign "advisors" and development agencies, with no skin in the game for their guidance. The overall situation in the region is dire!

But if you are wholly unprepared, you can seldom even see the forest from the trees; things become an ambiguous blur, and leaders end up making reactionary decisions based on fear and emotion—and, of course, on next-election politics. Therefore, in this setting, opportunities in this extant era of global socio-economic transition to the digital economy will be missed, as Caribbean societies remain distracted from applying intelligence in solving their problems.

Diversifying and moving forward with technology-platform architecture, conducive to building a sophisticated knowledge-based economy, is the only way forward to transformation and sustain prosperity. If this critical juncture of opportunity and transition is missed, history suggests that the region will be set back even further, and the prosperity curve will get further out of range. This situation will inflict pain and suffering, driven by a lack of opportunity in a *manual* regional economy that can neither connect with nor compete in the digital, globalized world—and future generations will inherit more intensified suffering. Moreover, with the reality of a warming climate, small islands in the Pacific and Caribbean regions are slated to be the first to be submerged by rising sea levels within the next 100 years or so. The probability is real, so we need to be thinking strategically now about our very survival as a people. We will examine this climate change risk to the survival of the Caribbean territory later on in the book.

FOR THE CARIBBEAN to achieve sustainable economic growth, we must look at the new growth and revenue opportunities outside of tourism. There are ample opportunities for tech-led growth within the Caribbean, as follows:

Healthcare:
212

The health care sector faces challenges of various kinds—financial, strategic, digital, and talent-related. These challenges are even harder to overcome in the Caribbean region. Exponential advances and interoperability in digital technologies are helping health care professionals to deliver services in ways that patients prefer to receive them. This trend is further fueled by unprecedented advancements in digital health solutions, "always-on" data, and open, secure platforms. Digital transformation is slated to play a major part in laying the foundation of new care delivery models; shaping predictive, preventive, and personalized futures; promoting closer collaboration among industry stakeholders—in short, driving cheaper, more precise, and less invasive treatments and therapies.

Economic Diversification:

A real vision must be articulated for building a robust digital architecture and infrastructure as the foundation for a digital economy, including:
The development of a Governance Regime for digital/data oversight;
Creation of policies, strategies, and backbone infrastructure to facilitate digital commerce; and
National implementation of e-government initiatives. There have already been improvements in the security of electronic payments and settlements, but not nearly enough to be taken seriously.

Food Security:

The Caribbean Community and Common Market (CARICOM) is currently confronting a burgeoning multi-billion-dollar food import bill. Only through private-sector activities can this bill be reasonably reduced, the better for Caribbean countries to be able to feed themselves adequately and to become export-driven in this sector. It is also necessary to develop a sustainable financing solution for investments related to the agri-food system and facilitate the introduction of more modern and climate-friendly technology into the agri-food sector.

There are six areas for potential private-sector technology investment in the agri-food sector:
- Automation Machinery
- Agricultural Science
- Genetic Engineering/Modification
- Livestock Processing Systems
- Crop Cultivation Systems
- Forestry
- Fisheries and aquaculture

Renewable Energy Production:

According to The International Energy Agency (IEA)'s *Renewable 2019* report, renewable energy capacity could expand by 50% worldwide by 2024, led by solar energy. The report found that solar, wind and hydroelectric projects are rolling out at their fastest rate in four years—though mainly elsewhere in the world, of course. Developing countries around the world continue to build clean energy systems, but the Caribbean region essentially has not even yet begun this transition in any meaningful way.

THE TASK OF CARIBBEAN LEADERSHIP now is to formulate winning strategies and to take meaningful steps that drive change. A plan for thriving and making Caribbean economies more resilient and resistant to future economic shocks and fluctuations must be the task going forward for all of the region's leaders. When we look back at this decade, how we fared will be based on what we either did or failed to do. Nassim Talib has also pointed out that "How you did in this pandemic, as a country, a village, a business, a group, or an individual, whether emotionally, economically, or morally, is an indication of how robust you are and how fit you will be for the next decades." Once again, it always comes down to what you do next.

For Caribbean economies, evidence-based decision-making must be brought to the very forefront. The corrupt bureaucratization of 'development' and its activities drains the economic lifeblood of entire populations and societies. The arbiters of development theories control local policymakers and business owners as well, because the former exploit their control of foreign development agency capital to control the latter's actions. The result is often the execution of absurd, non-free-market economy strategies that never work. Their charity-oriented development "projects" have no basis in real-world economies. The entire process becomes distorted, creating errors and imbalances, and genuine development gets pushed aside for the nonsense of top-down bureaucratic and academic development.

'Development' discourse has become preoccupied with "prestigious" journal publications, peer review, and instant gratification for academics trying to make names for themselves—a development monster, destructively generating a vicious academic circle of theories that prove to be inapplicable in the real world and therefore useless. Macroeconomics then becomes nn^2—an exercise in unchecked ritualistic theorizing and abstract philosophy, with no practical relevance to real people's problems or to those problems' solutions. Beware of those who are quick to tell you what to do but are not willing to put their own "skin in the game" alongside you.

No matter what type or quantity of international support the Caribbean gets, it ultimately always fails because only we can find solutions for ourselves. We must become less abstract and more focused on our thoughts and actions—become more purposeful, less distracted in our thinking, less timid and more courageous. Unless the

ai

region rises up and does something to help itself, nothing will ever happen to change the prevailing reality of our dependency and irrelevance in the universe.

We often let emotion overwhelm us when facing the enormity of the climb, so we must take small steps based on first principles in order to get our footing, and then identify the immediate tasks that can prepare us for long-term success. Then we can scale up rapidly, with speed and precision. We also need to stop spinning our wheels—so to speak—in anxiety and dwelling on past traumas; this mentality has only worked against us. The stress of anxiety can paralyze us in a constant state of inaction. In the end, our advancement as a people requires adherence to reality and focus on what we do next—period!

What we think or what we know or what we believe is at the end of little consequence. The only thing of consequence is what we do.

— John Ruskin

THE CARIBBEAN IS made up of many nations; but in the final analysis, it is effectively one body, a single unit with many dynamic functional parts. Never forget that we Afro-Caribbean peoples all originally came from Africa. Our prosperity must be intertwined and anchored in our moral concern for each other, our societal common bond, and our common humanity as people of African descent. Therefore, our future prosperity is dependent on our common actions in the present—on our determination to act in coordination and our will to secure prosperity and opportunity for future generations. Our success depends on our proximity to and use of science and technology, on our conscious reliance on quantitative thinking. Good character alone was not enough to achieve happiness and well-being, and that the pursuit of resources, opportunity, power,

216

and influence are all necessary and even virtuous pursuits. Without such pursuits, our sophistication of self-preservation remains dormant, and our existence would only be one of passivity and stagnation while the rest of the world passed us by. It would be a life filled with the greatest suffering and misfortunes. Therefore, learning how to cultivate acquired knowledge and developing new methods and learning streams helps us to strive for the life we want. In the universe, the making of our lives comes down to our own efforts—managing our executive faculties to make good choices.

For many in the Caribbean, the way we see ourselves, our capabilities, and our ambitions is all too often shaped by others. Our complicity in and self-imposed adherence to the hierarchical supremacy of others upon us is counterproductive to self-determination. The enduring legacy of the plantation slavery system, often invisible in our outward existence, is still very much deeply rooted in our inner selves, in our collective psyche. We continue to go about our daily lives relying mainly on our subconscious mind, which accounts for 95% of our decision-making. So our systemic environment can impose a submissive cultural mindset upon us if we do not make real efforts to live and act in consciousness. Our hindrances and barriers end up dominating our minds, preventing us from seeing the possibilities beyond the boundaries. It keeps us in a state of suspended subconscious mental slavery—a state of regression, confusion, insecurity, and trepidation. We do not aspire to become entrepreneurs and dream of changing the world; instead, we are timid, remaining at safe jobs to earn steady paychecks and remaining dependent on the system in the process. While other communities take risks, invest in each other, and write their own stories, we continue to let our story be written by others. Our identity becomes a uniquely Caribbean neuropsychological disorder—one of fragility, fear, self-doubt, manifested anxiety, and non-leadership of self.

Put all the distracting "development" theories aside; this is the objective truth about us. The real world is based on economic competition and conflict, so it is counterintuitive to believe that others are going to help you or share their wealth with you. All humans need to satisfy their basic needs, and self-preservation is first and foremost among those needs. Seeking prosperity is a natural part of the quest for security, so get over whatever moral dilemma is playing out in your head; without security, you will remain insecure in the human condition. Seeing the truth requires critical and strategic thinking, training our brains to be adaptive, self-interest-seeking, resilient, antifragile, and of course, always doing the math. Halting the region's timidity and finding its courage is a critical underlying requirement for its progress; but most critically, a deep and honest look inward at our internal engineering is also central to a future by our design.

Part II

CHAPTER 7

Quantitative Thinking & the Racism Disorder

Image by Eva Keiffenheim

"When you give up all the fictional stories, only then can you observe reality about yourself and about the world.

—Yuval Noah Harari

During the period of the European Enlightenment, in his 1637 work *Discourse on Method*, French philosopher René Descartes wrote, *"I think: therefore, I am"* as a first step toward demonstrating the attainability of certain knowledge. In other words, your existence in the universe is confirmed because you can think; there can be no doubt about that fact. However, merely existing is not enough; your success in the universe depends on how you think and whether you apply your intelligence effectively. For the people of the Caribbean, there can be no doubt that the current state of our existence is because we have been thinking ineffectively. And, if we continue to think and act *on Caribbean*

Time," we will continue to be late—always behind the prosperity curve, never catching up to ride the wealth wave. Here, we can put Aristotle in the same class as Bob Marley. Aristotle said that **"it is always up to you."** And Bob Marley said, **"Emancipate yourselves from mental slavery. None but ourselves can free our minds."** In the end, your mind is the ultimate determining factor in the quality of your existence—pay attention to how you think.

Our brains have been subconsciously programmed to think in a linear manner, which is the primary reason why it is difficult for many of us to visualize simple exponential growth concepts. Therefore, we must begin to understand that the more we can train our brains to think mathematically, the easier it will be to connect the dots, identify opportunities out of the white space, and act on them with confidence. We learn and create things by quantitatively applying knowledge; thinking trains our brains to see the problem-solving opportunities that exist, allowing us to see the broader implications. Even though every day seems to bring new challenges that seem insurmountable, each day also brings new opportunities. We must also learn how to put the trauma of the past aside and pursue our rightful place in the universe, approaching challenges by developing actionable strategies.

The Enlightenment period or the *Age of Reason* was an intellectual and cultural movement in eighteenth-century Europe that emphasized reason and science over superstition and blind faith. Rationalism became the primary source of authority and legitimacy: the idea that humans can use their faculty of reason for self-advancement.

Stoicism flourished throughout the ancient Roman and Greek world until the 3rd century AD; logic, science, and ethics bloomed. The Stoic Zeno believed that it was neither useful nor the purpose of reason to get rid of emotions. Instead, he argued, we should manage those emotions that are debilitating in our lives—control those emotions that lead to things like uncontrollable cravings, fears, or distress. Zeno also believed that emotions could become a "heaviness that weighs us down," eliciting sub-par performance.

Therefore, logic is optimal, and the more we approach critical thinking with logic rather than intuition, the better our outcomes will be. Enterprising individuals have always used logic to take advantage of their physical surroundings for personal gain; this is fundamental to economic growth and prosperity. They were able to quantify, mobilize, and control those factors of production and output, to gain profit and to continue to reinvest for more future gains, compounding returns over time and consolidating their wealth and power in the universe.

Quantitative thinking is about learning, application, and relentless iteration for better outcomes; it is dynamic and multi-faceted. Over the centuries, knowledge acquisition has enabled many enterprising individuals to identify and interpret the physical environment to build things that advanced their civilizations. Innovation enhances the efficiency and dynamic characteristics of product output, which leads to higher profitability, higher incomes for society, investment and reinvestment, wealth, and power.

Quantitative analysis, therefore, is essential for human development and social mobility; it acts as a cornerstone upon which to build securely. Knowledge empowers people and societies to transform themselves from within, creating organic ecosystems that improve outcomes. Therefore, quantitative thinking is the first step in forging a pathway to self-determination. Moreover, there has never been a better time than now for the people of the Caribbean to transform their societies. In the 21st century, knowledge acquisition and astute application of that knowledge are critical for positive growth outcomes.

In the information age, we have data analytics, AI, and ML to help us learn, gain insight, and get instant feedback, helping us to adjust and create new worlds. Power then can only be the highest form of understanding, so learning remains central to everything in the universe.

"I think we've entered The Exponential Age: an era where the digital and physical paths finally converge, and everything is disrupted- for good." —Raoul Pal

The main value of applying data science to our lives is to turn information into insight, and then to turn that insight into systems for personal gain. From an enterprise perspective, the better you are at applying insight, the better are your chances of creating value.

Identifying the competitive advantage function is central to the future prosperity of the Caribbean people. The knowledge-based economy is moving with breakneck speed, much faster than in past transitional periods. The industrial revolutions of history are prime examples of how knowledge and skill have transformed and utilized the key factors of production to create wealth by maximizing output. Mastering it as Britain did, for example—by applying knowledge and methods to extract resources from the Caribbean, then using those free resources and labour to generate trade and commerce globally for themselves, allowed the British to create great wealth and power for their society. That massive wealth was then strategically parlayed

223

into global power and influence—building the British Empire and white supremacy right along with it.

Of course, we know that the "Great" British Empire was built on thievery and genocide; but we must not allow that fact to distract us from our analysis and miss the learning opportunity. The point to focus on is the sophistication of self-preservation, the mastery of self-interest! Self-interest must have a system, a driving force, and that force is entrepreneurship, which is necessary for self-preservation. As discussed in the last chapter, to achieve economic security, one must pursue wealth. that is the way things happen in nature, and non-accept that reality will ensure your continued suffering.

The British understood what Adam Smith was talking about and they acted; accordingly, so whether we like it or not, they succeeded, and the British Empire was created and lasted for some time. The universe is inevitably full of winners and losers—another fact that should remind us that economics is not a morality; it is a power play. Therefore, you must think quantitatively in nature in order to win. Morality will not build intergenerational wealth and power; it will only put you on the other side of prosperity, which is poverty. The universe has never been about morality; it will continue to be about math.

Of course, Adam Smith never called for the genocide or other atrocities through which European colonizers acquired wealth, power, and privilege, to say nothing of their geopolitical domination of the rest of the world; but that, too, is nature at work. In the final analysis, we must remember that we live in a conflict-driven universe, where the priority is to achieve advancement. So do not be fooled today by the colonizers of the past trying to talk about morality after they employed brutal tactics themselves. The reality of our humanity is that the world is based on economic competition, a struggle for survival and scarce resources. So arm yourself for that struggle. It is a natural jungle out there, and survival in the future will be purely a function of the decisions you make in the environment in which you find yourself. Adaptation is central to survival and growth.

In the context of understanding the legacy of the slave plantation system and colonialism, it is time to address our history consciously in order to design our future. As hard as it might be, we must learn from our past traumas and use them as fuel for our future endeavours; otherwise, generations before us would've suffered for nothing. Learn from the Jewish community; they are good role models. Put emotion aside and think clearly and mathematically; let your primal drive be managed by your intellectual sophistication. That sophistication occurs naturally within you, but if it is not nurtured, it will be ineffective. The conscious, ruthless, and amoral application of economic decision-making to the benefit of every single group against all others is a theme that has played out time and again throughout history. It is not only Black people who have suffered historically; the Jewish people have been persecuted for 2,000 years!

Colonizers went all-in for their self-interest, establishing the Trans-Atlantic slave trade, the plantation slavery system, military imperialism, government-backed crony capitalism, and legislation to support the enterprise and institution of slavery. All of these things were done in the name of self-interest! So we must not get caught up in morality, which is never at play in economics. Trying to change hearts and minds with high-minded notions of equality, fairness, and what is rightfully owed to people of African descent is futile. No one is going to give up their gains. Instead, look at how those societies succeeded and learn what you can from their success; resentment and anger only hold you back.

From a learning perspective, the history of slavery and colonialism can provide lessons about human nature, as an omnipresent reminder of the reality of humanity. Conflict and scarcity of resources is a reality that we cannot change, so we must think rationally and quantitatively about the change we want and how it can improve our lives.

225

RACISM is not simply a function of individual attitudes; it is a perverse manifestation of the sophistication of self-preservation. It represents the extreme weaponization of tactics to achieve socioeconomic status, privilege and power at the expense of other populations. The ever-present competition for scarce resources predictably creates conflict, and racism is a naturally occurring part of that conflict. Competition between groups and the struggle for control of those scarce resources brings out the most primal and tribal instincts in us.

Shutting out others from sharing in your wealth is natural, and part of the history of humanity dating back to when our species began as nomadic hunter-gatherers and later transitioned to sedentary, organized societies. Nevertheless, even today, tribalism maintains itself as part of human nature—e.g., the U.S. and Trump supporters and the Republican Party, the war between Russia and Ukraine, and the ethnic genocide in the Balkans after the dismantling of Yugoslavia in the 1990s. As opposed to what you might have been led to believe, Europe, too—every bit as much as Africa—has been the territory of tribalism and war for centuries.

This is why wars and conflict never end. Be it tribal hunter-gatherers or Vladimir Putin seeking to bring back the glory days of the Russian Empire, the conflict-driven universe prevails; it is the same old story. In the modern era, racism has only become more abstract and surgical—but it still stems from that same primal instinct of self-preservation. The wealthy and privileged build barriers around knowledge and factors of production, creating closed networks and ecosystems to keep others out of the profit loop. The hoarding of profit, wealth, and opportunity underpins the human condition, and the sooner we as Black people fully recognize the prevailing reality,

226

the sooner we can begin working with our heads instead of our hearts.

THEREFORE, we must address the self-inflicted
DISORDER OF RACISM.

In the book *Living with Co-occurring Addiction and Mental Health Disorders,* author Mark McGovern, Ph.D, discusses how people with substance use disorders have at least one other mental health disorder—and how those who "struggle with this combination may be faced with a powerful recipe for destruction." For many Black people, racism can also become a destructive disorder if they only view it through an emotional lens and fail to see it for what it is: a white supremacist social construct, weaponized to wield power over us.

Nobel Prize, Pulitzer Prize, and Presidential Medal of Freedom-winning author Toni Morrison has so intelligently explained that "There is no such thing as race. There's only the human race, scientifically. Racism is a construct, a social construct." Morrison went on to point out that "money can be made off racism," so whites can benefit from racism. It can be used against the more emotionally reactive Black people to make them feel inferior, manipulating them into a negative state of existence. This inferiority complex weighs on their minds and creates insecurities, stresses, and anxieties, ultimately rendering them fragile—and this fragility contributes to a ***racism disorder***.

Mark McGovern describes a disorder as an ongoing condition that essentially contributes to human suffering. A disorder leads you to make irrational decisions that can be detrimental to the goal of living a healthy life. Racism can warp your thinking, making it more subconscious-based, driving up your anxiety levels and leaving you feeling inadequate. It can prevent you from being more assertive in

227

life, such as by starting a business or even simply enjoying other activities that whites take for granted, such as playing golf or skiing, because "that is what white people do." This racism disorder holds you back as you get stuck in the emotional abyss, interacting with the universe somewhere between something and nothing.

Therefore, if you remain in the emotional abyss, not applying intelligence, the abyss will eventually stare back at you, as Friedrich Nietzche so memorably said. You have essentially manifested your negative existence by adhering to the disorder of racism, by not intellectually facing these societal construct challenges. Racism is one of the major challenges in the life of a Black person. However, the key to overcoming racism is how you approach it—either through emotion and by letting it distract and overwhelm you or by applying intelligence and weaponizing your mind to overcome it. It is about what you do in the end. Success always comes down to how you apply *applied intelligence*!

The fifth edition of the book the *Diagnostic and Statistical Manual of Mental Disorders;* by the American Psychiatric Association lists a number of criteria for substance use disorder. Those criteria vary depending on the specific drug being abused; but typically, the symptoms of the disorder go to the inability to control how much of the drug you use over time, obsessing about the drug, and continuing use of it despite the negative consequences. The disorder of racism can have similar negative symptoms: an inability to control your reactions to racist events or becoming obsessed with—and distracted by—racist people, actions, and events. Emotional efforts to *fight racism* do not help your life, instead, focus intelligently on finding opportunities and taking the actions that can create value and power in your life. That power will put you in control of your life.

The interactions in your environment can add stress and physiological vulnerability to your mental disorder. The same can occur with your racism disorder, living in a white supremacist world, where the false narrative that "white is right" and the majority of the white population behaving as such can certainly have an impact on your mental health, and there is good research supportive of that conclusion. According to the organization Mental Health America (MHA), on its *analysis of racism and mental health,* people of colour and all those whose lives have been marginalized by those in power experience life differently from those whose lives have not been devalued. They experience overt racism and bigotry often, which leads to mental stress and develops a burden that is deeper than what others may face. Therefore, if we know this is reality, we must intellectually process it in our conscious brains, so it does not get dominated by our subconscious minds and become trauma, which becomes a direct line to racism disorder. We know that past trauma is the main reason that people experience addiction; so past traumatic experiences with forms of racism are similar to how people experience addiction and mental health disorders. It is all highly trauma-based.

Every day, people of colour experience far more subtle traumas (MHA):

- People who avoid them and their neighbourhoods out of ignorance and fear;
- Banks and credit companies who will not lend them money or do so only at higher interest rates;
- Mass incarceration of their peers;
- School curricula that ignore or minimize their contributions to our shared history; and
- Racial profiling.

Therefore, even non-overt racism can still be traumatic and not properly processed; it can contribute to one falling victim to the racism disorder trap. To avoid falling victim, we must apply intelligence and recognize the things that can cause us harm, and effectively deal with them so that they do not distract us from living the lives that we desire. In order to help us recognize it in full consciousness, here are the most common forms of racism we can experience living in society according to the MHA research article.

Racism: A broad term describing the combination of race-based prejudice and power. Without the power differential (in which one person/group/institution has more power than another), "racism" is simply prejudice and carries less weight and fewer consequences.

Systemic/Structural Racism: Systemic/Structural racism has three components: history, culture, and institutions/policy. Historical racism provides the framework for current racism. Any structure built on a historical foundation of racism will be a racist structure in itself. Culture, which is ever-present in our day-to-day lives, is what allows racism to be accepted, normalized, and perpetuated. Institutions and policies make up the fundamental relationships and rules throughout society, which reinforces racism and gives it societal legitimacy (which in turn makes it exceedingly difficult to dismantle).

Interpersonal Racism: This is racism that occurs in day-to-day interactions between individual people, when individual beliefs or prejudices are translated into actions that offend or harm others.

Institutional Racism: Institutional racism occurs within and between institutions. Institutional racism involves discriminatory treatment, unfair policies, and inequitable opportunities and impacts. These dimensions are based on race and produced and perpetuated by institutions (schools, mass media, etc.). Individuals within institutions take on the power of the institution when they act in ways that advantage and disadvantage people based on race.

Internalized Racism: This is when racism and white supremacy affect the minds of Black and Indigenous people and other People of Colour (BIPOC) to the point where they begin to believe that they are inferior because of their own race. This can sometimes lead to "inter-racial hostility" in which BIPOC treat other BIPOC in a way that mirrors how white racists might treat them. Another way internalized racism can manifest itself is by BIPOC accepting and internalizing Eurocentric ideals and values.

"Reverse Racism": This term is placed in quotation marks to emphasize that it is a fabricated term that should not carry any actual value. It was a term created by and for white people who want to perpetuate racism by denying their privilege in all its forms and by claiming that fighting to improve the lives of BIPOC is somehow "racist" against white people. MHA considers this term invalid because racism in any form depends on the presence of a power differential. White people have historically always fallen on the powerful side rather than the powerless side. Reverse racism is therefore impossible, as long as we live in a society that perpetuates white supremacy.

Oppression: The use of power (by a system/institution/group/individual) to dominate over another OR the refusal of a system/institution/group/individual who possesses this power to challenge that domination.

Racial Trauma: Simply put, traumatization that results from experiencing racism in any of its many forms. Importantly, this does not have to stem from one major isolated event; rather, it can result from an accumulation of experiences such as daily subtle acts of discrimination or microaggressions.

Depression, racial trauma, stress, anxiety, PTSD—all can manifest as a disorder that stems from experiencing the social construct of racism. They can also play a crucial role in determining the ways racism affects both physical, and mental health. According to the MHA, "Stress hormones are released during stressful situations, and research has shown that both the experience of and the observation of racial discrimination is stressful for children and adults who identify as BIPOC." Therefore, we experience racism as a weaponized social construct, and by dealing with it every day, we can fall victim to racism disorder. In order not to fall victim to it, we must apply conscious intelligence thinking to it from negatively affecting our lives.

As I write this passage, CNN is breaking the following news, which illustrates the stresses of racism in a society in which Black people constantly live under white supremacy culture. Read for yourself below:

Buckingham Palace official resigns over 'unacceptable' comments to Black charity founder
By Max Foster and Joshua Berlinger, CNN
Updated 9:32 AM EST, Wed November 30, 2022

"An honorary member of Buckingham Palace has resigned and apologized after a Black charity founder said she was questioned about whether she was really British at a royal reception on Tuesday.

The guest, Ngozi Fulani, is the CEO of Sistah Space, an organization that provides specialist services to women of African and Caribbean heritage affected by abuse. Fulani was attending a royal function on domestic abuse organized by the Queen Consort on Tuesday evening when she said a member of staff began a line of questioning that the palace called "unacceptable and deeply regrettable." Sistah_Space shared a rough transcript of the conversation on Twitter on Wednesday."

Nevertheless, if you have been unfortunate enough to be inflicted with *racism disorder*—as with other mental health disorders, such as addiction—there is a path to freeing yourself from it, and it all begins with your conscious mind. So unless you have made up your mind to find the will to change, you will remain suffering from this disorder. This means thinking differently, intellectually, and non-emotionally, building resilience and antifragility to combat the social construct of *racism*. New thinking may feel rather strange, but intelligence rules the world, as Marcus Garvey once said. So apply intelligence to your own surroundings and get in firm control of your life. Change takes discipline, so if experiencing racism has affected you or created deep satisfaction in your life, then move toward quantitative thinking, and your recovery will follow.

Also, therapy can be helpful—not in trying to understand racism, which we cannot change due to its embedding in human nature, but in finding an understanding of how the social construct of racism affects your mental health. Understanding how racism creates stress and anxiety, your ambitions, and your performance would be helpful in not letting *racism* get into your head.

CONTROL OF ECONOMICS can be parlayed into spectacular wealth and advantages, and the linear downstream distribution of wealth drives more advantages for those who focus on it—and greater inequality and suffering for those who do not. Inheritance exponentially reinforces the barriers to wealth creation for those outside of privileged groups, and the downstream wealth flow compounds the status quo even more. So wasting time complaining about how others accumulated their wealth doesn't help your wealth situation. It only distracts and wastes precious mental energy. We as a people must put feelings aside and think quantitatively about the nature of the game itself.

Discrimination is simply a constructed functional economic utility used against us by others to perpetuate their power and privilege in the universe. The question is, what are we going to do

234

about it? How are we going to go out and amass our own power and privilege in that same universe?

We can no longer blame others and systems for our success or failure. We are part of the system in which we live, and that system is not likely to change, so we must stop wasting our energy in that regard. Rather, the intelligent move is to adapt to the system and make decisions within the systemic environment for our gain. We have contributed to the architecture of the ecosystem itself by what we have not done and what we have allowed to be done to us—what we have accepted, and what we have not been willing to do for ourselves. We all have free will. So we must look inward with honesty, because our outer existence is a direct function of our inward engineering and outputs. Things come down to personal responsibility in the end.

Caribbean leadership and its people have not yet taken to the idea of personal responsibility as a major factor in success; too many remain on the veranda, blaming the system and the mango tree. What sense does it make for us to rely on top-down white supremacist culture and ideology and then wonder what the problem is? Prosperity is not a human right. The region has not come even close to creating a coherent and ambitious strategy for the 21st century to address digital transformation and new world economics. The process of building relevant knowledge-based economies doesn't require any fancy levels of knowledge or specialization; it simply requires quantitative thinking and basic ambition to begin.

Quantitative thinking is critical for human progression because it relies on logic and reason instead of emotion. The subconscious emotional thinker is susceptible to many fanciful things, suffering from imaginary thinking. The resulting anxiety makes one "comfortable" with one's position in life, fearful of change for one's own good, existing in a state of constant trepidation. One becomes fragile, lacking ambition, curiosity, and the inner strength to fight back. These self-inflicted dispositions have held the Caribbean back, and there is no possibility of correcting this stagnation unless there is a genuine mental shift from emotional thinking to quantitative thinking.

This complicit state of dependency culture—emotional and reactionary, not proactive at all, with adherence to Christian Bible stories—is exactly where and how white supremacy wants you to exist. As long as you "accept" that existence, white supremacy has defeated you.

The first step is the emancipation of the mind, which is to train it to minimize emotional thinking towards problem-solving, goal setting, and directional paths in your life. Lead yourself by a process of logic and ambition instead. More sophisticated reasoning is built on quantitative problem-solving, instead of culture and belief systems. Recognize the fantasy in Bible stories and the ideology in religious dogma and find power in spirituality instead. Freeing the mind requires addressing the many complex problems and stories into which the mind has bought.

One helpful source on this matter is Daniel Kahneman, winner of the Nobel Prize for Economic Sciences,, in his best-selling book *Thinking, Fast and Slow.* His main point is that S2 over S1 is the most effective way to think. Nevertheless, as we have previously discussed, for maximum competitiveness, artificial intelligence is a great *augmenter* of the human mind, maximizing its effective output.

So the case for using data science, AI, and ML to increase productive output is as important as what reading can do for you in this 21st century. As Kahneman's research shows, reliance on S1 in decision-making essentially means making decisions based on a "rule of thumb" method, which often turns out to be erroneous and unscientific. Furthermore, the brain can only remember a certain number of examples or things at a time anyway, so the "rule of thumb" becomes ineffective as a tool or method of decision-making. However, the machine can process hundreds of thousands of data points at the press of a keystroke, making it extraordinarily useful to people for deriving economic benefits. Therefore, we must raise our level of thinking and the use of technologies available to compete and win.

As a test, Kahneman addresses three specific questions that the individual who believes in intuition over data needs to embrace:

- **Is there some regularity in this area you can pick up and learn?** Do you have a firm method or data bank of experience shelved that can enable you to spot trends and patterns effectively? What specific areas can you identify that are sufficiently regular for our brain to process them efficiently and effectively?

- **Have you had much practice in this area?** Do you have a long observation of many environments with a high level of consistency and regularity? Following your gut instincts against the machine would require a phenomenal amount of practice, and capacity like never seen before.

- **Do you receive immediate feedback in the area?** Practice isn't simply about repetition; you can do something repeatedly and actually become worse at it. Therefore, you need coaching, learning, and feedback—immediate, scientific feedback. Speedy correction and iteration are critical.

If you were not able to answer all of these questions with a resounding YES, then you would do better to check your instincts at the door and adopt the *applied intelligence* process. Therefore, value is created by working with real information and finding those hidden asymmetries, through knowledge acquisition, critical thinking, and analysis. It requires applying a fact-based discovery process to leverage identifiable opportunities for economic gains.

237

Quantitative thinking requires mathematical analysis, using data-led insight. It requires accurate interpretations, relentless iteration, understanding of the contrast and comparisons, and detail, to spot patterns using real focused analysis. However, it is important to note that there can be pitfalls in data analysis, so remember to distinguish causation from correlation. Scientists themselves have this problem, so using data science is not that easy; augmenting your thinking still requires real iterative work on your part. You will fall into many errors and traps via data analysis—which is why ap^3 is helpful to the process of productive outputs. The idea that data provides all the answers is misguided!

Moreover, you should always be sure to know what you are looking at—to know the difference between insightful and clean data on one hand and useless statistics on the other. Being skeptical of data in general is a good idea! Faulty data or data analysis can lead down the road to rambling nonsense very quickly; before you know it, you can turn into Kanye West. Your human intelligence must still supervise your artificial analysis. Remember, AI is not conscious; you are the conscious decision-maker who is connected to nature. AI alone cannot connect with nature, and it will always be missing something. Therefore, the ap^3 discipline protects against the ignorance of artificial intelligence. AI knows nothing more than what it is programmed to know. So do not follow information flows blindly; information must be verified through a disciplined and rigorous framework of analysis, which still requires human executive intelligence.

Therefore, we must learn how to become critical thinkers, ourselves, and stop buying into what others want us to think and believe. We cannot continue to rely on academic top-down nn^2 that is not in our interest. Remember, everyone has an agenda, and conflict is everywhere. Foreign development agencies, governments, investors, etc.—everyone is seeking some sort of economic power over us. We must solve our problems. Taking personal responsibility and not handing off our problems to others is the foundation of self-reliance and self-determination. We must be completely honest about the part we have played in our own sub-par economic existence and recognize our failures and successes relative to other groups.

Both quantitative and qualitative measurements can be helpful and productive in identifying the objective truths about us. Honesty, above all, is a prerequisite for advancement, because you cannot build a future on a faulty foundation; the integrity of the structure will surely begin to show cracks, eventually falling apart. Put responsibility and accountability as first principles. Do not deflect; stand and deliver in truth, not letting the traumas of the past influence or control your decisions in the present, for it is your present that creates your future.

Quantitative thinking is the mindset shift that is necessary to perform in a complex and globalized world. So let us move beyond emotionally driven mediocre thinking and trivial solutions and strive for a higher dimension of thinking and performance. Hence building solid, technology-driven ecosystems and intelligent applications, and leveraging them for optimal change, is a must. The objective should not be to dismantle capitalism; you cannot change the system, especially given that that system has proven inherently beneficial to humanity. Capitalism works, and until we find something that can work better, there is no debate to be had. We can make as many excuses as we want, and hide from objective truths if we like, but reality will always prevail.

LET US combine HUMAN INTELLIGENCE WITH ARTIFICIAL INTELLIGENCE to demonstrate the importance of machine power in order to augment and maximize the human mind toward excellence. In the end, if you want to influence and achieve, it makes no sense not to use machines to power your prosperity outcomes.

The analysis below comes directly from research and development Douglas Blackwell Inc. have carried out in the Caribbean. The purpose of sharing this presentation is to demonstrate how intense and complex thinking can help to obtain the proper analysis and outcomes we want. The human mind cannot rival the processing power of a machine, so to win in the universe, finding the most effective competitive advantages is simply a sign of intelligence.

Background

Inflows of foreign direct investment (FDI) in Latin America and the Caribbean reached their highest historical value in 2012. The decline in FDI has been almost uninterrupted caused by the combination of macroeconomic factors and commodity price cycles. In 2019, they entered $160,721 million dollars of FDI, an amount 7.8% lower than that registered in 2018.

In addition, the impact of the current COVID-19 crisis will cause a profound reduction in FDI. Global markets could fall by 40% in 2020, and from 5% to 10% in 2021. This means that only in 2022 would there be a recovery in FDI in the world.

To help sustain and stimulate FDI in the Caribbean markets, a reform must be established. Our research shows these are the two driving factors of Foreign Investment reform:
- To first drive public discourse around the risk of losing foreign investment if targets can hide behind systems of corruption, mismanagement, and an indolent legal system, and
- To prop up the profile of organization in the region to promote interest in investment

We leverage decades of behavioral sciences and cutting-edge artificial intelligence while taking advantage of modern advertising technology to influence and sway public discourse.

Our Approach

Our team integrates a multidisciplinary methodology that incorporates psychological sciences, data science, and informational technology to maximize influence over public discourse.

| Leverage Behavioral Science | Establish a Content Supply Chain | Harness Big Data and Machine Learning | Utilize Modern Advertising Technology |

Douglas Blackwell creates a systematic strategy for influencing public behavior and conversation on an individualized level.

Change the Messaging from Informational to Behavioral

Informational messaging is formal and appeals to the logical centers of the brain. In contrast, behavioral messaging invokes core emotions which has a higher chance of influencing actions.

Informational messaging

Appeals to the logical centers of the brain and informs the reader but does not grab the attention of a passerby.

Behavioral messaging

Invokes a core emotion, in this case fear, which instantaneously plays out a cause-and-effect scenario in their mind.

Both messages intend to achieve the same outcome of keeping out unwanted traffic. The key is to predict which type of messaging will resonate with the target audience. Depending on the audiences' psychological profile, the content of the message will be received differently.

The Big Five Personality Traits: OCEAN

In classic psychological trait theory, the Big Five or OCEAN model is a factor analysis technique used to understand and analyze personality survey data.

Openness — *How open you are to new experiences*

Conscientiousness — *How much do you value structure and agenda*

Extraversion — *How much you enjoy interacting with others*

Agreeableness — *How often you put others needs above your own*

Neuroticism — *How much you are affected by negative emotion*

By leveraging psychological trait theory, Douglas Blackwell analyzes the target audience beyond basic demographics and behavior. It becomes an analysis on how the audience views the world and how it can be influenced.

Similar Demographics with Different Psychological Profiles

Douglas Blackwell analyzes the audience beyond basic demographics since people with similar age, gender, and nationality can have vastly different views of the world.

Different Content, Different Psych Profiles, Same Message

High neuroticism and High conscientiousness
(resonates with rational and fear-based content)

Low openness and High agreeableness
(values tradition and community)

Understanding what type of content resonates with the target audience is key in influencing action and conversations. In this case, **both articles point towards the issue of corruption in the Caribbean** but deliver the message in different ways. The article on the **left describes a climate of fear** while the article on the **right talks about a century old refinery being divested.**

Using Machine Learning to Predict Psychology

Douglas Blackwell will work with you to develop a machine learning model that is trained from big data and refined through expert data scientists to predict the psychological profile of every citizen.

Our team pulls in **psychologists and data scientists** to develop a comprehensive machine learning algorithm that predict levels of Big Five personality traits from behavioral patterns.

This can be accomplished by **analyzing thousands of datapoints per individual** and applying machine learning algorithms (such as regression with an elastic net regularization or random forest ensemble method) which **statistically predicts an individual's psychological profile from their data.**

Identify Sources for the Content Supply Chain

A digital content supply chain entails the whole process of planning, creating, managing and deploying digital content such as articles, videos, and images/photos to your desired channels and target audiences.

We've identified example outlets and authors to consider for sourcing content. Our sample list was generated by mining core/established publishing sources, large and recognizable publication houses, modern day influencers and thought leaders, and op-ed articles focused on experiences.

By curating a large variety of content from the large fact-base manuscripts to the small experiential anecdotes, we can rigorously analyze how the target audience receives different types of content and context.

Example Articles

- https://www.nakamews.com/2020/11/23/cdb-hosting-conference-corruption/
- https://www.theguardian.com/news/2018/jul/12/heres-how-the-worlds-most-secretive-offshore-haven-refuses-to-clean-up
- https://www.theguardian.com/politics/2004/jul/06/freedomofpolicy
- https://www.guardian.co.tt/news/idb-report-ti-corrupt-and-slow-6.2.1015187.9b29eacdfb
- https://www.roedslot.com/2020/08/14/rotten-to-the-core/
- https://corruim.uwalpay.ca/britstream/handle/19803/51727/9781552388501_chapter01.pdf;jsessionid=7\n\nMA03EGFF/808.1DBA3703Mdf396f5d4897;sequence=3
- https://freedomhouse.org/country/barbados/freedom-world/2020
- https://www.thedailystar.org/
- https://barbadostoday.bb/2020/12/08/corruption-matters-cdb-chief-urges/

Example Authors

- Brian Samuel, Jamaican Observer
- Maria Bradshaw - Nation News
- Emmanuel Joseph - Barbados Today
- Barbados Underground
- Brian Samuel, Jamaican Observer
- Sir Hilary Beckles, Vice-Chancellor of UWI
- https://www.cijn.org/ The Caribbean Investigative Journalism Network
- https://www.mediainstitute.org/thecaribbean_corrivision
- UWI, Dean of the Faculty of Law, Professor Rose-Marie Belle Antoine
- Professor Anthony Clayton, head of the Institute for Sustainable Development at The University of the West Indies (UWI)
- Professor Trevor Munroe, Executive Director NIA & honorary visiting professor Sir Arthur Lewis Institute, University of the West Indies, Mona since 2011.
- https://www.transparency.org/en/the-organisation/international-council

245

Our Approach for Content Source Identification

Douglas Blackwell automates the search for content by creating search & scrape tools that identify and amalgamates the thousands of articles/content at a time.

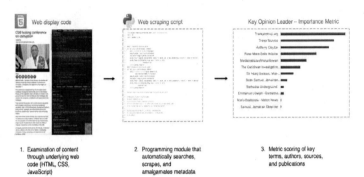

1. Examination of content through underlying web code (HTML, CSS, JavaScript)

2. Programming module that automatically searches, scrapes, and amalgamates metadata

3. Metric scoring of key terms, authors, sources, and publications

Machine Learning and Natural Language Processing

Natural Language Processing (NLP) is the intersection of linguistics, computer science, and artificial intelligence aimed at improving the interaction between computers and the human language.

Our team of data scientists embeds NLP into the content supply chain in order to better target individual audience preferences for content consumption.

The NLP component takes the raw text of an article and extracts:

- Entities (what is the article about?)
- Sentiment (how is language framed?)
- Syntax (how do parts of the sentence interact?)

In turn, we can then apply a multiclassification model to predict a content profile which can include metrics such as proponent for tradition, spontaneity, introspectiveness, hostility to foreigners, positivity. The presence of these traits in an article influence the amount of expected engagement from an individual.

At first, this will have to labeled manually – having people read the article and giving the scores to determine various metrics embedded in the article. The goal is to identify which factors resonate with each psychological trait. For example, someone with a high neuroticism score is more likely to react to an article with high negativity.

246

Natural Language Processing – Entity Recognition

Machines can detect entities within text such as locations, numbers, people, events, and organizations. This content extraction gives context to what the article is about.

Natural Language Processing – Sentiment Analysis

Machines can detect sentiment in the language of the article. This gives context to whether the article is positive or negative in tone.

ai

Natural Language Processing – Syntax Tagging

Machines can tag each word in a given sentence to further enhance the contextual and sentimental analysis.

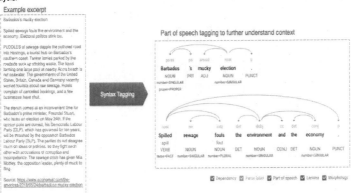

Putting the NLP Techniques Together

Once the machine reads and understands the article using various natural language processing (NLP) techniques, we teach the machine to classify the article in terms of receptiveness by psychological profile.

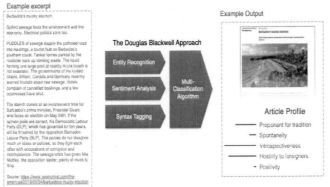

Matching the Psychological Profile with the Article

Instead of manually reading every piece of material, we teach a machine to read and understand using various natural language processing (NLP) techniques.

Psychological Profile		Article Profile
Openness	———	Proponent for tradition
Conscientiousness	———	Spontaneity
Extraversion	———	Introspectiveness
Agreeableness	———	Hostility to foreigners
Neuroticism	———	Positivity

By leveraging machine learning, Douglas Blackwell predicts on an individualized level how specific audience members respond to specific articles by matching their psychological profile to the extracted article profile.

Harness Big Data and Machine Learning

Top-Down Messaging is Inefficient and does not Resonate

Traditionally, advertisements and political messaging came from buying commercial time or newspaper space. A creative message is curated and pushed out to the masses in hopes that it resonates with an audience. This method is costly, inefficient, and outdated.

The way our audience communicates has fundamentally changed. In contemporary marketing, the audience leads the communication topics – they decide what is worth reading or watching.

The Douglas Blackwell approach analyzes hundreds of thousands of data points of the target audience to understand exactly what message appeals to exactly which audience way before the creative process for messaging even begins.

By leveraging Big Data, a marketing or political campaign can be fully informed of how well a message or campaign topic resonates with the crowd in real-time.

Big Data For Audience Segmentation

Audience segmentation is a process of dividing people into homogeneous subgroups based upon defined criterion such as product usage, demographics, psychographics, communication behaviors and media use. Audience segmentation is used in commercial marketing so advertisers can design and tailor products and services that satisfy the targeted groups. Everyone needs water to drink, but does everyone need bottled water? For companies to successfully reach their precise audience, they need to divide a market into similar and identifiable segments through audience segmentation.

Companies will not survive if the marketing strategy is dependent upon targeting an entire mass market. The importance of market segmentation is that it allows a business to precisely reach a consumer with specific needs and wants. In the long run, this benefits the company because they can use their corporate resources more effectively and make better strategic marketing decisions.

To effectively implement a marketing campaign, we first need to identify four pillars to clearly segment the public: demographic, geographic, behavioral, and psychographic data.

Four Types of Applicable Data

A combination of data types allows marketers to identify key audience segments to form targeted strategies that maximizes ROI on campaign spend.

Four Pillars of Segmentation

Demographics

| Age | Gender | Income | Education |
| Social Status | Family | Life Stage | Occupation |

Geographic

| Country | City | Density | Language |
| Climate | Area | Population | Region |

Psychographics

| Lifestyle | AIO activity, interest, opinion | Concerns | Personality |
| Values | Attitudes |

Behavioral

| Benefits Sought | Purchase Usage | Intent | Occasion |
| Buyer stage | User status | Life cycle stage | Engagement |

Behavioral Data

Behavioral data is data generated by, or in response to audience's engagement with a business, campaign or content. This can include things like page views, email sign-ups, or other important user actions. If we take social media, for example, how many followers do they have, how many people do they follow, how often do they share content, what kind of content do they share, how do they respond to a campaign, etc.. Also, if possible, their previous voting history might be informative.

This type of data is typically created and stored in the form of an "event," meaning an action that was taken, with "properties," meaning metadata used to describe the event. For example, an event could be "site visit" and a property for that event could be "device type." It may help to think of events as the "what" and the properties as the "who, when, and where."

Behavioral data is crucial in optimizing customer conversion, engagement, and retention. This goes beyond the "what" and "how" an audience engages with your campaign. When you have your audience's behavioral data at your fingertips, you can analyze the "why" of their behavior.

Psychographic Data

Psychographic data is information about a person's values, attitudes, interests and personality traits that is used to build a profile of how an individual views the world, the things that interest them and what triggers motivate them to action.

Douglas Blackwell analyzes the audience beyond basic demographics since people with similar age, gender, and nationality can have vastly different views of the world. We will use the OCEAN framework based on decades of behavioral science:

Openness — *How open you are to new experiences*

Conscientiousness — *How much do you value structure and agenda*

Extraversion — *How much you enjoy interacting with others*

Agreeableness — *How often you put others needs above your own*

Neuroticism — *How much you are affected by negative emotion*

This data does not currently exist with the targeted audience. We will first manually generate data by survey. Once we have enough data, we can leverage machine learning to predict psychographic data.

Data Sources we've Identified

We have identified examples of potential sources of data where we can leverage as drivers of the campaign strategy. Sources identified are both paid and unpaid access.

Public datasets

- Basic household data from state electoral registers: – Name, address, date-of-birth, Phone, Gender, Social Security No., Party affiliation, Voter history
- Donations data (available through Federal Election Commission and some NGOs)
- Census data
- Direct voter contact information (telephone, door-to-door, e-mail)
- Data from petitions

Purchasable datasets

- Statista
- StatCounter
- Datareportal
- Ourworldindata
- Consumer lists from commercial data brokers
- Offline Marketing Campaigns

Social media generated datasets

- Facebook/Instagram
- LinkedIn
- Email Marketing
- Data from website visits
- Google AdWords

What do we do with the data we've collected?

Once all available data is accessible, there next step is to clean and consolidate the datasets in a process called extract, transform, load (ETL). Everything is then housed in a central analyzable database.

Data Sources	Extract, Transform, Load (ETL)	Central Database	Analysis	Consumption
• Demographic	• Collect data from multiple sources	• Writing the data into the target database	• Predictive Analytics and Data Mining	• Data visualizations
• Geographic		• Database is cleaned and consolidated and is ready for all types of basic and advanced analytics including machine learning	• Classification	• Strategic recommendation
• Behavioral	• Convert data into the form it needs to be in so that it can be placed into another database		• Clustering	• Campaign and goal setting
• Psychographic			• Association	
	• Transformation occurs by using rules or lookup tables or by combining the data with other data		• Regression	
			• Forecasting	
			• Discovery	

Making sense of the data

Douglas Blackwell will create a custom centralized dashboard, accessible anywhere to constantly keep track of your metrics in real-time.

A data dashboard provides a centralized and interactive means of monitoring, measuring, analyzing, and extracting relevant campaign insights from the different datasets of key areas while displaying information in an interactive, intuitive, and visual way.

It offers users a comprehensive overview of the campaign's various internal goals, initiatives, and processes. These are ultimately measured through key performance indicators (KPIs) which provide insights into growth and improvement.

Furthermore, dashboards provide the ability for drill—down analysis which enables the users to get more detailed data on specific target areas. Drill—down capabilities enables the querying of specific data with little effort such as a click of a mouse button.

KPI/Metrics

Most important of all, we would need a way to keep track of the campaign performance. Initial thoughts on gauging public opinion would be to get polling data. Performance metrics can be extended to number of signed petitions, number of subscriptions, retention, etc. Some examples of KPIs are:

- Return on campaign spend
- Cost per conversion/ acquisition (is there Foreign Investment increase?)
- Conversion rate
- Impression share
- Lifetime Value of campaign

KPIs are not mutually exclusive. It's unlikely that the performance on one indicator is the best it has ever been while others are the worst. metrics will inform how effective the content "matches" the audience and we can build out how to optimize this matching process.

We will integrate machine learning with our KPI trackers to identify connections, trends, and insights that will help us understand the story behind our audiences, how effective our campaign is and what improvements we should make overtime. A contextual AI platform will help extract meaning from any kind of written content, including news, company investments, and forums.

It's all about data these days. Leaders don't want to make decisions unless they have evidence. That's a good thing, of course, and fortunately there are lots of ways to get information without having to rely on one's instincts. One of the most common methods, particularly in online settings, is A/B testing.

Multivariate testing (including A/B testing) is a technique used to identify the best performing campaigns on your marketing inventory. Such testing tools can be used to identify the ad copies, landing pages and even Call-To-Action (CTA) buttons that perform the best. Multivariate testing is a fantastic technique to measure customer experience and satisfaction metrics.

Machine learning in this case would be tied back to the audience segment, predicting what type of content "works" on what kind of audience segment.

Summary of Recommendation

 Leverage Behavioral Sciences

- Understand your audience beyond demographics and behavior; use psychological sciences to understand how they view the world to better influence their actions and decisions
- Use machine learning to to predict their psychological profiles to influence individuals on a national scale

 Establish a Content Supply Chain

- Identify sources of content that are both pro-reform and anti-opposition
- Use natural language processing to extract article context and sentiment and predict how they will resonate with individual psychological profiles

 Harness Big Data and Machine Learning

- Leverage big data both offline and online to more accurately identify key opportunities before, during, and after campaigns
- Use machine learning and big data to predict how well specific content resonates with target audience on an individualized level

 Utilize Modern Advertisement Technology

- Experiment with content (A/B) testing to further understand your audience
- Connect offline and online data by mapping offline information with online cookie or browser IDs for a comprehensive view of the audience

As you can see from the above example flow, making good business decisions or otherwise requires a significant intelligence-based process; so, failing to augment that decision-making with data science, AI, and ML in business as an example, is simply not intelligent!

CHAPTER 8

The <u>REAL</u> Truth Behind
European Wealth Creation

Liberalism has been the main theory accepted by the West for many centuries. Classical liberalism essentially says that we are all stuck with each other, so we need to act rationally and get along economically for everyone's benefit. Democracy and individual freedom underpin liberalism, they tell us. Liberalism is a political and moral ideal based on liberty, freedom of expression, free markets, equality, and the rule of law, instead of rule by the aristocracy. However, protectionist mercantilist policies and royal monopolies prevented free trade and imposed barriers on ordinary people. So liberalism allows anyone to obtain wealth through personal effort. Liberalism also dictates that in order for society to thrive, we need prosperity through free trade and commerce, entrepreneurship, and collaboration. Liberalism depends on many actors in society making their own contributions to the common good.

These liberal views originated in economic theories of scarcity, driven by the human condition and manifested by fundamental economic competition. Therefore, inherently, liberalism tries to add civility to the primal nature of self-preservation in a conflict-driven world. But the world is divided based on economic power structures, race, and ethnicity, underpinned by various actors using military force and other forms of power to secure economic expansion. There is often a divergence between what liberalism says it is and how societies actually behave. As always, theory and reality often do not align.

Liberalism helped Europeans justify the transatlantic slave trade, imperialism, and colonialism, all driven by the thirst for wealth and power of European states like Britain, Spain, and France. Liberalism attempts to insert morality into economics when it finds it useful to do so; but economics is innately not about morality and thus liberalism as a theory fails to operate smoothly in practice. European state policy during the imperialist/slavery/colonial era was all about economic and territorial expansion, and it was carried out only in the interests of Europeans. Economic gain was the main motivator. Again, Adam Smith was accurate about human behaviour.

In his book *21 Lessons for the 21ˢᵗ Century*, Yuval Noah Harari questions liberalism by observing that the once-dominant white Anglo-Saxon nations (i.e., Britain and the United States) are currently experiencing a period of "disillusionment" about liberal ideals. However, his analysis is faulty because there were never any moral ideals in the first place. What we are seeing today is not "disillusionment," merely fear of the white race losing power and control in the world. They see white supremacy being set back on its heels, so they use "disillusionment" as a guise for white supremacist anxiety. Liberalism was used to keep order by giving people the belief that things are fair and equal, when in reality, they never have been. The crimes of slavery and colonialism demonstrated the fraud of liberalism and the "New World" of the U.S. and the rest of the Americas. What existed then and continues to exist now is the raw conflict inherent in human nature, driven by the primal instincts of self-preservation and self-interest. All is geared toward economic gain in order to advance and preserve power and privilege in the universe at the expense of others. Racism is weaponized as a construct of the latter.

What do you think political slogans and agendas such as "Make America Great Again" and "Brexit" truly represent? They are nothing more than struggles over the dominance of the white race and culture! Look at the nationalist movements in Poland, or Vladimir Putin's delusional romanticization of Russian imperialism, his desire to become a 21st-century Czar—it is all the same old empire-building. Liberalism is only an idea, a philosophy trying to provide ideology to rationalize the self-declared supremacy of white Western culture. However, Europeans can never escape the constant war and uncivilized brutality, because liberalism is built on faulty ideas—a lie and false narratives through which to distract and pursue power.

The powerful actors in the universe are changing, and so are the old power structures. China is flexing its geopolitical and economic muscles for its own aggrandizement, and white supremacy feels threatened. The United States' population is diversifying, and white supremacist America fears losing power; that is why Donald Trump's message resonates with racially anxious uneducated white people. So these white Americans in the Republican Party are now willing to give up on the ideals of liberalism and democracy because those ideals no longer serve their interests. They are now willing to accept authoritarian rule if doing so enables them to preserve white dominance; this is what white nationalism is effectively all about. So, the real question Harari should be asking is "Will America still be a democracy 20 years from now or not?" This is not about "disillusionment;" it's about white supremacy!

While countries in Asia have been investing in education, technology, and infrastructure for years now, American society is focused on partisan spectacles such as Trump's plan to "build that wall" on the Mexican border and his instigation of the January 6th, 2021, insurrection. The whole thing is a never-ending reality show.

China, by contrast, is focusing on empire-building right now—geopolitical conquest through economic hegemony. The landscape has shifted; it is too late for the United States, whose decline has already begun. The election of Trump, however, has accelerated the decline, which is further fueled by stupidity. The U.S. has not kept pace with Asia in education and skill development. Harari also argues that the Brexit and Trump phenomena represent bewilderment and desperation for those nations and that these unskilled people are anxious in a transitioning world. History tells us that the rise of nationalism is predictable in these situations. It is what happened with Hitler's rise to power in Germany, for example; the fundamental underlying characteristics are similar. German nationalism and racism, the rise of Trump, and the shifting of the Republican party all have one core commonality: racism used as a tool to protect white privilege.

TECHNOLOGY HAS CHANGED the game entirely, and the Trump-supporter type is becoming more irrelevant to the globalized new economy. As a result, many of these people desperately latch on to Trump as their champion. He gives the willfully ignorant hope. Harari also identifies these types of people as the "useless class," arguing that algorithms have more value than they do and that they do not help themselves with their behaviour. This is an opportunity for Black people of the Caribbean, while this useless class in America remains desperate and distracted, to take the opportunity to make up ground by following the examples set by the Asian and Jewish communities—by investing in ourselves and our countries to become a relevant and meaningful collective player in the global economy. We must seize the opportunity to formulate long-term strategies to execute and succeed; we must not allow this opportunity to pass us by. The Trump and Brexit hysterias are simply reflective of the broader changing times. We must not be distracted by it. Trump and Brexit will go down in history as another last-ditch, failed white supremacist effort to hold on to the past.

ai

NIALL FERGUSON, the "celebrated" (among a certain crowd) British historian, is recognized mostly for his ability over the years to hang on to a much-diminished Britain as a force in the world. Ferguson is a writer of opinions under the guise of scholarship, and always through a white supremacist lens. To be clear, I am not in any way implying that Ferguson is consciously a racist; I am merely using his work as an example of the nuance and hidden symmetries that identify with white supremacy culture. His work about Britain's impact on the world reveals a white supremacist slant that is undeniable in my view.

In his book *Empire: How Britain Made the Modern World*, the title itself says it all. "How Britain Made the Modern World" is arrogant wishful thinking—short-sighted, not rigorous, opinionated, and self-serving, with a white supremacist tilt. Ferguson concludes in his book that Britain essentially "built the modern world" and that we should all be grateful for that, and put aside the little things like slavery, colonialism, and genocide of indigenous populations everywhere. Ferguson rationalizes away the bad by essentially saying that there was *more good* done than bad in his analysis, which is a weak whitewashing of history. Ferguson's views constitute romanticization and justification of autocratic rule, imperialism, and white nationalism—empire-building, nostalgia, and European cultural and racial supremacy.

Ferguson begins his 400-year storybook in a period of world history coincident with the development of slavery; make of that starting point what you will. He focuses on Britain's trade and commerce but trivializes it as merely stemming from the lust for sugar to satisfy the British sweet tooth. He romanticizes the Caribbean experience, glossing over and omitting the criminal and brutal acts of theft and murder, and conveniently forgets the use of military force against those without military means. He looks at the

260

role of missionaries and reformers, the church and its institutions as playing the role of "civilizing the savages;" yet he fails to address the church's important role in supporting slavery, colonialism, mass genocide, and other atrocities such as Canada's residential school system. This one-sided telling of history, unfortunately, appeals to the white supremacy crowd who comprise his primary audience—and they need not be the Trump-supporter type, either. Educated elites are capable of being every bit as racist as any of the hoi polloi. Ferguson sidesteps the proper telling of history with his version of it.

THE CHURCH robbed people of their identities, cultures, and traditions; but again, this was merely necessary collateral damage in the pursuit of building the Empire and modernizing, according to Ferguson. He goes on to paint colonial bureaucrats as "patrician proconsuls"—fancy words meant to obfuscate and obscure the truth. He associates Britain and its colonial administrators with sound military and political governance, necessary to bring the savage lands into the modern era. He goes all-in when he argues that if not for the stability of the British Empire, other hegemons like Germany or Japan may have come to dominate the world, God forbid—and that outcome would have been far worse. Ferguson is implying that *whiteness* is inherently better than other racial identities and tells us clearly that white European culture is the best thing that has ever happened to the world.

He devotes precious little time to the historical impact of the trans-Atlantic slave trade or the institution of plantation slavery, which created massive wealth for Britain and poverty and suffering for others. Massive inequalities, lasting economic imbalances, and political chaos were never covered by Ferguson in his book; therefore, a true telling of history was never his true purpose. But is scholarship not supposed to pursue the telling of objective truths? The cultural indoctrination of white supremacy makes it inconceivable for Ferguson to confront the truth about Britain and its ill-gotten gains, which it reaped by pillaging many parts of the world and leaving a swath of socioeconomic and political destruction in its wake.

Throughout the book, Ferguson grossly exaggerates the degree to which British imperialism was a force for good. His selective and biased use of evidence is highly subjective, used to make self-serving arguments about how the world benefited from British imperialism and its hierarchical structures. He makes these claims in order to support his underlying thesis about the legitimacy of white supremacy and state-sponsored slavery-based economies—a system crafted through force and thievery, and subsequent enormous intergenerational wealth transfers from those ill-gotten gains. All of this was good and honourable, according to Ferguson.

It is true—as we have already discussed—that the nature of the universe is such that things ultimately boil down to victory. However, we must always tell the truth about how those victories were won. We can accept the historical fact of British "success" (i.e., geopolitical and economic dominance) from the 17th through the 19th centuries; but we must tell the truth about that history as well. Making up spurious stories and pseudo-historical analyses for the rationalization of white supremacist culture and ideology must never be allowed to go unchallenged.

Ferguson is, in truth, a conservative pundit who spews right-wing ideology; he is not an intellectual, because intellectuals must hold truth as central, not personal opinions about history. Ultimately, Ferguson is an example of the perverse character of white supremacist academia, with its nostalgia for the white-privileged past. We must not allow such propagandists to go unquestioned as the authority and chief authors of history from the Western perspective.

The nostrums that figures such as Ferguson propagate under the guise of "liberalism," asserting that European culture is primarily responsible for the modern world, are dubious in the extreme. The falsehood of liberal rhetoric must be juxtaposed against the reality of the thievery, violence, and criminality that have characterized

European cultures ever since the era of the Vikings. We must talk about history holistically and truthfully, not selectively or self-servingly. *Empire: How Britain Made the Modern World* is little more than a compilation of Ferguson's controlled hallucinations and nostalgia. History, in the end, consists of stories written by those in power who have the privilege of being able to write it—which is why we must remain highly skeptical of historian storytellers.

The British Empire, while creating massive intergenerational wealth for the British people, also created mass economic destruction, enormous inequality, injustice, and even outright genocide. These are facts—but they are all too often selectively overlooked or even ignored in favour of romanticized and politically convenient narratives. One example of this disconnect came as recently as April 2021, when British Prime Minister Boris Johnson said something to the effect that systemic racism does not exist in the modern U.K. One imagines that he is likely also a fan of Ferguson's work.

The exploitation of people through racial and cultural oppression has always been used as a weapon in economic conflict—used as a sophisticated tool for entrepreneurship and wealth creation in the context of self-preservation and economic security. Conflict, division, and lies have been exploited throughout history by all sides for the sake of success and dominance. Thus white supremacy itself is simply a weaponized utilitarian construct that stems from the very primal nature of self-preservation! Hierarchical white supremacist structures, ideology, and doctrines have become increasingly sophisticated over time. Nevertheless, we can and must be vigilant about facts. Be alert to white supremacy narratives because it is embedded throughout our world, and what we read or are told about the past can influence our future negatively, if we do not make efforts on our own to get to the objective truth.

LIBERAL ideology, based on liberty and equality, free trade, and open competition, was devised by British intellectuals like Thomas Hobbs and John Locke. Liberalism as an intellectual concept "believed" in opportunity for all—except, of course, for Black and Brown people. So the liberal ideals of free trade and cooperation, treaties, and individual liberties, in which people should work hard and keep and enjoy the fruits of their labour and have the freedom to fulfill their dreams—none of it was ever real. Europeans created the slave trade and colonialism instead; that was their system for their own benefit.

America became the world's "first" liberal society, according to the dominant white supremacy storytellers. In the U.S. Declaration of Independence, Thomas Jefferson wrote, "We hold these truths to be self-evident…that all men are created equal"—except, of course, if you were Black. So we must identify and call out the many lies of white supremacy when it tries to wrap itself in liberal ideals. In theory, liberalism was a wonderful idea, but it could never be effectively applied against the primal nature of humans, and the belief that humans have been "civilized" themselves because of it has not panned out.

FOR THE CARIBBEAN PEOPLE, it is high time that we stopped being deceived by white supremacy culture. The central claim of liberalism and entrepreneurship—that wealth creation and the evolution of successful civilizations originates primarily in Western Eurocentric economic supremacy—is a false narrative. Black people had better get to know how the real world works, get to the truth, and get their collective heads out of the warm beach sand and into the cold hard world. Every day that we continue to live in delusion is another step toward irrelevance as a people. The overriding subconscious narrative that plays into Black people's heads is that "white is right" and that modernization is due to the brilliance of enterprising white men. We are meant to believe that Europeans and European descendants developed all the bright ideas, were innovative, hard-working, and honest, and have been solely responsible for the advancement of civilization—and are thus deserving of supremacy. These colossal false narratives continue to be passed down in the most elegant of forms, and they are often absorbed by Black people who are not aware of the truth. Author Joe Brewer, in an article titled "The REAL Story of Wealth Creation" explains this persistent underlying false narrative:

> Once upon a time, the world was full of unused resources. Clever businesspeople came along and found ways to add value to these resources by extracting them for use in industrial processes. Thanks to the invisible hand of unfettered markets (keep governments small enough to drown in a bathtub and only allow regulations that support the hoarding of wealth by holders of financial capital), this "value add" creates wealth in the form of rising GDP and the creation of jobs. All you have to do is let the wealth "trickle down" from the super-rich as they pile up increasingly huge masses of money.

This has been the prevailing or conventional wisdom story told, continually passed down like DNA. But the real story is one of white supremacy's use of brute force, lies, deceit, stolen people and stolen wealth, and abuse, under a rigged system that the colonizers created for their total control and self-interest. It is an inherently sophisticated and exclusive self-preservation system purposefully built to keep certain groups of people in control of all natural and human resources—the most significant factors of production, trade, and commerce. How could they possibly not win? Slavery and colonialism was the greatest wealth-generating system the world has ever seen, the legacy of which still endures today, in the power and the privilege being utilized.

> Poverty is created when the political expression of an economic system (for production and allocation of material information) takes sources of wealth away from some people and transfers it into the hands of other people, often changing forms (like the conversion of mass to energy) along the way.

Therefore, just like the clever transition from the slave plantation economy to the colonial economy, we must be cognizant of the changing systems that seek to oppress us. We must disrupt it and fight aggressively for our prosperity and self-created privileges in this world. No one else is going to do it for us.

If you want to use a historical starting point, seventeenth-century Britain can be seen as the more formal beginning of the flourishing of aristocracy, the institutionalization and dominance of power and privilege in the modern world. This power structure began to build a defined foundation, with barriers erected to keep others out—an inaccessible network of privileges and advantages based on race and class.

It goes a little something like this:

In the beginning, the King and the aristocracy held all the power. The nobility owned most of the prime lands, which contained an abundance of sustainable commodity-based resources, enabling activities such as fishing, hunting, and gleaning as well as offering shelter. The king controlled the army, so his royal authority was

266

backed up by military force. The land was the single most important source of wealth; therefore, those who controlled the land controlled the wealth. The aristocratic system channelled wealth toward the privileged few. Therefore, this system had nothing to do with merit, hard work, brilliance, or liberalism; it was essentially based on birthright.

Political power was centralized in the hands of the King and Crown, and the wealthy aristocrats circled the monarch, using their status as nobles to access wealth-creating opportunities. Eventually, the merchant class bought their way in when certain nobles became financially vulnerable and needed to marry outside of their class in order to maintain their status and wealth. And so it went. This closed-off system systematically began to privatize the land-based commons, evicting peasants or forcing them to rent the land from aristocratic owners in order to subsist. This, of course, is how cities like London formed as landless peasants moved into urban dwellings looking for work, forming the basis of modern urban poverty.

The aristocracy created an impenetrable and enduring wealth-creation engine and ecosystem by privatizing land ownership and keeping all the equity in the hands of the very few, the elite, and passing down that wealth and opportunity intergenerationally. Privilege meant wealth, closed to outsiders and firmly inter-generationally locked in. You were either in or out of it. Even after democracy finally shunted aside hereditary lords, ways were still found for the aristocrats to protect their extravagant riches through the maintenance of cultural traditions and social and political status structures. Of course, the monarchy was the driver of it all, and this power and privilege aristocratic group believed that the "hereditary principle" meant entitlement. The parliamentary system of government reinforced and secured the system through the enactment of statutory laws and the romanticization of tradition and culture.

So, behind the beauty of the British aristocracy's stately homes and the sometimes romantic and eventful lives they led, lies a darker story: a legacy of theft, violence, and unrepentant greed.

—Chris Bryant, The Guardian

From a historical perspective, the British aristocracy's most defining feature in an honest telling of history was not any virtuous aspirations to serve the common good, but instead, a desperate singular desire for self-advancement through stolen riches. They stole land under the pretense of religious reverence in order to legitimize conquest, expropriating and enclosing everything for their private use. They then corruptly carved out industries, commerce, and trade on a global basis for further self-enrichment and the linear passing down of privilege.

The transatlantic slave trade and the plantation slavery system were a hyper-extension of the aristocratic system in Britain; it was the original model on steroids. Slaves were simply seen as another economic factor of production, with extraordinary value—a super-asset of free labour. Slaves were more valuable than gold! With its long-term economic production and profit value, gold could not compete with the long-term production value of a slave. The hierarchical system that evolved in 17th-century Britain set the groundwork for the economic architecture for slavery and white supremacy—the expansion of the British economy and empire-building. Slavery, for all intents and purposes, was the hyperextension of the aristocratic nature of white men; institutionalized to ensure its longevity in whatever form it learns to cleverly transform and transition to over time. And it has worked and has endured, there is no doubt about that.

Britain executed white supremacy most elegantly—particularly in its clever use of the church—and fortified it into a rigged global economic system over the many centuries. The system was egregiously corrupt, yet it succeeded; so let it be a lesson about nature. For this system to persist, it must continue to be reinforced; therefore, it is a system within a system. The system uses the propaganda of liberalism to prop itself up, and uses monarchies embedded in religion to legitimize legacy, lineage, tradition, statehood, and nationalism.

God and King were the backdrops, using ostentatious and exorbitant spending on palaces, clothing, crowns, and jewelry, all of which was financed by the plantation economy. And the great plantation houses were erected as symbols to represent white supremacy. These were powerful measures and images as they subconsciously became embedded in the Black psyche over time, confusing Black people about their place and purpose in the world. These powerful hierarchical constructs in mind and structure further drove white supremacist cultural belief systems that both Black and White people bought into.

> The secret to the survival of the old aristocracy through the centuries was the mystique of grandeur they cultivated. They dressed, decorated, and built to impress so that nobody dared question their right to rule. The secret of their modern existence is their sheer invisibility.
>
> —Chris Bryant

RELIGION WAS THE SECRET WEAPON in this grand scheme, and missionaries became "Christian Soldiers." Building great churches to legitimize white supremacy was also part of the strategy of always showing superiority—great structures represented a great religion and an equally great and superior race of people. Christianity further ingrained white supremacy. The Barbados Slave Code used Christianity as the foundation for thievery. The code re-interpreted religious doctrines in a light favourable to slavery, and its ideas and renationalization were written into laws that reinforced the legitimacy of the plantation system. The Barbados Slave Code was the foundational document in a well-thought-out wealth extraction strategy that provided cover for the slavers, allowing white supremacists to live corruptly and immorally within the system they created to benefit solely them.

The institutionalization of entitlement allowed them to dominate all economic activity—land, natural resources, and human labour. The hierarchy propagated and perpetuated the system, and Christianity was used masterfully as a tool to instill obedience and placidity in its subjects. The picture below uncovers the epitome of the passed-down, pathetic, and fragile nature of white privilege, a culture of entitlement in which no one earns anything; everyone lives off of the work and production of others. This lifestyle is a direct result of past criminality.

The Duke (second left) and Duchess of Marlborough (right), with Alexander and Scarlett Spencer-Churchill, Goodwood. Photograph: Dave Benett/Getty Image.

As much annoyance, contempt, and disdain as the above photo evokes, we must keep our emotions in check. Emotion is not helpful here. Nothing we can ever do can change the past, so do not let past traumas take control of your intellect and prevent you from planning for a winning future.

In lifting the veil on the origins of wealth creation where Europeans are concerned, the purpose here is truth. Therefore, where trauma is concerned, we must use the truth as fuel to achieve a future that we design; we must not drain our energies in anger, but rather persevere. Use history as a guide to help you see around the curve and utilize your acquired knowledge of white supremacy to develop an offensive plan.

The organic nature of how power develops and how it flows must be fundamentally understood in order to win. The slavery-to-colonialism experience should sear into our minds the true nature of an economic conflict-driven world, and how the sophistication of self-preservation must be utilized to first survive before we can go on to thrive. There can be no illusions about nature.

Power must first be created and then applied purposefully. It is delusional to believe that you can achieve without firm pillars of success in place first. Within this natural universal ecosystem, energy is manifested towards extracting value from the surrounding natural world and creating various power structures that can combine and be aligned with winning outcomes. Accordingly, the frequencies you put out into the universe will attract others of similar pursuits to join forces for mutually beneficial achievements. Therefore, identifying resources, knowledge sources, and networks, supportive of value-creating pursuits, is the way forward.

The formation of sustainable and expanding power dynamics is central to the utilization of power. Concentrated power creates exclusive ecosystems that converge for the expressed purpose and ambitions of the group itself. Exclusionary knowledge systems of production begin to form, and information and opportunity become restricted to those on the inside of the exclusive group. Barriers go up. Information flow and knowledge ecosystems become increasingly privatized, shifting the productivity curve way out of the reach of those not in the network. As time goes by, this power group's core function becomes even more primal in maintaining these socioeconomic constructs and the status quo. The entire process develops into a self-serving cultural belief system of hierarchy and the divine right for the "superior race" to dominate another race of people.

This system is continually repeated and reinforced over generations, so diligently that everyone comes to believe it. It becomes subconsciously accepted, and Black people come to adhere subconsciously to their own mental subjugation. When you control the mind, there is no need for chains. As the colonizers shifted from slavery to colonialism, dominance remained the underlying objective; the master plan merely shifted, modernizing to keep pace with the changing times. Colonialism's purpose now was to remain economically dominant and continue to prosper. A less obvious and more sophisticated control of the entire supply and value chain was the objective now.

This is basically how Britain built its empire and continued to fuel its global expansion. The entire wealth creation system, in the context of the Caribbean historical experience, was created to leverage and maximize wealth, power, and socioeconomic domination for Europeans only. By systematically extracting natural and human resources from plantation-based economies in the Caribbean, the colonizers generated global trade and commerce for their enrichment. White supremacy's hierarchical operating system was now in full swing—a system perfectly calibrated to influence the minds of Black people toward the supremacy of white people.

> [...] [T]he West is rich because it took resources from other parts of the world. And the top earners in all nations accumulated their fortunes by extracting it.
>
> —Brewer

BARBADOS was the first society anywhere in the world to be built and sustained entirely upon the enslavement of Africans, according to the exceptional research work done by Sir Hilary Beckles, Vice-Chancellor of the University of the West Indies.

Professor Beckles explains that there were no alternative systems of economic development in Barbados during that prolonged period of history, and the system was ruthlessly enforced by the Barbados slave code. In the late 1600s, Barbados was the "richest" colony anywhere in the world. The hierarchical system and legal codes at the time were authored and enforced by plantation owners who were firmly backed and facilitated by the legislation and public policy of the British Crown. Therefore, imperialism, the slave trade, the plantation slavery economy, colonialism—none of these

273

constructs could have been so successful without the express support of the British state, underwritten by its military might. The "Triangular trade"—i.e., the pattern of "trade" in slaves, guns, and other goods, as well as crops such as sugar and tobacco, between Africa, the Caribbean and

Brazil, North America, and Europe—was the most significant socioeconomic event in world history. It helped shape the existence and circumstances of the world, particularly between rich nations and the continued plight of inequality and suffering of past colonized peoples. In the end, the British Empire had greatly been diminished by the mid-20th century. All empires eventually come to an end for one reason or another. However, by then, a massive amount of wealth, power, and privilege had already been amassed by the white supremacist system and passed down intergenerationally.

THEREFORE, AS CARIBBEAN PEOPLE OF AFRICAN DESCENT, we must be under no illusions about the importance of capital, and how the inheritance of wealth builds power and privilege. Many features of inequality have emerged from the structural socioeconomic wealth systems coming out of European aristocratic societies centuries ago. The impact of either having or not having capital is truly something that impacts societies for generations. This is why the socioeconomic impact of intergenerational wealth is so profound. Still, today, the legacy of the slave-plantation system endures positively for white folks and negatively for Blacks. The capital from that stolen wealth continues to compound and expand through inheritance. It spreads to social and political institutions, making one group powerful and another powerless, bolstering white supremacy and its hierarchical structures and agendas in the universe.

Effectively, the inheritance of capital also includes privilege and opportunity, which create incredible advantages for those doing

274

the inheriting. The lineage of wealth transfers over time has made all the difference in the world. Therefore, inheritance and one's general proximity to capital puts one at an advantage that is conducive to winning.

Wealth creation, at its core, is about satisfying the human condition by making us secure. It is about self-preservation, self-interest, survival, and prosperity. This is fundamental to nature in our metaphysical world. Unless Black folk can get with the fundamentals of human nature, stop being distracted by things that do not exist or work in nature, and get down to the sophistication of self-preservation (which is entrepreneurship), our socioeconomic circumstances will deteriorate even further. Our very existence as a people, like all other peoples' on the planet, depends on securing our future and that requires creating economic value. Wealth creation is at the very centre of it all: wealth = security. Therefore, our future relevance depends directly on the value we create and how effective we can become in influencing the global systemic environment. The world prizes value; without it, we cannot transact and leverage our worth in the universe. We can make as much noise as we like with the standard Black Lives Matter (BLM) type of narratives; we can align our emotions with nonprofit organizations in fighting for political power and social justice. But in the final analysis, things will simply come full circle, because everything boils down to wealth and power!

In today's world, inherited capital remains even more concentrated in the hands of very few—white males in the technology sector, for example. They are now arguably the most powerful and influential class because technology controls our lives whether we know it or not. Rich white nerds like Mark Zuckerberg run our lives, and Facebook's "Like" algorithms control many of our minds, emotions and behaviour. Much of the capital floating around the tech sector remains staunchly within the white male privileged VC and private equity hands. It is a closed network where capital is only truly accessible to them. Nevertheless, fundamentally, there is nothing new or revealing about this reality. It is merely the sophistication of self-preservation and how nature has always worked, going back thousands of years to our hunter-gatherer days.

Therefore, proximity to capital is a true force in nature; capital builds confidence in people and underpins wealth expansion. Wealth is created through new businesses and general investing, and it strengthens families, communities, and whole societies.

So when the narratives are spun about how brilliant individual white guys are in starting new ventures and building great businesses, changing the world, etc., just remember that it has nothing to do with brilliance on their part or anything of the sort. It has much more to do with proximity to capital. This is why, in the tech investing venture space, about 95% of startups do not make it past 3 years. The closed ecosystem network has so much cash that all they do is throw cash at the idea wall and see what sticks. Yes, that is how things transpire. There is no rigorous analysis, modelling, or due diligence being carried out; it is simply white men investing in other white men, as in a fraternity; like attracts like, and familiarity drives comfort and trusting relationships.

And if you do not believe that is the way things work, then look no further than the massive tech investing failures that keep occurring. Consider, for example, the major recent frauds, such as Samuel Bankman-Fried (also known by his initials SBF), the entrepreneur, investor, and former billionaire. Bankman-Fried was the founder and CEO of the cryptocurrency exchange FTX and cryptocurrency trading firm Alameda Research. In short, it was all one giant fraud; but everyone is blaming SBF. In reality, however, the entire white male-dominated tech investing network is to blame—including the noisy financial media, who are nothing more than entertainers reading scripts and creating hype. The main ones to blame are the big tech investor firms like Sequoia, an 85-billion-dollar company that always leads the hype. These guys say they are savvy investors, but obviously, they are not. They simply throw money at things they like, knowing that the rest of the herd will follow; they effectively control the Silicon Valley investing universe—deciding what to invest in. And what is really happening is that Sequoia is using its weight and market influence to get into deals early, expecting others to follow. "If Sequoia is in, then all must be good," was the assumption. No one does any due diligence, and the madness of the crowd overrides basic common sense. No one understands cryptocurrency or what they are investing in; but when the herd moves, it is a powerful force.

So along comes white boy SBF, from California, who went to MIT and whose parents are two Stanford University professors. Combine that with white privilege and proximity to capital, and the result is considered enough to be worthy of major infusions of capital. Others in the network join the herd, including talking heads and entertainers like Kevin O'Leary of "Shark Tank" fame, taking $15 million from SBF to hype the fraud even further. We can also go back years to convicted fraudster Elizabeth Holmes, the former biotechnology entrepreneur. In 2003, Holmes founded and served as the chief executive officer of *Theranos*, a now-defunct health technology company, which claimed to revolutionize blood testing but was really a massive fabrication. All of the usual suspects, the "smart money" investors took part in it. But again, Holmes was white and blonde and went to Stanford; so this shallow narrative was more than enough to create another billion-dollar-plus fraudulent valuation, without a single dime of revenue.

There are many more stories like the above out in tech investing land. The landscape is actually littered with failures and frauds; but the public only ever hears about the major ones, the ones the media identifies. So do not be fooled by the false narratives being spun about brilliance, talent, hard work, etc.; it is simply privilege and proximity to capital at work.

In another example further back in American history, much has been made of financier and industrial organizer John Pierpont

Morgan, one of the world's most prominent financial figures in the period between the 19th and early 20th centuries — "the Gilded Age," as it was known. J.P. Morgan was famous for helping to create the modern American economy. However, there was no exceptionalism or brilliance to J.P. Morgan. He was a sickly person throughout his life, lacking self-confidence in his early years, with a grotesque and disfigured nose (due to rhinophyma, a skin disorder that causes the nose to enlarge and become red, bumpy, and bulbous), which he insisted be covered with makeup in all his photos. JP originally did not even want to be a financier; he simply wanted to "rest and travel." Yet his father, Junius Spencer Morgan, a rich financier in London and New York, demanded that J.P. follow in his footsteps into the family business. So Junius funded the "start-up" firm J.P. Morgan in New York, consolidating his power between the two major cities.

Of course, the money handed down to J.P. from his father Junius to start the new firm was inherited from Junius' father, J.P.'s grandfather. JP's rise in the period of the Gilded Age, a period in American history marked by rapid industrialization, enormous concentrations of wealth, and privileged families in New York, the centre of the financial world. The Gilded Age was characterized by the extreme wealth of a few individuals and families, while many others lived in poverty. The era was also known for deep political corruption involving wealthy families and politicians, all the way up to the White House.

J.P. Morgan may be most famously known for "saving" the U.S. banking system at a period when there was a crisis stemming from the U.S. government lacking the gold reserves to back the U.S. currency. Through his political connections, J.P. Morgan was called in to fix the problem—and so he did, earning himself an oversized commission for saving the American banking system. J.P. also reorganized several major railroads and became a powerful railroad magnate himself, during his time, about 60% of the publicly traded companies in America were railroad companies. So, J.P. Morgan controlled the clients holding those shares and trading in them. He also financed industrial consolidations that formed General Electric, U.S. Steel, and International Harvester. J.P. Morgan was the most powerful and influential person in American business in his day, with consolidated power through a tight and connected network of investors and political connections. When Andrew Carnegie decided to sell his steel business, he contacted J.P. Morgan and sold it for $480 million in 1901, making Carnegie the richest man in the world at the time. The sale was financed through JP's network of wealthy clients, from New York and London.

So, objectively, all of what JP Morgan achieved or what made him "great" was made possible not because of his supposed brilliance or special talents. If anything, judging by the evidence, J.P. was below average—but his proximity to capital made all the difference. It was the inheritance lineage that took him from being someone who might have never been known to the public to becoming the great J.P. Morgan, business icon. Nevertheless, even after starting at the very top, and with all his vast privileges and connections, J.P. still was unable to grow his inherited wealth to any meaningfully great extent. J.P. Morgan died in 1913 in Rome, Italy on one of his annual several-month-long vacations. Upon hearing that Morgan had died with only a $66 million fortune, a most shocked Andrew Carnegie remarked, "… and to know now that he wasn't even a rich man."

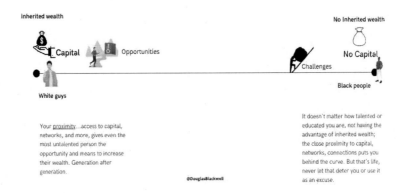

Proximity to Capital is what matters...

As time and generations passed by, J.P. Morgan Chase became a global financial powerhouse, which underscores the fact that wealth endures intergenerationally, compounds and expands exponentially, and consolidates in exclusive networks of less-than-spectacular white men.

Today, Jamie Dimon is the CEO and Chairman of J.P. Morgan Chase, and arguably the most powerful man on Wall Street and in global capital markets. But how does a "banker" who is essentially a manager become a billionaire? He has never created anything; he is not an innovator or an entrepreneur. Again, being a white male in a white male-dominated industry places him in close proximity to the capital and wealth-creating ecosystems, which often allow the least talented among us to achieve great wealth and power. It is like an aristocracy, where one's wealth outcome is dependent on one's birth status—white male. So do not believe the white supremacy hype; there is no American exceptionalism, only the mighty inheritance variable. As with J.P. Morgan, Jamie Dimon, and others, in the final analysis, it all comes down to positioning and advantages. If you are conveniently positioned right on the one-yard line, the likelihood is that you are going to score a touchdown! Therefore, the long-term impact of inherited wealth, access to capital, and political connections underpinned by exclusive networks of wealth should never be underestimated or improperly weighted. This is where the power lies in the world and what drives and dominates political economy everywhere! It might be helpful if we think about things more mathematically, and if we can fundamentally understand things as being part of nature, we may be better equipped to deal with our challenges less emotionally.

See illustration:

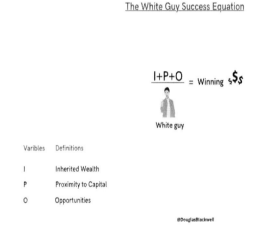

The White Guy Success Equation

$$\frac{I+P+O}{\text{White guy}} = \text{Winning } \$\$\$$$

Varibles	Definitions
I	Inherited Wealth
P	Proximity to Capital
O	Opportunities

@DouglasBlackwell

Nevertheless, we should never dwell on the past or make excuses. Black people need to take responsibility for our own lives and grasp the nature of things, reality, and the way the world really works.

Achieving real power requires pursuing prosperity and security in the long term. It requires sound strategic thinking and decision making—that is, applied intelligence. It requires the sophistication of self-preservation, which is entrepreneurship, and not holding our hands out begging governments for money to improve our lives; only we can better ourselves. Black people need to recognize how other groups like the Jewish community have fought discrimination and adversity. The Jewish people have been dealing with annihilation and persecution for at least a couple of thousand years. Black people need to understand that we exist in nature; so, as the Jewish community has done, we must muster the resolve to change our positioning in this economic conflict-driven world. We must create value for ourselves and use it in our own interest. We need to build resilience and become antifragile people with resolve and determination. As the Jewish people know, security comes through focusing on the sophistication of self-preservation—enterprise development towards wealth creation. It takes money to buy weapons and build a top army to survive in the desert, on the edge of the sea, surrounded by your sworn enemies. So you either survive or die. It is up to you.

We have way too many examples of how capital and opportunities are squandered in the Black community—by Black professional athletes, for example. If they are not buying gold chains and new cars and supporting their entourages, attempting to be rappers and spouting nonsense on Twitter, then they are now investing in "Pickleball." This includes the likes of LeBron James, Kevin Durant, and Draymond Green, to name a few—even former tennis star James Blake as well, even though he attended an elite Ivy League university like Harvard. It just goes to show that when you fail to understand how the universe works, regardless of education, you can easily squander capital and miss real opportunities to drive change. So because Tom Brady is recreationally investing in Pickleball, other uninformed Black athletes want to invest in Pickleball as well. We need to set priorities and start developing our intergenerational wealth and power base, by applying some intelligence to our decision making. Investing in Pickleball does not get your foot in the door of the mighty tech sector. Real Black technology experts are not interested in Pickleball. Perhaps pooling their capital and creating venture and private equity funds for the capital-starved Black tech entrepreneurs who actually have great ideas would make more strategic sense. We cannot continue to make foolish moves with no idea of what we are doing, with no long-term power-creating strategy. If we continue to stand for nothing, we will always fall for something! These pro athletes' advantage, namely their proximity to capital, continues to be wasted. We cannot create Black tech entrepreneurs—Black millionaires and billionaires—if we cannot even think effectively.

Fundamentally, achieving personal security is part of the human condition, and capitalism is a functional way to secure ourselves through prosperity. Intrinsically, pursuing security is self-preservation at play, which requires putting self-interest first and engaging in entrepreneurial behaviour. Simply stated, building towards individual security requires building wealth. So to secure our families and communities over the long term, we must build wealth and pass it down intergenerationally. Capital is the functionally active catalyst for wealth creation, allowing those near it to take advantage of it.

In the post-George Floyd era, we have seen where everyone and their grandmother creates a nonprofit to "help the community." But go back and listen to all of that talk and weigh it against the results today, and you will find that nothing of any meaningful economic value has been achieved. These top-down organizations are not conducive to producing any real and sustainable growth outcomes; they lack the knowledge, experience, capacity, or capital to be effective in private equity and venture. We must stop this. It will not work. However, these organizations can help set up foundations to provide the capital to every Black youth who wants the opportunity to seek out the best education streams, to prepare for the future of work and entrepreneurship. We need to fund pre-university programs with focuses on math, science, engineering, business and entrepreneurship programs, strategy and political science and history, producing well-rounded graduates who can gain entry into the very top universities in the world. They can compete and win if they are well-prepared and well-funded throughout. Another core area where nonprofits can be helpful is in the area of Black mental health. We are in a real crisis, and if we cannot become mentally healthy, we will not be able to compete and become high performers.

If we are going to continue to bury our heads in the sand and continue to exist opposite to nature, to how success is achieved in the real world, then we should simply stop complaining. It is up to us to change ourselves and uplift ourselves. No one is coming to save us; we must think and act for ourselves and rescue ourselves. Thinking long-term, like astute investors, and understanding and adhering to finding ways to improve our overall proximity to capital is vital. The world is unfair; and yes, there is massive inequality; and yes, we as Caribbean people of African descent have endured slavery, colonialism, and Neo-colonialism, leaving us significantly behind the wealth curve. All of the above is true! But we cannot change the past, and complaining about it will not help our circumstances either, thinking strategically and taking real actions will.

Chapter 9

Economics | Decision Making

Douglas Blackwell Images

Freud compared the conscious mind to the tip of a large iceberg, representing about 5% of those decisions made in consciousness. The other 95% is the unseen subconscious mind which is below the water. However, that 95% influences most of our daily decisions and judgments. According to Freud, our feelings, behaviour, cultural beliefs, biases, motives, and decisions are most heavily influenced by our past experiences, which are stored in our subconscious. So the critical decisions we make are made more by emotion and intuition rather than by intellect, reason, and logic. The unconscious mind has enormous processing power and instinct, and based on S1, it allows us to live our daily lives without thinking much about it. We do not have to tell ourselves not to run into walls, how to drive to a destination without using a GPS, or how to avoid dangerous predicaments. We do not think about how to breathe or chew food, because the unconscious mind does all that for us, guided by our past experiences.

Research tells us that the average person makes 35,000 decisions a day, most of which are economic or linked to socioeconomic situations. Therefore, economics-based decisions are the most frequently made decisions in people's lives. Hence, life is intrinsically about economic decisions, first and foremost. Behavioural economics and neuroeconomics are disciplines that concern themselves with how people make economic decisions and how they assess and manage risk. The conscious mind information processing system—that 5% of our brains—only has so much capacity, holding as much information as can fit onto a Post-It note.

That visual analogy was devised by Dr. Renée Richardson Gosline of MIT's Sloan School of Management, where she is the principal research scientist at the Initiative on The Digital Economy, and a Black woman to boot. Dr. Richardson Gosline is an expert on the intersection between behavioural economics and technology and its implications for cognitive bias. She is also a leading thinker on the science of digital brand strategy. Therefore, she provides critical insight into how our social structures and technology interact and how they affect performance and self-perception. Her work highlights how technology, particularly AI, augments human intelligence. We simply need help from intelligent technologies to perform optimally, she argues. Dr. Richardson Gosline calls it the need for "The Outsourced Mind." She goes on to provide great insight into why and how enterprises, organizations, and developing nations must utilize AI and machine learning in a disciplined process to optimize performance—a.k.a. *applied intelligence*.

Outsourcing the mind simply means recognizing the scientific fact that we need more conscious processing power, awareness, and analysis in order to perform optimally. Caribbean leadership must put the primitive nature of ego aside and focus on the efficacy of science. We cannot afford to waste time with counterproductive theories in economic development discourse that are primarily driven by emotion and "wokeness." We must create value if we want to achieve wealth, influence, and relevance, and also forget about all the nn^2 regarding global racial equity and fairness. Do not be deceived; there is no such thing as the right to racial equity. These are not human rights; they must be gotten in an entrepreneurial fashion. It is always about value through the sophistication of self-preservation!

Behavioural economics is about decision-making, but the quality of information and decision-making systems that we have in place are of low value. Therefore, *applied intelligence* tries to position itself at the intersection between behavioural economics and artificial intelligence, to be helpful in the discipline of good decision-making. Therefore, the ap^3 framework makes plenty of room to accommodate *The Outsourced Mind* in its equation.

More and more, we come to rely on algorithms for our daily tasks, whether we realize it or not; so how much control do we have in our daily lives in any case? Again, the answer is not to fear intelligent technology, but to adapt to it. We are still very much in control because we make the decisions to use the things available to us to satisfy our needs and wants. Therefore, without the utilization of intelligent transformative technologies in our lives, we will severely lag behind other societies around the world, which we can in no way afford to do. There is no chance for economic prosperity in the Caribbean without an aggressive and strategic application of knowledge, coupled with intelligence-based technologies underwriter our future; there will be no future prosperity worthy of mention.

IN THE WORLD of investment and business, the unconscious mind must be put in the back seat, and a conscious and weaponized mind must take the wheel. The future prosperity of the Caribbean region depends on the proper and aggressive use of scientific decision-making processes and methodology. Whether in the fields of business, education, healthcare, social service delivery, crime prevention, etc., *applied intelligence* must be applied strategically based on its augmenting value. Nonetheless, we do need to move faster and go further than most, as the rest of the world is way ahead of us. We must apply intelligence strategically and leadership courageously if we are going to succeed at transforming our legacy economies in this decade of digital transformation and to survive as a viable society over the next century or more.

The pursuit for all Caribbean stakeholders (political, economic/business, social/environmental activism, etc.,) must be to outsource complex problems increasingly to disciplined intelligence decision-making systems. We must be consciously aware of the transformative effect that knowledge and technology applications can have on our societies and push as strongly as possible to make digital transformation happen for us. Nevertheless, technology is not a magic bullet; strategy must underpin it all. The increasing evolutionary process from manual to digital will increasingly require

288

more sophisticated knowledge systems, and we must keep pace with it all to thrive in the 21ˢᵗ century.

So, Dr. Richardson Gosline has termed the phrase *Homo Techologicus,* which means that our minds are co-creating with technology. Algorithms are tools that essentially mediate human decision making in order to achieve desired outcomes. Algorithms are simply extensions of our brains in the same way that a hammer or a screwdriver is an instinctive extension of our hands; but everything flows from the mind. So, by combining human and artificial intelligence, Caribbean society can seek to find its competitive advantages and its pathway to success by riding the wealth curve—through pursuits in AgTech and the zero-emissions-based economy, for starters. Self-reliance is a virtue!

ECONOMIC decision making has always been a mainstay of human civilization, and the success of any society depends on good economic policies and decisions. Societies with strong socioeconomic fundamentals always include a culture of entrepreneurship and innovation. We need not engage in any debate or explanation; the point is that technology and innovation are central to sustainable and dynamic long-term economic expansion.

None of the many problems the global economy faces today—global warming, the pandemic, and rising nationalism in developed countries like the United States—are conducive to the Caribbean getting meaningful help from the Western world anytime soon. No one is coming to save us; it is up to us to save ourselves. As the pandemic vaccine rollout revealed, the West always takes care of itself first. Therefore, Caribbean people must take off the rose-coloured glasses, shed the remnants of the dependency culture, and stop participating in paternalistic "development" experiments that Western agencies and countries continue to push on us. If we know better, we ought to do better.

A main characteristic of courage is persistence. If you can bring resolve to your situation and begin to effectively lead people, courage will naturally manifest through purposeful intentions. So finding that courage and that life requires that you get out from under the shady mango tree, step into the bright sunlight, and go out and "get the bag," as today's slang has it. It is time to be more proactive, even aggressive. We must stop being victims, stop listening to the academics and the people who simply talk; as one Caribbean expression puts it, "Talk don't cook rice." Informed action-based self-reliance-based is the only way.

This decade will be a decisive and consequential one, so if we do not get our act together with speed and precision, acute suffering such as we have never seen before will become the prevailing reality. If the regional leadership continues to sit idly by twiddling their thumbs, then extinction awaits us.

The Caribbean continues to consume more than it invests and produces; these huge imbalances and a fundamental lack of investment create a system of diminishing productivity. Also, the investments that have been made do not align with 21st-century growth patterns and dynamics. Leaders do not understand the connection between technology and growth, which is why they blindly continue to push tourism. Staying wrapped up in the old economy and groveling for the same old hotel projects is not aligning with the reality of the 21st century. In addition, a lack of inclusion within Caribbean societies, stemming from the legacy of hierarchical colonial structures, reinforces old colonial mindsets and pits people against each other. The typical light-skin-vs.-dark-skin dichotomy still exists in the region, sadly.

We know better now, so let us do better and cease the self-hatred, as well as other backward practices such as the continued

290

exclusion of our LGBTQ+ community. These things demonstrate backwardness and are counterproductive to progress and prosperity, resulting in a vicious circle of never-ending self-inflicted suffering.

EPICTETUS, the enslaved Roman, turned inward to exercise the power of his free mind, once his outward freedom was no longer possible due to his imprisonment. Internally, we all have the power to control our minds and the way we think, regardless of the circumstances in which we live. Nothing is predetermined. Changing how we think is the first step toward determining our own outcomes. We need to imagine boundlessly, but within the reality of our natural existence.

Underinvestment in knowledge leads to underinvestment in innovation, technology infrastructure, entrepreneurship, education, science, and technology. Therefore, seeking a knowledge-based economy must be priority number one, because there is no chance for you to exist in a new digital globalized world with an old manual or analog economy. The Caribbean is desperately flat-footed in a rapidly transforming world. If this does not worry the region's leaders, then it should, because it means that they do not understand the urgency of the situation—and worse yet, they have no idea how to go about getting things done. The pandemic has shone a bright light on the state of our preparedness. Prosperity is not something that simply happens; it cannot be installed from the top down by development agencies. Bottom-up thinking, intelligent application, and investments in thought must be made before making any attempt at tinkering with the economy. Faulty thinking is dangerous, and without the application of *applied intelligence,* the execution risk will be significant.

Executing without maximum preparedness leads to fragility and failure, because it is not the smartest players, but often the best-prepared players who usually win the game. Socioeconomic

291

ecosystems of development towards profit and wealth creation must be engineered from within. We must do it ourselves organically and from the bottom up; top-down approaches do not work, and they tend to exclude the broader population, causing problematic imbalances in those local economies.

TOURISM, for example, was touted after independence as the future growth engine for the Caribbean; this was the thesis of the colonizers at the time in their wisdom. However, it only ended up being an extension of the romanticized legacy of the colonial-era plantation slavery system. The only difference is that today, we have ostensibly "free" Black workers serving tourists. Tourism perpetuated old white supremacist attitudes; the role of Blacks now was one of hospitality, maintaining their subordinate positions.

Nevertheless, Caribbean leaders continue to trip all over themselves to promote the next sham "Tourism Project," seeking photo-ops with shady deal-making with foreign developers, and misleading local populations about the jobs it will create and the boost it will have on local economies. Well, the reality is…not so much! Tourism has not delivered middle-class growth economies, only low-income ones. The sales narrative simply does not pan out, but it usually works out for greedy politicians padding their bank accounts. Local folks get screwed as foreign investors get ridiculous government tax concessions which take revenue away from the government treasuries. The fact is that tourism has not proven to be the engine of growth for Caribbean economies and should not be relied on as such any longer, a new growth-informed direction is required.

Note that there is simply no evidence that shows that these massive tax concessions and other incentives influence investors' decisions. The reality is legitimate and quality investors make decisions based primarily on the long-term return potential, this is

292

how they do it in western markets, so why are we not informed about how investing happens? Again, the uninformed are ill-prepared to negotiate with the well-informed. Like taking candy from a baby. It is the corruption and greed, the ineptitude of local politicians and their operatives that benefit, and the people suffer.

Sandals, for example, have directly contributed to the underdevelopment of the Caribbean. Sandals, known as a "great business," the king of the all-inclusive. However, as the real facts are laid out – Sandal's "success" has been driven meaningfully by state-sponsored tax concessions, taking advantage of politicians who know nothing about business. Sandal's ability to navigate and manipulate inefficient and ineffective political systems in achieving enormous concession packages from Caribbean governments has become an art form.

> To lay, with one hand, the power of the government on the property of the citizen/ and with the other to bestow it upon favoured individuals to aid private enterprises and/ build up private fortunes is nonetheless a robbery…

> ~ Samuel Miller

Take Grenada, as a prime example. Sandals 2012 was looking to put another all-inclusive resort in the region, and Grenada was the optimal location, known for its natural environment and beauty, Grenada was perfect for the Sandals brand. So, the Government of Grenada saw fit to award Sandals with multiple multi-million-dollar tax breaks (waives corporate taxes for 29 years, property taxes for 25 years, customs duties on all capital inputs for 25 years and an extension of the duty waiver on alcohol for 25 years too). Those astronomical tax breaks embody the tomfoolery of government Ministers in the region in general. These concessions are just nuts, the government treasury and the people of Grenada suffered socioeconomically because of such actions. To date, there has been no economic development beyond the gates of Sandals, no meaningful fair wage growth or middle-class employment growth for "Black people" in Grenada, via the Sandals giveaway.

The growth problem is further exacerbated by Sandal's all-inclusive brand, where all economic activities associated with tourism-hospitality are confined inside of Sandal's walls. Economic activity does not reach the real Grenadian economy.

However, we can't blame "Butch," he was a businessman after all and only acted in the best interest of his business. It was not his job to negotiate for the Government of Grenada and its citizens, that's the government's job. So, Butch as a businessman must be a businessman, don't be mad at him, place your anger on the corrupt and incompetent government leaders who negotiate these deals with regularity.

INTERNATIONAL TRADE STUDIES by the World Bank, United Nations, and various other similar institutions, found that tax incentives do not increase the aggregate amount of foreign investment available to developing countries. Caribbean nations, like all other nations, must welcome and seek out foreign investment, all nations need foreign investment to grow. That's a given. However, the investment cannot only benefit the investor, and it must be done responsibly in benefiting local communities as well.

The research tells us that "Tourism-Hospitality" is the number one promoted industry in the region. With the wonderful natural environment of sand, sea, and sun, how could one resist the Caribbean? However, we must use our intellect and not our emotions, to make critical investment decisions. I'm in no way saying not to invest in tourism, in the future, what I'm saying is that based on the evidence and analysis about sustainable economic growth outcomes, tourism has not proven to be what it has been touted to be. Tourism is not an inclusive middle-class income growing sector, it is a low-knowledge, low-tech, and low-income-producing service sector. Therefore, not conducive to growth and wealth creation in the new global economy. Further, in 2022, the lack of plans around the digital transformation of the sector leaves the sector way behind the new economy profit curve. Therefore, if the industry does not strategically and digitally transform itself, the Caribbean tourism product will get further degraded and commoditized. Generating the lowest income and growth differential relative to other travel destinations around the world, but we're already in that boat, sadly.

Tourism is an easy sell to the people, but it's not what will create prosperity in the 21st century. So, under an old-economy tourism-focused profile, sustainable growth will continue to be elusive. The stubborn fact remains, that not focusing on a knowledge-based economy in an increasingly digital world is detrimental to the regional economy.

SINCE THE TURN of the century, Caribbean tourism growth HAS tripled (United Nations World Tourism Organization [UNWTO], 2019) and is expected to continue to grow over the next decade (World Travel and Tourism Council [WTTC], 2019). Just before the pandemic, tourism industry reports indicate that the Caribbean was gearing up for another tourism growth burst, attracting new hotel investors and well over 31,000 new accommodations in the construction pipeline (Britell, 2020). The Caribbean is indeed one of the most tourism-intense regions in the world, with international tourism contributing meaningfully to GDP (gross domestic product) labour (WTTC, 2019). Likewise, tourism accounts for at least 13% of capital investments (WTTC, 2019), but is one of the most resource-intensive industry sectors too.

The data, however, shows that regardless of all the above-reported activity, those island economies have not grown effectively enough to create the type of growth profiles necessary for sustainable middle-class growth. The evidence tells us that if the region does not urgently transform in this decade of transformation the aspiration for a needed successful middle-class-driven economy might be lost. Possibly for another one hundred years, as history has taught us. The region is vastly **unprepared** for knowledge acquisition, and technology investment, it is significantly under-skilled and under-educated.

In short, although there has been increased volume in tourism over the decades, pre-pandemic, it has not translated to real meaningful GDP growth that increases people's standard of living. And that's the point!

In *Caribbean Island Tourism: Pathway to Continued Colonial Servitude,* Alfred Wong summarizes the situation honestly:

> Tourism has been an important component of the Caribbean Island economy for more than three decades. The business model is based largely on the deployment of low-wage workers in destination surroundings that mimic the past colonial plantation era. Moreover, mass tourism has resulted in stretching the carrying capacity of some smaller island states to the limiting end. Large transnational tourism corporations operating cruise ships and/or hotels are coercing sovereign governments to offer ever more fiscal concessions as incentives for business continuation. Additionally, as the competition for tourism revenue is heightened by destinations outside the Caribbean, regional states are struggling to find new means to maintain and

expand the tourism trade. Alternative tourism venues such as sex, gambling, tax evasion, medical, sports, culture and ecology are being implemented. Some of these offerings are indeed degrading to the people and their cultural traditions. And they do not improve the economic well-being of the people satisfactorily. A new strategy to replace classical as well as alternative tourism is urgently needed.

Therefore, the narrative that tourism is or can be an engine for sustainable growth is not supported by any credible evidence.

ai

PART III

Chapter 10

FOOD, MONEY & POWER

If your stomach is lacking nourishment, it also lacks satisfaction; you simply will be unable to be productive in your endeavours because all things require energy. Remember, the universe is "matter, energy, and emptiness." So you have to nourish yourself in order to function effectively. The first necessity for a productive and sustainable existence is the ability to maintain your energy level. Remember the simple lessons your parents taught you, such as "How do you expect to learn if you are too hungry to concentrate?" These simple truths are foundational: If a population cannot properly keep its collective bellies fully then how can they possibly have the energy to be a productive society? Food production and healthy communities are the very foundation of societal growth and long-term sustainable prosperity. Every society must have the capacity to feed itself, first and foremost. The Agricultural Revolutions of the past made continuous technological improvements to the tools used in farming and continued to strive forward with more sophisticated farming applications and production methods. Societies that farmed and produced their food were able to support their expanding populations. Self-sufficient economies continuously introduced new technology improvements and methods—knowledge ecosystems systems contributed greatly to the advancement of agriculture and socioeconomic sustainability.

Farming and agricultural science improvements provided increased food supply and better-quality food; better growing proficiency, and more surplus to go beyond feeding individual families—to feeding communities and profiting from that surplus. Therefore, surplus production has always represented business opportunities for thousands of years—agricultural growth has always been led by technology and science, and that sector growth has usually permeated into the broader economic growth outcomes of rapidly advancing societies. Therefore, land has always been valued as a productive asset to generate wealth. Surplus drives profit and wealth creation. Agriculture, therefore, has always represented opportunities for future prosperity in any country and remains the basis for the **Wealth of Nations**. Accordingly, the path to sustainable growth is through the efficient production of agriculture—trade and commerce—high-value-added food production and exportation. You simply have to create quality surplus and export markets to earn healthy profits to create wealth.

Exports of high-value food products will lead to hard currency receipts for island producers. Hard foreign cash circulating in local Caribbean economies will lead to increased local spending, spurring increased entrepreneurial development to meet the new demand created by increased economic activities. Therefore, agricultural and food production driven by technology adaptation is a fundamental prerequisite for the development of thriving Caribbean economies. In the end, technology and innovation must be the main driver of future prosperity for the entire region.

Europeans masterfully understood the relationship between agriculture and economic expansion, and how to utilize and leverage it to create wealth and power in the universe. They organized the slave trade and plantation system for the sole purpose of economics—to secure food supply, trade, and commerce, supportive of expanding European populations. The *triangular trade* construct was designed specifically for European wealth creation, power, and privilege—slavery paid for all those castles in Britain. Slavery, this single move, shaped the entire history of power and race in the world, which of course has been continuously bolstered over the many centuries and its legacy still endures in Europeans' favour. So again, everything matters in the universe, and those who control the economics and enterprises remain masters of the universe. It is no more complex than that. Therefore, the world has always been and will always be about **food, money, and power!** If the Caribbean people of African descent remain willfully ignorant of these fundamental realities of life. Continue to rely on nn^2 and others instead of themselves, and continue to make excuses for their predicament in life, then the reality is that they will remain acutely impoverished and powerless in the universe!

IN NEWLY EMERGING economies around the world, technology investment represents over 90% of new enterprise development and growth. In the domain of global farming, technology investing soared to $7.9 billion in 2020 according to AgFunder's latest Farm Tech Investment Report. However, for the Caribbean, we find no substantial data that shows any meaningful or quantifiable information that shows capital flows for investment to the Caribbean. This simply means that while the rest of the world advances, the Caribbean is at a standstill, moving backwards in a new globalized world.

For example:

- Total investment in Indian agri-food start-ups for FY2020 stood at $1.1 billion, with 133 deals. ASEAN agrifood tech start-up investing reveals that investors are driving the region's nascent industry aligned to the emerging mega-trend in food production.

301

- Israel, a tiny desert territory, has utilized technology to become a major player in agriculture, giving itself the ability to create food security and export profit; and at the same time create high-quality, highly-skilled, high-earning jobs—building towards a strong middle-class that spends in its local economy and exerts its power in the world. Israel saw $800 million last year in investment, spread across 278 deals, producing some of the industry's most innovative start-ups.

"FoodTech" and "AgTech" data reveal mega economic opportunities in farm-based food production. This optimism is supported by investment dollars circulating in all parts of the globe, except the Caribbean. Even though the region has the most optimal growing environment for significant agriculture outperformance. It has not been unable to organize and strategize to lure credible foreign investment capital to execute on the opportunities right in front of them. So unless the regional business leaders and policymakers start to get serious and begin to demonstrate competence and visionary leadership, the Caribbean will continue to fall behind in this decade of transformation.

Currently, like it or not, global investors view the Caribbean as too laid back, and not serious enough about investing in technology infrastructure and developing proper capital markets infrastructure, compliance, and governance to facilitate high-quality institutional-type foreign investment. Another big factor holding back the region from being seriously looked at by big capital investors is the fixation on tourism as the "main thing" for economic growth. Again, tourism has **not** delivered the Caribbean a middle-class economy. Tourism only maintains and bolsters the status quo of a dependent culture—sitting and waiting for others in lieu of being proactive and enterprising towards becoming a self-reliant, export-driven, AgTech-led economy.

The exit volume of VC-backed agritech companies reached 49 deals in 2021, up 81.4% YoY, while the exit value totalled $22.8 billion. Over the past decade, the exit count has increased steadily, led by acquisitions, which represent 67.3% of total exits in 2021. Agriculture is one of the oldest areas of technology and innovation in existence, and that fundamental profile has changed little throughout history. Modern AgTech start-ups began attracting venture funding roughly one decade ago, with the industry raising $230.1 million in 2010. Since then, VC funding in agtech has grown to $10.5 billion in 2021, a 41.6% CAGR. This explosive growth results directly from two primary factors: population growth and climate change.

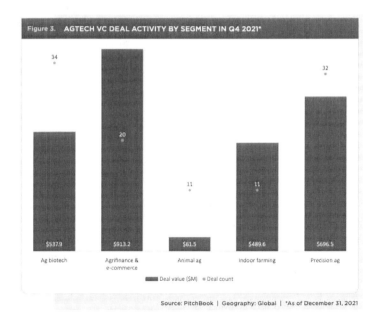

Figure 3. AGTECH VC DEAL ACTIVITY BY SEGMENT IN Q4 2021*

Source: PitchBook | Geography: Global | *As of December 31, 2021

The global population is expected to swell to 9.8 billion by 2050, driving more demand for food. At the same time, greenhouse gases and climate change are creating increasingly frequent extreme weather events that threaten crop yields (Pitchbook Research, 2021 Annual Agtech Report). Therefore, the Caribbean has a significant opportunity to leverage its natural resources—land, sea, and sun—as its major competitive advantage, to drive a zero-emissions-based agricultural export economy.

It is imperative that the region leap into the new economy, harness knowledge-based ecosystems, and utilize advancing technologies to create future prosperity for the region. Value creation can only happen by first developing a unique value proposition through the utility of innovation and technology applications. In the end, everyone has access to the same technology, but it is what you do with it that counts. The data-driven insights on agriculture tell us that for the Caribbean, agriculture is the best hope for the region to ever ride the global prosperity curve. The best opportunity for generating broad economic activity in the region. Leadership continues not to put time into the right areas of economic development, continuing to go to regional conferences and spend taxpayers' money on *talk shops*, filled with unqualified, uninformed bureaucrats who know nothing about venture capital and private equity.

Real-world economics and entrepreneurship are what is needed to lead this regional economy forward in this decade of transformation. AgTech is the new frontier for the pursuit of a high-performing middle-class Caribbean economy. Demand for food—particularly personalized, clean, healthy foods—is growing exponentially, so this requires robust intelligent technologies and automation to scale local economies for export growth. Successful development requires us to act on real substantiated information, aligning growth precisely to the identified and verified demand megatrends taking place in the world today.

Technology is increasingly allowing many more players from around the world to enter the agricultural space, regardless of geography, environment, and climate. These ventures, and expansions, are attracting global investment capital by the boatload because they can present compelling money-making business models. So far, the Caribbean simply sticks to top-down academic "development" agency and paternalistic charity-tinted nn^2 that only garners laughter and ridicule from the rest of the world. Nobody wants to deal with those that position themselves with those who do not know what they are doing, will not get the qualified people, and are always playing the victim card. The latter, sophisticated investors know, is the easiest way to lose a lot of money. Therefore, investors simply do not take the region seriously, and this is why it cannot attract serious tech-based investment capital.

Unless the Caribbean steps into the real world, with doable strategies that can demonstrate real bottom-up money-making enterprise opportunities, not top-down and waste-of-time constructs, there is **no chance** for long-term sustainable prosperity in the region.

The natural agriculture environment represents a strong-standing opportunity to create wealth for nations in the region. However, the lack of bottom-up entrepreneurship with a culture to match remains the biggest barrier to prosperity. The continued acquiescing to over-academicized, top-down development discourse in the region has kept it away from real-world economics, and success. Failure has been normalized in the region—timidness has also become part of the Caribbean identity and no serious investor wants to be a part of that. Leaders need to shed their cowardness and display some lion-like courage to move this staleness forward into freshness. As this decade of transformation moves rapidly along, at this time, the region remains wholly unprepared and exists in a state of bewilderment about the reality of what to do about creating a resilient and prosperous new economy.

ai

ENTREPRENEURSHIP AND CAPITAL are the main things. Capital looks for big transcending opportunities to invest in and to create more wealth from. Capital seeks innovation and big visions to build confidence before they decide to invest. Nobody seeks mediocre or charity-tinted situations. So the regional leadership must stop the victimhood dispositions and academic development nonsense; neither one has been helpful.

The region's natural agriculture and renewable energy competitive advantage opportunities are real. You only need technology investments to harness it. However, time and opportunity are being squandered by an **all-talk, no-action** Caribbean community leadership profile.

Therefore, we cannot continue on like this, we are driving right to extinction. We exist in a state of controlled delusion, believing that we can achieve prosperity without even understanding how prosperity is even created, to begin with. This is an extraordinarily counterproductive existence. Without capital investment and the development of regional capital markets to boost global investor confidence, there can be no real business activity and no meaningful growth outcomes. Where there is no tech investing there will be no growth, no future opportunities, and no prosperity. We cannot stand by passively while our economies degenerate permanently into the abyss, irrelevance, into the economic wilderness to die from acute willful ignorance. It is everyones' moral responsibility to produce and set conditions for intergenerational opportunities and wealth outputs, not to saddle our children with future poverty and despair. We must become fed-up with a subservient and timid existence, an existence not conducive to high productivity and profitable economies, one that burdens future generations instead of developing future wealth opportunities. We must find the intestinal fortitude to fight back, with the courage and skill necessary to generate some ambition and aggression, formulate

306

strategies and not be controlled by our emotions, while being trapped in our past traumas.

Again, Black populations have been willfully ignorant of how the real world works and have shown a propensity not to learn but to rely on emotion and religion instead for escape from reality. Leave *Wokeness* at the door, exercise intellectualism, and logic, and focus on science and technology to build the future. Emotional words might be good oratory and may make us feel good in the moment, but it does not produce lasting wealth. Case in point, the George Floyd event sparked world demonstrations and outrage, both Black and White people passionately articulated for political change, and many new *woke* organizations shot up overnight. Black community leaders and activists suddenly anointed themselves as the woke leaders for all things "Black." In Canada, for example, organizations like the "Black North" in Toronto, jumped on the bandwagon, with a stated mission of: ***"...to end anti-Black systemic racism throughout all aspects of our lives by utilizing a business-first mindset."***

Nevertheless, as of right now, the Black North organization remains nothing more than a confused, misdirected, and begging organization. After George Floyd, Black North leadership got big Canadian business CEOs to sign a convoluted reactionary pledge to *"commit to the removal of anti-Black systemic racism...that is negatively affecting the lives of Black Canadians."* CEOs signed it because it was good PR at the time, and of course, no CEO wants to appear as if they are "racist." So the signing was easy, but there was no follow-through; it was simply convenient PR for them. As expected, nothing of any meaningful impact has come out to date from the Black North. The Black North leadership continues to display a willful ignorance of history, human nature, and an understanding of self-preservation and power—real-world economics. The notion that White CEOs and their associated networks would suddenly give up their white privilege, or share it with Black people, is a fantasy. Black North is ignorant and anti-intellectual, driven by emotion and ego rather than logic and quantitative thinking. Again, economics is not a morality play, it is a power play!

Reactionary and woke organizations like Black North have become harmful to Black entrepreneurship, Black professional growth, and business progress in general. It has painted Blacks into charity corners of the universe, giving the impression that we are unable to compete in the real world. Systemic racism is a fundamental problem, of course, however, there are no quick fixes. But not recognizing or not adhering to the laws of nature, of self-preservation, shows ignorance to the reality of the Black experience. Things will not be solved overnight, and they certainly will not be solved with morality and emotionally driven methodologies. Also, the Black North leader has fallen into the same failed top-down development trap, which has been going on since the independence of the African and Caribbean colonies. The same trap which has failed diversity and inclusion programs in the US, failing to get Black businesses into the business mainstream.

Change occurs through disruption, first on the side of the one wanting change, so how you think and behave is critical to driving change. Change does not happen by appealing to the hearts and minds of others in power. Organizations like Black North are intellectually lacking in logic and strategy, becoming harmful to Black communities and progress, because they are fundamentally not understanding the hard truths about *nature!* And the first enduring truth about nature is that the universe cannot be anything other than what it is; that the nature of self-preservation remains steadfast, regardless of the time and place. In the end, it always comes down to *YOU.*

Therefore, the hard objective truth is that so-called self-declared Black leadership organizations need to first know the *truth* and then tell the truth—that our prosperity and power come down to what we can do for ourselves, and what we do next. Not about what others can do for us, that is wishful thinking and willful ignorance. Power creation is a long-term thing, never overnight and never top-down; it is always bottom-up. So we should forget about useless, harmful, and willfully ignorant organizations like Black North, and focus instead on the reality of the universe—evidence, data, and science. Everything flows bottom-up through economics, and wealth and privilege are created from successful economics; accordingly, political power is inherently derived from economic power.

In addition, when you do not adhere to primal first principles which are intrinsic to successfully navigating the universe, you tend to fall for every new concoctive delusional theory floated by unread and delusional leaders. Human consciousness is based on the phenomenon of decision-making, based on past experiences in the context of the metaphysical universe. Therefore, when you lead with emotion, you may believe that what you are doing is correct, but the way things seem is often not aligned with what they really are. Therefore, errors in judgement, distraction, poor decision-making and following misinformed leadership will continue to plague Black populations in the Caribbean if they continue to live in a culture of past trauma and emotion. So the way forward is to go back to the first principles of survival and find firm mental footing. Establishing core values, understanding how the world works, separating fact from constructive delusion, and focusing on core principles to build wealth, this is foundational to success. And building foundations of education, math and science, technology, entrepreneurship, self-interest, and investing in each other, for the good of the whole society, is also fundamental.

Having a strategic perspective with a long-term outlook is the only way forward. Woke organizations like Black North are a big distraction, and not helpful, they become part of the problem. These organizations promote fragility in Black people, a weak identity culture instead of the required resilience and robustness, antifragility. Progress requires always telling the truth, seeking a scientific understanding of things, quantitative approaches and applying measurement to things. Therefore, applied intelligence methodologies are required, and intellectualized and mathematical foundations of thinking are essential to human progress.

QUICK CASE STUDY: **AppHarvest**

A recent article from CNN, titled: *Is the biggest greenhouse in the U.S.the future of farming?* by Liz Kang (video by Dan Tham, CNN Updated 3:19 AM ET, Wed October 6, 2021), features AppHarvest, an AI-powered greenhouse in the foothills of the Appalachian Mountains in the US; the article asks if this greenhouse is the future of farming? The answer is yes!

The facility is more than simply an oversized version of a backyard greenhouse; this high-tech operation uses robotics, artificial intelligence (AI) and data to grow up to 45 million pounds of tomatoes per year. The global population is headed toward 10 billion people by 2050, and the UN predicts that we will need to produce 70% more food to feed them. It is not possible to meet this demand with traditional farming. So AppHarvest is the future of farming—representing technology and innovation with AI-powered greenhouses.

Jonathan Webb, founder and CEO of AppHarvest, says, "We have to figure out how to grow a lot more food with a lot fewer resources, all the while in the middle of climate disruption," says Webb. "We can do that by using technology."

Built-in 2020 and set across 60 acres, AppHarvest says that its state-of-the-art greenhouse yields 30 times more per acre than open fields while using 90% less water. "The facility allows you to control the light, the heat, and the nutrition of the crops," says Josh Lessing, AppHarvest's chief technology officer. "When you have that much control over the environment, you can do a lot of interesting things," he says. Using 300 sensors and AI, the facility collects data from over 700,000 plants, and growers can remotely monitor the microclimate to ensure that crops receive the ideal amount of nutrients and water. AppHarvest's robots assess which tomatoes are ripe enough to be harvested, and then pick and prune them using their robotic arms.

311

"Building technology to forecast, steer the crop, and create absolute stability in the food supply allows us to grow locally and control our food destiny. That is the real opportunity with robotics and AI," says Lessing. Global food production currently accounts for a third of greenhouse gases, 80% of deforestation, 70% of terrestrial biodiversity loss, and 70% of all freshwater use, according to the WWF. Therefore, demand is not the issue, the issue is having the foresight and determination to build an enterprise to capture demand and create wealth while reducing fossil fuel usage?

The global food shift happening is presenting another related opportunity in the trending personalized foods market. As scientists decode the molecular impact of food on the body, personalized nutrition is emerging as a potential treatment for obesity, diabetes, and cardiovascular disease. The Caribbean's natural environment is uniquely positioned to take advantage of this emerging business opportunity if it can organize quickly, and engineer branded demand accordingly, towards becoming a meaningful world supplier of clean and healthy personalized foods.

> Scientists in the emerging field of personalized nutrition are decoding the cellular and molecular impact of diet on individual health, and they are finding that food is more than simple sustenance. Its ingredients and nutrients can be customized to support a diet that helps prevent or treat diseases such as obesity, diabetes, and cardiovascular disease.

—Scientific American

Technology is driving more designer foods, cleaner, tastier, and more nutritious, and demand is coming directly from the richer countries around the world with expanding middle-class demographics and from the exceptional emerging demand trends from China. The globalized economy is driven by highly informed consumers, particularly the millennial demographic, they are the trendsetters, in product demand and how they transact. So smart businesses must align to consumer values and habits to take advantage. Traceability of food products: where their food comes from, harvesting, processing, carbon emissions released during production, logistics, human labour practices etc., are all important to today's informed consumers.

Consumer choice is driving the supply side more and more, particularly when dining out. Vegetarian and vegan foods centered around plants are achieving exceptional growth. In Britain, the number of vegans more than quadrupled from 2014 to 2019. In America, sales of organic food which people take to be better, both for themselves and for the environment rose from $13.3bn in 2005 to $56.4bn in 2020. Restaurant menus now name the farms that supply their food, as it is important for quality assurance and branding and giving diners a greater sense of connection to what they are eating. More and more people are attaching moral consciousness, health, and well-being to the foods they are eating. All of this presents ample and diverse agritech, consumer-driven commercial opportunities for Caribbean entrepreneurship towards regional 21st-century growth.

Therefore, the region is naturally aligned to capitalize on this multi-billion-dollar mega-trending opportunity in high-value-added, Caribbean branded food production. And given the available technology and knowledge acquisition capabilities, Caribbean farm-based food enterprises can be engineered to align operationally to the technology universe.

THE EMERGING PLAYBOOK in the digital age is first to identify the existence of real market demand opportunities while avoiding the distractions, the mirages, that lead to errors in judgement. Finding and understanding the potential of significant market opportunities first, and then utilizing digital enterprise applications to capture them, is the optimal path for achieving sustainable enterprise growth. Embedded data-science assets as critical parts of the overall enterprise digital architecture will act to level the playing field for ambitious and forward-looking Caribbean entrepreneurs. The application of knowledge and technology will raise their confidence and elevate them onto the global wealth curve.

The intelligence factor in enterprise farming can be an exponential win for business operations. AI, big-data-driven automation and demand intelligence on the sales and marketing side create holistic enterprise value opportunities. Therefore, comprehensive digital platforms that can run entire enterprises are part of the future of business operations in the 21st century!

Professor Hon-Ming Lam teaches climate-smart and sustainable agriculture, and plant and agricultural biotechnology at The Chinese University of Hong Kong. He believes greenhouse farming can help ensure food security and says that building greenhouses on land that is inaccessible to field farming, or near a city where the product will be consumed, can cut costs and carbon emissions tremendously. So companies like AppHarvests provide a good example of industry using renewable energy sources as much as possible to minimize carbon emissions.

Currently, AppHarvest's tomatoes can be found at grocery chains and restaurants around the US, sold at around the same price as a standard tomato. In the coming years, the Morehouse facility plans to grow other types of vine crops such as cucumber or peppers. A new facility is being built in Kentucky to grow leafy greens and herbs, and another for berries.

High-value production and sales for a food-secure regional economy and high-income earning exports, simultaneously, is the answer! Therefore, we must begin to apply quantitative thinking and find the functions that can produce the wealth outcomes we all want. Therefore, the utilization of the *applied intelligence* framework to

314

execute fact-based non-static solutions and adhering to a bold vision, within the framework of a sound strategy, is how success occurs.

So to in in a globalized world, the region must uniquely position itself for the emerging global food demand shifts. This means intensive investment in greenhouse infrastructure technology. In places like Israel, as mentioned earlier, advanced greenhouse technology ecosystems have elevated that country to become a relevant player in global agriculture. Plant-based food exports also created food security for the nation of Israel. So if a small desert territory like Israel can get it done, and relatively quickly, then what is stopping the Caribbean? Only excuses.

The last 5 years of AgTech start-ups in Israel have been phenomenal. The Netherlands, another small territory, a country in northwestern Europe, is known for a flat landscape of canals, tulip fields, windmills and cycling routes, 185th the size of Australia but produces 810 times more export earnings per hectare. So if it is being done elsewhere, and with similar square footage landscapes, what is holding back the Caribbean? The main point here is that technology is allowing many more players into the agriculture space, **regardless of geography, environment, or climate.** So if these new ventures and countries can continue to attract capital funding to grow their operations, and if the Caribbean continues to stand still. It will only find itself even further behind the wealth curve, moving closer to increased irrelevancy, and eventual extinction. Boundaries only exist in the mind, nothing is ever predetermined, and ordinary people can achieve extraordinary things, but the first step is a mindset shift—first believing you can and then take real steps and actions towards doing.

A REPORT (November 2020) from the Caribbean Export Development Agency about organic beauty products, aged rum, and hot pepper sauce, "Caribbean producers have a lot to offer the European market" the report says. The report also highlights a "growing trend for Caribbean food, beverages, and natural products across Europe...Caribbean food is now worth almost £100m." However, this latter number is grossly understated, and if the opportunity was only £100m, one may even question, why bother? The real opportunity, however, according to the data, is in the billions of dollars.

If you consider **Grace Kennedy Foods (GKF)** out of Jamaica, for example, you will see that it is a company with significant potential, but one that has not been able to properly seize upon the huge global opportunity in authentic ethnic foods. This market opportunity for GKF alone is in the billions, but GK remains a "meager" US700-million-dollar company when it should be worth billions. The management team at GK has not been able to come up with a bold strategic plan to capture global opportunities, and has not been able to present a credible new economy digital strategy plan also to its shareholders. GKF's website mission statement says, "To deliver the taste and experience of Jamaican and other multi-cultural foods to the world…"

If delivering to the world is the stated business objective, then why, according to their 2021 financial statement, does 53.4% (US$729 million total revenue) of their revenue come from Jamaica? Jamaica has a population of only 2.9 million. By contrast, North America and the U.K. represent a total market of over 430 million people. In the U.K. alone, "the ethnic populations" (i.e., non-white communities) represent over 20% of the national population, or 13.2 million people. So intelligent thinking leads to the conclusion that our focus must be on the global market. Research also supports that *ethnic foods* are a growth opportunity for the wider mainstream market, so there really is how you turn GKF into a billion-dollar-plus global enterprise.

New demand capture in these markets could easily make GKF a multi-billion-dollar operation within a relatively short period. GKF has a significant number of natural competitive advantages that are not properly utilized. GKF, therefore, is only lessening the value and potential of the Caribbean food brand as a whole. Worse yet, because GKF's product line consists mainly of highly processed, sugary, unhealthy foods, it does not appeal to the new health-conscious consumer around the world, not to mention the health damage it is causing at home. This is not conducive to building a healthy Caribbean society. GKF makes cheap, artificial-flavoured food products, with lots of additives and preservatives, and this is antithetical to the natural Caribbean profile we need to build and promote around the world if we want to develop and profitable high-value-added export market. GKF does not, in its current form, hurt the Caribbean food brand.

Therefore, limiting things primarily to the Jamaican market is not business sensible, and positioning the brand at the lower end of the food market is also not growth-oriented.

The Caribbean is already a global vacation destination brand, known for its natural environment, so it would make perfect sense to utilize and leverage "the brand" and build a high-value nutritious Caribbean brand profile, and this will also help other regional food supplies break into global export, which is the only way towards sustainable and profitable growth.

In comparison, McCain Foods in Canada generates approximately $7 billion in annual revenue, but they are not resting on that because they know upstarts and technology can unseat them in a flash. So McCain, for example, made one of many big investments in the emerging high-demand food products space, by making a $65 million investment in a start-up Canadian greenhouse operation "GoodLeaf" a company that focuses on greenhouse-grown healthy greens. Leafy greens are trending in demand and are the *#1* demanded plant/green food products in the world. The McCain example is important relative to GKF and the Caribbean's food industry going forward because it demonstrates that successful companies in leadership positions must never stand still, and must innovate and continue to invest in technology,

ACCORDING TO *SCIENTIFIC AMERICAN*, as scientists decode the molecular impact of food on the body, personalized nutrition is emerging as a potential treatment for obesity, diabetes, and cardiovascular disease. On-going research indicates that the general one size fits all 'nutritious' diets of many food guides are ineffective and misguided towards personal health and well-being. Certain nutrition may be good for one person but less effective for another—we are all different, so it is illogical to assume a standard nutrition regime is good for everybody. Mounting scientific evidence shows that meals that are perfectly healthy for one person could be another person's fast-track path to diabetes, obesity, or heart disease, the article says.

At the Nestlé Institute of Health Sciences in Lausanne, Switzerland, scientists are mapping the relationship between personalized nutrition and individual health. Nestle, a global food giant, is seeing where the lucrative future market opportunities are. Corporations large and small, and start-ups are all racing toward personalized food distribution enterprise models. The ongoing research and clinical trials could inform a new generation of nutritional concepts and solutions very soon, which will transform the entire food industry. Dr. Jörg Hager (J.H.), Head of Nutrition and Metabolic Health Unit of the Nestlé Institute of Health Sciences, points out that: "We strongly believe that the food we consume daily comprises the largest single influence on our health."

Personalized plant-based foods can have benefits not only for the export market but also for Caribbean food nutrition and security holistically. Unfortunately, the region suffers from its colonial past where imported processed and sugary foods are over-consumed, resulting in bad nutritional health, and high food import bills. In Barbados recently, Dr. David Bynoe, a government programme coordinator said that Barbados is spending too much money at an unsustainable pace on healthcare food imports, he added that the importation and consumption of low-quality, unhealthy, processed foods are significantly contributing to the developing crisis in healthcare in Barbados.

However, it does not have to be that way. Geography puts the Caribbean in an advantageous position regarding agriculture and has more than enough capacity to produce all the healthy foods it needs for regional food security, and for a highly profitable export market too. So the region has enough potential to effectively feed itself and make profits. The GKF example discussed earlier, highlights only one of many ways that the Caribbean can utilize technology with its natural environment attributes.

THE PLANT-BASED food market is expected to grow retail sales of plant-based food alternatives that may reach $162 billion by 2030 — up from $29.4 billion in 2020, according to a new report from Bloomberg Intelligence, titled, "Plant-Based Foods Poised for Explosive Growth."

The Report Highlights many of the opportunities for Caribbean enterprise development:

- Global restaurant chains, plant-based market leaders and health and sustainability benefits drive the long-term adoption of alternative food options.

- Plant-Based Foods Poised for Explosive Growth identifies growth expectations for the plant-based foods market through 2030.
- Industry leaders including Beyond Meat, Impossible Foods, and Oatly are driving an increase in plant-based food options as they partner with restaurants and major chains.
- More traditional and established competitors, like Kellogg and Nestlé, are looking to gain an edge by ramping up their distribution of plant-based products and producing promotional campaigns that showcase their variety of options. As consumers become familiarized with plant-based products and initiatives, BI foresees an evolution in consumer habits over the next decade.

Jennifer Bartashus, senior consumer staples analyst at Bloomberg Intelligence (BI) said:

> "Food-related consumer habits often come and go as fads, but plant-based alternatives are here to stay – and grow. The expanding set of product options in the plant-based industry is contributing to plant alternatives becoming a long-term option for consumers around the world. If sales and penetration for meat and dairy alternatives continue to grow, our scenario analysis suggests that the plant-based food industry has the potential to become ingrained as a viable option in supermarkets and restaurants alike. Meat and dairy alternatives could even obtain 5% and 10% of their respective global market shares in the next decade."

BI expects that population growth causing a strain on resources will contribute to more plant-based food growth. The Asia-Pacific region is particularly vulnerable to the limited food supply, with an expected population of 4.6 billion by 2030. As a result, the region is likely to dominate the plant-based protein market reaching $64.8 billion by 2030, up from $13.5 billion in 2020. The majority share of that market in Asia and the Pacific will be dominated by alternative dairy products, at 57% by 2030. Comparatively, Europe and North America will see roughly $40 billion in sales, with Africa, the Middle East and Latin America all seeing between $8-9 billion each.

International restaurant chains, including Taco Bell, Chipotle, Jamba Juice, and Starbucks will be significant players in increased sales and consumption of plant-based alternatives. Large chains offering burgers, sausage and milk alternatives will encourage consumer habits to adjust to plant-based food products. BI expects "faux chicken" to be particularly primed for growth over the next year.

Drivers

- Increasing Incidences of Intolerance for Animal Protein
- Growing Urbanization with New Consumer Aspirations Significant Venture Investments in Plant-Based Product Companies Increasing Vegan Population

Opportunities

- Research & Development and New Product Launches by Plant-based Products Manufacturers
- Organic and Clean is the new demand trend
- Emerging Economies- Asia-Pacific, Latin America, the Middle East, and Africa

Trend

- Rising Industry Concentration with Growth in Mergers and Acquisitions in the Plant-Based Products Space. There exists a robust exponentially growing market opportunity in the all-natural personal body care space as well. People want clean organic natural products. Therefore, a huge market opportunity exists for producers right up the product value chain—plant-based health and beauty and wellness products—both body and hair.

- The global natural and organic personal care products market is said to reach $23.6 billion by 2027, growing at a CAGR of 9.3% over the analysis period 2020- 2027. Amid the COVID-19 crisis, currently, the global market for natural and organic personal care products is estimated at US$12, according to ReportLinker.

- Skin Care, one of the segments analyzed in the report, is projected to record a 10.9% CAGR and reach US$9.4 billion by the end of the analysis period. After an early analysis of the business implications of the pandemic and its induced economic crisis, growth in the Hair Care segment is readjusted to a revised 8.3% CAGR for the next 7-year period.

- The U.S. The market is estimated at $3.4 billion, while China is forecast to grow at 16% CAGR. in the segment of global cosmetics, the USA, Canada, Japan, China, and Europe will drive the 8.6% CAGR estimated for this segment. These regional markets accounting for a combined market size of US$1.8 Billion in the year 2020 will reach a projected size of US$3.2 billion by the close of the analysis period. China will remain among the fastest growing in this cluster of regional markets. Led by countries such as Australia, India, and South Korea, the market in Asia- Pacific is forecast to reach US$3.6 billion by the year 2027, while Latin America will expand at a 10.5% CAGR through the analysis period. The 189-page report presents concise

- insights into how the pandemic has impacted production and the buy-side for 2020 and 2021. A short-term phased recovery by key geography is also addressed.
- In the U.K. alone, total personal spending on skincare, bath & shower products, shampoo, deodorants, and hair is worth north of $9 billion. Therefore, based on the demand for organic plant-based natural products, it is more likely than not that the shift to all-natural, clean products will be seismic. Given the choice, and all things being equal, most reasonable people would choose all-natural over synthetics.
- Vegan hair & beauty has seen a 175% increase in product launches in the past five years. "Natural is the key to Spanish consumers and 72% of Spanish women claim to use little make-up and prefer a more natural look. Younger consumers aged 17 to 24 years old, associate a more natural look with a well-groomed appearance." According to the Dutch Cosmetics Association.

The **bottom line** is that the global market is there and expanding quickly, it is a function now, of what Caribbean enterprises and policy-makers are going to do to build a profitable high-value-added, tech-supported, export-led growth economy to lead itself into a transformational 21st century.

An "Organic Certification" Opportunity for Caribbean AgTech Growth. There is a growing organic movement taking place in the world, to reduce the use of agrochemicals, such as synthetic fertilizers, pesticides, and growth hormones in food production. People want *clean* foods! However, there is very little evidence that agriculture in the Caribbean is getting the message.

In 2004, in a report titled *Establishing an Organic Certification System in the Caribbean*. The report pushed for adopting organic standards based on the Food and Agriculture Organization's CODEX Alimentarius guidelines for organic farming. However, to date, no coordinated system to deliver this standard has been developed and there is no existing established methodology to inspect or certify agriculture-based products for organic certification. The leading organic agricultural association in Barbados, the Organic Growers and Consumers Association (OGCA) was very supportive of this, however, it had no tangible way to verify that growers' practices met the standard and merited recognition. The report further highlighted that "The situation was compounded by the lack of a credible, sufficiently independent entity responsible for conducting inspections and awarding organic certification to existing organic growers and farmers who wanted to convert to organic agriculture."

In short, to build an industry in the organic space an organic foods certification mechanism must be in place, and it can only function digitally.

A single regional centralized digital hub is required, with an operating model for efficiency, with local "offices" under the authority of a central organization. Underpinned by artificial intelligence and machine learning, the system should incorporate compliance and verification measures, knowledge portals, training programs, sales and marketing online programs, analytics, and business intelligence and more. Building capacity and accelerating business development for the exponential growth of organic Caribbean brands must be the objective. This organization should be aligned with international certification standards, so the *Caribbean Seal* can be accepted with credibility anywhere in the world.

In the future, AgTech production to a large extent will be intelligent and autonomous. AI solutions will significantly improve farms' profitability, sustainability of production systems, and machines will make production decisions on the operational supply side on the data gathered from the demand side. Providing harmonized and automated hyper-efficient enterprises of the future. In simple terms, on the supply/operational side, AI provides farmers/producers/manufacturers with real-time insights allowing them to identify areas, for example, that need irrigation and other treatments. Also, innovative farming practices like vertical greenhouse agriculture will help increase food production and quality dramatically while minimizing the use of natural resources like land and water.

On the demand side, the focus is on using information – big data, AI, and machine learning to provide valuable *real-time* analytics for decision-making while remaining flexible and staying ahead of the demand curve. This provides the opportunity to adjust quickly to identify and capture emerging opportunities for continuous enterprise growth. AI helps with the pursuit of differentiation and low cost, while opening up new markets around the world, creating new demand, and capturing uncontested market space. This is based on the studied view that market boundaries and industry structures are not a given and can be reconstructed by market evidence and actionable insight towards becoming a major industry player in a relatively short time.

So we must not waste valuable time in conferences doing presentations that do not lead to anything meaningful. Instead, we must move timely and with coordinated action. Research by Douglas Blackwell Inc., titled: *CARICOM, agriculture and the Digital Age,* lays out how the Caribbean can best position itself in the massive global organic market and build global market share.

FROM THE DATA we know that food safety is the *#1* issue for global consumers! "Our 2020 survey looks at organic sales in 2019 before the coronavirus outbreak and it shows that consumers were increasingly seeking out the Organic label to feed their families the healthiest food possible. The pandemic has only increased our desire for clean, healthy food," — Laura Batcha, CEO and Executive Director of the Organic trade association.

Furthermore, from the same survey above, 81% of shoppers, both online and in-store, view the transparency of their food as either important or extremely important. Especially in the age of information, consumers are focusing more on their health and well-being, and are preferring organic foods over conventional increasingly. Also, knowing exactly where their food comes from has been identified as very important to consumers in the same survey.

Agriculture enterprise development in the context of Certified Caribbean Organic is at the very core of future economic growth and prosperity for the region, in the context of new global economy business. It is also the pathway for social development, food, and nutrition security at the grassroots level will build a more healthy, sustainable, productive, and highly profitable regional society.

We have moved very far in biometric applications, these applications can be used through a simple smartphone to monitor and measure quantitatively, the large numbers of nutrients in our bloodstream. The data can then be used to generate personalized dietary recommendations, and design food intake menus and programs for consumers, allowing consumers to place specialized food orders to arrive directly—farm to table! Applications to monitor dietary intake, voice and barcode capture, digital ordering, payment ecosystem technology and more. Artificial intelligence will get to know your body, medical and family history and recommend diets with a preventative function to your health metrics – with the necessary data the algorithm will be much more reliable than any doctor. Developing and positioning a future AI-driven Caribbean organic plant-based food industry, to become a meaningful global supplier.

Algorithms can now accurately predict an individual's response to any given food, measured by continuous blood-glucose monitoring with a small device attached to the upper arm. The algorithm is used on lifestyle data, medical background, and the composition of the microbiome. Simply defined, the microbiome is the genetic material of all the microbes – bacteria, fungi, protozoa, and viruses that live on and inside a human body. The number of start-ups offering bespoke nutritional advice by algorithms has soared. All these apps have the same business model. Their algorithms identify what people should eat and what they should avoid, and keep track of what is in their cupboards, refrigerators, and online shopping carts. Again, the opportunity for the Caribbean is to link and leverage these tech-led opportunities to become the branded global supplier.

AI-generated recipes use flavour combinations, coming from the leading chefs around the world. These apps also analyze restaurant menus and recommend which dishes to order—another opportunity for specialized farm-fresh foods. Makers of kitchen appliances, such as Philips and Samsung, have been central to the personalized nutrition ecosystem. At Davos, their chief executives talked about the challenges and opportunities for public health by developing more affordable appliance models for emerging markets, where the number of middle-class households is growing fast. The executives see a future where most households will have smart fridges linked to personal nutrition accounts with automated ordering, directly linked to suppliers anywhere in the world.

In short, the specialized opportunity exists, and with intelligent technology, local enterprises in the region that invest in knowledge ecosystems can compete with anyone from anywhere else in the world. Everyone has the same ability to access the same knowledge systems and associated tech, so nothing is holding anyone back. Agriculture enterprise development is at the very core of growth and prosperity in the new global economy and is vital for the region's future. In a nutshell, the opportunity has the potential to:

- Create employment opportunities for younger generations in organic agriculture through a high-up value chain approach, utilizing public-private partnerships within the key economic sector of agriculture.

- Enable scaled-up enterprise growth underpinned by technology to become commercially viable, and export-focused, through the establishment of value-added processing facilities that also provided skills training, knowledge transfer ecosystems, and high-income earning employment opportunities.

- Strengthens the institutional capacity of local organizations, stakeholders, and government policy towards the agricultural sector, by understanding the global regulatory environment to inform local enterprises, cutting red tape, and increasing the efficiency of enterprise and industry holistically.
- Commit (through the building of related databases) to a significant improvement in information technology ecosystems and knowledge access and sharing region-wide.

Chapter 11

Understanding The Economics of Racism

After independence, the conventional wisdom was that the new era would bring prosperity and growth to the region. However, as things played themselves out it became increasingly clear that the enduring legacy of the slave-plantation system would not be so easy to overcome. Social, economic, and political systems of oppression would continue to endure. The systemic environment of embedded white supremacy power structures of exploitation and domination is still working its way through, even to the present day.

Kwame Nkrumah's book, *Neo-Colonialism: The Last Stage of Imperialism*, a book first published in 1965, was groundbreaking in its analytical thought and is still relevant today. Nkrumah defined the independence transition as nothing more than neo-colonialism, which was the classic statement on the post-colonial condition. Newly "free" African, Caribbean, and other previously held colonies of Black and Brown people that transitioned to "independent" nation-states were in flag independence only. Things never were as they seemed, nor were they aligned with the narrative told by the post-colonizers. Power and privilege remained firmly in the hands of the past colonizers, so in reality, they were still in control of everything. Therefore, independence was very much merely another chapter in a well-thought-out white supremacy system of dominance. Caribbean "independence," therefore, was an adjustment to continue the economic exploitation and dominance of the region, merely more cleverly and less direct.

The era of the multinational corporations, technical advisors, and *experts* that came in after independence was simply an orderly transition from direct control (colonialism) to indirect control (neo-colonialism.) So from Nkrumah's time until now, times have changed—but the fundamentals of white supremacy dominance have only become more sophisticated, more difficult to identify.

After the independence ceremonies, the multinationals, technical, and managerial experts replaced the imperial colonial bureaucrats—dependence remained the prevailing reality. Also, we have witnessed the phenomena of the delusional "new Black elites," coming out of independence, hungry for status, fooled, and buying into the hierarchical white supremacy narratives. These new flag-state elites came primarily in the form of politicians, ambitiously seeking political power, and politics became the path to ill-gotten gains. The new Black elite foolishly traded the economics and potential of their new nation-states for the status of political office and titles. This effectively left the colonizers with exactly what they wanted, to hold onto and control the economics of the islands, while giving the elites the false belief that they had power. Trying to achieve political power without first securing economic power simply does not work. Real power flows through enterprise, profit, and wealth. But blinded by the shine and fake prestige of political office; many, not all, but enough, have fallen for the trappings of title. Trading value: economic opportunities, real money, land and agriculture, control of enterprise and industry for "status." So in the post-colonial era, whites cleverly increased their power and dominance focusing on maintaining and expanding their economic power.

According to Nkrumah, the strategic aim of neo-colonialism was to maintain the structural economic systems of domination from the imperial past. Nominal independence only gave Caribbean countries the illusion of freedom, while whites shrewdly maintained power and control through industry and enterprise. Multinational corporations like Nestle intensified their marketing in the region and turned their products into Caribbean staples. People became addicted to sugary, unhealthy foods like Milo, Fanta, sodas, and processed cheese. Jamaicans, for example, came to make highly unhealthy processed "Easter Bun and Cheese" into a part of their culture, regardless of how utterly poor the quality of the food was and without understanding the negative colonial history behind it. These unhealthy foods unwittingly pushed locals to believe in the status of Western culture, eating "Western" foods, and driving Western companies' sales in local Caribbean markets way up. Black populations in the region created cultures and identities based on the "supremacy" of Western culture, seeking to gain the acceptance of the white elites whom they subconsciously believed to be superior to them. People's psyche was out of sorts, emotionally aspiring to be part of Western culture.

THE CARIBBEAN CONTINUES to import low-quality unhealthy foods, and with a current CARICOM food import bill north of US$10 billion, it is slated to grow even more over the next five years, according to FAO. Food has become a health and financial crisis for the region. The region remains hooked on sugary junk foods, such as sweet biscuits as a staple, while an entire natural fruit juice industry could be created through agricultural technologies. Without change, no sustainable local food manufacturing can emerge if people keep choosing unhealthily processed and sugary foods over healthier, unprocessed local foods. Full self-awareness of health and well-being must come to the forefront of consumer behaviour, and supply will change when demand does.

Whether you know it or not, white supremacy culture remains embedded deep in the Black Caribbean subconscious. Unless we come to full consciousness of it and take action to change that mindset, nothing will ever change.

Once again, according to Nkrumah, the post-independence era is simply a continuation of colonial-era policies "under the guise of achieving freedom." Caribbean nations were made to believe that they had freedom, but the imperialist nations simply adjusted their strategy and tactics for the appearance of freedom. The white supremacy playbook has always been the same, it is simply updated and more sophisticated over the generations, recalibrated relative to the times and present objectives.

Nkrumah in his time promoted economic unity and local industrialization for nations and regions, he declares, *"Quite obviously, therefore, unity is the first requisite for destroying neo-colonialism."* This statement is still so relevant today, and a requisite mindset for sustainable prosperity. However, without a clear understanding of the reality of economics as the foundation for self-determination, not much can be achieved. Vision, purpose, and ambitious entrepreneurship is the only path to economic success. Caribbean people must stop continuously being fooled by top-down development theories that are pushed by the West and focus on authentic self-reliant bottom-up development objectives.

Bold national and regional economic growth strategies are required through an entrepreneurial culture, to engineer growth and leapfrog the region to ride the global wealth curve. Planning and attracting foreign capital to invest in technology ecosystems that can fuel high-value, tech-driven enterprise growth is the correct move. The overriding purpose is to help Caribbean nations strive for economic self-determination and halt the suppressive nature of the dependency economy and cultural confusion.

The Caribbean must integrate into the global markets if it wants to create value and equity for itself, otherwise, sustained prosperity and happiness can never be achieved; Nkrumah declared that "[...] economic unity, to be effective, must be accompanied by political unity. The two are inseparable, each necessary for the future greatness of our continent, and the full development of our resources."

IT IS IMPORTANT TO understand the economics of the slave trade in order to understand the methods of colonialism, neo-colonialism, and white supremacy. In 1543, the Spaniards created the "Asiento," which was a contractual agreement to supply enslaved African people to the Spanish colonies. The origins and details of the transatlantic slave trade are essentially the story of the colonizers' quest to achieve great wealth and further economic expansion. The white supremacist system is based on economics, power, control, and cultural dominance. Racism then was and still is a functional and convenient tool to drive wealth for one group at the exclusion of another. The enduring system of racism has created a constraining structural environment in which Black populations in the Caribbean continue to live, one in which they embrace their suffering and inequality by adhering to white supremacy culture.

The knowledge website "Understandingslavery.com" offers a brief but solid chronological account of how slavery, colonialism, and imperialism are inherently linked:

- By the 16th century, the Portuguese and Spanish dominated the slave trade economy, which meant that competition for riches would soon develop among competing European nation-states. So by the beginning of the following century, others would begin to position themselves in the slavery economy too. The English were the most aggressive. By 1618, King James gave.

- a charter of monopoly to 30 London merchants to engage in the trafficking of Africans, and the slave economy began!

- By 1640, tobacco, coffee, cotton, and most importantly sugar became hugely profitable cash crops cultivated on the slave economy plantations in the Caribbean and the rest of the Western Hemisphere. Demand exploded as Europeans experienced the benefits of the exponential production function of free slave labour—building extraordinary wealth through the economic engine of slavery. The British government, through legislation and state-sponsored capitalism backed by military force, began to institutionalize the slave economy. Slavery now was on the way to becoming the single greatest wealth creation system for any group of people in the history of the world.

- The slave economy helped to transform Britain from a primitive Dark Age society into an empire! All the great castles and other symbols of extravagant wealth seen all over the U.K. were essentially financed by slavery and colonialism in the coming years. The exploitation and institutionalization of slavery was the most productive economic input capitalism ever saw.

- Barbados remains the best example of this. Barbados was the birthplace of the British slave society model. The British made fortunes through the plantation society they set up in Barbados. Sir Hilary Beckles has brilliantly described Barbados as *"the first Black Slave Society...anywhere in the world,"* developed between 1636 and 1876. By the late 1600s, the Barbados slave society was the richest colony for the British Empire anywhere in the world. Sending the multiplier of compounding returns back to London through continued intergenerational wealth transfers, which cannot even be quantified in dollar terms today. Those transfers translated to more opportunity, more profit, more wealth, privilege, and power for Europeans.

Note: Regarding the talk on reparations, although I agree in principle with Sir Hilary Beckles, who is a major proponent of reparations, I respectfully submit that it is, alas, a major waste of time, a distraction with no possibility of ever happening. The reparations pursuit is counterproductive and builds the wrong cultural mindset; we need a proactive mindset geared toward victory, not one of victimhood. What has been done cannot ever be undone. And if it is not helping us build toward self-reliance, socioeconomic resilience, antifragility, and wealth achievement, then we must not waste time with those endeavours. Engaging in wishful thinking is regressive and not helpful to the objective of winning. Let us focus instead on what it takes to ride the new-economy wealth curve. Sir Hilary has argued for reparations directly to the political decision-makers in the U.K.; but those politicians represent the economic interests of the U.K. first and foremost, so it is hard to imagine any scenario where British politicians would go for a reparation package. Besides, it is naive to believe that anyone would willingly share their wealth with us, whether that wealth is ill-gotten or not. Hence, pursuing reparations for any purpose other than to correct and complete the historical record is a distraction from building Black progressive momentum.

Nonetheless, Beckles must be respected in his role as a scholar and for being genuine and purposeful. His work continues to be honest and adds a major contribution to the proper telling of history. The endurance and profoundness of the Barbados slave society still lingers and shapes Bajan society today, unfortunately.

Barbados has a distinct social character and cultural identity that remains rooted in its slave society past. Barbados' plantation system experience is so abiding in Bajan society and has become a major and prohibitive factor to growth and prosperity for the nation. Bajan public perceptions of the universe steam from their slave society past. The culture and tourism industry in Barbados is successful, precisely because of

ai

their subservient acceptance of the British hierarchal, aristocratic, white supremacy culture. Many in Barbados subconsciously prescribe to aristocratic ideals without even knowing why they are behaving in such a way, the impeded nature of white supremacy culture in Barbados, makes them accept and in many cases puts whites ahead of Blacks.

—Sir Hilary Beckles

THE BARBADOS SLAVE CODE of 1661, officially titled "An Act for the better ordering and governing of Negroes," was a law passed by the colonial English legislature to provide a legal basis for slavery in Barbados. It has been described by one economist as the Caribbean model of the *pure plantation*—the first jurisdiction to be reformatted as a black slave society. Barbados remains the last to loosen the political psychological stranglehold of the plantocracy.

Beckles says that the code "economically transformed the colony and redefined its social environment and that of other Caribbean colonies. Critically, it accelerated the pace of mass enslavement of Africans as the basis of Europe's colonial projects in the Atlantic world." Mass enslavement of Africans imported into the Caribbean territories was an economic strategy with long-term and far-reaching intergenerational consequences.

Sir Beckles's work is highly useful because it goes to the core of the slave plantation system and the lasting mental impact it has on Caribbean people. The slave economy system was built entirely around "legally" assured principles of property rights of African bodies; Beckles calls this "innovative and transformative." All Africans bought were classified as lifelong chattel property. The slave code culturalized and reinforced the slavery economy. Slave laws were intended not to protect lives but to secure the investment value in those lives—to ensure that they served the investors' profit creation

336

objectives over the long term. This was the sole purpose of a slave. According to Beckles, "There was no corresponding discourse on the inhumanity, immorality, and brutality of the national reliance on slavery, and the enslaved became the principal source of England's new wealth. A new England came into being with Barbados, and a new Barbados was created by England."

By the mid-1650s, the "Barbados investment" was beginning to pay off handsomely for the British; the island yielded breakthrough profitability and exponential returns never seen anywhere else before. The period of slavery and colonialism was an institution, an industry, an economic machine, and a system that was working extraordinarily well, and creating great wealth to boot. Therefore, slavery became the leading economic growth model for Europeans, the most important model for intergenerational wealth creation, assuring self-preservation and gain for their people, for centuries to come.

The success of the tourism industry in Barbados, for example, is a *de facto* direct descendent of the romanticizing of the remnants of the slave-based society. I wonder what our ancestors would have said about profiting off their backs this way—their humiliation, brutalization, oppression, and subjugation all being romanticized for the enjoyment of white British tourists, descendants of slave owners. "In these politically engineered ecologies of environmental enchantment, golden sand beaches and sugar barons' bungalows mask a persistent black poverty polarized in communities of crumbling chattel houses," says Beckles.

The suppression of the hard truths about your society is a disrespect to those that had to suffer. Political leaders rush to suppress those evident truths for their ambitious political interests, and the Barbados brand has become synonymous with happy servitude. The Barbados tourism psyche is one of acceptance of constant humiliation. The subconscious undignified environment that Bajans have created for themselves, boosting as the standard of

Caribbean tourism, is nothing more than ignorance of the enduring legacy of their slave-plantation system history. This romanticization, intrinsically embedded, reinforces white supremacy cultural adherence.

Descendants of the colonizers continue to soak up all the profit and wealth, the prime lands in Barbados, anchored from their criminal past, unrepentantly, and the Bajan tourism industry simply continues to be trained to say "Yes, please," which demonstrates nothing more than the embedded colonial nature of their thinking. Barbados today stands as the historical and enduring English symbol of global enrichment through white supremacy achievements.

According to Beckles:

> Despite their political ascendancy in contemporary society, black descendants remain marginalized within the wealth-management and ownership structures and cultures of the national economy. Political power has been no balm for the physical and

> psychological pain associated with three centuries of plantation tyranny. Passions from the past continue to shape social understandings of the present. The discontent brews beneath the social surface. It boils and spews periodically in the form of popular protest but quickly evaporates; the society settles again, and the sins of slavery sink once more to the bottom. But they are not forgotten.

> The Barbados slave code was the official legal codification of slavery and the structural, institutionalization, and justification of the development of the white supremacy global economy. It served as a basis for other Caribbean slave colonies to

adopt the system. This white supremacy economic system, based on fundamental first principles in economics – scarcity and conflict were the underpinning of the slavery economy. Slaves were the main factor of production which created economic advantages for those who had them, state-sponsored enterprises prospered, ultimately creating great intergenerational wealth transfers for Britain.

Investors representing the English royal family and its ruling elites, including the military and clergy, rushed to the island to secure their share of the wealth.

That wealth and property accumulated multi-generationally; the remnants can still be found in the social and economic fabric of the entire Caribbean. Institutions that govern countries are intertwined with European economic institutions based on white supremacy. The slave trade was purposeful and skillfully executed, requiring discipline, advanced management, complex economic systems and arrangements, and well-structured investment instruments. Organization, cooperation, and resource allocation in the slavery economy were necessary for it to function so well. For example, the creation of joint-stock venture companies found its stride in the era of slavery and colonialism. Small-time merchants now had the opportunity to buy their way into the aristocracy, which controlled access to the slave trade, and thus wealth. Exclusive enterprise networks, and partnerships, forged powerful monopolies that controlled entire sectors of the global economy: agriculture, minerals, manufacturing, trade, and commerce. The lure of the enormous wealth creation opportunity drew other European nations in to join the enormous wealth pursuit. Fortunes were forged, and castles were built. All on the backs of slaves.

Modernization and Industrialization

It is without a doubt that the economic utility and functionality of slavery allowed Britain to maximize industrial revolutions that came on later. The raw materials from colonies supplied the factories at home, which made the goods for trade and commerce. This process fueled profits and reinvestment and compounded wealth and opportunity over the long term.

Banks and insurance companies fueled investments which saw the City of London become the centre of the economic universe. In the 1740s, when British merchants joined with West Indian sugar planters, the first sugar trading organizations became all-powerful, significant enough to gain a voice in the British Parliament. The British individuals who became planters made fortunes. After 1791, the British Caribbean islands produced the most sugar and the British people quickly became among the largest consumers of it. And the profits of slavery were plowed right back into their economy, now going towards increased industry diversification to further expand their economy.

Manchester, for example, became an important textile centre, where factories made cloth from slave-picked cotton. Between 1630 and 1807, slaves produced about 75 per cent of exports of raw goods from the new colonies. Bristol quickly became the centre of a booming sugar import trade. Sugar was the most profitable of Bristol's industries. Bristol had 22 sugar houses.

With a booming British market for sugar, Bristol grew in prominence and civic stature. Bristol was home to groups of prosperous sugar merchants, as well as planters who returned home to retire to grand houses in the West Country. Bristol still contains important architectural monuments to its links with sugar and the slave trade. Glasgow also boomed during the 18th century with profits from the slave economy. A small group of Glaswegian merchants dominated the rapidly expanding transatlantic tobacco trade. These Scottish merchants became known as Tobacco Lords. They created tobacco trading networks in Virginia and by 1760 Glasgow had overtaken London as the main importer of tobacco. The merchants' enduring influence can be seen in some of the major roads and buildings in Glasgow. Many of the old streets of Glasgow - Buchanan, Glassford, Ingram and Dunlop are named after Tobacco Lords.

Slave traders used the trade to elevate themselves into the upper echelons of society. David and Alexander Barclay, enslavers from Jamaica, for example, married into the banking families of Gurney and ultimately created Barclays Bank.

Fitting out a slave ship for the triangular trade was an expensive and very time-consuming business. Ships could take over a year to return to Britain to realize profits. To afford such voyages, merchants needed money to cover their initial costs. The Bank of England made capital available for slave voyages as the City of London became the financial centre of the slave trade. Slavers also needed to ensure their cargos, Lloyds of London became formative during that era, by ensuring slave and merchant ships. Barclays Bank began investing directly in the slave trade. In 1762, Francis Baring, another slaver, founded Barings Bank. Thomas Leyland, also another slave trader, became a partner in one of Liverpool's oldest banks in 1802, and after multiple series of takeovers, Leyland Bank eventually became HSBC. So on it went—and as you can see, it would be rather difficult if not impossible to capture the true quantifiable intergenerational economic value of slavery. The enormity, exponential and transformative dynamics of the entire apparatuses of the slave economy brought European people and government together for the sheer pursuit of wealth and power, with the extension of privilege over Black people through the engineering of white supremacy.

Development and the Reinforcement of Neocolonialism

The wealth and power accumulated under colonialism transcendently enriched the Western world while under-developing the colonies and putting up barriers for them. In the post-independence era, Western nations switched to the *"development"* of the *"less developed countries"* as a recalibrated tool and narrative, but it was essential for maintaining white supremacy culture and power throughout the world. For the rest of this chapter, we will be concerned with the analysis of intervention to demonstrate the disingenuous nature of the "development" discourse.

IN THE MODERN ERA, socioeconomic cultural dominance by Western capitalist systems has remained steadfast; Western nations that fund and control institutions like the World Bank maintain all of the power. These types of organizations backed by Western funding nations have promoted Western ideals of modernization and liberalism as the path to development for those classified as *underdeveloped*. However, there has been no revelation or acknowledgement of how these nation-states became underdeveloped in the first place. Colonialism and its enduring legacy destroyed Black societies and prevented them from future organic growth. Therefore, it is not logical to conclude that you can take liberal economic ideals and simply apply them to Caribbean states, and like magic, they will work. The fundamental and dynamic conditions for liberal-led growth are starkly different for developed versus underdeveloped. There is no way around historical economic facts and events that shape different civilizations, the variables and differences are paramount to the understanding of white supremacy.

The imposing of "development" in a non-inclusive top-down way makes development interventions doomed from the start. The development machine has become an industry all to itself, both Black

342

and White people have created livelihoods on "development" discourse. This is a class of development professionals...Western experts, technicians, and advisors, all make handsome livings promoting something that does not work. In the real world, if companies or organizations continuously fail, they go out of business but in the domain of "development" discourse failure means success, because they get to get paid to fix the mistakes, including the ones they created in the first place. This is a racket! The bureaucracy of development gets paid to fail, not to succeed. Failure creates more work and more salaries for advisors.

As AN EXAMPLE, the 1980's Latin American debt crisis revealed the true motives behind those institutions, particularly the World Bank and the IMF. Their advertised role was to ensure order and prosperity for economic and financial systems around the world, but they are only really there to maintain Western capitalist interests through the support of the Western banking system. For example, the case of Brazil and the debt crisis in the 1980s was a prime example of the latter. The IMF and World Bank functioned as supportive of the Western banking system during that crisis and not as the honest brokers that they publicly portrayed themselves to be.

To provide some brief background: from 1974 to 1985, Brazil engaged in an ISI (Industrial Substitution Industrialization) growth strategy. This period was highlighted by the import substitution of basic inputs and capital goods, to expand the supply of domestic manufactured goods. ISI was seen by Brazil at the time (pushed by academics of course) as a path to rapid industrialization. It had a big population and domestic economy, so the ISI strategy seemed like a good idea at the time. However, the price for that growth would come with huge borrowing from Western banks – massive amounts of sovereign debt to foreign private bank creditors began to pile up.

343

With relatively 'cheap' and available US dollars, coupled with stable interest rates created the optimal US dollar lending environment for Brazil and other Latin American countries at the time. However, going into the 1980s things began to change.

First, the U.S. Federal Reserve decided to combat inflation by using its monetary tool of raising interest rates. Higher interest rates now meant it was more costly for Brazil to service the rising debt load, and to add to the misery, rising interest rates began creating greater demand for US dollar-denominated debt instruments. This rapidly elevated the value of the U.S. dollar—up 44% over a very short period. Brazil now had to find more money in its economy to service its quickly rising debt and also had to convert Brazilian dollars back to US dollars to pay, which it had previously converted to invest in its ISI growth strategy. What a mess! In short, the combination of higher US interest rates, coupled with a significant rise in the value of the U.S. dollar, meant a full-blown debt crisis was set upon Brazil and other Latin American countries.

External agencies, the World Bank, and IMF, which were run out of Washington DC, began to intervene to manage the Brazilian debt crisis…posing as the honest brokers. The IMF was said to have been brought in to manage an orderly process to get Brazil back to economic equilibrium, however, as time went on, it became increasingly clear that the IMF/World Bank was there to represent the interests of the foreign private banks. The failure of Western banks, they believed, would hurt the U.S. and other Western economies greatly. This was their main concern, and they could not let that happen—in the language of a later era, these institutions were "too big to fail."

The IMF/World Bank was essentially there to ensure global monetary stability. The Western private banks which loaned billions in sovereign debt to these developing countries broke all the norms of lending. But because it was sovereign debt, the private banks knew that their Western governments would not let their banking system fail back home. They were right. The IMF intervened to ensure the solvency of the global banking system so that those private banks could continue to operate. What that meant for countries like Brazil was that they continued to receive loans and would have to adhere to strict IMF-imposed austerity measures. Brazil had to curb its domestic spending sharply and begin to raise taxes. Once the IMF twisted their arms and got the austerity process underway, the IMF then gave the private Western banks the all-clear and they turned on the lending taps once again.

The IMF was the guardian of the international monetary system, but it primarily represented the interests of the private banks and their respective governments. This type of environment meant that the World Bank came down on the side of the creditors. It was anything but fair to Brazil and its economy and people. Brazil continued to drown in debt servicing and did not have much monetary policy flexibility with the IMF pushing austerity and trade liberalization down its throat.

The Brady Plan was then implemented in 1989; it was a debt securitization plan to secure private bank lenders. The Brady Bonds, as they would be called, were essentially sovereign debt securities denominated in U.S. dollars, issued by developing countries and backed by U.S. Treasury bonds. In other words, the U.S. created and secured tradable debt securities to ensure liquidity and confidence in these private banks.

"The very existence of the World Bank is based on the realist assumption that there is a common interest between the developed and the developing countries. The debt crisis, however, was defined by conflict of interests between the debtor and the creditor countries." (Pereira, pg. 121)

IN ANOTHER EPISODE, World Bank intervention in the form of "projects" is another example of the adverse effects of "development." In his ground-breaking book *The Anti-Politics Machine*, author James Ferguson explains that the primary motive of the World Bank is to foster new markets for developing countries through development intervention. Ferguson used the joint World Bank/CIDA project in the Thaba-Tseka area of Lesotho as one of many examples to illustrate his point.

The Canadian government had an interest in promoting rural development in Lesotho because it would help Canadian corporations find export markets for farm machinery and other related equipment. Canada's objective interest as an actor in the system was tied to its political economy and self-interest. The World Bank presents a narrative of helping people, helping poor, small farmers, and women farmers; however, in the case of CIDA and the Thaba-Tseka project, CIDA/WB catered to the large, highly capitalized farmers at the expense of the poorer, more vulnerable ones. This was primarily because smaller, more rural farmers could not afford the pricey farm machines and related equipment that Canadian companies were selling; nor could they afford to hire "farming experts," technical advisors, or consultants.

In short, the Thaba-Tseka project was an unremitting failure, and in typical fashion, WB/CIDA development intervention produced no good results and created unintended negative "side-effects" for the local populations. No consultation with local populations ever took place; instead, top-down implantation based on liberal Western ideals and agendas was implemented. The planners of CIDA/WB in Lesotho never interacted or accepted input from local knowledge-holders, so nothing worked out; indeed, more errors and problems were created. The arrogance of the West created ignorance toward the project, and unforeseen effects of bad development intervention and policies plagued the project from the start. The attempt to engineer economic transformation became incoherent.

346

The lack of a basic understanding of the history of colonialism and the imbalances it created, more specifically, not understanding the economic activity and flow of the southern region of Africa made circumstances worse. The World Bank wrongly assumed that Lesotho was a "subsistence" economy, but the economy was a producer of cash crops for the South African market mainly, not a traditional peasant society, as the World Bank experts in the atmosphere and ignorance of white supremacy culture wrongly concluded. The assumption was made that Lesotho was isolated, untouched by any modern economic activity. Ferguson points out that the "scholarly" work used by the World Bank to draw those assumptions was laughable: "The World Bank Report is simply an error, the sign of gross ignorance or incompetent scholarship."

A review of the World Bank Country Report on Lesotho also shows biases and made-up justifications for project intervention through "staggeringly bad scholarship," as described by Ferguson. Colonialism as described earlier is a purposeful and organized system of wealth extraction and political control; therefore, like most colonies at independence, there was no naturally occurring economic infrastructure to speak of. By 1966, Lesotho's economic activity was primarily linked to the southern African regional economy—60% of Lesotho's male labour force worked in South Africa. This is, of course, a significant economic factor that should have been incorporated into the World Bank Country Report analysis; but it was not. The entire process and assumptions were wrong.

The result was a failure that had unintended negative consequences for the people of Lesotho; it was they who mainly paid the price for these errors. The Lesotho development intervention experience demonstrates the constraints on effective development—the hypocrisy, the systemic environment, and the prioritization of the power players' interests over the interests of the vulnerable. The "strings-attached" development models are reflective of the wider Western growth agenda under the guise of development.

The development discourse and professional "development" industry underpinned by the institutional monster of the World Bank and the IMF, embedded in white supremacy culture, supportive of the global banking and capitalist system, is what "development" is all about!

A FINAL EXAMPLE is the Inter-American Development Bank (IDB), packed with advisors and bureaucrats who command Caribbean economies and run Caribbean economies right into the ground with failed top-down development approaches. The IDB recently issued another "call for proposals" in November 2022. So let us take a look at a very recent project of theirs:

REQUEST FOR EXPRESSIONS OF INTEREST
CONSULTING SERVICES

Selection # as assigned by e-Tool: RG-T4017-P001
Selection Method: Fully Competitive
Country: International
Sector: Integration and Trade
Funding – TC #: RG-T4017
Project #: ATN/CO-19236-RG
TC name: SUPPORT TO ECONOMIC RECOVERY IN THE CARIBBEAN THROUGH TRADE AND INVESTMENT IN BLUE ECONOMY
Description of Services: Design a Blue Economy Investment Promotion Strategy and Action Plan for selected OECS countries and provide ad-hoc capacity building in blue economy investment attraction to investment officers.

Link to TC document: https://www.iadb.org/en/project/RG-T4017

The first thing that needs to be pointed out is the top-down command approach, where academics rather than entrepreneurs are the ones identifying problems—solving them not with entrepreneurship, but with "consultants" writing useless reports. What we need instead are direct entrepreneurship activities funded directly by the IDB. The entire consulting industry is a racket, and the

348

consultant-IDB relationship is corrupt. The IDB officials keep devising academic development ideas to justify their existence; they feed the consultants who get large contracts to write meaningless reports, and the gravy train keeps rolling for those two groups. Meanwhile, the Black people of the Caribbean keep suffering.

In Point #1 of the "Background and Justification" section above, IDB mentions how "Foreign Direct Investment (FDI) helps economic growth." However, their approach is not to find FDI for local entrepreneurs and businesspeople to fund their good ideas and digital transformation. Instead, they paternalistically take it upon themselves to decide which economic problems are important, then frame and classify it for us, commanding us as to what to do and how to do it. This, of course, goes against everything we know about entrepreneurship and business-leading growth. Institutions and agencies can direct growth, but the "bank" side of it can invest directly in it—not with loans but with venture and private equity capital. Why should what happens in the rest of the world not also happen in the Caribbean? As the "Description of Services" section of the announcement says, IDB wants to "Design a Blue Economy Investment Promotion Strategy and Action Plan for selected OECS countries"— in other words, with those countries with which they have cozy relationships, as well as those who do not object to the corrupt nature of these relationships. The description goes on to say that it wants to "provide ad-hoc capacity building in blue economy investment attraction to investment officers." Again, nothing goes into the hands of young entrepreneurs and business people; instead, funding goes into the hands of the institution's "investment officers."

The "Blue Economy (BE) Strategies" talk about "economic structuring" to "build resiliency" as if they have a magic hand or some type of mechanism to fix these regional economies. They even bluntly say, "Setting the policy and institutional frameworks for the BE sectors to operate is crucial." All of this is more of the same meaningless nonsense; nothing ever happens. The real world pursues growth through entrepreneurs; capital invests in them because they get things done!

Caribbean economies keep suffering while consultants and IDB employees continue to benefit financially. At the same time, institutions like the IDB force local governments to comply with these bogus projects that are not in their nations' socioeconomic interests by holding capital over their heads. The entire process is humiliating and harmful; it also creates significant imbalances in these economies and builds more acute problems and suffering into them. These interventions must stop!

IN THE FINAL ANALYSIS, the Western-dominated development discourse is controlled by the systemic environment: structures, constructs, organizations, institutions, and programs. The system is rigged against the ones it says it seeks to help. The Caribbean must understand the systemic realities it faces. Only then can we create a game plan to advance within that systemic environment; survival requires adaptation! Again, knowing how the universe works will help to avoid distractions, frustrations, and disappointment so that we can get things done. We must get away from the notion of *equality*; there has never been an equal society anywhere in the universe. Everyone must play the cards they have been dealt; that is the way the world works. Black populations can no longer live in fantasy about changing the hearts and minds of Western nations. Racism cannot be eradicated by changing hearts and minds. Adaptation to the systemic environment, strategically and with self-interest top of mind, is central to improving prosperity outcomes. The history of civilization teaches us that economics and entrepreneurship, creativity and innovation, endurance and the resilience of the human spirit are the best ways to face challenges, break boundaries, and reimagine the future.

Riding the global wealth curve requires entrepreneurial leadership. Prosperity is not a right; it must be created. Dependency is a state of mind, so change your mindset and you will change the reality of your existence. The constant veranda complaining is wasted energy. It is time to get off of the veranda and compete in the real world, taking personal responsibility for self, family, and community. Your prosperity must become normalized, and the victim mentality must end; antifragility must prevail. Realism is the conscious realization of what the universe simply is, not fantasies about what you wish it to be. Remember that we cannot change nature. Our universe is based on scarcity, conflict, and power! A powerful identity awaits those with courage, perseverance, and imagination, and those with a willingness to embrace lifelong learning and self-improvement.

Chapter 12

Do Not Blame China

China represents one of the greatest threats to the future of the Caribbean. China is on a mission to become a geopolitical superpower. With its massive population, technology, ambitions, and state-controlled economy, China is an undeniable force with which to reckon on the world stage. China is embedded in global financial markets with great influence and is the number one holder of U.S. sovereign debt in the world. A quick search on Bloomberg of Western firms like Morgan Stanley and Goldman Sachs clear U.S. dollar payments in Hong Kong annually; last year, it reached record levels of $11 trillion. Hong Kong is an international financial hub that remains firmly under Chinese control.

China's attitude is one of ruthless domination of the factors of production, and its government believes that this century belongs to them. In China's eyes, this is simply a restructuring of the global geopolitical power structure away from white supremacy. It also represents another power shift in the global capitalist system. China's method is hyper-state-driven capitalism—but upon closer inspection, it is little different than what past imperialist colonizers did for many centuries. China is no better or worse than any other global power; they merely happen to be succeeding at the moment. Nevertheless, where the Caribbean is concerned, it had better keep its eyes wide open and understand the geopolitical power climate and China's ambitions and determine how best to deal with China.

China alone accounts for 18% of the world GDP, a country where technology is utilized significantly as a tool for global economic expansion. Huawei, for example, leads the race for 5G conversion with a share of more than 15.39% of global markets, and we know Huawei is a *de facto* "state-owned" enterprise, so all Chinese companies are closely tied to the geopolitical ambitions of the Chinese government. The sheer audacity of Beijing's plan to roll out the 5G system in particular and next-generation wireless technology in general is globally significant.

Therefore, the Chinese neo-colonization 2.0 happening in the Caribbean region now is a massive existential threat to Caribbean nation-states—to the very existence of the region, its culture, and its way of life. History repeats itself, especially for those who do not pay close attention. George Bernard Shaw once said, "If history repeats itself, and the unexpected always happens, how incapable must Man be of learning from experience." Chinese neo-colonialism 2.0 is already underway in Africa and the Caribbean.

The British dominated the first two industrial revolutions by using its colonies in the Caribbean to supply raw materials, then sending them back to Britain for processing and manufacturing, trade, and commerce. The wealth created from that process was what built the British Empire. China has similar ambitions, with a similar playbook—and once again, Africa and the Caribbean will be used to create wealth for others.

There are tens of millions of Chinese strategically placed around the world. In many cases, these Chinese are housed in huge barrack-style dorms in many countries in Africa and the Caribbean. China is a major power in the global economy, and its tactics and lack of shame make it a particularly difficult challenge to tackle. An economic engine with huge geopolitical ambitions, China has its eyes set on the Caribbean—strategically located right between North and South America—as an asset in its plans for economic and geopolitical expansion in the Western world.

Caribbean states must have a specific strategy for economic growth, which necessarily includes how to deal effectively with China—and that strategy cannot consist of simply standing still,

353

frozen in fear, allowing China to ride roughshod all over us. Instead, we must understand that what China is doing—conquering and colonizing territory—is entirely normal in history. So we must not be amazed; rather, we must inform ourselves about how to protect our national interests, playing our cards correctly and ascertaining how we can emerge victorious and prosperous in the end. China is asserting itself in the hyper-globalized and capitalist economy, and that is precisely the way the world functions. China is taking what it believes to be its rightful place in the universe, and why should it not? It is also offsetting centuries of Western white dominance. China is rising, which is the nature of things. However, Black populations of the Caribbean should understand how the universe unfolds and develop our playbook to make our economic ambitions into reality.

We as a people are not helpless; our fate is not predetermined, so we must stop constantly behaving like victims and play some offense for a change. We must begin to be more cerebral, to think critically, and to apply intelligence and technology to assist us in achieving our economic goals. We live in a globalized world now, and globalization within the capitalist system will only intensify. So just as China has devised a strategy to pursue its ambitions, why can we not do the same? Why do we always be fragile? Why can we not set goals for our growth and power and work towards it? Are we immune to self-reliance? We cannot continue to beg governments like China's to give us money and then cry about how they are dominating us.

The fact is that Caribbean leadership has failed to secure long-term economic security and prosperity for its people. Further, in this transformational and defining decade, failing to transform the region's economies will only seal its fate, and the continued subjugation of Caribbean peoples will remain the greatest probability. Other past colonies have managed to fare better and do extraordinarily well. The "Asian Tigers," (the Four Asian Tigers are the developed East Asian economies of Hong Kong, Singapore,

South Korea, and Taiwan. Between the early 1960s and 1990s, they underwent rapid industrialization and maintained exceptionally high growth rates of more than 7 percent a year.) Singapore particularly has been able to organize and execute their economic ambitions most exceptionally, to rise as one of the richest countries in the world. So why can we not aspire and work to achieve similar? What excuse do we have this time?

The region can certainly benefit from trading with China, and indeed it must; foreign investment is something every country needs, and China has plenty of capital. However, how a nation deals with China on the investment front is central to getting positive outcomes from the relationship. We can benefit from Chinese investments greatly, but those investments must be aligned with a specific and articulated economic growth strategy, laid out in the national and regional interests. The strategy must be devised in the context of digital transformation over this decade. It must be intelligence-based, transparent, measurable, and accountable to the people. Anything else is purely a waste of time and will fail miserably.

The Chinese Belt and Road Initiative (BRI) is a clear example of Chinese activity and geopolitical strategy, where poor countries are being lured in by sweet loan arrangements, but the bitterness will come later. Countries in Southeast Asia, Africa, and Latin America have already experienced the Chinese strategic debt trap playbook, and Caribbean leaders continue to jump headfirst into this poisonous trap.

Slavery and colonialism fueled European economic expansion; Chinese colonialism 2.0 will do the same, only in a more sophisticated manner. Raw materials such as aluminum, steel, and various minerals and agricultural commodities are all needed to fuel the Chinese domestic economy, enabling it to dominate global exports. Like the European colonizers, China extracts vast resources and sends them back to Chinese factories for processing, manufacturing, trade, and commerce. Then it sells cheap, low-quality goods right back to African and Caribbean countries.

An article in the magazine New African, **"*Viewpoint: Why we should be aware of China's new colonialism"*** by African businessman Benedict Peters argues that "we are now slowly awakening to the growing menace of China's plans for economic supremacy. In Africa, it is clear that China's campaign of foreign investment is a new form of colonialism."

In the article "Belt and Road: Colonialism with Chinese Characteristics," author Anthony Kleven points out: "While China's tens of billions of investments and loans are greedily gobbled up by cash-starved African states, they are not as bereft of strings as is often claimed. The BRI is trapping numerous countries in unsustainable levels of debt." For example, China has set its sights on Guinea's bauxite reserves, which are among the world's largest. China needs such a vast resource to keep its aluminum industry running profitably. China provided Guinea with loans twice the size of its GDP, and so they are now unable to service the resulting debt. An abundance of related Chinese companies has now taken control of Guinea's bauxite reserves as payment in lieu of cash. This, of course, is an abundantly better return for China in the long term, because control of natural resources has a significant multiplier effect on the Chinese economy and Chinese wealth, while the Guinean economy and people suffer in poverty, unable to capitalize on their vast natural resource in order to create any wealth for their population. Yet whose fault is that? Corruption and mismanagement by Guineau's leaders allow for the nation to be played and exploited. This is the nature of our conflict-driven world; what do we expect to happen?

The types of outcomes described above have everything to do with leadership, bad decision-making, selfishness, greed and corruption, and plain stupidity on the part of Black leadership! In the Caribbean as elsewhere, people must be honest with themselves. Politicians will never change, so it is up to us, the people, to take control of our situation and flip this miserable script—begin to write our own stories. We cannot blame China; in truth, we are doing it to ourselves.

THE DEBT TRAP can be summarized as follows: China lends desperately poor countries millions and billions for investment in infrastructure-type loans, knowing perfectly well that the borrowers are incapable of paying back. Deals often stipulate predatory terms and conditions that include penalties for failure to repay, allowing China, contractually, to seize vital public infrastructure assets as collateral if those set terms are not upheld.

Let us examine a few examples.

A recent article titled ***"China's Opaque Caribbean Trail: Dreams, Deal, and Debt"*** by the Caribbean Investigative Journal Network (CIJN) is filled with examples of the Chinese debt trap strategy. One of the most visible, expansive, and expensive ways in which Beijing engages with Caribbean countries is through its financing of large-scale infrastructure projects. The CIJN investigation unveiled a trail of official secrets, questionable procurement processes, and the always-looming threat of potentially insurmountable debt. The Chinese playbook is the same everywhere: huge, impractical, and unnecessary hotel projects, highways, agriculture projects—even building a Prime Minister's fancy new house. According to CIJN, "China's Caribbean portfolio is extensive. It
includes highways and bridges, housing, energy, mining, air and seaports, tourism projects, hospitals, and even official residences, forming a part of that country's strategic thrust into Latin American and the Caribbean."

357

The investigating team discovered that in most cases, the precise terms of agreements are not routinely publicized, and the procurement processes and concessions are a mystery. The Chinese often end up with all of the labour contracts, and their labour practices lack adherence to any type of building code or other health and safety standards.

In another example, a VICE documentary on YouTube titled *"Undercover In Guyana: Exposing Chinese Business in South America."* The documentary shows how China's growing presence in South America has reached Guyana, and how VICE's undercover operation exposed the significant corruption in deals between the two countries. This video is certainly worth watching.

A 2012 independent forensic audit of the Jamaica Development Infrastructure Programme (JDIP) and the Palisadoes Shoreline Protection and Rehabilitation Works Project concluded that there was non-adherence to allocations approved by Jamaica's Parliament and the Ministry of Finance. The audit also uncovered the arbitrary issuance of Variation Orders and selection of sub-contractors, along with the unprogrammed and arbitrary allocation of funds for institutional strengthening in Clause 13.3 of the contract (a $630 million North-South Highway project signed with the China Harbour Engineering Corporation [CHEC] on June 21, 2012): "The Government shall unconditionally and irrevocably waive any right of immunity (to the fullest extent permitted by applicable law) which it or any of its assets now has or may acquire in the future in any jurisdiction."

To add insult to injury, a case study conducted by the Caribbean Development Bank (CDB) found that there was "no way costs could be recouped through toll payments." China then argued that since the cost of the investment could not be recouped through toll payments, land adjacent to the highway should be turned over as compensation. Jamaica, of course, had already agreed to those terms in a previous contract clause. China predictably enforced it, and the

Chinese company promptly brought in more than 1,000 Chinese workers to begin work on a commercial project. The result was free land for China, no Jamaican worker participation, no contracts for Jamaican firms, and no economic benefit to Jamaica. This type of scenario has a significantly better multiplier effect on China than a low-interest rate return. These moves produce employment for Chinese workers; Chinese real estate properties are being built on free Jamaican land; and new Chinese landlords are now entrenched in the Jamaican economy with no cost basis for land assets. It puts the Chinese in a massively advantageous position with respect to Black Jamaican land and real estate owners and developers as well as other entrepreneurs; it is Colonialism 2.0. Again, we cannot blame China when our own stupidity created the situation.

In practical terms, the precedent set is that the Jamaican state has allowed China, in a case of sham breach of contracts by the Government of Jamaica (GoJ) or actions that the Chinese have themselves determined result in non-performance, would now be actionable against Jamaica. When contextualized, the clause essentially requires the GoJ to forfeit any current or future owned assets to China for debt recovery via seizure. It is a blatant encroachment on Jamaican national sovereignty.

"New roads, new businesses, new hotels, and booming Chinese immigration have led to many companies being staffed with more Chinese workers than local Bahamians." —Forbes

In Trinidad and Tobago, the sudden termination of the Government's $71.7 million projects between China's Gezhouba Group International Engineering Company and the Housing Development Corporation (HDC) in 2019 has also drawn attention to a lack of transparency in the awarding of the contract—what has been described as overly generous concessions to a Chinese company.

In Suriname, there are rising fears that mounting debt to China, spanning decades, risks stalling future development and exposing the country to liabilities far beyond its ability to pay. Nevertheless, it is not China's responsibility to look after our interests; that is the responsibility of Caribbean leadership. The highly skilled Chinese negotiators need to be matched with equally skilled negotiators on our side—not greedy, desperate, and inept politicians trying to enrich themselves through public office.

China's engagement in the region does not necessarily have to be a negative; it can be a major positive for growth. That, however, depends on how the region plays its hand. Understanding the historical colonialism playbook of foreign powers and developing our own countervailing strategies is essential to winning. Being proactive rather than reactive and setting economic and other strategic objectives for our nations is the key to bringing about eventual positive outcomes. Remember, China needs to forge and maintain global relationships in order to expand. So the Caribbean has something to offer, and we must make it our very nature to focus on obtaining the best business deals for ourselves, first and foremost.

What these local politicians fail to understand is that China is fundamentally an investor; so ultimately, the most critical consideration is what Caribbean leaders can negotiate successfully with them. The Chinese are involved in the region for a reason: they see an opportunity that is aligned with their long-term strategic goals, and so they need the Caribbean to help execute their overall ambitions. Therefore, China is practical, and it will do whatever it can get away with doing—i.e., whatever local leaders and stakeholders let it get away with doing. If the latter continue to hand over their people's natural resources and other national assets, then China will smartly seize those assets and take over, as part of its geopolitical objectives. Neither China nor the rest of the world has any moral obligation to the Caribbean region in their economic and political dealings. We exist in a conflict-driven universe with scarce resources;

this is what one is supposed to do. If we do not understand that reality, then extinction is in our future.

The nature of the universe shows us that it is impractical to believe that any actor would or should behave differently. So do not blame China, for it is simply another actor in history doing what it is supposed to do. Remember, the sophistication and extension of self-preservation is entrepreneurship and conquest. This is about winning, nothing else, and Caribbean leaders must first understand the game before the play, or they will be slaughtered!

ASSETS BELONGING TO THE PUBLIC, to the people, are being offered by unintelligent and corrupt politicians as collateralized property in business deals with China. This is beyond the pale—egregious, anti-democratic, anti-patriotic, illegal, and moronic in epic proportion! Sovereignty represents a state's most precious right and freedom under international law. It is rooted in basic humanitarian principles and the essential concept of human dignity. Nonetheless, it is happening in the Caribbean right now. According to attorney and chartered accountant Christopher Ram, in Guyana, for example, Article 8.1 of one project contract, signed January 9, 2017, shows how fragile Caribbean nations' sovereignty has become: "The borrower hereby irrevocably waives any immunity on the grounds of sovereignty or otherwise for itself or its property in connection with any arbitration proceeding…or with the enforcement of any arbitral award pursuant thereto." Ram say that "this is Guyana dangerously agreeing to cede sovereignty. It plays into the Chinese strategy of using economic weaponry in the pursuit of influence and domination." In short, these governments have "signed away their nation's sovereignty, dignity, and basic self-respect to China. China could simply walk in and take control of Guyana's assets through its preset debt trap," says Christopher Ram.

In July 2020, an appellate court in Kenya halted a construction deal by simply pronouncing that the $3.2 billion contract between Kenya and China for the construction of the Standard Gauge Railways (SGR) was illegal! The judgment effectively lifted the lid on the "dragon's debt-trap diplomacy." China had been pressuring Kenya to pay the huge debt, even while in the middle of battling the COVID-19 pandemic.

This came to a head because, since 2013, Kenya has saddled itself with more than $5 billion in loans from China for the project. However, in its very first year of operation, the project reported losses of about US$98 million, making servicing the debt impossible. And of course, the terms of the deal made it such that if Kenya could not repay, it could end up giving China control over some of its most important assets. In this case, it would have been Mombasa Port, Kenya's largest and most valuable port—the gateway to Kenya and the landlocked neighbouring nations of Burundi, Congo, Rwanda, South Sudan, and Uganda. Therefore, it is easy to see how losing control over the vital port would mean erosion of Kenya's sovereignty. The implications are frightening; thousands of port workers would have been forced to work under its Chinese lenders. Fortunately, Kenya's judicial system saved the day, delivering a wake-up call to all those involved in similar entanglements with China.

CARIBBEAN NATIONS are headed down very similar paths; but I would not trust the Caribbean courts to have the wherewithal to protect their countries from this type of sovereign encroachment. Based on existing information about China's involvement and momentum in the Caribbean, I would estimate that there is a better than 50% chance that Caribbean states, for all intents and purposes, will be essentially owned by China at some point in the next several decades.

COVID-19 has provided us with a pause, an inflection point at which to shift our thinking and strategy to focus on a better future. We cannot remain stuck in the past any longer, betrayed by amateurish, thieving politicians with nothing to offer but stale ideas and desperation. If we stand still, we will perish; we must move in the same direction in which the rest of the world is moving or be left tragically behind yet again. We cannot afford another 100 years of misery and despair. Extinction is next. Like Africa, the Caribbean desperately needs Foreign Direct Investment (FDI) to develop its economy in order to transition into the digital age. However, the specifics of every deal and financial structure must be transparent to the public. Furthermore, the basic economics supporting each investment must be presented ahead of time, including performance-based metrics, data sources supporting the investment case, critical data-driven analysis, specific modelling, and advanced predictive decision-making algorithms. Most importantly, deals must be inclusive of the broader population, and deals must always pass the common-sense *"What is in it for us?"* smell test. A digital transformation agenda can help us turn the tables—help underwrite a future of prosperity. Resources must be mobilized in triple-time, with the stated objective of catapulting the regional economy onto the path to joining a prosperous global economy. Ambitions must be focused, and we must think ambitiously; we cannot afford to sit idly by and remain spectators, watching ourselves become extinct.

A real strategy is required, a fundamental change in mindset and approach, rooted in the underlying variables of the new economy, driven by the goal of achieving Caribbean-centric growth. The Caribbean needs a new common Investment Policy Statement: a new operating paradigm, one that is progressive and inclusive, and with a drive toward sustainable socio-economic development. Politicians should no longer be placed in charge of investment decisions; instead, a professional, data-and-applied-intelligence-driven, performance-based, team-oriented approach to execution is the correct move. A common 21ˢᵗ-century socioeconomic vision, specific to the digital revolution, must be our targeted transition growth strategy. It must be about entrepreneurship and sustainable bottom-up approaches that are results-oriented. Scientific ecosystems, coupled with highly qualified investment committees who work with real information and are accountable to the people, is the push! The process must be driven by intelligent, scientific data-based decision-making and predictable modelling, powered by data, artificial intelligence, and machine learning. It must be followed up with fearless actions and implementation, transparent and measurable. We know that the best ideas are the ones that are supported by real information and are improved through an iterative process.

The *applied intelligence* process identifies and determines the correct problems to solve. It defines solutions based on evidence and selects the right technological applications to solve them. This involves filtering ideas down to the optimal potential for success, using computational, quantitative, and qualitative measures to evaluate growth outcomes for business ideas through rigorous testing. This is inherently a bottom-up process that uses data for effective decision-making, enabling leaders to be confident in those decisions. This new paradigm includes an advanced level of due diligence, all of which must be brought to the forefront of the investment decision-making process. This is necessary to examine potential opportunities based on their merit, particularly their identified and quantified exponential growth function. All of these measures must be made to fit within a developed and transparent Investment Policy Statement. This requires ***applied intelligence***!

Therefore, knowledge and technology underwritten by capital is the way forward—the tried, tested, and true pathway to prosperity through self-reliance, building a resilient economy, and achieving authentic happiness. We cannot blame China if we fail to learn and execute.

364

Chapter 13

The Power Transition

Many of the world's economies today are consumed by the necessity of digital transformation—and rightly so, for the new economic era is the most consequential socioeconomic transition period of our lifetime. In addition, the COVID-19 pandemic has created an opportunity to shift our strategic thinking and focus toward a better and more resilient economic future. At the same time, however, we cannot lose sight of the other critical transition taking place in parallel: the transition from fossil fuels to renewable energy production. This shift is creating transformational geopolitical energy dynamics, so Small Island States (SIS) must become cognizant of the shifting power dynamics taking place in the world and figure out how best to position themselves to gain from it.

"Energy is fundamental to our civilization and the prosperity of nations. Its production, distribution, and utilization are deeply embedded in the fabric of our economies and central to the relations between states."

–Adnan Z. Amin, Director-General of IRENA

The International Renewable Energy Agency is an intergovernmental organization mandated to facilitate cooperation, advance knowledge, and promote the adoption and sustainable use of renewable energy.

The growing deployment of renewables has been set in motion, which will fundamentally change the global energy power complex. Canada, for example, in its own "Build-Back-Better" strategy, is now setting economic policy based on transitioning to a green economy. In the U.S., NextEra, a clean-power utility, has surpassed ExxonMobil to become America's biggest energy firm. While the index of American energy companies has declined by an average of 47%, NextEra has jumped by 112%, more than the broad S&P 500 index. In the past four years, venture capital (VC) deals have more than doubled in this space, and governments like Norway have been using their oil revenues to build a future based on a zero-emissions economy. Saudi Arabia, while it continues to sell its oil to the world, has embarked on an ambitious long-term strategy for a clean energy existence. They know oil is not a long-term solution because of its incompatibility with the natural environment, and humankind needs the natural environment for our survival.

According to The Economist magazine, U.S. President Joe Biden wants to spend $2 trillion to build an American green economy. The European Union has earmarked 30% of its US$880 billion COVID recovery plan for climate measures, and the president of the European Commission, Ursula von der Leyen, used her recent state-of-the-union address to confirm that she wants the EU to cut greenhouse-gas emissions by 55% in the next decade.

So where are the CARICOM Community's bold plans? How is it going to transition to the green economy? Based on geography, sunlight is an abundant free resource for the Caribbean region; it receives hours of daylight to generate significant amounts of energy. Furthermore, with battery technology improving, storage is another significant opportunity. Imagine the energy independence and the financial gain for Caribbean societies if they could only coordinate proper enterprising strategies and get something meaningful done for a change. These types of opportunities are currently evolving around the world, and in regions without the natural advantages of geography that the Caribbean enjoys. So why can the region not get our collective act together and do something?

The Caribbean Sea itself is another resource for wind energy generation. Moreover, as island geography would have it, desalination plants in strategic locations around the islands will be necessary to deal with the scarcity of freshwater. At some point, there will be a need to turn seawater into good drinking water, or water for household and industrial use, at least—thus making it necessary to preserve freshwater sources. There is no reason why a zero-emissions-based economy cannot be a reality for the region, no reason at all. Yet stale old politicians in suits, uninspiring, unmotivated, and backward, are holding back real progress. Good, virtuous, visionary, and capable leadership at the helm is what it takes; unfortunately, that remains scarce. SISs have an opportunity to self-sustain
themselves if they can build a long-term investment strategy, and aggressively apply tactics to accelerate build-outs of renewable energy production assets.

Therefore, a serious and comprehensive, holistic, detailed strategy is required! A well-positioned and disciplined approach—relevant to the times, with meaningful investment criteria and goals—is critically needed. Creativity and bold innovation, underwritten with courage, must be combined with both human and artificial intelligence to optimize decision-making for beneficial outputs. We can no longer afford to waste precious time going around in circles with the same old lame talk, with non-plan-based, false agendas led by useless and equally false politicians.

We cannot let history repeat itself and remain as sitting ducks, this time by foreign renewable energy giants like NextEra, who will eventually find their way into the region. Like the fossil fuel energy companies before it, it will monetize our free natural energy resources, such as the sun, and sell them back to us. NextEra shareholders will enrich themselves on the backs of the Caribbean people, and Colonialism 2.0 will be right back in the driver's seat. Essentially, we are allowing others to come in and exploit our free resource, instead of thinking innovatively and entrepreneurially and capitalizing on it ourselves. If we continue to sit on the veranda and do nothing but complain, we are assured of accomplishing nothing but delivering ourselves right back into the hands of Colonialism 2.0. We must get off the veranda! We cannot continue to be suckers, repeatedly! The preverbal doormat for the rest of the world to use and abuse, yet again. At some point...some point...we must realize that enough is enough, find some intestinal fortitude, basic courage and go after the future ourselves because the future surely will not simply come to us.

A RECENT REPORT by the International Renewable Energy Agency (IRENA) reveals how geopolitical dynamics have become a key driver of renewable energy transformation. Those nations that cannot grasp shifting global power politics will become collateral damage and remain dependent and fragile. This means that Caribbean peoples will be perpetually relegated to the bottom rungs of
the global economy and society. We need to create a zero-emissions based economy, primarily to fuel our local economies at dramatically lower costs. This is frankly common sense: if we can run a household, a business, with low or no energy costs associated, then that simply means we have more money left in our pockets. And in the high-inflation era in which we live in today, lowering costs of operations gives us an obvious advantage. Therefore, the evidence indicates, and logic and basic common sense dictate that if the Caribbean wants to see prosperity, it must become a low-energy-cost producer of goods and services. But first, it must build that zero-emissions-based economy by attracting foreign investment,

368

which requires demonstrating a sound growth plan in which investors can make money, and a vibrant entrepreneurial class and openness to the entry of foreign entrepreneurs. There is no way around this; without a detailed long-term strategy in place and capable people to execute it, nothing will happen, which has been the story of the region. In order to change that state of affairs, we must first change our mindset.

Renewable energy is extremely well-suited to be the underlying fuel for long-term, sustainable growth, because cost is always relevant. For SISs especially, renewable energy can underpin magnificent growth outcomes simply by lowering energy costs, leaving more cash in people's hands to spend in their local economies and to make investments. IRENA points out, a mere 25% shift to off-grid renewable energy production and consumption will translate to an estimated annual saving of US$9 billion in fuel costs if all 31 countries in the Caribbean move to a 90% clean energy objective by 2030. Imagine what a $9 billion annual cash injection spread amongst the population would do for GDP growth?

"As Caribbean countries continue to respond to the impacts of COVID-19, they have a once-in-a-lifetime opportunity to 'Recover Better' with sustainable energy to support greater energy resilience and security," says Damilola Ogunbiyi, CEO and Special Representative of the UN Secretary-General for Sustainable Energy for All and Co-Chair of UN-Energy. However, until now, the region's leadership has simply squandered this once-in-a-lifetime opportunity!

The new *Recover Better with Sustainable Energy Guide* the UN Secretary-General for Sustainable Energy puts out, highlights key policies that Caribbean governments should adopt to ensure a successful energy transition in this period, including:

- **Robust policies and institutions in support of renewables and energy efficiency**: To deliver strong growth of renewables and energy efficiency, governments should establish or empower institutions such as regulators and other relevant agencies and ensure that the right frameworks are in place to drive the successful development of renewables and energy efficiency.

- **Shifting electricity sector investments to renewable energy plus storage**: For power generation, new investments in renewables are cheaper than new investments in fossil fuels in all major markets today. By adding storage, Caribbean countries can increase resilience, use homegrown energy, avoid creating future fossil fuel-stranded assets, and reduce the significant negative consequences both to public health and to the fragile ecosystems of the region. With continuing cost reductions, renewables plus storage are now cheaper for many Caribbean countries than conventional fossil fuels, providing reliable power for up to 14 hours a day.

- **Invest in energy efficiency**: Investment in energy efficiency cuts energy costs, creates jobs, and offers the cheapest way to reduce emissions. For instance, cold chains are integral to the tourism and agriculture sector of the Caribbean region. Energy-efficient cold chain systems would not only ensure significant cost savings for businesses but also strengthen food security across a region that is vulnerable to various climate risks.

- **Ease of doing business**: Several activities can be put in place to ensure that investments are made as rapidly as possible, including speedier approval processes and transparent investment policies (price discovery, reverse auctions, etc.) for renewable energy and energy efficiency. Fiscal incentives such as reducing or eliminating import duties and value-added taxes (VAT) for renewable energy equipment and energy-efficient appliances should also be considered.

If we can source energy for free, i.e., from the sun, then why would we continue to pay to import dirty fuel oil? Why would we continue to invest in fossil fuel infrastructure when the world is transitioning away from it? Why would we not look to develop a renewable energy technology infrastructure relevant to the changing economic times?

Investing fundamentally represents an optimistic look toward the future with imagination and vision. So why would reasonable people agree to invest counterintuitively in the past, in fossil fuel energy sources, when these sources will contribute to their territorial extinction over time?

Accordingly, there is no reasonable economic argument, evidence, or otherwise which exists that would hold any sensible nation back from making an aggressive push for a renewable energy transition. Citizens must demand this push from their leaders, or see their nations fall further behind the global wealth curve. However, this cannot be done without a proper practical strategy that includes engaging in global capital markets to find investment.

In 2019, global investors poured a record $36bn into climate-related technology investments, according to Cleantech Group, a research firm. Half the money flowed into North America; so with China encroaching on the sovereignty of nations in the region, it would be wise to think of how to engage the U.S. investment market strategically. The geopolitical and economic competition between China and America could be used to garner U.S. government support for private banks and venture capital investment in the Caribbean. It has been done before, i.e. in Latin America; however, we now have the advantage of experience, which we can use to ensure that we make proper deals so that we will not cheat ourselves out of success. I would guess that the United States would be more than willing to promote development and economic investment partnerships in the Caribbean around renewables in the name of "national security." It would simply need to be framed as a counteroffensive against a rival power that is moving in on its geopolitical territory, the Western Hemisphere. Playing major global powers off against each other in order to achieve geopolitical objectives is nothing new for state actors on the global political chess board. Our only objective must be to capitalize on existing power dynamics and look after our own interests.

The renewable energy transition is already well underway, and technology-related "green jobs" will be a major dimension of that process. Therefore, education and skills training must be aligned with the future of work and must be accelerated over this decade. Economic change can often begin with state-sponsored entrepreneurial policy initiatives, research and development, and the deployment of technologies toward real enterprise creation. Public policymakers and businesspeople must work in concert to develop and promote a zero-emissions economy. The renewable energy business is fundamental to the change and to our future prosperity.

THE PURSUIT of a zero-emissions based economy can spur the growth of entire industries. Consider, for example, the electric vehicle (EV) industry. The average EV has a range of 300 miles or 482 km, with many Tesla models specifically traveling well over 700 km. To put it into perspective, Grenada, for instance, is 12 miles (18km) wide and 21 miles (34km) long and covers a land area of 120 sq. miles (440 sq. km). It is safe to say that any EV would have a significant range around Grenada. So why is an EV-transportation sector not being promoted and developed in the region? The EV sector also happens to be the top-performing index in global stock markets (2021,) so the markets are telling us where the big opportunities are and what they want to invest in. But of course, the region's "brain trust" continues to promote the usual white-elephant hotel projects instead.

It would also seem logical that if governments were to work to attract and facilitate investment in charging stations and related software applications, this would further a knowledge-based economy. In addition, it would make sense to formulate a development policy in which 90% of new vehicles—both personal and commercial—that are imported into the country must be EVs. We would immediately see the beginning of a shift towards renewable energy industry infrastructure development—towards a zero-emissions economy. All the existing fossil-fuel car dealerships on the island would have no choice but to begin the transition toward EVs with their foreign manufacturers following close behind. So it is a question of strategy and policy. Bold policy moves would create new and robust areas of job growth, technology research and development, IT servicing, and, most critically, *entrepreneurship!*

Vehicle owners would then be motivated to install solar panels on their homes (which public policy would help encourage as well) to fuel their EVs free of charge. This change would stimulate increased activity in the home solar installation market and force financial institutions to adopt more responsive and innovative financing practices. The policy should open the region up to new financial technology or "fintech" firms with innovative financing while bypassing traditional banks. All of this is possible through progressive and economically inclusive policymaking. We need to move on from the theories and move into real economic activities to make prosperity in the 21st century a reality for Caribbean peoples.

Almost overnight, the laws of supply and demand would begin to take effect, and we would begin to see the beginning of long-term transformation trends forming for SIS economies. Effective government policy can essentially spearhead long-term economic change and future growth outcomes that can create wealth for nations and be passed down intergenerationally.

Consider the success of the Asian Tigers, where government facilitation policies for entrepreneurship and transformation have proven to be most effective for growth and wealth creation for those countries that made up their minds to focus on winning. The Asian Tigers are a good role model for Caribbean governments to emulate.

Prosperity outcomes begin with how we think; they require creativity, innovation, vision, courage, and the proper application of policy leadership. Technology advancement also requires constant research; Caribbean islands could promote themselves as research centers for tech-based companies and attract their activity. Drawing young brainpower to our shores will boost our intellectual property growth and entrepreneurial environment. Who would not want to work on a Caribbean island? In the age of remote work, this can be a reality if you go after it.

Most universities and colleges in the region do not have real industrial engineering, data science technology, or Masters in Entrepreneurship programs. This must become a priority for Caribbean institutions of higher learning, because without an educated and innovative base, it will be difficult to build a zero-emissions economy. For example, St. George's University (SGU) in Grenada—a for-profit institution owned by a Canadian private equity investor, Atlas Partners—continues to turn healthy profits since the university was purchased in August 2014. SGU needs to give back to the local and regional economy by aligning itself more with Grenada's 21st-century, new-economy growth aspirations, providing research and development for the new economy and digital transformation. In Canada and in other developing nations, domestic students pay considerably lower tuition fees than international students do. In Canada, wealthy international students essentially subsidize domestic students' tuition. In the province of Quebec, for example, students pay the lowest tuition in the country—less than CAD$4,000 per year at last count. This is specifically a result of provincial government policy; charging foreign students high fees allows Quebec schools to charge Quebec students lower tuition. I myself benefited from that practice when I attended McGill

University many years ago. Why can Caribbean policy not be structured similarly, so as to help build a suitably educated workforce in furtherance of a knowledge-based, tech-driven economy?

SGU in Grenada is in an optimal position to implement such a policy, because it attracts wealthy medical school students from all over the world. It is a for-profit university that continues to generate healthy profits. I am not aware whether SGU pays taxes or not, but I would not be surprised if they concocted some excuse not to pay. Nevertheless, they certainly ought to pay taxes like everyone else. They also need to subside local students significantly in their undergraduate programs and develop more programs geared towards the national economic development interests of the region.

We need to get organized and become proactive, innovative, and aggressive in our approaches to engaging legitimate global investors and capital markets development in the region. We must negotiate proper, transparent, and mutually beneficial investment deals. To lure the type of savvy investors that we need in order to transform, we must present a real value proposition, because international investors have many other places to put their money. So we need to be competitive. To compete effectively, we must present compelling opportunities that can create long-term value creation for investors. We must be highly organized and competitive; otherwise, we will fail to attract any credible investors.

Addressing these problems, strategically, tactically, and transparently, with concrete policies and measurable actions, will demonstrate—especially to global investors—that the region is serious about foreign direct investment. We must fully understand the paramount importance of creating an opportunistic and fruitful investment environment for global investors to take us seriously.

We recognize that this shift will not be without execution risk; nothing ever is, but inaction means certain extinction. Complacency and acceptance of the status quo will destroy our common Caribbean society, and the continued acceptance of acute corruption and incompetent leadership simply drives us straight to extinction. We, the people, must demand better from leadership and ourselves. Authentic and qualified leadership is crucial at this critical juncture in time, and serious and highly skilled people who know what they are doing must be brought to the forefront—now!

Investors and entrepreneurs are best at commercializing new ideas, but facilitative government policy plays a key role in that process. The more economic activity is produced, the more likely it will be that global capital markets will notice. Institutional investors always find their way to good financial opportunities anywhere in the world. Nowadays, global pension funds and the like have the mandate to put a meaningful portion of their investment portfolios into climate change mitigation technologies, projects, and investments that impact climate change mitigation. More and more, companies and billionaire-backed funds are eyeing climate-friendly investments in less developed regions around the world. There are great transformative opportunities and billions of investment dollars available, which could leapfrog the region's economy and bend our prosperity curve steeply upwards in our favour. However, without bold-thinking, qualified, skilled, tech-savvy people at the helm, armed with a sound and well-articulated vision, no investors will risk capital in the region.

Improved technologies and methodologies have led to improved efficiency and commercialization over many years. As world populations continue to increase and land becomes scarcer, the ability of SIS to achieve food security and grow export markets is becoming increasingly out of reach. Nevertheless, there still is a pathway to profit for small island farmers through the coupling of renewable energy capacity like solar with AI technologies as an operational engine to drive growth. So small and medium-sized farming and food-producing businesses can utilize technology ecosystems and platforms for more efficient and profitable farming and production ecosystems. AI and data tools are being utilized

376

intelligently all over the world for sales and marketing, for finding new global markets, and for guiding entrepreneur farmers to the more profitable, higher value-added demand side of the business universe.

AI combined with renewable energy becomes a powerful economic growth engine. In short, the inverse relationship between growing revenues exponentially and dramatically driving down costs is good business math for exceptional profit outcomes.

We, the people, must become policy advocates, pushing governments to enlightenment, encouraging transparency, innovation, and entrepreneurship within our society as a cultural norm. We must drive a socioeconomic renaissance! We cannot leave it to others; it is our responsibility to take ownership and take care of ourselves and demand more from our leaders.

We must work with sophistication to dismantle old legacy systems of the past, both mental and physical. We need to engineer our own prosperity, building foundational technological infrastructure to create the winning conditions. The Caribbean as a whole must awaken to a higher state of consciousness, with honesty, putting *applied intelligence* to work for effective economic ecosystem development in support of entrepreneurship-led development, for our sustainable prosperity in the 21st century!

EXAMPLE OF A PRIME BUSINESS OPPORTUNITY BASED ON THE COMPETITIVE ADVANTAGES OF THE REGION

ZEGE Inc. (Zero Emissions Green Economy)
New Eco Homes for Holistic Sustainable Living...

Land, water, energy, materials, interior, landscape integration, clean, vision, innovation, living, transportation...

ZEGE INC., is a constructed business model developed by Douglas Blackwell Enterprise Engineering

Chapter 14

Caribentricity

Emancipate yourselves from mental slavery/
None but ourselves can free our minds.

—Bob Marley

The above quote is profound and enduring. Marley captures the central theme necessary for Black self-determination: **mindset**. In this vein, the book *Mental Slavery* by author Barbara Fletchman Smith provides a critical cultural psychoanalysis of the enduring and complex effects of slavery. She references Black families who have settled in the U.K. to make her point. Her analysis of Caribbean cultures offers insight from a psychoanalytical perspective—how slavery embedded varying degrees of trauma and stress in the Black collective psyche, trauma and stress that persistently lurk in the subconscious mind. So while whites passed down wealth intergenerationally to their descendants, Blacks passed down the trauma of historical subjugation and discrimination, the legacy of which still plays a role in limiting their mental existence and performance in the present. Trauma, Fletchman Smith says, is passed down like a genetic trait, influencing how Black individuals relate to themselves and to others and how they perceive the world and behave in it. It narrows their expectations of themselves.

In the present, we must consciously address this "passed-down" trauma, which in this generation has become learned behaviour. We must consciously acknowledge the traumas, intellectually deal with them, and get past them. This is absolutely indispensable to moving forward mentally. Smith's incisive analysis demonstrates how looking back beneath the surface of the past to gain clarity about our present can meaningfully help us navigate into the future. Mindset is the most important thing; it sets the direction of our thinking and actions.

Smith points out, "[...] [S]ome people not only survived, but have thrived despite the passed-down experience of slavery. Others have not been so fortunate." Therefore, how one thinks is critical to how one behaves, and the outcomes that come from that behaviour.

THE FIRST STEP is to understand the systematic environment and formulate your approach to reality, establish clear objectives, and know your opponents and their tactics. Smith says:

> White supremacy exists on the European man's certainty of his 'rationality'. This self-assurance dates back to the eighteenth century, a time at which the dominant European culture became strongly identified with 'rationality,' considered the best quality bequeathed by fifth imperial Athens. Irrationality, on the other hand, was consigned to "the other"—those on the margins of society or outside it. The contribution of psychoanalysis to this state of affairs has been a systematic description and problematization of this "splitting." It has brought back to us the Euripidean possibility of the rational alongside the irrational, the uncivilized within the civilized.

Smith provides insight as to how some of the very early Eurocentric views of the universe came about, which also represents the earliest identification of white supremacy culture. Logically, the ramifications of the enduring white supremacy culture have created individual and societal disorders for people of African descent—mainly those living a subconscious existence, not focusing their minds on conscious awareness. The heavy concentration of trauma in the Caribbean colonies seems to have created a dysfunctional society, stemming from the *mental slavery gene*, Smith says. This has unfortunately become part of our Black Caribbean identity. The overbearing weight of Western thinking with its superiority/inferiority complex is embedded in the Black experience. However, if we sit in place, drowning in trauma, how can our predicament ever change? To the contrary, it will only get worse. Therefore, it is of no value to lament the injustices of the past, for we cannot change the past. We can only focus on what can be done next and how to build the winning conditions for a prosperous future. This will be a more productive use of time, so we must put our energy into our future, not into our past.

Among the many legacies of slavery, which remains stubbornly omnipresent in our culture, is *fear,* the fear related to our past, projected into our present and future. However, that type of fear is imagination-driven, not real; it is driven by past experiences and trauma. Again, we must be careful in how we think. The fear of racial discrimination alone can hold us back from attempting things that white people take for granted, and that creates a big psychological advantage for them. This reality is an enormous subconscious barrier to growth, both economically and socially. This deep-seated anxiety felt as a racialized person in a white supremacist culture can wear us down; but we do not have to be victims. Victimhood is a choice. Anxiety and stress can be addressed in consciousness and remedied through therapy, which many in our community do not pursue but nonetheless desperately need.

Like many immigrants from the Caribbean wishing to show their children their roots, I spent my fair share of time at all-inclusive resorts on several different Caribbean islands with my family over the years. One of my most vivid memories was observing European hotel guests as they watched the hotel's cultural show one evening. This was in Grenada, and we shall leave the hotel unnamed. Grenadian dancers at this high-end resort performed dances in "traditional garb." The dances were inherently depicting a happy slave-plantation life where these women were happy to exist there, which of course is simply ridiculous!

At the time, it did not occur to me that these performers were being trotted out to give visitors the illusion that they were experiencing authentic Grenadian culture. Now, it is truly disheartening to think about foreigners walking away believing that they have just experienced authentic Grenadian culture. Those dances in no way resembled Grenadian culture; the whole spectacle was fabricated to advance a false narrative that romanticizes the legacy of the plantation system for entertainment value. This example reveals one of the many unpalatable truths behind the Caribbean all-inclusive resort-style vacation. It was a tourist product developed solely for the consumption of white Westerners. No self-respecting Grenadians would have created it willingly; it was done because their employment or income depended on it. It simply consisted of putting locals in positions of subservience, entertaining foreign guests for poor compensation, and promoting false narratives of the happy natives to make guests comfortable.

I've travelled the world, crisscrossing Europe and Asia; but in all my voyages there, I cannot recall ever having all my meals and activities at the hotel. The purpose of travel is to experience other cultures and to see the sights. A good friend of mine, an avid foodie, recently returned from a two-week vacation in Croatia. His Instagram posts are full of shots of marketplaces, small villages, restaurants, and coastlines. They suggest that he was able to experience authentic

Croatian culture and hospitality, particularly through the local cuisine. However, in the Caribbean all-inclusive experience, you encounter none of those offerings. Local culture is deleted; you are eating bacon and eggs rather than saltfish and bakes for breakfast. You mainly experience bad buffets, crowded and unclean swimming pools, and absurd nightly entertainment. Even the Pope recognizes that Caribbean "holiday centres offer a reconstructed ethnicity that humiliates both tourists and the host community."

Today, close to 40% of the average Caribbean economy or GDP derives from tourism and its associated activities, according to a Douglas Blackwell analysis titled *Genesis Green Growth, G3*. The analysis points out that although tourism is the major GDP contributor, the quality of that contribution is low-income generating, which does not contribute to building a middle-class economy. And the dominance of the all-inclusive package has propagated a system designed for Western resort owners to generate revenue locally and funnel the profits out of each country. Cultural critic Ian Gregory Strachan provokes the question in his scathing assessment of the tourism industry, *Paradise and Plantation*, arguing that "the Caribbean finds itself again coveted for its natural resources—this time, though, not for gold, silver, pearls, tobacco, cotton, or sugar, but for sun, sand, and sea." So although the region might have achieved political independence, economic dependency is still firmly entrenched. If tourism-hospitality is the largest economic sector and the all-inclusive model continues to dominate, our economies are nothing more than a source for the continuation of wealth extraction and entertainment for foreign interests. Whether through the extraction of sugar under colonialism or foreign exchange through the tourism industry today, the nature of it all is fundamentally the same.

Dependence on large foreign corporations that own and operate many of the hospitality assets in the region, including—but not limited to—hotels and resorts, villas, airlines, tour operators, cruise ships, travel agents, restaurants, and service providers: these entrenched ecosystems control local economies. They create diseconomies of scale and imbalances and negative investment in local communities.

Social exclusion occurs as a result, especially on islands like Barbados; it is not unusual to find "whites only" establishments in trendy tourist areas in Barbados, catering to white tourists and local whites. Blacks know they are not welcome, regardless of their middle-class status. The lack of indigenous business owners and stakeholders in the tourism hospitality sector in Barbados also leads to environmental neglect and an absence of corporate social responsibility. Labour breaks down along racial lines: senior managers are white, and workers are Black.

Furthermore, many of the labour opportunities that tourism offers are in the low-skill, low paying service sector, keeping the economy off of a middle-class development trajectory. After independence, tourism was touted as the deliverer of prosperity for indigenous populations, but this promise never materialized. In the era of globalization and the increasing digitization of economies, the Black local workforce will continue to be marginalized and exploited. They will remain unskilled and thus unprepared to transition to the new digital economy, where wealth-creating opportunities can be found.

Even in 2023, the legacy of slavery and the plantation system invisibly underpins the regressive Caribbean socioeconomic hierarchical structures that are part of the legacy of the plantation slavery system. Nevertheless, there still exists a path forward that will allow the region to take back control of its cultural offerings and to participate in the new global economy with respect and dignity.

THE DEFINITION OF "EUROCENTRICITY" is a focus on European culture and history to the exclusion of a wider, more diverse view of the world—a mentality that implicitly regards European culture as preeminent and the most rational. In other words, the term *Eurocentricity* denotes a worldview that posits European history and values as the standard, superior to all others. It is a worldview that helps to simplify Europe and the United States as the most rational and important actors within the global capitalist system.

Caribcentricity, by contrast, seeks a shift in mindset by first asserting our Caribbean culture in the lineage or descendants of African people. This sets our individuality and our ambitions based on what we want and where we want to go, instead of following Eurocenticity as the standard or superior culture to aspire to. Setting our economic ambitious to what is critical for our prosperity and happiness in the 21st century, our growth agendas, based on our understanding that only through value creation can you have value and exert influence in the world. Caribentricity seeks to write its own story, design its future, and carve out its own place in the universe. It is a platform for comprehensive progress through the advancement of knowledge, science, and cultural revitalization!

What we need is to build the Caribbean identity through bold, transformative, technology-led economic growth systems. Cultural advancement is based on accelerating entrepreneurship growth, challenging and changing dynamic power structures in a way that makes us relevant and equal in the world. The *Caribcentric* mindset strengthens and prepares us for the most competitive environments in the world. It is a culture of entrepreneurship and innovation, pride, and the relentless pursuit of our rightful place in the universe.

IN A 2021 article published in Now Grenada, titled *Grenada Tourism: Why are we killing the goose?*, author Brian Samuel argued correctly that the future of Grenada's tourism economy should not be oriented towards low-end, mass-market, mega-resort-type projects, but rather to a higher-end tourism growth model encompassing the natural environment and culture of the island. Samuel gave the example of a Chinese-backed tourism project on the north end of the island, at Levera Beach, a pristine location. Another example given by Samuel was the Mount Hartman project in the south of Grenada. Both projects represented giant, unnecessary development projects not reflective of the trending tourism themes, particularly the trend away from mass-market mega-resorts.

If one takes the time to examine the global tourism landscape, one will find that Samuel's fundamental thesis makes sense and reflects what is trending in the global tourism universe today. The two aforementioned projects are ill-considered when viewed against the backdrop of the current global marketplace. Such huge projects on a tiny island territory will lead to disastrous environmental outcomes and will end up "killing the [golden] goose" of tourism, argues Samuel.

Grenada's natural environment is what the island is known for, its best tourism asset—the reason why people come. So the market evidence presents a negative general outlook for mass-market mega-resort tourism in Grenada. Regardless, the government of Grenada seems to remain a raving fan of such projects. Amid the transformative events of the COVID-19 pandemic, which has exponentially sped up the global economy's digital transition, the Grenadian government, in its infinite wisdom, has decided to ignore the factual information and pursue a product type that the data indicates is in decline, with a detrimental environmental impact.

Therefore, new technology-led sectors must be developed, particularly in the knowledge-based economy, to free the Caribbean from this plague of backward thinking. The hard realities and challenges that the region faces are exacerbated by its dominance and dependence on large foreign corporations that own and operate many of the all-inclusive mass-market products in the region. In effect, foreign interests have created a self-serving system that controls local economies, politicians, and people. The diseconomies of scale that it creates further contribute to **negative investment** (any investment that costs more to hold than it returns in payments can result in negative carry.) So foreign companies taking their profits out of the Caribbean instead of reinvesting them locally is a form of negative investment, which adversely impacts social structures and puts imbalances into local economies and communities.

The lack of inclusion of indigenous business owners, budding entrepreneurs, and stakeholders in the tourism hospitality sector leads to a disproportionate concentration of wealth and power in the hands of a very few, most of them foreign or local whites. For many locals, the only labour opportunities remain in the service industry, which offers no possibility of advancement to the middle class. This disrupts the family dynamic, as men increasingly must often depend on women to be breadwinners, putting strain on the social fabric of the nation and region as a whole. Without a dignified economic growth agenda and strategy, Caribbean families will increasingly despair to the detriment of our society.

A New Paradigm: Locally Inclusive Hospitality (LIH)…
(LIH is a proprietary tourism business strategy developed by Douglas Blackwell Inc.)

Barbados Food and Rum Festival

Grenada Sailing Week

Festivity

Food

Rum

Authentic Experiences

Locally Inclusive Hospitality (LIH) promotes Caribbean culture in a non-caricatured and dignified manner. It promotes and leverages the warm, inviting, hospitable nature of Caribbean peoples.

In his book *Behind the Smile*, anthropologist George Gmelch describes how tourism fails to make a meaningful economic impact on the islands. In his study of the inner workings of Caribbean tourism, Gmelch explains how the industry's effects are measured in "leakage." He explains that "the real economic benefits of tourism to a country are not revealed by gross foreign exchange earnings, but by what is left over after deducting the amount which stays or returns overseas." Furthermore, the density factor of large and concentrated all-inclusive resort operations contributes negatively to local environmental ecosystems and biodiversity. The supposed economic benefits of large all-inclusive resort projects that politicians regularly tout actually have negative long-term impacts on local economies—low-wage jobs, no meaningful impact for local vendors like restaurants, and other hospitality-related services. In Grenada, since Sandals arrived in 2012, there has been no economic development to date beyond the gates of Sandals itself. That means no meaningful fair wage growth for the service employees, no

388

meaningful senior management advancement for local individuals, and no measurable benefit to the middle class.

The very ethos of the mass market all-inclusive model inevitably inflicts suffering on the local environs. All accommodations, meals, drinks, tips, recreational activities, and entertainment are included in the flat rate, disincentivizing local spending by travellers. Guests are not encouraged to stop sipping tax-free rum punch in their hotel infinity pools and patronize local businesses, thus supporting the local economy. Close to US$50 billion is spent each year on vacation leisure activities in the Caribbean region, according to the World Travel and Tourism Council (WTTC), 2020 report on global tourism; but how much of that spending really ends up in the local economy?

A more inclusive approach, would steer away from the cheap, undignified, mass-market resort setting and towards an ***Independent Boutique Hotel and Villa Rentals (IBHV)*** vacation experience business model. The core supply-side asset of the Caribbean hospitality industry continues to be the IBHV, which represents the region's largest and most intimate part of the hospitality market. Ranging from the single luxury villa to the intimate 100-room-and-fewer boutique hotels. The IBHV category forms the very foundation and fabric of authentic Caribbean tourism hospitality, representing the most logical and practical business growth opportunity on which to build. The demand side is further bolstered by an annual US$39.3 billion in leisure activity spending (based on pre-COVID numbers), according to the WTTC. The growth strategy is bolstered by a long-established tourism-hospitality market of selective IBHV properties to choose from. The global middle-class "experience-based travel" is the key demographic driving high growth in travel today.

Moreover, as demonstrated by Airbnb and Accor Hotels, transformative disruption underpinned by innovation is the factor that will continue to drive extraordinary enterprise growth in this sector.

The problem is that the Caribbean tourism-hospitality market is currently unbranded and fragmented, making it hard to extract significant value from it. The hospitality product is severely lacking in technological sophistication, relying on applications that align with global tourism growth trends. It particularly lacks the ability to make use of enterprise technology—including data, artificial intelligence, and machine learning—as tools to create value for the enterprise, and industry. Local hospitality stakeholders, too, have failed to recognize the rapidly changing global business environment. The playing field has already shifted. Due to their failure to capitalize on enterprise technologies, these operators are highly vulnerable to upstarts and disrupters. That provides the Caribbean with a tremendous long-term value creation opportunity.

Therefore, by leveraging the existing IBHVs and applying a foundational cloud-based Platform as a Service (PaaS) enterprise-building approach, we can harness many intelligent technology stacks to form an enterprise geared toward generating growth. We should build capacity in order to get service partners and suppliers onto the platform and persuade customers to use the application as the preferred booking tool in the world for Caribbean experience-based vacations. On the demand side, we should empower vacationers and local populations alike with digital applications so they can easily book vacations, services, and activities. On the supply side, we should empower IBHV rental property owners, local hospitality and entertainment, and all related activities operators with a platform to grow their business. This is the way forward.

Disruption is happening now, happening in the global tourism-hospitality market—but the Caribbean seems to be still in a slumber, oblivious to technological transformation. The acceleration of innovation and the velocity of disruption are changing everything, with new ways to add value to the vacation experience, particularly through digitization of the booking and itinerary processes.

The IBHV approach represents the ideal inclusive growth opportunity, because independent properties need to find capital for technology improvements and digital platform building in order to drive sales effectively. There are many aging owners and founders who are looking for palatable exit strategies but are unable to find them. Therefore, we need a vibrant capital markets sector in the region to do deals that will reposition the sector to flourish in the 21st century. Low-budget, American-style, all-inclusive mass-market resort products are not conducive to the promotion of the Caribbean's natural environment, unique culture, and hospitality. Furthermore, the large foreign interests that control these properties and industry could not care less about promoting an authentically Caribbean branded product.

Therefore, a grand opportunity exists in which the region can lead in amassing an impressive and genuine Caribbean collection of hospitality properties and vacation experience products. These hospitality assets will be supported by a technology-servicing ecosystem—the digital platform. The combined *LIH and IBHV* model harnesses local hospitality assets and leverages them through an end-to-end, all-encompassing, intelligent sales and marketing system, including guest bookings, servicing, and a centralized system shared amongst property owners. This platform will provide the hospitality service sector with the efficiency of operations, and the ability to onboard their products and services online through a secured e-commerce platform. In short, this will move the region up the value-added supply chain and into the 21st century.

If there is any doubt that the future of travel has changed forever, one need only consider the success of Airbnb, which has now become the de facto largest accommodations company in the world without owning a single property. It has also forced sluggish rental brands like VRBO to transform themselves to stay alive and compete. The LIH model allows for leveraging demand by accessing the trending information on market preferences and growth and using data to make business decisions. Evidence shows that the cheap, mass-market, all-inclusive resorts are losing out to the experience-based industry, which is more naturally suitable to the Caribbean environment.

CHAPTER 15

The Fierce Change of the Digital Now

On March 2, 2020, I wrote an article titled *"AI and the Rise of the Creative Class—the Demise of the Useless Class."* The purpose of the article was to show the ever-increasing role that artificial intelligence is playing in our daily lives. The core theme of the article was how the future of work is rapidly changing through AI. As we are seeing now, due to the impact of COVID, the natural evolution of technology and change is happening exponentially more rapidly; virtual is the new norm. As acknowledged by Upwork CEO Hayden Brown in a New York Times article titled *What Bosses Think About the Future of the Office,* "We just listened to the workforce, and everybody said remote work was working really well." Those of us who can leverage digitization and can work from home will make it through this crisis smoothly. Those who cannot do so are bound to experience challenging financial and anxious times ahead.

It is the same for communities, societies, countries, and regions. How you make it through the pandemic and come out the other end will contribute meaningfully to determining your long-term prosperity curve trajectory. Transitional periods in history have always been a big determinant of future outcomes, so we need to pay attention and do the work.

In his book The Art of War, the ancient Chinese General Sun Tzu says: "Amid a crisis, there is an opportunity." We must always recognize the significant transcending forces at play in our times and determine how we can make the most of those opportunities. Seize them, learn to embrace volatility, figure out a strategy and move forward with confidence. Accordingly, expect more digitally focused solutions and innovations to be a major part of *everything* going forward.

Adapting and preparing for an economy and lifestyle that is increasingly being executed through digital technology is where the entire world is headed if not already there. There will be winners and losers, inequality, that is the nature of things. We need not fear change; change is natural, so instead, we must embrace the change and ride the trends. The onus will remain on us to up-skill and retool ourselves to remain relevant to the times. The ones who understand this prevailing reality of the future of work are the ones who will be best suited to thrive in the future.

Another article, titled *China Focus: Digital economy helps offset coronavirus impact*, points out that "some industries in China have been put into temporary stagnation due to the sudden coronavirus epidemic outbreak; the country's booming digital economy, however, is playing an increasingly important role in hedging economic risks and uncertainty." In short, China's quick economic bounce back from COVID-19 can be directly attributed in part to its possession of a strong and rapidly growing digital economy. They were well prepared! China has been intensely investing in the "digital now" for some time, so it is no surprise that China can rely on its digital economy to remain ahead of the curve.

The pandemic has made society more mindful of both the inefficiencies of the old economy and the efficiencies and possibilities of the new economy. Therefore, one thing is now certain: the post-COVID world is being set up for significant new economic advances, driven by digital technology. If societies do not spend the necessary time over this decade, to align with the new digital world, good outcomes will be difficult to achieve. Do not live in delusion or merely pray for things to get better; "God" will not save you, so focus on saving yourself. It is always up to you in the end. We will see a slew of innovations and processes to come, the regulatory environment will dramatically shift to accommodate the *digital now*, and there will be collateral damage, of course, there always will be and that cannot be avoided, we can only try to minimize it. Those who choose to stand still will simply get run over, left by the side of the road and no one will come to save you. Consequently, not being aware of the rapidly changing environment coupled with not having a plan, will only ensure suffering. So be aware and use this period wisely and begin to prepare your kids for the future of ethe future of work.

IN THE PERIOD around 1665, the time of the Great Plague of London, Isaac Newton, too, had to work from home. So history shows that most things happening now have already happened at some point in history. The study of history, therefore, is one of the most beneficial things you can do towards learning and critical analysis. Likewise, Newton used his time away wisely, studying at home while the universities were closed. Even without his professors to guide him, Newton thrived during that time, which he later referred to as his *annus mirabilis*, the *years of wonders*.

I do not mean to demand that anyone accomplish anything as great as devising the theory of gravity and defining the laws of motion as Newton did, which changed the world of science. The important insight here is that we must not sit and wait on others, or get caught in the vise of paralyzing inaction; helping ourselves is the most important thing.

Do not be distracted by the noise; focus instead on the overriding megatrends happening around you. Self-awareness is key, lest we can become bogged down in our subconscious existence—which can end up being one of delusion. Delusion often leads to misunderstanding of your surroundings and the universe, accompanied by stress and anxiety, which inherently leads to negative manifestations and results, which in turn lead to errors in judgement.

395

The mind's capacity to rationalize can be a powerful force that can lead you in the wrong direction, so be aware of what is real and what is not. After all, "The mind is everything; what you think, you become," said Socrates.

There is no sense in wasting time contemplating things or searching for a new philosophy; the ancients gave us all the answers to life already over 2,000 years ago. Take some time to read these universal classics to gain knowledge from their wisdom. In the future, the value will be given to those who can create value for themselves and their community. The digital economy is about maximum efficiency, and there is nowhere to hide; so if you cannot produce value, you will be exposed sooner or later by the new economy. Machines will increasingly do task-oriented jobs, and less economic value will be placed on manual and managerial-type work. Even higher education in specialized fields will be devalued by AI and automation.

Someone who has spent years in their education to specialize in a particular area may wake up one day and simply find AI replacing them—value and efficiency are the name of the game. For example, highly paid investment analysts, those who analyze companies in order to make stock recommendations, will be replaced by specialized AI algorithms that can compute and connect hundreds of thousands of data points, and simply do a better job of it. The computer will provide much better, fact-based, insightful value than the task-driven specialist can ever achieve. Besides, these analysts are seldom right in any case, so logic dictates that the computer, a massive processor of information, will produce better outputs—unless the analyst can invent a functioning crystal ball, one supposes. Ultimately, a human cannot perform hundreds of thousands of computations per second, detect patterns out of ambiguity, or form conclusions in short order.

Currently, value-creating entrepreneurs and innovators are forced to pay investment banks and law firms millions of dollars for what amounts to cut-and-paste template advisory work. Specialized algorithmic programs can do regulatory work in seconds. Why would any firm continue to pay an analyst to do granular work—such as legal work—when a computer can do it better, in a matter of seconds and at a fraction of the cost? This will work itself out through the value evaluation process and change will happen.

In two of his best-selling books, *"21 Lessons for the 21st Century"* and *"Sapiens,"* historian Yuval Noah Harari predicts that just as mass industrialization created the working class, the AI revolution will create a new "unworking" class. Harari's work poses a simple but bracing question: "What should we do with all the superfluous people, once we have highly intelligent non-conscious algorithms that can do almost everything better than humans?" Harari points out that as old professions became obsolete, new professions come into play. He argues that the idea that humans will always have a unique ability "beyond the reach of non-conscious algorithms is just wishful thinking," and gives many good examples to back up his statement in the two books.

Too much specialization can lead to the elimination of one's job or lower the monetary compensation that one once could demand. A taxi driver and a cardiologist may have more in common than meets the eye because of their narrow focus or specialization. They may be easier to replace by AI. AI can execute specific tasks in cognitive fashion, more effectively and more accurately than a human can. For cardiologists, for example, AI can execute specific tasks and pattern analyses to provide a more accurate diagnosis than a doctor can. I do not mean that we ought to get rid of cardiologists altogether—only that those machines could make them better at their jobs. As for taxi drivers, Uber has already dramatically cut into their market via technology, and the future of driverless cars may make the taxi driver a thing of the past. These things are difficult to predict; but it is clear that many professions are at risk of becoming redundant in the future, regardless of their level of education and training.

CONTENT CREATORS: There is still hope for humans, however, depending on one's ability to adapt and learn in new environments. Specific groups that might not immediately come to mind are well-positioned to rise and thrive in the digital age. I call this group the *Content Creators (C²)*; these are the entrepreneurs, innovators, artists, cultural thinkers, thought leaders, trendsetters, trailblazers, and dreamers—the C^2 creative class. Those with imagination can apply it to the reality of the natural world and see what is possible. These C^2 individuals, aided by technology, will become true creators and leaders; they will be the designers of future worlds.

Historically, this group has always added value to society, shaping the way we live, work, and play; from business to the arts, C^2's contribute to the betterment of our society. However, in the past, much of their entrepreneurial wealth potential has been consumed by lawyers, investment bankers, and other professions that live off of the creativity of entrepreneurs. This group I call the *taskers*. They latch on to these value-creating entrepreneurs and make considerable money by cutting and pasting tasks. Going forward it is inevitable that computers and machines will play an increasingly important role in tasking, and their value will not be denied along the value chain. In short, AI and machine learning will be able to add incredible value at minimal cost.

Harari defines the future of value through the evolving technology landscape of artificial intelligence:

> In the 21st century, we might witness the creation of a massive new unworking class: people devoid of any economic, political or even artistic value, who contribute nothing to the prosperity, power and glory

of society. This "useless class" will not merely be
unemployed — it will be unemployable.

This quote is not only relevant to individuals, but also hyper-relevant
to societies, countries, and regions, particularly the Caribbean. If the
region does not dramatically respond to protecting its own survival
through transformative growth, then the "unemployable" reference
will amount to irrelevance for the Caribbean in the global community.
Right now, the Caribbean is dramatically behind the global wealth
curve, and there is no identifiable evidence to the contrary. The
region is immaterial to the global economy, unconnected and on the
periphery, neither here nor there. And the idea of using tourism to
catapult us into global economic relevance is a non-starter. So the
stark possibility that the Caribbean can be headed to becoming a
"useless society" in the context of an advancing global community, is
a total reality!

Doing nothing and engaging in wishful thinking is the first
sign of future extinction. In the end, if you cannot recognize the
environment in which you live and cannot create value in it, then you
are of no value to the universe. This is the undeniable and
quantifiable reality of economics, conflict, and scarcity. It applies to
all societies.

MOST of what today's schoolchildren are learning in schools will
probably be irrelevant in the future, if it has not become obsolete
already, or it will not provide any real economic value towards the
future of work and earning a desirable income. Back in September
2013, Oxford researchers Carl Benedikt Frey and Michael A.
Osborne published a paper, *The Future of Employment*, that calculated
that an estimated 47% of U.S. jobs are at high risk of being taken over
by computer algorithms and automation within the next 20 years.

This prediction is trending in the right direction. Henceforth, one's value in society comes down to the economic value one can create for oneself. This is the cold, hard reality.

The nature of capitalism has created its own highly complex organic algorithm for recognizing and rewarding value. AI is simply intensifying the value equation with greater precision. And some "expert" thinkers have warned that once artificial intelligence surpasses human intelligence, it may exterminate humankind or our humanity. They see AI controlling the planet and transforming the entire known universe into one giant supercomputer. I do not subscribe to such unfounded fears; instead, the trends do tell us that AI and machine learning are here to stay and will improve our lives considerably. However, if we choose not to align ourselves, if we fight this natural evolution to digital reality, our economic value and earning power will decline greatly, and we will become truly worthless in the 21st century. Therefore, how you think about the reality you face will be critical to how you behave, and that behaviour will determine your outcome.

At the May 2019 Digital Enterprise Show in Madrid, a global consulting firm, McKinsey & Co. McKinsey Global Institute (MGI), presented a report titled *Twenty-five years of digitization: Ten insights into how to play it right*. The report focused on how countries, sectors, and CEOs face an increasingly complex world where new digital technologies are affecting productivity and performance while causing disruption. "[In]this world, the rewards for success—and the penalties for failure—are ever greater," the report said. This represents the new reality in business. Are Caribbean leaders thinking or asking similar questions?

Among the core themes of the MGI report are the growing digitization of business, the critical investments and strategies that corporations must embrace in order to stay relevant, and the reality that digital transformation will lead the future. These are all questions that Caribbean stakeholders must be asking now!

MGI lists 10 key insights from their extensive research on digitization, digital technologies, big data, and artificial intelligence (AI) in particular, which all form the core of an evolving new-economy business playbook. Agile firms will reach higher productivity and profitability levels, while irrelevancy and lag will be the reality for firms that do not. Digital culture will change behaviour and culture and create new norms; so, if Caribbean countries are not keeping up with the times, they are behind it, unable to create value, and ultimately becoming increasingly useless to the global community.

Some of the broader themes in the MGI report are as follows:

- An additional $13 trillion could be added to global GDP by 2030 through digitization, automation, and AI, and these technologies will also create major new business opportunities and productivity gains.
- "The digital natives are calling the shots": significant growth in start-ups is effectively competing with incumbent companies for market share.
- "Digital changes everything—even industry boundaries": digital platforms are crucial for developing digital ecosystems, creating diversification beyond sector borders, and providing clear profitability growth. For example, through digitization, Chinese insurer PingAn has started many other innovative businesses such as OneConnect. This company develops and sells financial technology solutions in sales, risk management, products, services, and operations around the world. In this case, AI technologies have created new business lines and revenue for the insurer.
- Agility is the new way to compete: according to MGI, "in virtually all industries that we have analyzed, digital natives are more agile at developing and scaling businesses—than

incumbents. In general, digital natives make bolder moves such as owning a platform or allocating more capital expenditure to digital plays in adjacent markets." The research indicates that simple agility can be a particularly profitable strategy during transformations, particularly when greater uncertainty exists. In short, agile incumbents have higher profit margins and growth acceleration than those that do not.

- All about the Platform: 70% of companies with a digital platform strategy achieve higher growth than the average firm that does not. The research shows that creating a global business platform gives a company a substantial earnings boost.

- Professional expertise and effective management of digital transformation are vital: knowledge and specialization are required to implement any digital strategy. Most companies do not staff digital transformation engineers; and using your IT guy to implement complex AI technologies has ended up setting companies back, according to the MGI report. It is imperative to seek out experts in the field of AI and Industrial Engineering who can, first, identify the complex problem, then develop the right digital strategy, create the necessary algorithms, and execute and manage the unique digital ecosystems for growth. Complex data programs require qualified individuals; MGI's research also indicates increased incidences of failure when companies try to "do it in-house."

- The first step toward digital transformation begins with properly identifying the business problem; if not, failure is often baked in right from the outset. Identifying mistakes or problems after going live often leads to an ever-mounting collection of errors and unnecessary spending of money. MGI points out 5 critical points for the effective management of the digital transformation. They are: (1) advisory mobilization, which requires shared ownership, accountability, and responsibility; (2-3) clarity of commitment to the digital transformation, and sufficient resources devoted to it as a core organizational priority; (4) the right investment in the technical talent needed in data analytics and digital technology, with chief analytic and digital officers playing a supervisory role; and (5) anchoring everything with agility in case initiatives prove to be difficult to scale.

An article in the Economist titled "Rise of The Machines" reports that the main subjects that MBA students today study are all AI-related. And according to Brian Uzzi, who teaches a course on AI to MBA students at The Kellogg School of Business, "AI has become a key tool for businesses in all industries. By harnessing the power of computers to analyze data rapidly, detect patterns, and suggest courses of action, businesses can work much faster and with fewer overheads." It is not surprising, then, that AI can be found in the most successful businesses around the world. British supermarkets Tesco and Ocado use machine learning to help improve the routing of delivery drivers and to detect fraudulent transactions. Businesses like Virgin Holidays use algorithms and big data to tweak marketing messages based on real-time feedback. Uber harnesses machine learning to forecast demand and help direct its drivers to customers ahead of time. It has also used AI to determine the level of price increases individual customers are willing to tolerate—and on and on!

Business schools, then, are rightly following where the future of business is headed. According to the article, "When the professor began incorporating AI into his research a decade ago, all but a handful of the 3,000 students he taught knew what AI was. Now, almost all do." For years IBM has been using AI to help doctors diagnose patients more quickly and accurately; similarly, in business, AI helps executives make better fact-based decisions. AI technology has simply become an indispensable business tool used to gain

403

meaningful competitive advantages. Those destined to lead these firms in the future will not be writing the algorithms themselves; they will be hiring engineers to do so. Yet even so, algorithms are now writing their own algorithms. So the next generation of business leaders and managers will rely more on information, analytics, and intelligence to effectively make decisions. Again, if Caribbean leadership is not acting with the same business intensity towards their economy and about the future, only suffering and regret lies ahead.

According to *CB Insights,* "The next wave of digitization is coming through new frontier technologies including general ledger technologies like blockchain, automation, and a large set of smart, artificial intelligence (AI)-based technologies." China has already attracted 50% of global investment in AI start-ups, ahead of the U.S. and Europe. This is the intensity that the region must proportionally try to maintain, or those nations' upward directional momentum will create an inverse growth relationship for the Caribbean.

This further suggests that companies that are early adopters of AI and that apply industrial engineering practices have experienced strong profit growth. Effectively, AI is the specific technology that is directly correlated with higher financial performance, underpinning each firm's ability to boost and accelerate its performance through automating intelligent tasks.

According to MGI analysis, professional services and retail companies that do not deploy AI are reporting cash flows that are 15-20% lower than their AI-embracing peers. In financial services, the gap is 30%, and in high-tech, a substantial 80%. These figures demonstrate not only that the gap between the performance of nonadopters and adopters is a large one, but also that that gap is more significant in sectors that are more digitized and globalized. The analysis by MGI of several hundred AI use cases provides evidence of widespread benefits to operations and profitability from embedded AI and data science-related practices.

The digitization journey began a quarter of a century ago; today, it is ever-present. Standing still and waiting to "see what happens" as traditional practice in the Caribbean is not a business strategy, it is simply foolish. Based on the evidence, investing prudently in advanced technologies creates significant long-term value for the enterprise, countries, and regions. Caribbean prosperity and power will depend on how they use data science and AI to create real value to prosper in the 21st century.

ESTONIA is a small country in Europe that recognizes that its small size can be an advantage in transforming itself quickly to capitalize on digital economy efficiencies for the sake of better productivity and growth. This is the type of offensive thinking the Caribbean needs to implement, just as we must determine how to play the geographic cards that have been dealt to us to our advantage. Briefly, residents of Estonia use their digital identities to vote, fill prescriptions, and start businesses. Increasingly, Estonia is becoming a country of convenient digital identity, transitioning effectively to the new economy. People's data is shared when it is needed; the pharmacy knows instantly what doctors are prescribing in Estonia, and tax returns are automatically generated. From kindergarten website access for daily info to normal online banking, technology makes lives easier in Estonia, providing more time for leisure, downtime, health, and wellness. "You cannot imagine how spoiled we are with that. When you try to do something in another country, then you start to understand how privileged we are" (Watts, WSJ, 2019).

According to Watts in his Wall Street Journal article, Estonia's 1.3 million citizens all have a mandatory digital identity that serves as the primary way citizens access services, whether it be making a utility payment, buying or selling a car, or using loyalty cards in department stores. Children are given a unique identification number and added to the grid from the moment they are born. Life events, such as

405

deaths and marriages, are entered into databases. The government is now testing real-time monitoring of economic output by analyzing tax data that is automatically uploaded by Estonian companies.

If tiny Caribbean states can even begin to think like Estonia, it will be a start. Thinking about efficiency and better systems will trickle down to more efficient and productive business practices. The future cannot be stopped, so the best thing for the region to do is to jump aboard and take part in it before it passes us by. Leveraging technology for the benefit of all citizens is a long-term winning move.

Governments must help people deal with technological change, and the impacts it will have during the transition and thereafter. Technology continues to change the way we interact with each other and will provide great efficiencies for our economies, giving us more spare time in our lives. However, there will be difficulty in transition for a meaningful part of the population, which will have a political impact on domestic political economies. One of the most significant tech-related challenges is the effect of artificial intelligence on labour markets. One study published by the Brookings Institution in 2019 report on artificial intelligence estimated that roughly one in four jobs in the U.S. was "highly vulnerable" to automation. As humans are becoming less required in the workforce relative to machines, more governments will face social and political pressure about the negative effects on the most vulnerable people in our population. People will be left behind and inequality will grow, there can be no doubt about that. Yet we cannot hold back change, for technological advancement serves the greater good. We must push forward, or our entire Caribbean society will perish.

Hard and wise decisions must be made, quickly! Governments must create an effective strategy and policy that advances technology for sustainable long-term growth while addressing the social inequality fallout. Government must promote and utilize technology efficiency gains, but also adjust regulations to protect communities from the potential downside where it can.

Nevertheless, the progress train must not stop, not even slow down. Governments and institutions must make society aware of the impacts of digital transformation and leverage innovations in socially responsible ways.

Cybersecurity must also be a top priority as the world becomes more digitally interconnected. Digital infrastructure and architecture must have real cybersecurity strategies to protect nations, enterprises, and people.

Why is strategy so important? Because a "vision without a strategy remains an illusion," says Lee Bolman, author and educator.

With the relentless forces of globalization at play, having a strong strategy for development is paramount. Understanding the forces that shape change is the starting point for developing strategy at critical junctures.

A quick review of business strategists by author and Harvard Professor Michael E. Porter offers some good insight. According to Porter, Operational Effectiveness (OE) means performing similar operational activities better than rivals perform them. "Operational activities" means any number of practices that allow a company to better utilize its inputs—for example, increasing efficiency and productivity through technology inputs in order to develop better products more quickly. Those activities can easily be copied from one firm to the other, so they cannot represent a competitive advantage. Strategy, on the other hand, means performing different activities from your rivals, or doing them similarly but in a meaningfully distinct way that creates real value. As Porter argues, strategy positioning attempts to achieve sustainable competitive advantages that clearly distinguish the company from the crowd.

This same approach can be applied to an individual country or region to navigate at this critical juncture of transcending global change. This is how strategy can allow nations to carve out their piece of the economic pie in the global economy.

Porter's three key principles related to underlying strategic positioning are as follows:

- **Strategy is the creation of a unique and valuable position, involving a different set of activities.** Each SIS in the region can look at its own resources and determine on which resources it should focus activities in order to develop a competitive product for distribution.
- **Strategy requires you to make trade-offs in competing—to choose what not to do.** In times of upheaval and change, it is often the things that are not done that make the greatest difference. SIS leadership and policymakers must be very analytical and avoid being reactive, making the same mistakes made in the past, or relying on faulty information to make decisions in the present.
- **The strategy involves creating "fit" among a company's activities.** "Fit" must be identified. For example, is agriculture a "natural" fit for smart farming? Does it involve using AI to move up the global value chain? Can technology be used to create high-value food products, bypass middlemen, or maintain a greater percentage of the profits?

Bold, transformative strategies are required to develop sustainable, long-term competitive advantages. An effective competitive strategy is about differentiation—deliberately choosing a distinct set of activities to deliver a unique mix of value that results in greater expansion of market demand in order to grow profitably. For example, Grenada is known as the "spice isle," so would it not make sense to leverage that commodity to implement a strategy that brands the island's spice products for global sales? Why not use intelligent digital technology to market products—create new demand and profits where none existed before?

The strategy edge requires leadership, differentiation, innovation, and focus. It requires that decisions be made on real information and solid research rather than intuition and ego, a clear intellectual framework, and a business process to guide the strategy. This is the applied intelligence process. The strategic agenda must be a power agenda; it demands discipline and continuity while remaining flexible and open to new information, and continual improvement of the organization's or country's strategic vision. Looking at the changing global forces that impact industries is key, and developing a strategy that can ride those changing tides is critical. Change is also an opportunity for local industries and companies to evolve along with the rest of the world. We must align strategies to technology investments that together can drive efficiency gains and boost long-term sustainable competitive advantages and profitability growth.

Leadership must quickly study the new digital landscape in the context of globalization and lead with optimism and courage, not regress to the same old backwards thinking. Policymakers must identify each country's natural industries and their competitive advantages, adjust and align to move up the global value chain, and anticipate and exploit opportunities in their nations' favour. They must always be strategic and think and analyze before acting.

Change offers opportunity, but only for those paying attention. Opportunity-spotting through fact-based discovery is a process that must be undertaken in an organized and disciplined way; that process must use and leverage valuable insights in order to capitalize on economic opportunities with confidence. Governments working with industry leaders can shape outcomes through effective policymaking, implementation, and facilitating enterprise growth. But they must "stay in their lane," so to speak, and leave entrepreneurship to entrepreneurs; governments should confine themselves to promoting and supporting business owners with sound policies and resources. In this environment, innovators can prosper by using

409

favourable public policies to identify new enterprise opportunities for growth. Government investment agencies and alike can also work to reinvigorate growth in favour of incumbents and facilitate capital investment into tech-related disruptive actions for transformation.

For example, when identifying relevant and natural competitive advantages in the field of agriculture, the question should be: Is it a natural competitive advantage to exploit via technology investment? Strategies can be created to move the agriculture industry forward, particularly up the global value-added supply chain.

Creating a High-Value Industry...

- Which products have high-value export-earning potential?
- What technologies and platforms can we leverage to create competitive advantages and extraordinary value?
- Who are the key suppliers and stakeholders that can help in the process?
- Identify major global forces, competition, and potential disruptive entrants.
- Identify the underlying forces that drive profitability in any industry or business.
- Identify key risks and devise risk mitigation strategies through data science analysis/artificial intelligence and machine learning.
- Seek out foreign direct investment to expand local capital markets and spur growth.

Blue Ocean Strategy

Blue Ocean Strategy (BOS) is one of the most effective business growth strategies around, one that can easily be applied to any industry or country's development aspirations. BOS was developed by Professors W. Chan Kim and Renée Mauborgne, INSEAD business school, Fontainebleau, France and based on a study of 150 strategic moves (spanning more than 100 years and 30 industries). BOS development models show that lasting success comes not from battling competitors but from creating "blue oceans": untapped new market spaces ripe for growth. Effectively, the iconic BOS argues that *tomorrow's* leaders will succeed *not* by battling competitors, but by creating "blue oceans" of uncontested market space ripe for growth. This "value innovation" factor allows firms and countries to LEAPFROG over its competition... rendering them obsolete. BOS coupled with and powered by **ai | applied intelligence** application which embeds the power of machines...data science, artificial intelligence and machine learning, augmenting human intelligence to do things in nanoseconds instead of days, months, and years. Will enable the Caribbean to accelerate its development, and not be left behind in this decade of transformation.

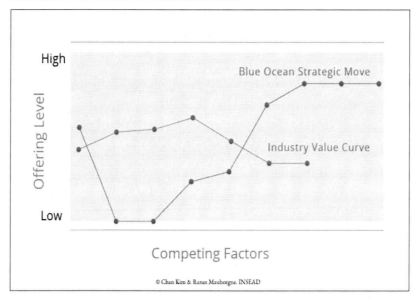

© Chan Kim & Renee Mauborgne. INSEAD

Creating blue oceans builds brands that are so powerful, that a blue ocean strategic move can create brand equity that lasts for decades.

Fundamentally, the Caribbean region needs to think like an incumbent business that must first transform to survive, and then it must begin to think like a start-up to create new growth opportunities for itself.

A business purpose must be formed, and then leaders need to focus on overall regional strategy, and priorities and lead their nations to figure out how to get things done with a new mindset—the kind of mindset that can be a catalyst for sustainable change. Advanced data-based technologies today make it possible for the region to create that space, its unique value proposition, new demand, and an operating platform model to execute its competitive advantages.

Sailing to blue oceans means making the competition irrelevant by expanding markets based on new product offerings and innovation. This moves us to find untapped market potential, develop new product categories, and create new and authentic Caribbean brands. Successful BOS businesses usually go on to dominate their market for an average of 10 to 15 years, according to BOS research. Therefore, the region must always think long-term in its development pursuits.

Some key highlighted points of BOS

- The best way to drive profitable growth is to stop competing in overcrowded industries. In those "red oceans," companies try to outperform rivals to grab bigger slices of existing demand. As the space becomes increasingly crowded, profit and growth prospects shrink. Products become commoditized. Ever-more-intense competition turns the water bloody.

- How to avoid the fray? Sail to blue oceans, finding those oases of uncontested market spaces. In blue oceans, you invent and capture new demand and offer customers a leap in value while streamlining your costs. The results are handsome profits, speedy growth, and brand equity that lasts for decades while rivals scramble to catch up.

Understand the Logic of BOS

The logic behind the blue ocean strategy is a counterintuitive one:

- It is actually not based on technological innovation; blue oceans seldom result from that. Often, the underlying technology already exists, and blue ocean creators simply link it to what buyers' value most.
- You need not venture into distant waters to create blue oceans. Most of them are created from within, not beyond. In the red oceans of existing industries, incumbents often create blue oceans within their core businesses.
  - Never use the competition as a benchmark. Instead, make the competition irrelevant by creating a leap in value for both you and your customers. And reduce your costs while also offering customers more value.

Red ocean versus blue ocean strategy

The imperatives for red ocean and blue ocean strategies are starkly different.

Red ocean strategy	Blue ocean strategy
Compete in existing market space.	Create uncontested market space.
Beat the competition.	Make the competition irrelevant.
Exploit existing demand.	Create and capture new demand.
Make the value/cost trade-off.	Break the value/cost trade-off.
Align the whole system of a company's activities with its strategic choice of differentiation *or* low cost.	Align the whole system of a company's activities in pursuit of differentiation *and* low cost.

Currently, Caribbean business competes with a Red Ocean mindset that holds them back.

A strategy that involves creating competitive advantages must be put into practice. The need to create blue oceans intensifies as global digital transformation accelerates. It is time to think strategically, creatively, and innovatively. It is time to bring strategic thinking into full consciousness. Once corporations realize that the strategies for creating and capturing blue oceans have a different underlying logic from red ocean strategies, they usually go on to create blue oceans of their own. Caribbean nations must behave like corporations when it comes to economic and enterprise development.

The Cart Before the Horse

In a March 13, 2019, Harvard Business Review article titled *Digital Transformation Is Not About Technology*, authors Behnam Tabrizi, Ed Lam, Kirk Girard, and Vernon Irvin observe that companies are pouring millions into "digital transformation" initiatives but a high percentage of those fail to pay off. that is because companies put the cart before the horse, focusing more on a specific technology rather than doing the hard work of fitting the change into their overall business strategy first. Caribbean nations must do the same when it comes to development; they must understand that technology is only an enabling tool. Entrepreneurs, investors, and policymakers can often get caught up in the idea of *"Digital Transformation"* (DT) and forget that you still need a real business idea first at the end of the day.

The authors above give several key lessons that have helped organizations through digital transformations, and they can be equally applied to countries and their development plans:

- **Lesson 1**: Figure out your business strategy before you invest in anything. Leaders who aim to enhance organizational performance using digital technologies often have a specific tool in mind—devising a machine learning strategy, for example. But digital transformation should be guided by the broader business strategy. There is no single technology that will deliver everything; the best combination of tools for a given organization will vary from one vision to another.

- **Lesson 2**: Design customer experience from the outside in. If the goal of DT is to improve customer satisfaction and intimacy, then any effort must be preceded by a diagnostic phase that includes in-depth input from customers. Leaders often expect that the implementation of one single tool or app will enhance customer satisfaction on its own. The only way to determine where and how to make changes is to obtain extensive and in-depth market analysis and to measure market the leader's digital transformation performance. This can easily be applied to the tourist industry.

- **Lesson 3**: Recognize peoples' fear of being replaced. When employees perceive that digital transformation could threaten their jobs, they may consciously or unconsciously resist the changes. It is critical for leaders to recognize those fears and to emphasize that the digital transformation process is an opportunity for the country to upgrade to better compete globally, which will benefit society as a whole over the long term.

- **Lesson 4**: Bring technological entrepreneurship culture into business and government. Silicon Valley start-ups are known for their agile decision-making, rapid prototyping, and flat management structures. Outsource work to qualified, enterprising people to help get the job done. Find those who can write strategies and who can be a partner along the way. The process of digital transformation is inherently uncertain: changes need to be made provisionally and then adjusted. Decisions need to be made quickly, and transparency and measurement of performance are a must.

  As a result, traditional hierarchies get in the way. It is best to adopt a flat organizational management structure that is kept somewhat separate from politics. The last thing needed is politicians commenting or trying to score points in areas where they have no expertise. Leaders must decide on priorities and base them on practicality and feasibility. We need things that work now; let the entrepreneurs do the R&D, then bring working solutions to the government.

The role of leadership
The challenge of developing or re-establishing a clear strategy often depends on leadership; a clear intellectual framework to guide

416

strategy is necessary to make decisions. Strategy renders choices about what not to do every bit as important as choices about what to do. However, the leader's job is not the operational effectiveness of day-to-day decisions, but the bold, visionary, and transformative competitive advantages that must be pursued.

A strategic prosperity agenda demands discipline and continuity while remaining flexible as new information is learned and knowledge acquired, for continual improvement and making decision trade-offs to drive the region's core strategic vision.

It is time that all Caribbean stakeholders adapt to the reality of globalization and devise a strategy based on what the world is, not what they think it should be. They must stop standing flat-footed and constantly complaining, and stop depending on development agencies like the UN, the World Bank, and other similar institutions that have been so unproductive to date. As a people, we have been stagnating for far too long, unable and unwilling to lead ourselves. Enough is enough; the time for excuses is over. It is now time to strip away the negative legacy and mindset of dependency and move toward self-reliance and self-determination.

Mindset is a choice, and so is the growth trajectory that a nation chooses. Decisions matter, and the critical decision facing the Caribbean today is one of acceptance of the prevailing reality of a digital future. Historically, the future wealth of any nation is directly correlated with its productivity gains, derived through technology investments and driven by efficiency, innovation, and growth. The region now stands at a critical juncture in time, at a crossroads, whether to be transformative or not to be.

Technology and business strategy are intertwined, and government facilitation of entrepreneurship-led growth is critical to development; so that relationship must be strategic in nature, addressing technology holistically. Technological architecture and implementation choices support overall growth strategies. Proper human resources must also be put into place for effective execution,

417

continually monitoring the underlying strategic choices and assumptions and adjusting as needed. Ultimately, all stakeholders—both public and private—NGOs, academics, and social advocacy groups must unite behind a strategy and recognize it as essential to the survival of the Caribbean species.

Collaboration amongst stakeholders around critical technology infrastructure that supports growth must be pushed, and proper frameworks for analysis and knowledge ecosystems must be advanced. Monitoring and measurement tools must be in place to ensure the efficacy, performance, and necessary strategic adjustments that will have to be made along the way. Agile strategy development, flexibility, and execution are the objectives. To generate effective results, stakeholders must apply intelligent functions as foundational tools geared to empowering efficient execution.

All stakeholders should have a broad understanding of the critical technologies that should be invested in, to gain competitive advantages and build critical economic resilience. Change can only happen if we change ourselves first. The Caribbean needs to work together holistically and strategically in order to organize effectively, choose the right technology platforms and ecosystem partners, and carefully align with those identified core growth objectives.

To compete in an ever-more complex new-economy world, not only are strategies becoming more complex and engineered, but the processes of developing and executing strategies effectively and monitoring them for successful outcomes are essential. In the new world, leaders are forced to consider a wider range of options, operational functions, variables, and future scenarios. Tech-enabled strategy platforms to lead growth are becoming the rule. We must think more expansively and precisely about the problems we face. This new economy playbook must be underpinned by the scientific *applied intelligence* approach.

CHAPTER 16

Emerging Markets & Industrial Engineering

According to Pitchbook's online publication *Private Equity News and Trends*, over the last two decades, less money has been raised through the stock markets and more activity has come along in the private equity space instead. Private equity also happens to be more conducive to a developing country's growth profile. Private equity (PE) investing gives the investor one more lever of control over the investment, and there is less volatility associated with PE investing. PE has more options for efficient tax planning, has generally longer-term hold horizons, and provides for more direct communication between investors and management. In short, it works better for pre-emerging markets like the Caribbean, in the favour of both the entrepreneur and investor.

Technology investment has always yielded efficiency gains, contributing greatly to localized increases in productivity and GDP, raising profitability, and creating longer-term value. So investors are motivated to allocate more of their portfolios to private markets. Moreover, investors believe that private markets have become necessary for getting better overall diversified risk-adjusted returns.

Capital is still the grease that makes the wheel turn, and it has become more forced on technology-based investing over the decades. Thus, investors have rightly concluded that technology creates efficiency gains for enhanced profitability. Technology investing, therefore, remains associated with the best returns over time. New companies must adjust their offerings to ensure that technology is a major part of their growth. To achieve transformation successfully, the region must begin to disrupt itself because our inability to compete successfully for global investor capital is simply driving us

419

toward extinction. In no uncertain terms, the lack of focused capital investment is holding the region back from prosperity.

According to McKinsey's 2019 *Global Private Markets Review*, private equity's net asset value has grown more than sevenfold since 2002, twice as fast as global public equities have. Now even those large traditional institutional investors that have previously avoided PE and venture investing are now allocating more meaningful capital to it. So the money is there and trending in the right direction; but Caribbean businesses and governments have not done nearly enough to position themselves to capture any of that PE capital. The Global Infrastructure Initiative, led by McKinsey Global Institute, estimates that the world needs at least $4 trillion of annual investment through 2035 to keep pace with its transformational change. A major portion of that will be filled by PE investing, and if the Caribbean does not meaningfully get into the game, it will be permanently excluded from it.

Investing in real businesses and real communities has always been the universal formula for wealth creation, so PE and Venture (PEV) are broadening their appeal to universal growth norms. "Savvy general partners (GPs) have expanded their firms' abilities to take advantage of today's most prominent sources of value creation. Leading firms have also pioneered several digital techniques to find greater efficiencies in operations, deal sourcing, due diligence, and other core activities" (McKinsey, 2019). Again, it is up to Caribbean leaders to learn about PEV and create the conditions to attract motivated capital from around the globe. The private investors and institutions alike will all come if they believe there are profits to be made in the region. However, if the region presents itself as unprepared, and unknowledgeable about global capital markets, it will not be taken seriously.

The major opportunities always stem from uncovering unique pockets of growth, and for the Caribbean, it is the digital infrastructure—everything from government services to business platforms. Every sector needs to be disrupted and overhauled; there are fortunes to be made for local entrepreneurs and investors alike. However, none of this will ever come to fruition with regional policymakers remaining mired in top-down, project-oriented development. That approach does not work; it never has, and it never will. Sophisticated capital wants technology-focused investment because technology and innovation have proven to be the greatest creators of wealth in the world. Without such an understanding of investing, the region is only engaging in delusion.

The Caribbean has tremendous upside from an investment perspective as it represents a massive infrastructure play, and the region's small size can actually be a significant competitive advantage if its leaders can recognize and plot the right course forward. As in the aforementioned example of Estonia, a total digitization economy is necessary for a small state to achieve maximum competitiveness. The region's capital markets infrastructure and global presence are non-existent, irrelevant to the world and to foreign capital pursuits. Again, global investors have a "show me" mindset: Show me that you are organized, that you know what you are doing, and that you have engineered a climate and enterprise opportunities worthy of investment.

The financial services industry, for example, is witnessing a significant technology-led change. Consider, for example, Special Purpose Acquisition Companies (SPACs), which today actually outnumber traditional IPOs coming to market. Increasingly, collaboration is required in a hyper-competitive marketplace, and data analytics within investment programmes are allowing investors to catch key trends and design new investment product offerings and solutions. The Caribbean enterprise of the future will thrive if it can align itself with innovation and capital.

Approach & Strategy

421

Without capital, good ideas simply die on the vine; accordingly, the main priority for Caribbean business leaders and public policymakers should be to change the investment narrative. We must put forward real 21st-century strategies and actions to attract real capital. No longer can we allow ourselves to be classified as "developing"; we must rebrand ourselves as **emerging.** Emerging markets are where global investors are looking, so we must align ourselves with where the capital is flowing. The term "development" carries negative connotations, associated with other terms such as "the Third World." The latter expression dates back to 1952, when the French historian and anthropologist Alfred Sauvy coined the term to describe economically "underdeveloped" countries whose needs were largely ignored by the more advanced, powerful nations of the world.

> As an emerging market economy progresses, it typically becomes more integrated with the global economy, as shown by increased liquidity in local debt and equity markets, increased trade volume and foreign direct investment, and the domestic development of modern financial and regulatory institutions…with significant penitential for growth through modernization, which presents significant investment opportunities in all facets of those economies, for oversized returns.
>
> –Investopedia

Does the above *"emerging markets"* description not sound significantly more attractive and investable? "Emerging" connotes potential; "developing" smacks of charity work. Investors do not invest for charitable purposes; they invest in real opportunities through which they can make large sums of money. This is how the real world works!

Therefore, allowing others to classify us as "developing" and accepting that narrative will continue to hold our economies back, well behind the wealth curve, never to catch up. Again, we cannot change the past, but we do have the power to control our narrative in the present. So it is time to stand upright and advance confidently; it is time to begin articulating our own interests, with bold efforts and equally bold and well-thought-out policy agendas. This must be clearly articulated to the citizenry as well, so that they can understand how their lives will improve with the investment strategies put forward. They will then be more likely to support their leaders, and investors will begin to take the Caribbean more seriously with a real bona fide, executable strategy in hand.

BUILDING ROBUST capital markets is an essential start. We will not accomplish that mission overnight, but investing is a long-term endeavor, and markets know it. Therefore, we must act according to what pays the greatest dividends. We need a long-term, sustainable, and profitable investment environment, with increased transparency and compliance. The regulatory environment is key. Forget about the constant promotion of development projects driven by aid agencies; focus instead on what has proven to work for civilizations over the many centuries: **investment in technology, innovation, and enterprise to create profit and long-term wealth.** We have no need for advisors and academics whose theories only work in the classrooms to come and experiment and waste time.

To alleviate these many challenges, leveraging emerging market footholds to integrate and align with the existing growth opportunities globally is where we must collectively head. For example, Caribbean businesses must integrate themselves into international markets through global value chains, by identifying and offering themselves as suppliers of high-value-added goods and

423

services. We must extract ourselves from the low-income commodity business and into the high-income value-added business.

Once again, it is important to keep our minds on taking the actions necessary to create the conditions for a renaissance in prosperity to occurring in the Caribbean, a renaissance in thinking and actions must occur first. The fetish of dependence on the foreign development agenda must be obliterated from our minds. We must become bold in thought and action, set strategy, and rely on our intellectual capacity to innovate, build long-term enterprises, and boldly and adventurously insert ourselves into the global value chain. that is the required thinking!

The purpose must be to leapfrog the region into the new global economy through investment. There is no time for reiterations of the failed development strategies of the past. The global economy waits for no one. The critical need is to capitalize on opportunities for economic transformation to secure sustainable prosperity for generations to come. Nevertheless, attracting foreign investment capital remains the central focus of fueling productivity and growth in the region. Developing a global capital markets presence to bring deals back home will fuel dynamic growth. Hence, massively emerging sectors like Fintech, Agritech, and Biomedical Engineering can all thrive in Caribbean jurisdictions, and robust PEV deal-making can make that a reality. Why not? Other emerging-market countries around the world are doing it, so why ca we not do likewise?

We must be actively committed to recruiting local talent, talent from the Caribbean diaspora, and foreign as well. Where the knowledge and talent exist, we must go. We need engineers, software developers, business school graduates, business owners, and entrepreneurs in our economies. We must engage in local collaboration with regional universities in science and technology, research, and innovative joint MBA business and technology programs, as well as create new programs like Industrial Engineering. We must seek to assemble a practical team of futurists, scientists, engineers, and investment managers to put foreign capital to work for us and invest foreign capital responsibly in our regional economies. These actions will be underpinned by both human intelligence and AI—quantitative data-driven investment analysis and management—to verify and test intuitive thinking and new business ideas.

Identify existing local, regional, and international opportunities to expand the export-oriented business agenda that would benefit from modernization and transformation. This will work to fuel the desired digital and zero-emissions economic profile as part of the region's agenda. The Caribbean's geography is highly conducive to renewable energy and a zero-emissions economy. Therefore, the addition of practical and economically viable green technologies and applications can become the one-two punch for a regional growth offensive.

Oversized and sustainable return opportunities must be the priority, pursued by promising technology-focused opportunities for good profitable companies that can grow and extract extraordinary value for investors, entrepreneurs, and communities alike.

The foundation of our strategy must be to help ourselves first. Therefore, local Caribbean institutions such as pension funds, credit unions, trade unions, and successful business owners must become the first investors in the Caribbean growth story. If international investors see that local capital does not have its own skin in the game, they will ask why they should risk theirs. Local pension funds especially need to step up in a major way and invest in the future of their own economies, and also become better and more strategic investors in the regional economy.

THE TERM **"industrial engineering"** was coined almost 100 years ago, when engineers began to develop techniques to improve production systems in factories. According to the Institute for Industrial and Systems Engineers, industrial engineers design processes and systems that improve quality and productivity by eliminating time wasting, money, materials, energy, or other commodities.

However, in the 21st century, and specifically in the new digital economy, industrial engineering has become more broad, contemporary, and aligned with overall business management engineering to include other domains such as finance, business intelligence, information systems, and supply-side and demand-side analytics. Industrial engineering incorporates the integration of software systems for design and implementation relative to the objectives of the enterprise. It is also extraordinarily useful in assessing entrepreneurial opportunities relative to decision-making, construction of enterprise, and commercialization.

New product development under the industrial engineering process...

Technology definition process:

Determine the correct problem to solve → Define the solution → Evaluate and select technology

This process involves filtering the ideas down to the optimal potential of success, using computational, quantitative, and qualitative measures to evaluate enterprise and entrepreneur business ideas through rigorous testing across different analyses.

applied intelligence

Idea Generation   Idea Screening   Concept Development & Testing   Market Strategy & Business Analysis   Product Development   Market Testing   Funding Models   Market Entry/ Commercialization

Concept development & testing considerations:

Gain/Pain Ratio   Competitor Analysis   Key Features   Value Proposition   Concept Testing

idea generation

Creating a set of ideas that can use the defined technology.

This stage of new product development is generating a lot of potential ideas focused around innovation. This will help form the foundation for your new product development for the defined technology.

Idea generation process:

| Discretionary | Quantamental | Quantitative |

- Web scraping
- Text extraction from reports
- Table extraction from reports
- Semantic Search
- Topic Model
- Data extraction from unstructured text

AI powered research capabilities to:
- Spot emerging trends
- Surface customer insights
- Analyze an investment space
- Stay ahead of the competition

- Alternative Data
- News Sentiment
- Nonlinear correlation analysis
- Time Series Analysis

Identifying the proper white space for the defined technology

ai

Marketing considerations:

Concept Over Product	UX Design	Brand Voice	Conducting Webinars
Create an emotional connection with the target group by making them realize that they need your products to solve their business challenge. • What is your unique selling point?	Create a UX experience that is both user-friendly and attractive. Looking at the latest UX design trends in the market will give some motivation to your design.	Establish an effective communication style that represents the brand in the best way possible. This could be blogs, emails and website content.	Hosting webinars is a way to attract high quality leads. Effective marketing takes place when you focus the conversations around the consumer's problem and then the benefit the product provides to the consumer.

11

Market & business strategy considerations:

Product	Price	Promotion	Placement

Market testing process:

Alpha testing	Beta Testing
The test engineers from the CARICOM region use and judge the product based on performance. The test engineers also map the marketing mix results with the product created. In case of any issues, the changes are planned and implemented before the final go-ahead.	Performed after the alpha testing phase. The target groups or customers identified in CARICOM as well as internationally. It is about listening to the voice-of-customers. If any issues are reported, they are moved back to the development team for fixtures.

428

roadmap

The optimal path to a decision.

Should we invest in this, or should we not?

Act

Create a plan for implementation. This involves identifying what resources are required and gaining support from employees and stakeholders. Getting others onboard with your decision is a key component of executing your plan effectively, so be prepared to address any questions or concerns that may

Weigh the Evidence

Evaluate for feasibility, acceptability and desirability to know which alternative is the best. You will need to weigh the pros and cons, then select the option that has the highest chance of success.

Identify the Decision

Recognize the investment decision and address why it will make a difference to customers and employees

Gather Information

Make the decision based on facts & data. Determine what information is relevant and involve the necessary stakeholders to make the decision.

Choose among Alternatives

When it's time to make your decision, be sure that you understand the risks involved with your chosen route. You may also choose a combination of alternatives now that you fully grasp all relevant information and potential

13

Our AI Engines

 Engine 1   Engine 2   Engine 3   Engine 4

Structure	**Ensemble**	**Event**	**Context**
The first step in knowledge extraction is to identify all of the entities and structural data within a set of documents: the people, places, concepts, numbers, sentiment and quotes. A series of custom classifiers extract and resolve those entities and store them in a knowledge base. We then identify relationships between pairs of entities using unsupervised methodologies. Every piece of data that we capture retains its provenance, giving us full transparency on the decisions made by downstream algorithms.	We construct models of reality based on streams of millions of documents. By de-duplicating and reconciling statements made by multiple observers, we create an ensemble version of the corpus. For any given event, there can be thousands of varying descriptions, from the people involved with the tiniest details. Taking a multi-document approach allows us to capture this variation as signal rather than noise. The multi-document approach improves performance metrics of the structuring engine compared with single document approaches.	This engine looks for evidence of real-world events based on a set of documents. It analyzes a set of structured data extracted from the documents. It is then able to cluster together entity relationships as a function of time. The result is a time-directed graph of inferred real-world events from any given corpus.	Information is best understood in context with all the other information around it. The context engine can be used to analyze any claim, fact or assertion and identify any supporting evidence or any contradictions and return these to the user to better contextualize the information. On a larger scale, the context engine allows us to connect together events based on an inferred chain of probable causality. This allows us to see how a set of events is connected and evolves through time, and to additionally enable us to identify the origin and spread of information over time.

10

AI engines will serve three key purposes. *1. **Understanding the Landscape,*** which is the first step in knowledge extraction, means identifying all of the entities and structural data within a set of documents from the targeted industry. *2. **Confirming our PoV*** refers to the construct of models of reality based on streams of millions of documents. *3. **Identifying Opportunity Areas & Risks*** means asking which areas of R&D are the next big things. Using the mapping and validation created in steps 1 and 2, we may then identify hot spots of innovation through the mathematical patterns within patents, scientific papers, and capital allocation, and more.

Therefore, *applied intelligence* builds capacity and range to cover as much of the universe on a given topic as possible—to come as close as possible to devising effective solutions to complex problems with the assistance of AI. The use of machine learning (ML) gives applied intelligence a tremendous advantage over human theoretical modelling or intuition. The simple utility of applied intelligence becomes an immediate competitive advantage to the user. Additionally, machine learning provides more cognitive power to constantly learn and do better.

AI platforms dramatically speed up the entrepreneurial process. A robust platform strategy and AI-led enterprise architecture speed up entrepreneurial development. Comprehensive digital commerce strategies underpinned by operational AI & ML, geared towards building businesses in optimal industries identified, and aligning with consumer behaviour trends in targeted countries or regions for export distribution, is the new business intelligence normal, moving the entrepreneur forward with purpose and focus.

- Knowledge-based environments will help empower Black entrepreneurs in the region to take advantage of these types of learning opportunities and environments—to face a faster and more complex world.

- Industrial Engineering, used for development to discover new insights, optimizes performance and results, which is central to sustainable and inclusive long-term enterprise construction.

- The successful application of AI technologies becomes a fundamental game-changer, an indispensable profit tool. That makes it almost impossible to compete successfully in the 21st century without AI-driven platforms in place.

- This will require significant generational digital infrastructure investments, but the holistic ROI will be unquantifiable compared to the initial investments, transitioning Caribbean economies to heights unimaginable in the present.

ENTREPRENEURS usually find new ways to have positive social and environmental impacts on communities. Entrepreneurs have always tackled society's greatest challenges and solved them through business applications; therefore, entrepreneurship is central to the process of socioeconomic change.

Innovation is the process of turning new ideas into quantifiable economic value—into new products and services, new ways of doing things more efficiently and effectively. Innovation must be inherent and aligned with entrepreneurship to extract real and sustainable value. Entrepreneurship drives innovation, creativity, and efficiency development and turns good ideas into ones that are useful to society. Innovation fuels most of the world's long-term productivity and is responsible for economic gains; it is the key to profitable outcomes. According to the *World Economic Forum (WEF) Global Issues Report* says that "innovative firms significantly outperform non-innovators, in terms of both revenue and employment growth." The same can be said for countries! The entire

Caribbean region must understand that only through a cultural shift to an entrepreneurial and innovative culture can we have a realistic chance to create prosperity for ourselves in the 21st century.

WEF goes on to say that innovation requires a diverse cast of characters, and does not function in isolation; in short, innovation requires many actors, and it is a team effort:

> *"Innovation tends to involve a lot of players; innovation systems are composed of research institutions, universities, national laboratories, hospitals, corporations, startups, venture capitalists, and patent attorneys. The public sector can play a key role, in the form of funding bodies and intermediary organizations like technology transfer offices and accelerators (programs designed to turn raw startups into young companies)."*

How these participants interact is critical; efficiency is the core goal of operation and interaction. Therefore, intelligent technology platforms will be critical to the efficiency and in facilitating good communication and strategy formulation. Knowledge systems (publications and standards) from which entrepreneurs can benefit is one example of things that must be included in the dynamic strategy. New savvy players are disrupting, so the old transform to the new and improve or die.

Stakeholder "Activism" a Requirement for Growth

While corporate activism has been a widely successful method of creating value in North American and European markets for a while now, it has not been on the radar in Caribbean capital markets. The Caribbean business community and industries as a whole are very inefficient, and technology has not been integrated enough to change that situation. Capital markets leadership is very lackadaisical. Jamaica, however, has shown some leadership in advancing the capital market in the region. Unfortunately, Jamaica has been very inward-looking and narrow-minded on the whole, content to be a big fish in a small pond.

In short, given that it has such a large population by Caribbean standards, Jamaica is not living up to its potential, and it is not recognizing its responsibility as a leader. Therefore, it is holding itself and the entire region back. The attitude of Jamaican capital markets leadership also blocks the natural growth progression to globalization and higher activity and more growth and profitability. Jamaica must stop thinking small, tribal, and open its eyes to 21st-century opportunities. The more investors and people that can participate in the regional economy the better it is for everyone, and more wealth will be created all around. Jamaica must stop its provincial thinking and start thinking globally! Everyone must participate and contribute towards regional growth; the Caribbean is too tiny to be divided, and division will be our death knell.

Jamaicans must fundamentally understand that they are not merely "Jamaican"; Jamaica was not a state created out of any common or shared values of a people and/or ethnic group, as nations are normally created. It is simply a territory where boatloads of enslaved Africans were shipped by the slavers, and Black Jamaicans are descendants of those enslaved people. So we should not allow ourselves to be fooled by randomness. Hence, a pan-Caribbean attitude must prevail. United, we can stand; but divided, we will continue to render ourselves irrelevant, simply driving faster towards extinction.

THE ABILITY TO USE forms of social media communication to propagate one's message is a powerful tool for the integration of activism. Corporate activism has become mainstream in Western markets and is also acting as a check on corporations. Governance

433

issues can be brought up through social media, such as examination of corporations' track records on environmental and social responsibility. The rise of the activist investor has taken on a whole new meaning in driving stock performance and creating shareholder value. The bright light of activism is a force to reckon with; increasingly, corporations must react to the activism or see their stock sink.. Therefore, larger incumbent corporations in the Caribbean must have leadership in social responsibility and operate with a more purposeful existence for the common good. They must operate with heightened awareness and responsibility towards their business operations. How business interacts and innovates with other economic actors, and what they do to foster a more symbiotic and mutualistic ecosystem, will produce good social benefits for their societies—for the common good.

For the Caribbean, the task is to facilitate two phenomena:

1. **Social activism,** wherein the focus is on digital transformation, opportunities for young people, environment, and social responsibility—the impact businesses have on local communities; and
2. **Investor activism**, in which an individual or group buys a significant stake in a public company to influence the board and the running of the company. Many publicly traded

Caribbean companies are mismanaged, plagued by poor performance, excessive cost operating structures, and nepotism; many of them could be run more profitably if they were taken private.

The most significant issues for many Caribbean companies right now are digital transformation, social and environmental impacts, and technology infrastructure investment. Private equity firms, hedge funds and wealthy individuals, family offices, local investors, and local pension funds are the types of investors that can lead shareholder activist movements in the region to garner investment, restructure and digitize operations, and improve profitability and shareholder value. Investor activism fueled by foreign capital is a natural fit, and exactly what the region needs now to force real change. By driving transformation and innovation, the entrepreneurship culture can help in shifting the region towards global commerce.

Over the past decade or so, hundreds of billions of dollars have been poured into companies via activist investing activities around the world, and there is no reason why the Caribbean cannot tap into that market to find investors. A significant number of companies in the region are old, slow, and bewildered, and have no clue how to transition to the new economy. Moreover, these incumbents hold back the modernization of the regional economy by contributing to underlying inefficiencies and imbalances in these local economies. Grace Kennedy Foods out of Jamaica is the best example. Massy Wood Group Ltd., Caribbean Airlines Limited, Angostura, A.S. Bryden & Sons (Trinidad) Ltd. are only a few of the incumbents that are preventing the region's entry into the 21st-century. Their leadership enjoys old-school elite privilege and suffers from the big-fish-in-a-small-pond syndrome.

Grace Kennedy Foods: A Prime Example

- GK's mission, as stated in its annual report, is to deliver the taste and experience of multi-ethnic Caribbean foods and culture to the world. GK seeks *"to be a Global Consumer Group, delivering long-term consumer and shareholder value through brand building and innovative solutions in food and financial services."* Yet so far, GK has failed to accomplish this mission.

For GK to elevate to the status of a global company, it must first disrupt and transform itself through innovation, then equip itself with robust technology through an operational enterprise platform. GK has failed so far even to forge an operational AI-driven platform for its business. It remains wholly unprepared and behind the technology and transformation curve relative to its global competitors—flat-footed in responding to the global consumer trends and changing demographics in the food business. Other global tech-savvy business leaders in the same space are rapidly engaged in advanced analytics, AI, and ML in order to meet the challenges of the 21st-century economy. New upstarts in all industries continue to disrupt traditional players like GK, so maintaining the status quo is not helpful to GK or to the region's economy. By contrast, Tyson Foods, Heinz, McCain, and many other food companies are all involved in new innovative startup initiatives—embracing transformational change and leveraging their wide existing distribution channels so as to maximize shareholder value.

McCain, for example, invested $60 million into a healthy greens greenhouse operation called Pure Leaf, a Canadian startup. McCain recognizes the transition of the global food environment towards healthier plant-based foods, and the new greenhouse technologies are available to advance that market. So they make the necessary investment appropriately.

At last count, Grace Kennedy generated approximately US$729 (as per 2021 annual report) million in revenue, with over 53% coming from Jamaican operations alone. Jamaica has a population of only 2.9 million people. By contrast, North America and the U.K. represent a combined market of over 430 million people. In the U.K. alone, "the ethnic [non-white] populations" represent over 20% or 13.2 million people. Research shows, and common sense too, as the world *darkens* everywhere, the normalization of ethnic cuisines is an expanding growth industry. These markets could easily make GK a multibillion-dollar operation in under 5 years, a relatively short period.

Leveraging insights from an abundance of data on trending millennial food tastes on the demand side, coupled with implementing operational automation on the supply side, would be an excellent strategy for extracting extraordinary value from the global economy.

Shareholders must demand that GK step into the 21st century and build a real, quantifiable growth strategy for the times. Activist investors and social impact activists must combine efforts to ensure that large companies like GK, so influential in local and regional economies, are acting intelligently and responsibly to bolster Caribbean growth. Is GKF building towards zero-emissions operations, using electric vehicles, supporting local farmers, and investing in local entrepreneurs? If not, why?

ENTERPRISE SINGAPORE was formed to champion entrepreneurial innovation and oversee standards and accreditation for Singapore's economic development. Enterprise Singapore is a statutory board under the Ministry of Trade and Industry formed to support this Southeast Asian country's small and medium-sized enterprise development, to upgrade capabilities, innovate, transform, and internationalize. Its overriding mission objective is to facilitate and champion enterprise growth in Singapore...see: Enterprises.govv.sg

"Enterprise Singapore is the government agency championing enterprise development. We work with committed companies to build capabilities, innovate, and internationalize. We also support the growth of Singapore as a hub for global

trading and start-ups. As the national standards and accreditation body, we continue to build trust in Singapore's products and services through quality and standards."

The world is changing at a rapid pace; technology is disrupting companies, industries, and the way we do business. Asia is the world's current growth engine, and Singapore is right at the centre of it all, one of its leaders. In this environment, companies need to act nimbly and integrate ecosystem capability to innovate and globalize and prepare their businesses for the future. Enterprise Singapore was formed with this purpose in mind many years ago. Growing Singapore companies, either locally or overseas, has always been at the heart of the work of Enterprise Singapore. They work with businesses, from start-ups to SMEs in leading high-growth sectors, or with companies that will have a meaningful impact on continuously building a country's wealth.

> *To enable businesses to navigate today's enterprise landscape, Enterprise Singapore adopts a company-centric approach. We do so by providing programmes and support catered to your company's stage of growth, the industry you are in, and the overseas markets of your interest.*
>
> *Together with our extensive network of local and overseas partners, we support the efforts to enhance industry and enterprise competitiveness through the 23 Industry Transformation Maps (ITMs). We will work with your company to capture new market share through upgrading and innovation; adoption of new technologies to improve productivity; facilitating expansion into overseas markets and strengthening leadership capabilities to build a talent pool. Beyond growing enterprises, we will continue our efforts to*

build trust in our products and services through quality and standards, as well as establish Singapore as a leading start-up and trading hub.

In no uncertain terms, for Caribbean survival, a similar **Enterprise Caribbean** model must be adopted! However, the Enterprise Caribbean model must be 10 times as intense and focused and with a fully operating resource hub for business development in the digital era. The March 29, 2015, article "How Singapore Became One Of The Richest Places On Earth" by Jim Zarroli highlights that many see Singapore as a free-market success story. However, the role that government and policymakers have played has been a key factor in its success. Zarroli says, 'Singapore has been called the 20th century's most successful development story. A tiny island-state became one of the richest places in the world and a role model for other governments in Asia and beyond."

If Caribbean leaders are not paying attention, their willful ignorance is putting future Caribbean prosperity at risk. "I do not think any other economy," says Linda Lim, an economist at the University of Michigan, "even the other Asian Tigers, have that good of a statistical record of rapid growth, full employment, with very good social indicators—life expectancy, education, housing, etc.—in the first 20 years."

"We have had, since 1965, an undivided society, solidly behind a meritocratic system, pushing for higher standards of education, higher standards of performance, and meritocratic at every level," the late prime minister Lee Kuan Yew Lee told an audience of college students in 2013. Singapore, like everywhere else, has its issues with inequality; however, economic growth and prosperity for its people is the primary responsibility of the state and other actors. It delivers on that commitment and uses surplus funds to create a strong social system and safety net. Singapore has little land and no natural resources! It is basically a rocky peninsula. But after its independence in 1965, the former British colony was transformed into a major manufacturing and financial centre. The late economist Milton Friedman described Singapore as an example of how to do development right. Singapore looked to financial services and manufacturing back then and continues to invest in technology and adapt and lead the changing times. They figured things out and became an enterprising culture.

Caribbean policymakers and enterprises need a role model; Singapore is it! The Caribbean region's leadership needs an entrepreneurial growth mindset and a strategic, fact-based growth model on which to build. What Singapore has done is create an incubative, facilitative ecosystem, underwritten by quality economic policymaking of high utility, performance, and sustainable results. Many have called Singapore an "economic miracle." However, the main factor contributing to its standout success is that it simply built a strategy and executed on it.

Chapter 17

Knowledge is the New Money

"Intellectual capital will always trump financial capital."

Paul Tudor Jones III

Before the 21st century, wealth was mostly defined in the form of physical resources: land, real estate, property, gold, etc.; all capital-intensive sectors with very high barriers to entry. However, since this century and particularly this decade began, it has become as clear as daylight that the knowledge-based economy is where great wealth is increasingly being created. No sophisticated analysis is needed to arrive at this conclusion; it is obvious from the fact that the wealthiest people in the world and the largest and most influential companies are tech-related enterprises. In the 21st century, technology, digital assets, and intellectual property have taken over from physical assets as the dominant creators of wealth in the universe.

We are at the beginning of a period called the 5th Industrial Revolution (5IR), where AI is changing the future of work. Renowned futurist Peter Diamandis calls it *rapid demonetization*, in which technology renders previously expensive products or services much cheaper—even free. And human labour's worth to the enterprise is now increasingly being measured against the value that machines can deliver.

For example, not too long ago, video conferencing was a paid service only affordable to large corporations. Today, video conferencing is everywhere and essentially free. Educational institutions are finding better ways to deliver education virtually through innovation. Better diagnostics via artificial intelligence increase diagnostic accuracy at a fraction of the cost to human resources. AI is lowering the average cost of healthcare by focusing on prevention. Accordingly, increased efficiency through intelligence and automation is becoming fundamental to business and to life in general. Yet

Caribbean economies have not yet even investigated efficiency gains through technology in any meaningful way. They have not paid attention to the most critical growth sector opportunities that can propel their economies forward.

Just as blue-collar workers lost jobs to automation between 2000 and 2010, when robots began to replace 85% of manufacturing jobs, white-collar workers in this 5th Industrial Revolution are facing the same fate. Managerial jobs will become increasingly obsolete because of the augmentation of the machine; machines can do certain tasks incredibly better, faster, and at minuscule costs. Therefore, it is a question of simple math: producing more at lower costs equals increased profit, and profit makes the world go around.

The diagram below explains how AI fits into the job market; by changing its dynamics, AI replaces the jobs at the bottom of the relative *skill-for-value-metric,* and the new high-skilled and new economy jobs move to the top. These new, more relevant skills have greater value in the economy, so they demand higher pay. The most skilled knowledge workers can be 100 times more valuable to the enterprise than the average unskilled worker. Accordingly, those who occupy the top of the skill ladder are essentially at the top of the economic food chain, so to speak. They become the most-sought-after, best-paid workers. Premiums are now being paid for the new-economy skilled knowledge worker. These relevant and useful knowledge holders move to the C^2 group of people, as discussed earlier. They are the innovators, content creators, entrepreneurs, and the gig economy, aligning their pursuits with the prevailing knowledge-based economy. These C^2 workers are no longer seen as costs but as assets and revenue generators for their employers.

The chart below illustrates the *value-metric*:

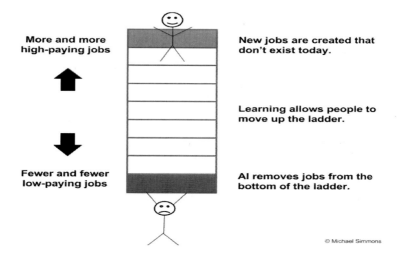

More and more high-paying jobs

Fewer and fewer low-paying jobs

New jobs are created that don't exist today.

Learning allows people to move up the ladder.

AI removes jobs from the bottom of the ladder.

© Michael Simmons

Relative to the above illustration and for explanation purposes, we can simply replace people with countries. As a result, the Caribbean rests at the bottom of the global knowledge economy, garnering the lowest incomes and growth dynamics.

The process of digitization often worries us about AI and automation taking our jobs. But it does no good to worry about things we cannot control or about progress and advancement that is happening. We often become distracted by our self-manifested hysteria about change and the evolutionary process that technology brings. This is how the world continuously unfolds, so continuously complaining and seeking to place blame is self-defeating. Focus instead on adapting to the evolving reality and you will be better off. Therefore, newer technologies replace the old and inefficient ones, and you must adapt; economies become more resilient the more they rely on technology. Technological change is continuous, so you cannot simply sit and hope for the best, because you will only end up getting the worst of it. Natural selection is everywhere.

Caribbean nations are becoming increasingly marginalized as more technological advancement takes place all over the world. The 5th Industrial Revolution represents the Caribbean's greatest growth opportunity, but also a huge risk to the region if it does not advance in triple time. Other nations are utilizing AI exponentially, and their economies are increasingly widening the wealth gap relative to Caribbean economies. So while other nations are building back better, Caribbean political leadership continue to grin and bathe in the blissfulness of their own ignorance and selfishness They cling to their countries' low-income and commoditized economic profiles and behave as victims when they are not, doing nothing to help the people for whom they were elected to create growth and security.

INFORMATION FROM a Data Watch article, Sept 30th, 2021; titled: "Japan races to hire 270,000 artificial intelligence engineers," puts the urgency of digital transformation into perspective. Even a nation as renowned for its technological sophistication as Japan appears behind the curve and intensifies its efforts to move ahead in the 5IR. "We cannot develop a system to forecast demand for products—though we need it—without a ramp-up in AI infrastructure," lamented a Japanese food company executive in charge of digital transformation. Japan has a considerable number of IT workers: 1.22 million engineers in 2020, according to the Ministry of Internal Affairs and Communications. In the U.S., the number stands at 4.09 million; in India, at 2.32 million; and in China, at 2.37 million. However, in a rapidly evolving digital world, it is the specific IT skills or assets that matter most. In Japan, based on 2018 statistics, conventional IT workers, those who develop websites and apps, accounted for about 90% of all IT workers. Cutting-edge IP workers, those who specialize in AI and smart devices that connect to the Internet of Things, only made up 10%, according to the Ministry of Economy, Trade, and Industry. So Japan's current stated mission is to close the shortage by finding 270,000 digital transformation skilled workers by 2030.

Professor Ken Sakamura of Tokyo University says that people capable of working with AI and solving AI and IoT problems will be increasingly in demand; so this bodes well for the C^2 class who are enthusiastic to work with intelligent technology, to get tasks done. In the world of digital competitive rankings, a survey put together by the International Institute for Management

Development, a Swiss business school, found that Japan's overall ranking dropped to #27 from #20 over the last few years. However, as we see, "Japan, Inc." is not standing still. The Japanese government, with cooperation from universities and companies, has an all-out plan to take countermeasures to improve Japan's competitiveness in the new global economy.

Adaptation of the knowledge-based economy is the only thing that will fill that ***knowledge-to-profit*** chasm. Knowledge intensity is shaping the future of the global economy and the ecosystems that underlie it; knowledge remains the main thing, the fundamental underpinning of future growth.

So in a changing and increasingly competitive world, Caribbean leadership must speak less and act more on digital transformation. Act with extreme urgency and build a strategy. To put things in perspective, if Japan, of all countries in the world, can appear to be behind the AI curve, then where does that leave the Caribbean? Again, everything comes down to what the region does.

IN TODAY'S NEW ECONOMY, intellectual property is the optimal "capital," the underlying and ultimate driver of the enterprise. The new world brings new realities and challenges, but it also creates magnificent new opportunities. Traditional simple supply-and-demand analysis has not yet caught up to the new economy's relevant economic and efficient systems. The whole equilibrium analysis approach is no longer terribly useful in practical terms, nor will it be relevant to real-world economic decision-making in this new digital economy. There are so many variables to consider now—not because they did not exist before, but because access to information, analysis, and opinion is happening in real time now. Therefore, it is impossible to return to static classroom models to explain the world today and how things will flow. It was always difficult to predict, but it is harder than ever now.

In this more complex, data-rich world, logic dictates that the enterprise can be more efficient and effective, more profitable, and sustainable in the long term if it considers the demand side first. In brief, with the availability of data science, AI, and ML, it is simply more sensible, risk-adjusted, to use business intelligence as much as possible in everyday business. It is more sensible to rely on data than on intuition or worse yet, the traditional philosophical theories of supply and demand that economists still continue to push. So business intelligence must be embedded in the decision-making enterprise architecture if it wants to compete effectively in the 21st century. The old manual world is gone.

As the illustration below shows, before digitization (BD), there was a great deal of cost built into the practice of business—countless layers of it. By contrast, after digitization (AD), we end up with two main cost layers, namely **Creator** and **Platform**—dramatically minimizing the layers and costs and increasing profits and enterprise value.

446

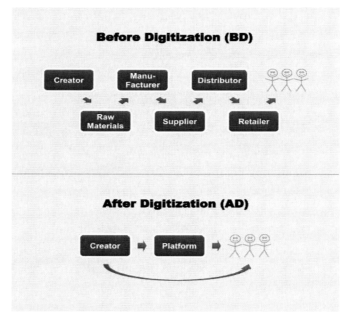

@Michael Simmons, Accelerated Intelligence

In the digital world, many of the necessary processes can be done through digitization over the platform, adding hyper-efficiency to the enterprise, which also adds more value to the final product, contributing to the firm's brand building and profitability. So in the digital value chain ecosystem, the focus must be on intellectual property (IP) development—which is the optimal value creator, the software, automation, data analytics, and social media assets for real-time analysis, including instant feedback. This is fundamentally how enterprise value will be created in the 21st century.

Platforms like Netflix, Airbnb, and Amazon have taken traditional businesses and brought them to the quantum in the global business universe. Netflix is the biggest chain of movie theatres and content creators in the world, all without owning a single theatre—the most efficient and direct distribution model. Airbnb is

447

ai

the largest accommodations and hospitality company in the world without owning a single physical piece of real estate. And Amazon…well, you get the picture.

Moreover, embedded analytics in the very platform allows for each transaction to be an opportunity to collect customers' data. Machine learning allows for faster intelligence gathering, continuous building of knowledge systems, and better overall delivery of the customer experience.

Identifying unique competitive business advantages is where the region must start. The Caribbean's geography and climate make the region a highly hospitable "growing" environment for AgTech and renewable energy enterprise development. Combining the two creates tremendous optimal operating environments will help the region leapfrog onto the global wealth curve through effective and efficient economies.

The universe is not static; new knowledge creates new technology, which requires new learning, which then creates newer more advanced technologies, and so on. Identifying valuable knowledge ecosystems that can be leveraged for specific enterprises has become ever more important. Opportunity windows can close very fast; leaders must take advantage of new knowledge and new technologies, and rapidly find substantial capital in order to get things done. Caribbean leaders must inspire and push their nations to identify and capture the opportunities in a transforming world. The more quickly our entire society embraces a knowledge-based economy culture, the sooner prosperity will appear on the horizon.

Caribbean leaders and stakeholders must become realistic and understand what is really at stake—survival! All actions matter, and inaction matters as well. So we must think long-term—at least 200 years into the future. Otherwise, our thinking will not be optimal, and our decisions will be more expedient than anything else. History tells us that what we do or neglect to do in our time and place in the universe will impact our families and societies for generations to

448

come. Therefore, as Caribbean people of African descent, we have a moral obligation to our ancestors who suffered so greatly and to our future generations to work intelligently in our time to lay the foundational tenets for intergenerational prosperity.

Imagine a Caribbean where political and tribal discourse are muted in the economic interests of the society...where the acceptance of the latest nonsense academic theories is not allowed to seep into our discourse...where reality prevails, and solutions are built effectively based on reality...where we become immune to nonsense. Imagine a Caribbean where critical thinking, self-reliance, personal responsibility, and self-determination become the fundamental characteristics of our society.

Leveraging Your Competitive Advantages

> The central event of the twentieth century is the overthrow of matter. In technology, economics, and the politics of nations, wealth in the form of physical resources is steadily declining in value and significance. The powers of the mind are everywhere ascendant over the brute force of things
>
> — George Gilder

Adapting our societies to a changing economic reality is essential for good outcomes and plays a critical growth function in our civilization. Hence, technology adaptation has always been at the helm in eras of profound change, and the ability for societies to expand economically requires them to feed themselves through those expansions. Therefore, as in the industrial revolutions of the past, agricultural technology and knowledge advancement always underwrote expansion. The first Agricultural Revolution (circa 10,000 BC) brought about the prehistoric transition from hunting and gathering to settled agriculture (also known as the Neolithic Revolution). The Arab Agricultural Revolution (8th–13th century), the spread of new crops and advanced techniques in the Muslim world and copied by Europeans later which helped them out of the Dark Ages.

Between the mid-17th and late 19th centuries, those agricultural revolutions in Britain, for example, were essentially continuous technological advancements in farming, ushering in an unprecedented increase in agricultural production, including increases in labour and land productivity. These advantages help create wealth for privileged aristocrats by shutting out common people. Agriculture has always been a wealth creator, and technological advancement has been the efficiency factor to optimize production and value. So let us not fret about it or reinvent the wheel; it continues to roll very nicely. We need only seize these opportunities as they present themselves. Let us utilize our land and agriculture astutely by harnessing those resources to AI—maximizing our natural competitive advantages to create wealth for ourselves.

Chapter 18

In Long-Time

Technological innovations—what some economists might call general-purpose technologies—have always been the main drivers of transformation and growth. The Industrial Revolution, for example, included the steam engine, electricity, and the internal combustion engine, to name some of the top examples. Each period's intense innovation catalyzed new waves of complementary innovations and new opportunities.

Today, the most significant general-purpose technology of our era is AI. AI and its impact on how we work is called the 5th Industrial Revolution (5IR). The significance of AI in business is irrefutable, but it remains misunderstood by many. Based on the history of general-purpose technology, we can relate AI as positioning humanity for another extraordinary leap forward, and those who will benefit most from the 5IR will be the ones who embrace it most.

1st Industrial Revolution	2nd Industrial Revolution	3rd Industrial Revolution	4th Industrial Revolution	5th Industrial Revolution
Mechanisation	Electrification	Automation and Globalisation	Digitalisation	Personalisation
Occurred during the 18th and 18th centuries, mainly in Europe and North America	From the late 1800s to the start of the First World War	The digital revolution occurred around the 1980s	Start of the 21st century	2nd decade of the 21st century
Steam engines replacing horse and human power	Production of steel, electricity and combustion engines.	Computers, digitisation and the internet,	AI, robotics, IoT, blockchain and crypto.	Innovation purpose and inclusivity.
Introduction of mechanical production facilities driven by water and steam power	Division of labour and mass production, enabled by electricity.	Automation of production through electronic and IT systems	Robotics, artificial intelligence, augmented reality, virtual reality	Deep, multi-level cooperation between people and machines. Consciousness.

The sequence of the five industrial revolutions

A Phenomenal Journey Towards the 5th Industrial Revolution

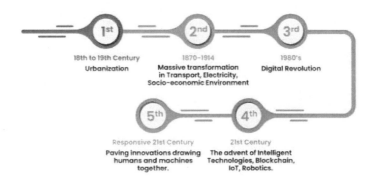

It is apparent that in the Caribbean, SIS cannot scale traditional farming enough to compete with the large landmass territories in Latin America, California, India, etc. Therefore, the only realistic way for these SIS to become relevant players in the agricultural sector of the new global economy is by embracing the 5IR—by combining human intelligence and artificial intelligence.

Strategy is the process of identifying, quantifying, and mitigating any risk that affects or is inherent in the strategic objective. In agricultural enterprise pursuits, we must use strategy for differentiation, to maximize our natural competitive advantages. We must create maximum operational efficiencies for productivity and enhanced profitability, with the objective of opening and capturing new and uncontested market spaces.

Still, the 5IR is no magic bullet; it still comes down to human decision-making in the end. AI simply and dramatically shortens the time it takes to learn and execute tasks, and it improves on those tasks. Nevertheless, AI is also not intelligent on its own; it is not conscious and has no idea for what purpose and from whom this information is being provided. It always needs instructions from humans—in other words, programming. Therefore, AI coupled with human intelligence creates optimal productivity and output dynamics.

Since machines are not conscious, they cannot interact with or interpret their surroundings, either. Here is where human leadership and sound strategy come into play, and how humans and artificial intelligence can combine most optimally as a powerful force in the universe. Still, it is important to remember that machines are never free from human bias, because it is humans, after all, who program machines. So AI can often reinforce biases that already exist in any given society.

Accordingly, "clean is not the same thing as accurate, and accurate is not the same thing as actionable. Problems on any one of these vectors could impede an A.I. model's development or interfere with the quality of its results." Marianne Belloti, *A.I. Is Solving the*

Wrong Problem. Belloti goes on to explain that data can be problematic, because from the beginning, it can be factually incorrect, corrupted, or improperly formatted, with the result that the message can be distorted and misinterpreted. For example, a piece of data captured in a particular context and being reused inappropriately, with the wrong level of granularity for the model's purpose, can be problematic.

Solving all of these data problems in any organization of any size is difficult, and once the data asset becomes corrupted, it can affect analysis or applications greatly. So we must recognize that innovation creates opportunity, but it also creates vulnerabilities. We must sober ourselves to the objective realities of AI and be hyper-focused in our application of it, recognizing that systems are dependent on the quality of the inputs. So human intelligence must still override and manage artificial intelligence.

In the end, it is still up to human intelligence to make sound decisions employing *applied intelligence.* Therefore, it provides the framework to combine artificial intelligence with human intelligence for maximum problem-solving and sheer usefulness. Strategy again is critical in everything and in every decision—effectively all decisions are strategies. So *applied intelligence* is essential in any Strategy-Leadership framework which aligns with data science for the central objective of optimal decision-making. No matter how much data we get, how fast we get it, or how powerful these machines become, a strategic framework remains essential to positive outputs and outcomes.

We must strip things down and get to the most effective utilization of business intelligence assets. We should be consciously aware of the specific problems that we are trying to solve, and having a disciplined operational strategy framework in place helps tremendously. If we do not utilize *applied intelligence*, we leave much of what we do to chance, thus increasing the risk of errors in judgement. Hence, we must build a road map to improve our chances of getting where we want to go more quickly. The functions and insights provided within this process also identify the hidden asymmetries that lurk, and those asymmetries can be enormously helpful in problem-solving and in connecting the dots.

CLIMATE CHANGE is an existential threat—but contrary to common belief, climate change is not a moral issue, it is an economic issue. Climate change is deeply rooted in unavoidable economic conflict, because it is driven by the laws of nature, and the scarcity of what nature provides for our existence is fundamentally about economics. Therefore, the Small Island States (SIS) of the Caribbean must be wary of how the global "fight" against climate change plays out and how it impacts our own economic future. Do not be fooled into acting "morally" by wealthy countries and being distracted from what must count most for the Caribbean people—prosperity!

Caribbean leadership must keep its eyes on the prize: sustainable growth and enterprise development. So when the West offers to "help" or pay for "projects" to help the region fight climate change, be aware that they are not helping you, but themselves. They are essentially executing their climate mitigation strategies and obligations throughout the region, but in such a way as to meet their own climate reduction targets. Remember, there are no free lunches in this world. These funded projects are in the West's interests first and foremost, based on signed agreements on emissions reduction.

Climate change is a global issue, and we are all affected by it; but not all situations are identical, and the Caribbean's contribution to pollution is minuscule compared to the industrialized countries. So do not be suckered into bearing the disproportionate weight through so-called "climate mitigation projects." The region cannot have the same climate priorities that Western nations have; our priorities must be growth-oriented, first and foremost. Leaders in the region must still address climate change;

455

however, it must be with a view to advancing its economies not hindering it. Solutions must be put forward towards fostering zero emissions, green-growth regional economy.

Climate change risk mitigation strategies must be built into the regional economy and made a part of the naturally occurring reality of transformation. Most importantly, decisions concerning how best to combat climate change must never come at the expense of economic growth and digital transformation. Fighting climate change must be coupled with economic growth strategies.

We must see climate change not simply as a "problem" to be solved independently, but rather as an opportunity to grow our economy efficiently. Most major problems entail major opportunities, and with crisis usually comes opportunity. So we must capture those opportunities by thinking quantitatively about how to extract value and wealth from them. The solutions must be enterprising enough because that is how wealth is created, and history shows that entrepreneurship usually solves most of the world's most pressing socioeconomic problems. Therefore, entrepreneurial pursuits underpinned by technology and innovation must be the focus for the region.

For example, Russia's government has recognized and is capitalizing on the economic opportunities that climate change is delivering, and so, has begun leasing thousands of square kilometers of land in the country's far eastern region to the likes of China, South Korea, and Japanese investors. Much of this land was once unproductive, but it is now used to grow soybeans, which account for 65% of all the protein fed to farm animals. Sergey Levin, Russia's deputy minister of agriculture, has predicted that soy exports from its far-eastern farmlands may reach US$600m by 2024. that is almost five times what they were in 2017.

The government of Newfoundland and Labrador, a northeastern province of Canada, is also trying to promote the expansion of agriculture to attract similar investors, like Russia is

456

doing. In Canada's western province of Manitoba, a company called Bonnefield Financial is investing to capitalize on the ways that climate change is changing the Canadian landscape and agriculture. The company is buying tillable fields and leasing them out to farmers. The big bet here is that an increasingly warmer climate will steadily increase the asset value of large areas of farmable land. So the long-term business objective is for farmers in Manitoba to transition from more cold-weather crops like wheat and canola to denser, more profitable staples like corn and soya.

To provide some context on the science of this matter: these opportunities stem from the process by which plants and some bacteria produce glucose from carbon dioxide and water using energy from sunlight: photosynthesis, through which plants grow and feed themselves. In short, more carbon dioxide in the atmosphere means more plant growth. The build-up of carbon dioxide in the atmosphere over the past century due to global industrialization has led to a "global greening," since plants benefit from higher carbon dioxide levels. This helps boost crop yields and is part of the investment calculation that farmland investors in the north are making. In short, green plants grow faster with more CO_2. Many also become more drought-resistant because higher CO_2 levels allow plants to use water more efficiently. More abundant vegetation from increased CO_2 is already apparent. For further information on this as I know it sounds counterintuitive, please see the following publication: *Carbon Dioxide Benefits the World: See for Yourself* @ CO2Coalition.org.

Therefore, as the planet warms, lands that were once frigid and unproductive can now become more valuable and become available assets for farming. The amount of area that is used for farming has been increasing for centuries, and since the 18th century, it has expanded fivefold. Most of the growth came throughout the 20th century, as industrialization and carbon release warmed the planet and technology added to more efficiency and production in farming, generating increased output.

More recently, technologies such as genome editing, and better data crunching have helped raise crop yields significantly. Northerly countries with large landmasses such as Canada, Russia, and China are warming at least twice as rapidly as the global average. This development plays well for these land investors; but for tropical regions like the Caribbean, it is not good news for their future commercial farming aspirations. Because of the Caribbean region's geography, physically vast countries like Canada and Russia can increase food production by taking advantage of global warming to grow crops they previously could not. Therefore, because of geography, globally competitive large-scale farming in the Caribbean is not realistic, if not impossible as a viable enterprise and contributor to GDP growth for the region.

The only realistic way for these Caribbean SIS to become relevant players, relating to agribusiness, is through the sophistication and application of advanced intelligence-based technologies and automation—**AgTech.** The evidence tells us that modern farming is inefficient, and climate change is reducing the amount of arable land available in the Caribbean region, which does not have much of it in the first place. The reality of geography is front and centre in agricultural business contemplation.

In addition, data analytics, AI and ML are being applied to demand-side activities to find new demand trends, opportunities, and new markets—along with automation to run the supply or operational side effectively. SIS that continue to engage in traditional farming will see their future economic prospects diminish if they do not align with the new economy. Major transformative thinking and actions are required right now! And AgTech is the future of farming, and prosperity for the region.

For example, Vertical Greenhouse Technology Farming Systems, as explained by Douglas Blackwell strategy report, titled, *Greenhouse Technology Farming Systems*:

- Grow 75 times more food per square foot than traditional ones and requires 90% less space
- No need for pesticides
- Allows crops to grow year-round
- Isn't affected by outside weather
- Uses 90% less water than traditional farming
- For every technology greenhouse built, you save 31 acres of land, 62K lbs of wasted food, and 18.3 M gallons of water.

We must think quantitatively and understand that new technology systems and applications are central to our very economic survival. The first principle is always first to survive because there is no situation in nature where you can ever thrive without first surviving.

In the domain of global farming, technology investing in farming soared to over 20 billion dollars in 2020, according to AgFunder's latest Farm Tech Investment Report. However, the Caribbean was more or less excluded from receiving any of those investment dollars. Total investment in Indian agri-food start-ups for FY2020 stood at $1.1 billion, with 133 deals. ASEAN agri-food tech start-up investing reveals that investors are driving the region's nascent industry, as they see the existing mega-trend for personalized, clean, healthy foods taking shape.

Israel—again, a tiny desert country—has used technology to become a major player in agriculture/AgTech through the effective use of greenhouse technology systems. This has enabled the country to create food security and high-value export income while creating high-quality, highly skilled, high-earning jobs, building enormous wealth and growing a strong middle class. The land-space similarities between Israel and SIS of the Caribbean are obvious. Israel is a tiny country, much like Caribbean states; but the major difference is that the Israelis have decided to take their future into their own hands, relying on, and doing for themselves first. The Israeli agriculture sector has masterfully used technology in the context of developing knowledge-based ecosystems for not only transforming the business of farming but their entire economy, which is primarily tech-based.

The Caribbean's leadership continues to flounder with backward thinking, relying on useless UN-based institutions that continue to apply discredited top-down projects and disingenuous advice. Israel, on the other hand, with only a minuscule 22,145 km² of land to its name, has been able to become one of the fastest-growing AgTech economies in the world because it is self-reliant and resilient. So success has nothing to do with size and everything to do with mindset and strategy.

FoodTech and AgTech data reveal a mega-economic opportunity in high-value farm-based food production for those paying attention. This optimistic outlook is validated by real investment dollars circulating around the world—except in the Caribbean, of course, since its leadership lacks a credible plan to compete for those dollars. Even though the region has the optimal environment for agriculture, investors are not taking the region seriously because the region is not doing anything to help itself, to position itself to raise serious capital from global investors. And as we know, perception is reality, so unless the regional business leaders and policymakers demonstrate seriousness through a strategy to create a solid investment climate for AgTech, the region will continue to ground itself while others, like Israel, fly higher.

THE ONGOING COVID-19 pandemic has disrupted the food supply chain and has provided a stark reminder of the benefits of an efficiently producing agricultural sector. The Caribbean region, with its significant food import bill (more than US$10billion per year and growing), could reduce that bill dramatically through a "homegrown" production approach, via effective enterprise development focused on high-valued export growth.

There is also a natural and significant business opportunity with the links between the agriculture sector and the tourism-hospitality sector. It is simply unbelievable that the tourism sector imports most of its food. With such a natural environment for agriculture and tourism, it is a wonder why they have not figured out how to work and brand together. Each sector could support the other for mutual benefit. The non-branding of the region's natural environment in food and all-natural plant-based personal care products, for example, is a classic example of mismanagement of the natural assets of its environment and competitive advantages.

Unfortunately, global investors view the Caribbean as too easygoing, not investing in technology infrastructure, and too focused on tourism. Technology is the name of the game, but the region continues to attend the wrong dance again and again, never finding the right investment partner. Investors invest in good ideas, people whom they see as smart, ambitious, and aggressive, and the designers of the future. Bold moves need to be made, and bold and courageous people are needed to make them. We are now almost a quarter of the way through both the century and the decade of transformation, but the Caribbean is not even in the 21st century yet.

Based on the region's geography and the natural environment, AgTech is the logical, rational, and plain common-sense path for export economy-led growth for the entire Caribbean. No more mealymouthed "development" agencies and charity-tinted nonsense projects! We do not want non-profit, we want profit! The demand for food, particularly personalized, clean, healthy foods, is growing exponentially, according to the demand-side analytics. Therefore, successful investing requires us to act on real, substantiated information, not theoretical wishful thinking. We do not need more advisors and bureaucrats who do not know what they are doing; we need more entrepreneurs and capital to get the job done! Technology is increasingly allowing many more players to enter the agricultural space very quickly, regardless of geography, environment, or climate. The global venture space is filling up and expanding, and investment capital is constantly seeking to put capital to work; but if we desire capital, we must create the winning conditions to get it.

LONG TIME separates *time* into two investment classes or paths: first, there is *theories-narrative-hype-time*, which is reactionary, emotional, social media-driven and news-driven pontification. It amounts to useless noise. Then there is *data and market-time,* which refers to predictability, based on real information and insight that yields positive outcomes in investing, generating greater overall returns over the long term, both for the investor and society. So we must set our thinking quantitatively, and always with a Long Time framework geared towards investing.

The return dynamics look like this:

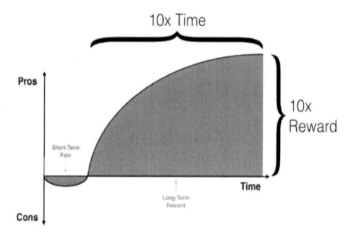

@Simmons

In the above chart, there will be some discomfort and pain in the beginning when investing in technology transitions; but the rewards compound exponentially over the long term, so we must invest in *Long Time*, not cater to short-term time frames or thinking. Short-term thinking leads to errors in judgement that can destroy the substantial potential for gains in the longer term.

    In short, failing to invest in technology in an evolving technology universe or failing to be an early adopter can lead to a lifetime of regret and pain if you miss certain opportunities due to procrastination. If you are afraid to act, you will suffer for it.

    Rapidly evolving trends tend to take on a life of their own and the trick is to get in early with the businesses that are transforming and leading the trends, industries, and whole sectors, or creating new ones. And looking at these opportunities in Long Time rather than through short-term thinking is most optimal for significant returns over time.

The Jeff Bezos/Amazon story, for example, is a very simple one. Essentially, Bezos was researching markets in his capacity as a hedge fund manager, and he then discovered a fascinating thing happening—a new tool called the Internet, which was growing at an incredible rate of 2,300% per year according to Bezos. Alarm bells went off in his head. He found that industries simply do not accelerate that rapidly; so, he realized that he had better find a way to leverage this amazing growth momentum and dynamic, and quickly! Bezos first used research, analysis, and strategy to get on his way—to determine whether the Internet was really growing that rapidly, or if it was a mirage. This is exactly what *applied intelligence* seeks to do: think toward prosperity. Bezos then sought out a business model that he felt would best capture and monetize the trending opportunity; *applied intelligence* does that as well. In short, the idea of Amazon emerged from his quantitative thinking process, and then with the confidence of the analysis, he did not hesitate to act. And the rest, as they say, is history!

Every single day, we are faced with decisions about opportunities in an evolving universe—and as always, technology application usually holds the key to success. Selling books was nothing new, but the technology application, method, and mechanisms by which they were sold proved to be the key to Bezos's *long-time* success. So the moral of the story is, you need some type of disciplined process
of quantitative thinking to identify and analyze opportunities, or at least a flexible framework through which to make decisions. Also, exploring what you do not know instead of what you already do know is central to successful outcomes. The odds of making large returns by building a business from the ground up are extremely low, so the intelligent entrepreneur or investor will use intelligent means such as data and AI to augment their thinking and applied intelligence to improve their success odds.

THE CHART BELOW maps out major technological breakthroughs in the last 250 years; you will observe that there is a direct correlation between those industries and wealthy people like Jeff Bezos over a *long-time*. Today, the chart shows that a tidal wave is developing trends and enterprise opportunities in the diversified technology space.

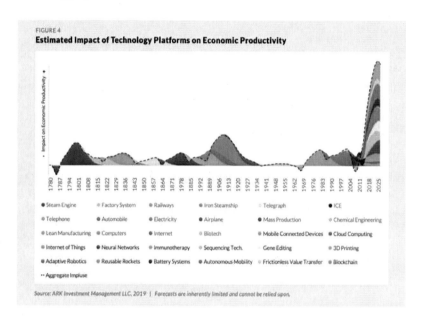

Therefore, thinking and decision-making processes involved in successful enterprise building require intelligence-based systems to carry good ideas forward to reality. Everyone can find usefulness in decision-making mechanisms and processes, and so *applied intelligence* strives to be useful to people above all else.

AS COUNTRIES GROW, they reach a certain point where the activities that were once relied upon to create value can no longer do so. At these strategic inflection points, we need to improve our decision-making, because errors in judgement impact negatively over a long-time. The Caribbean stands at that inflection point now, the point at which digital transformation becomes imperative; so we cannot return to the same old lame tourism projects of the past. Agriculture and renewable energy, underwritten by technology, are the future of sustainable growth and prosperity for the Caribbean people. It is simply illogical to continue along with old-economy behaviour; doing business in the 21st century requires 21st-century thinking.

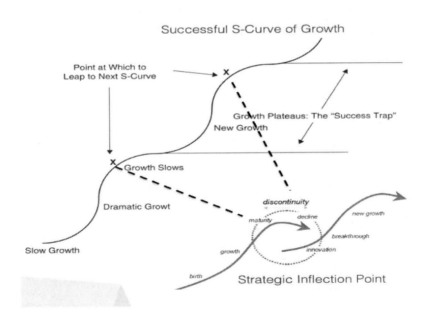

Leaders who can successfully take their respective countries through inflection points can reenergize those countries, underwrite technological infrastructure, promote positive investment climates for investors, facilitate growth and collaboration, cultivate new capabilities, and develop entrepreneurial talents.

Science and common sense tell us that for SIS with limited landmass, the opportunity to benefit from climate change mitigation while utilizing knowledge-based technology in the factors of production, is most intelligent. The future of a robust and profitable export-oriented agriculture sector and nutritional food security will be heavily reliant on building toward a zero-emissions-based economy. The identified growing demand trends also tell us that the global demand for plant-based foods is accelerating rapidly, and consumer preferences are shifting. Artificial intelligence is transitioning the world away from inefficient farming and transforming the greenhouse industry by putting game-changing technologies into play. AI will speed up the transformation of the agriculture industry around the world, so Caribbean leadership must decide if they are going to bring their people into the 21st century or not.

Digital technologies are increasingly powering business operations. Digital technologies have moved beyond adoption silos to become an enterprise requirement. This sector is the entry ticket for doing business and prospering in the 21st century.

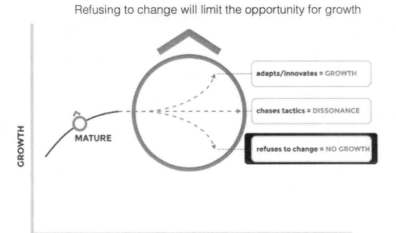

Refusing to change will limit the opportunity for growth

Doing things with a long-term view, and in *Long Time,* reaps the biggest gains; short-term thinking, on the other hand, yields miniscule gains, if any at all. In other words, you obtain small successes and instant gratification, which creates a false sense of achievement, while the big *Long Time* gains go to those who apply an intelligent process in search of their prosperity. The applied intelligence path requires rigorous, fact-based research and analysis in the quantitative function. The process also requires relentless iteration, because seeking optimization is the most viable path forward to delivering useful growth solutions for people and countries. Past transitions in history have always happened with the *growth function of long time,* and no meaningful socio-economic transition has ever taken place in the short run.

PART IV

Chapter 19

Success is a Mindset

In their ground-breaking book **Why Nations Fail,** authors Daron Acemoglu and James A. Robinson provide an evidence-based analysis of the "origins of power, prosperity, and poverty." Acemoglu and Robinson tackle some of the most important questions in development. Questions about how economic development, wealth, and power flow and transcend the universe. They provide analysis and good answers by looking at *why nations fail.*

Why are there national income differences within regions? For example, why is Botswana prospering while Sierra Leone is not? As they take you through history, the authors conclude that strong inclusive institutions often lie behind successful civilizations. Those political institutions drive economic growth and positive social outcomes, and they provide a solid analysis showing that without *inclusive institutions* within a sound strategic framework, it is improbable that sustainable economies can prevail. Their research also shows that authentic free markets supported by solid democratic institutions are the best-suited underpinnings to spur entrepreneurship and innovation.

Why Nations Fail is a lesson in human history; it pulls no punches and is well-researched, evidence-based, honest, and clear about the hard objective truths. It teaches us that in the end, it is the quality and veracity of the decisions leaders make that determine their nations' fate; good decision-making frameworks are extremely helpful in generating good outcomes.

As the authors point out, "[…] [P]oor countries are poor because those that have power make choices that create poverty. They get it wrong not by mistake or ignorance but by purpose. […] [To understand this,] you have to go beyond economics and expert advice…study how decisions get made, who gets to make them, and why those people decide to do what they do."

Traditional economics has ignored the study of the political processes relative to socioeconomic outcomes. This is mainly because economics itself has turned into philosophy, over-engaged in theories like perfect competition that do not exist in real-world economies. This philosophy-economics creates automatic errors in judgement from the very outset when these theories are then used to inform development strategies. Development economics not only becomes useless for the development of SIS, but even harmful. Therefore, for the Caribbean's purposes, development economics is not helpful! As economist Abba Lerner once noted sometime in the 1970s: "Economics has gained the title 'Queen of the Social Sciences' by choosing solved political problems as its domain." Therefore, it provides the wrong formulas and cannot even identify the real problems to be solved, so errors, mischaracterizations and misjudgments become the norm for these Western-led development agencies and academic institutions. They become part of the problem, and a bygone part at that. *Why Nations Fail* crushes the conventional academic discourse on development by exposing the bogus non-explanations that economists often offer: "[M]ost hypotheses that social scientists have proposed for the origins of poverty and prosperity just do not work and fail to convincingly explain the lay of the land."

The authors provide many centuries of the economic history of different civilizations, and the evidence shows "that the engine of technological breakthroughs throughout many different economies is innovation, spearheaded by new entrepreneurs and businessmen eager to apply their new ideas. This initial flowering spread…people

471

saw the great economic opportunities available in adopting the new technologies developed…they were inspired to develop their own inventions."

Therefore, the Caribbean must drive towards and foster a real-world, innovative, and entrepreneurial culture, an inclusive and knowledge-based society with strong and genuine facilitative leadership with inclusive institutions.

A mindset reset and a recalibration of political institutions to service this entrepreneurial culture is among the most important things to move the species forward. However, self-serving institutions stand in the way of this progress—corrupt dealings, status, political power-seeking, and incompetence are major barriers to growth. Efficiency, scale, and innovation are the driving forces behind dynamic economic growth, but inefficient institutions retard progress. Therefore, when efficiency collides with inefficiency, efficiency must prevail in order for societies to become the best they can be, so that they may benefit from efficiency and make progress. Inefficient, ineffective, and corrupt institutions filled with superfluous, selfish politicians strangle prosperity. Technology and innovation have been the one mainstay or common denominator of growth, as history shows; but inefficient environments obstruct the path of growth. So let us maximize our factual insights, awakening and revitalizing the basic needs of our human condition: self-preservation, prosperity, and happiness.

"Happiness is the meaning and the purpose of life, the whole aim and end of human existence." — Aristotle

A Caribbean-led renaissance movement is necessary to build inclusive economies and to stop settling for the economy that others have imposed on us. We must forge aggressive and calculative societies; otherwise, we will remain fragile and vulnerable to shocks that threaten our survival. Using technology to create opportunities to transform existing industries and to replace those legacy hierarchical socioeconomic structures that hold us back is critical. We must recalibrate our institutions to create growth and risk-taking incentives and to reward innovation and creativity, entrepreneurship, and independent thinking—in other words, individualism. We must also create an environment that allows everyone to participate in the economy. Governments in the region must get their collective acts together, for people's humanity is at stake. Hold yourself responsible, and accountable to your citizens above all else. Find some honour and courage. We need virtuous leadership more than ever!

Government cannot do the job of entrepreneurship, but it can certainly facilitate it through policy decisions and establish the conditions for long-term sustainable economies. Past efforts are no longer good enough; we must do better once we know better, and it starts with creating sensible knowledge ecosystems and strategies for digital transformation. A Caribbean renaissance movement in thoughts and deeds must be based on a commitment to an all-out push for our peoples' future survival. Self-determination means exactly that: "self-determining" our future, being antifragile, and not leaving that future in the hands of others. Life-long learning, realignment, and adaptation are fundamental to human progress.

NOW we must revisit religion again on the premise of being a root cause of why Black people often hold themselves back. After what was discussed in parts I and II, we do this for the purpose of driving home the point about intelligent decision-making as the path to finding our individuality, spirituality and ultimately our happiness in our time and place in the universe.

Many Black people have been trapped subconsciously in the acceptance of White Supremacist Christianity (WSC), which is essentially the use of Christian-based religion to perpetuate white

473

supremacist dominance and the narrative of Black inferiority. WSC plays on the legacy and past traumas of slavery and colonialism to control the minds of Black people into believing that seeking wealth is not good; after all, the Bible says that *money is the root of all evils.* But the Bible does not actually say any such thing; it is simply a part of the WSC narrative. Nevertheless, this dogma is buried deep in Black Christians' psyche, which aids in keeping us subconsciously docile, accepting our "lot in life."

Adherence to religion as a "cure" for past traumas plays right into the hands of WSC. False narrative solutions to our problems leave us stuck in the mud, while white supremacists drive right on by, keeping all of the economic advantages for themselves. The worship of something that is inherently built to subjugate us is nonsensical. Leaving us in a constant state of confusion is a clever control tactic of WSC, using religion to have us believe in the suffering culture while whites pursue profit, privilege, and great pleasures.

The impact of WSC on the Caribbean psyche is profound! But we as Black people have yet to come to terms with the fact that we cannot fix racism by appealing to the hearts and minds of our oppressors, and that putting our efforts into fighting "racism" is a waste of time, and only holds us back from achieving prosperity. It is also critical to understand that we should not care about what racists think of us, because if we produce strong economic conditions for ourselves and multigenerational wealth outcomes, these folks cannot or will not be able to control our lives. Therefore, as logic and basic common-sense dictate, the pursuit of economic security—a fundamental need of the human condition—will ensure the survival of our people; fighting racism and inequality will not.

Where in the history of the universe have you ever heard that one group of people would be willing to share their wealth and privilege with another group? That is not nature, not self-preservation, and not reality, so why do we make efforts to bring about that state of affairs? Again, we fail to understand the nature of the universe and we continue to suffer from our willful ignorance of it. The nature of economic conflict and the struggle for scarce resources have demonstrated throughout time that the personal gain of the individual is helpful to the tribe. And so the ***sophistication of self-preservation is entrepreneurship***, which is an instinct inherent in our nature and must be acted upon in order to thrive in nature.

Black people have not been unable to separate religion from spirituality, clinging to obedient WSC doctrines—deeply ingrained ideologies that have systematically worked to keep them down. Amazingly, when you try to explain this to them, they fight you by rationalizing their own suffering and arguing in favour of their subjugation through WSC. The Black psyche remains in a state of constructed delusion via adherence to Christian dogma, indoctrinated to the point that Black people no longer have open minds. They persist in the belief that *there is only one God*—even if that "God" subjugates them and casts them as inferior.

WSC is based on fear and punishment, mystery, suffering, damnation., i.e., going to hell. Fear works very well to keep people under control. WSC dominates with terror inflicted on the subconscious mind. And with this, Black people's lives become a controlled hallucination, reinforced every Sunday or Saturday morning!

The Jewish people freed themselves from slavery and devised their own self-determination agenda. They endured the Holocaust and vowed "never again." In the Jewish community's case, they used religion for the advancement of their tribe, not for adherence to suffering; they had had enough of that! And look where they are today. So instead of resenting them, we should learn from them.

Other races around the world have their religions as well—Islam, Hinduism, Buddhists, Sikhs, Taoists/Confucianists/Chinese traditional religionists, First Nations/Indigenous. Meanwhile, 1.93 billion people, or 15.58% of the global population identify as Secular, Nonreligious, Agnostic,

475

Atheist. For interest's sake, worldwide, more than eight-in-ten people identify with a religious group. A comprehensive demographic study of more than 230 countries and territories conducted by the Pew Research Center's Forum on Religion & Public Life estimates that there are 5.8 billion religiously affiliated adults and children around the globe, representing 84% of the 2010 world population of 6.9 billion—according to Pew Research Center, *The Global Religious Landscape*, Pewresearch.org.

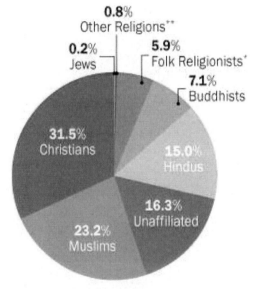

Size of Major Religious Groups, 2010

Percentage of the global population

* Includes followers of African traditional religions, Chinese folk religions, Native American religions and Australian aboriginal religions.

** Includes Baha'is, Jains, Sikhs, Shintoists, Taoists, followers of Tenrikyo, Wiccans, Zoroastrians and many other faiths.

Percentages may not add to 100 due to rounding.

Pew Research Center's Forum on Religion & Public Life • Global Religious Landscape, December 2012

Black people are the only race of people who subscribe to a religion that they had no part in creating and that has been systematically used against them; yet they still relish the suffering culture of that religion. Unbelievable! So whose fault is it that we are on the bottom rungs of the universe? If we choose to live in the darkness of willful ignorance, fearing truth and logic and failing to understand the nature of the universe, then we will remain in a perpetual state of constructive delusion, hallucinating ourselves into nothingness. That nothingness then becomes our behaviour. It is like staring into the abyss while the abyss stares right back—so we become our behaviour. We fail to advance our understanding of the universe because we exist in a self-imposed fantastical-suffering existence, never facing up to objective truths. If we are afraid of asking hard questions, we will always end up with soft answers, never able to forge a real existence.

If you are still clinging to religious doctrines in the 21ˢᵗ century, then you are accepting suffering; so you should stop complaining, for you have made that choice of your own free will. The culture of suffering driven by religious dogma is what you are doing when you adhere to *the Scriptures*. Your subconscious mind dictates about 95% of your thoughts and actions daily. The white supremacist suffering culture is deeply embedded through the indoctrination of religious texts and culture over your lifetime; all that teaching, and preaching is dominating your existence. So if you are not making a conscious effort to live in consciousness, aware of your surroundings and the influences in your life, then suffering becomes your life. Happiness will be forever elusive.

Adherence to WSC leaves you passive, non-seeking of gain, preferring to be dominated because instead of believing in yourself, you believe what others tell you about yourself. You become the ideal sucker, the useful idiot in a conflict-driven universe, convenient for others to use for their economic advancement.

Black men especially have become the universe's sucker in the present day. They have become domesticized, weak-minded, and

477

fragile, and they have shamefully left their Black women to clean up their messes. They have not devoted themselves to any identifiable purpose, showing incredible weaknesses, some succumbing to drugs and alcohol in order to drown the shame and pain. They are always falling for distractions, living without a plan, with no fight in them, unable to control their own emotions. Being governed by your raw primal emotions, without conscious governance, is a weakness. Therefore, strength and resilience must be developed and underpin our existence, because existence in fragility is no existence at all.

So when it comes to the issue of drug addiction and incarceration, we should not worry about the excess of Black males in prison. The hard truth is that if these men were not fragile, or if they were resilient, we would not have this problem. So do we want to put our efforts into men in prison, or do we want to think in *Long Time* and focus on educating our younger people for the future of work, and putting our time into developing an entrepreneurial culture? Will we do the things that will push us to prosperity, or will we do the things that pull us back into negative territory?

We must forget about running around after the fact with Band-Aid solutions and proceed directly to the root cause of the problem: Black men must change their thinking and behaviour! The hard truth is, we devote too much time to saving the unsavable, saving the unproductive members of our community. We need to think carefully and cut our losses whenever it threatens our long-term survival.

What should concern us is how to build a Black middle class, put Black families in positions to succeed, and provide the resources that can build multigenerational wealth. If we do not change our collective mindset and behaviour, then change for the better will not occur; we will simply end up perpetuating our own suffering. Instead of creating intergenerational wealth, we will manifest intergenerational suffering—a legacy of poverty, dysfunction, and mental illnesses such as stress and anxiety.

478

AMAZING GRACE

Free will and the ability to think critically while applying intelligence are core to a prosperous Black existence. Thinking carefully and critically about the mental subjugation trap of Christianity is central. For example, let us consider the song *Amazing Grace* to analyze some not-so-conscious thoughts and understandings about religion versus spirituality.

During the COVID-19 crisis, many were faced with unique challenges. Everyone, in one way or the other, might have had to change something in his or her life in order to navigate through the pandemic. COVID accelerated the transition to the new economy, so the resilient ones were able to adapt and thrive. Some had to face greater challenges; nevertheless, transcending change is in our midst, and such transformation may require a total reinvention of self for some. Undoubtedly, however, it will also require finding untapped internal strength to do so.

The human condition has always dealt with adversity through adaptation, driven by inspiration. Appropriately, the song *Amazing Grace*, one of the most iconic songs in the world, played over 10 million times a year, is a story about inspired change and doing better when you know better! Yet many may not know the story behind this amazing song. It was written over 300 years ago by English poet and clergyman, John Newton, who was also a former slave trader.

As a clergyman, Newton was looking for a hymn to go along with his New Year's Day service. He was looking for a simple song, one that simple people could enjoy, consisting of heartfelt words that would inspire. Newton had already selected the scripture for his sermon that morning: First Chronicles, Chapter Seventeen…, in which King David asks himself with wonder, "Who am I… that thou hast brought me here?" Newton then said to his congregation that Friday morning…, on the 1st of January 1773: "The Lord gives us many blessings, but unless we are grateful for these, we lose much of the comfort from them." So Newton uttered, "Never mind David. What about you and me? Where were you when the Lord found you?" For himself, Newton answered, "I was a wretch."

Hence, the first words of the song would be *Amazing Grace,* which sounded right to him; indeed, Newton then wrote, "how sweet the sound." While writing, he began to reflect on his former life and the fact that he was once a slave ship captain, trafficking in human cargo. During that time, Newton had been captured by a rival ship and forced to work as a "slave" himself for a short while, on a small island off the coast of Sierra Leone.

After his release, Newton went directly to live so depravedly that even his shipmates were shocked. What a wretched life I have led, he said. He then began to ask the Lord for grace and forgiveness to "save a wretch like me." He realized how far he had moved away from God, and the life God intended for him in his former life: "I once was lost, but now am found." Newton then reflected more intensely, reflecting on his life of sin—both as a slave trader and in his own brief enslavement experience: "Twas Grace that taught my heart to fear." Newton continued to pray and reflect: "And Grace, my fears relieved/ How precious did that grace appear/ The hour I first believed." Spirituality, purpose, and redemption seemed to be where Newton was headed.

For the rest of his life, Newton would mark every March 21st as a day of humility, prayer, and praise for his great deliverance from the life of sin that he had been living. Newton's conversion set him on a long, winding path that would take him to a new life—not in one great leap, but step by step. A sinner sought Grace from God, and God gave it gracefully.

It was then Newton's life began to transform completely. Again, the transformation was a prolonged process, not one that took place all at once. "If I had any light then," Newton said, "it would be at the first faint streak of dawn." Pastor John Newton dipped his quill once again to sum up this long journey. He began to lament: "Through many dangers, toils and snares/ I have already come." He wanted to sum up that this was not a single event, but something that remained with him every day: "Twas grace that brought me safe thus far/ And grace will lead me home." The onetime slave ship captain did not only go on to renounce slavery, but worked actively to abolish it. Nineteen years before his death, Newton's *Thoughts upon the African Slave Trade* was published, including his personal experiences and eyewitness accounts of the appalling conditions on slave ships and the other atrocities of slavery. This book provided British abolitionists and parliamentarians like William Wilberforce with the evidence they needed to educate a misinformed public.

As Newton approached death, he gave his close friend William Jay his now-famous declaration: *"My memory is near gone, but I remember two things: that I am a great sinner and that Christ is a Great saviour."* Newton died in 1807 at the age of 82.

In the years following his death, Newton's songs would have an amazing journey. By now, in its original form, the hymn was all but forgotten in England. However, as grace would have it, nearly a half-century after Newton wrote the song, it began to appear in the American South, sung to a new, soulful melody. This new music is today so much a part of the hymn that one could not even imagine it any other way. Newton's simple words had enormous new power in life; it became a quantum source
of power that brought some comfort to the indignity of slavery. Through brutality and subjugation, *Amazing Grace*—ironically written by a former slave trader—now became the salvation and hope for slaves themselves.

However, the salvation that the plantation slaves found had *nothing* to do with religion, nothing to do with its doctrines and ideology. Slaves saw the song purely for what it was: a source of **spiritual strength**! The spiritual words that Newton wrote based on his transformation were now being used by slaves to find the strength to stay alive under the brutality of their enslavement. It had nothing to do with adherence to religious dogma, nothing to do with Christianity, and everything to do with satisfying the needs of the human condition—the need for **spirituality!**

"Amazing Grace" was sung often on civil rights marches in the American South; it was sung when Martin Luther King delivered his "I Have a Dream" speech at the March on Washington in 1963. The hymn was also sung joyfully in South Africa when Nelson Mandela was released from prison in 1990. It was sung throughout the American South and the Caribbean whenever its comfort was needed, the story of "Amazing Grace" reminds us all that the same grace that transformed the life of a former slave ship captain three centuries ago can still change lives today. The true story of Amazing Grace, however, is a spiritual story that continues, and as long as there are people in need of hope and deliverance, its grace will have no end! Therefore, the grace in *Amazing Grace* is one of *spirituality,* not religion, because religion is a specific set of organized beliefs and practices, usually controlled by organizations and institutions, primarily the church. Spirituality on the other hand is an individual practice flowing through your natural human energy, and has to do with having a sense of peace, purpose, and individuality.

The slaves were able to separate the usefulness of spirituality from white supremacist Christian doctrine. Our ancestors knew how to find strength and perseverance to survive, and they laid the spiritual survival foundation for us; we cannot afford to waste that Amazing Grace that they bequeathed to us.

Unlike our resilient ancestors, Blacks today have been unable or unwilling to distinguish religion from the usefulness of spirituality;

they swallow religious doctrine whole, blindly acquiescing in and adhering to WSC. Therefore, today, by our own free will, we Blacks defeat our own selves through a lack of understanding of the true nature of how Christianity doctrines work against them.

At its core, the story of "Amazing Grace" is about finding inspiration to fill the soul; we must be astute enough to understand that and not conflate religion with the usefulness of spirituality. We must live in consciousness, not get caught up in WSC stories or fall for ideology wrapped up in Bible stories. Not making those stories the centre of our belief system is critical to having a successful existence. Here, we must use our free will and our individuality and dare to express ourselves freely with logic, critical thinking, and common sense. The internal power to unbecome, or to become what you desire to become, can be found through spirituality. Spirituality is our natural sense of being. We think, therefore we exist, which requires energy—and that energy can energize our spirituality to useful ends in our humanity.

RELIGION IS "the opiate of the masses," as Karl Marx famously said; it is used to confuse and dominate for the express purpose of wealth, power, and privilege of WSC. Adaptation and change, whether through necessity or from what is deep in our hearts, require inspiration and purpose. So regardless of what you think or what you choose to believe about Newton's transformation, the main point is that during a crisis of the soul, there are often spiritual opportunities for growth. For the enslaved Black people of the American South, their soulful rendition of the song "Amazing Grace" was a survival technique, fueled by their perseverance, their need for spirituality and hope. Let us neither squander this legacy nor romanticize it. Let us rather learn from it and honour it by the application of objective truths, logic, and common sense about separating religion from

483

spirituality. Questioning and discomfort combined with honesty are requisites for progress.

Enough with the Romanticizing of racism, it is time to apply boldness and assertiveness. — time to think mathematically, quantitatively. "What is in it for me?" should be our main question. We must choose strength over weakness and apply *applied intelligence* to our everyday lives. We need to be systematic, not emotional. The universe operates based on power, so a mindset of weakness and suffering does not help you. Black populations have continually misunderstood the directional flow of economic power and influence; as a result, their misguided and naive political approaches continually come up short. We continue to think incorrectly about the realities of the creation of prosperity and power, the components of happiness. Happiness is about the freedom to express yourself, and your individualism, not being constrained by societal belief systems that do not serve your interest. So leave the WSC herd! Abandon excuses: acknowledge the hard truths and do not shy away from them. Address those truths with critical thinking and free will. Choose reality over the fantasy of Bible stories. Choose prosperity over suffering and spirituality over religion; have we not suffered enough?

Chapter 20

You Simply Cannot Get Around It...

One of the most remarkable phenomena in the history of the universe is the utter "big lie" of Christianity. The man-made doctrines and cult-like context of Christianity and the institution of "The Church," all things considered, are responsible for some of the most atrocious and wicked things in history, both directly and indirectly. Christianity has been responsible for mass genocide and suppression of humanity throughout history. How, then, do we evade the hard facts about the Christian Church? We simply cannot evade it. We must confront facts.

So using basic human intelligence, how can one possibly defend the institution of the Christian Church without acknowledging its historical atrocities? No reasonable person can engage in a serious conversation about Christianity without dealing with the historical record of the institution itself.

Let us begin with the Crusades, the massacres of the Jews and Muslims of Europe, the Arabs, and even many of the Church's own followers. All in the name of "God." Consider the Inquisitions, including their persecution of the Jewish people, the transatlantic slave trade and the plantation slavery system, and the overrall colonial and imperial pursuits of WSC. Consider the subjugation of women, the forced conversion and genocide of the indigenous peoples of the Americas. Consider even the Church's dubious treatment of science, such as the Roman Catholic Church's persecution of Galileo—wherein, on 26 February 1616, Galileo Galilei was subjected to house arrest by the Roman Catholic Church for teaching and defending the view that the Earth orbits the Sun. What about the

485

Catholic Church legalizing torture in the name of God—"the truth," as the church referred to it? In the 20th century, the Church was silent during Hitler's "Final Solution to the Jewish Question," the grand plan to annihilate the Jews of Europe. The massacre of Byzantine Christians in the 4th Crusade; the murder and forced conversion of Serbian Orthodox Christians in the Balkans during the Second World War; the residential school system in Canada, including the systematic rape, torture, and murder of children; institutional child abuse and paedophilia, which the church continues to protect those paedophiles in the present day—the sins of the Church are too many to catalogue. How can one possibly get around all that?

Where is the responsibility, the shame? Can the abuse, rape, and torture of children truly be chalked up to only a few bad priests? What of the persecution and rejection of gay people—are gay people not God's children as well? The doctrine of the Catholic Church preached anti-Semitism until as recently as 1964, accusing the Jewish people of the murder of God in the form of Jesus of Nazareth. And do you honestly believe that the church has not played a meaningful role in influencing attitudes and hatred against Jewish people? In Rwanda, the most Catholic country in Africa, priests, nuns, and bishops were put on trial for inciting the massacres of their own people during the Rwanda Genocide. Here, too, the Catholic Church remained silent. It is amazing even to think that the Church criticized condoms, calling their use immoral even when AIDS was ravaging Africa.

Where is the humanity in the church? How can the church claim any moral standing in any capacity? From the time of the slave trade to the present day, the church has been responsible for the deaths and suffering of millions of African people, both directly and indirectly, which makes it incredibly difficult to quantify the evil done. How can such an institution have any legitimacy, let alone the credibility to call itself a moral symbol or actor in the world? It cannot; so how can any reasonable human rationalize the doctrines and ideology, the teachings of Christianity, as good and moral? Human intelligence and individualism must rise to the forefront of our thinking, above storytelling and lying; the truth must always reign supreme. Truth must be the moral standard in our society.

Therefore, intellectually, if you make your decisions based on anything other than reasonable evidence and critical analysis, it will be very difficult for you ever to see the objective truth. You will simply continue to be dominated by the vulnerabilities and weakness of your emotions, unable to express yourself intellectually, based on logic and common sense. You will suffocate your free will, bury your individualism, and always be cowering sheep in a herd, merely waiting to be slaughtered.

IN HIS BOOK *Guns, Germs, And Steel,* Jared Diamond details the story of the Spanish penetration and conquest of large swaths of South America, all "in the name of God." But is God about mass genocide? For those who continue to preach "the word of God" no one has been able to explain the ungodly acts of genocide committed in the name of Christianity? Diamond's chapter "Collision at Cajamarca" details a dramatic moment in Spanish colonial history, namely the mass murder of thousands of indigenous men by the Spaniards. In short, the Spaniards overtook the city or area of Cajamarca—in the name of the Roman Catholic Church, of course. Here, again, we see the use of "God" to justify crime and genocide. The objective, as the Spanish told it, was to "cause joy to the faithful and terror to the infidels;" this is terroristic language, is it not? The "fight" to conquer was in the name of the "Catholic Imperial Majesty," for the "glory of God because they have conquered and brought to our holy Catholic Faith so vast several heathens, aided by His holy guidance." In that case, was God a murderous white supremacist? A conquering general? Well, it certainly seems so, based on the Church's justification for murder. "Such battles have been won, such provinces discovered and conquered, such riches brought home for the King…and such terror has been spread among the infidels, such admiration excited in all mankind." The "battle" at Cajamarca epitomizes the many narratives and rationales for the justification of mass murder by WSC.

However, I always prefer to look at what was done rather than what was said—to look at the evidence rather than listen to nice Bible stories. When you combine "in the name of God" and the "name of the King of Spain" (or the King of France, Britain, Belgium, etc.), and when the written record of the history of the event says, "I am a Priest of God, and I teach Christians the things of God, and in like manner I come to teach you," this only tells us that for those in the Caribbean who identify as "Christian" do not know the true history of a religion they did not even choose for themselves. Are you satisfied with being willfully ignorant of facts? How have you reconciled yourself with the sheer falseness of Christianity?

Consider the "battle" of Cajamarca: how is sneaking up and murdering thousands of unarmed men a battle? It is cowardice! Christianity is about white supremacy, which uses "God" to justify murder and thievery. "We come to conquer this land by this command, that all may come to a knowledge of God and of His Holy Catholic Faith; and God permits this, in order that you may know Him." And there it is: "God permits this." Permitting mass genocide—rape, pillaging, and stealing wealth and raw resources from lands belonging to others. Christianity is a fraud, propagated for the economic advancement of WSC, which simply makes up the lies it needs as it goes along in order to justify the atrocities.

In the end, we know the story: In the Americas, Africa, Asia, India—WSC and the Church were the combined underpinnings of global genocide, socioeconomic conquest, and massive injustice in the world over many centuries. This is how Europeans fueled their global expansion, but this we already know., The question for Black populations of the Caribbean is, can we accept facts or not? Can we make decisions based on evidence, on science, instead of the fantasy of Bible stories? Without the application of critical and quantitative thinking in our collective lives, the region will not even know how to point itself in the right direction. For Black populations of the Caribbean, WSC was not our choice, nor has it benefited us in the last 400-odd years, to say the least. WSC is about making economic gains for white supremacy alone, for continually calibrating to keep white populations on top and Black populations at the bottom; this is in human nature. Therefore, acceptance of the dogma of Christianity is acceptance of White supremacy and Black inferiority.

If we believe that spirituality is necessary for the nourishment of the human condition, and if we also believe that religion is based on satisfying unsettled souls, then we rightfully must believe in the need for a spiritual existence. So it would be reasonable to conclude that religion was created to explain things that we could not explain thousands of years ago when we did not have science to help us. Therefore, these stories never left us, even making it through the enlightened periods of human history. Belief in supernatural stories remained strong, but mainly because people are lazy and do not take the time to do the work of searching for objective truths in life.

HOWEVER, THE DISCUSSION now must turn to the human condition's need for spirituality and how it became overrun by religion, because all of this will help our understanding of the universe. All societies, dating back many thousands of years, were hierarchical and functioned as hunter-gatherer tribes before evolving to sedentary societies. In those societies, it was the men who stood at the top of those social structures, particularly the religious leaders that wielded the moral authority, and power was derived from that authority. These men would soon evolve into representatives of

"God" here on earth: priests, bishops, the Pope, noblemen, and of course the king. These men simply wrote and continued to write the governing laws that control sedentary societies; and of course, power corrupts, so they wielded power in their own favour. Hierarchical societies based on religious laws began to form, and those "closest" to God became the morality makers in these societies.

So to return to spirituality and away from religion, the first place to start is how we think about our natural existence in the universe—realizing that we are a part of nature, not any divine creation based on a fantasy story. So as in nature, we use our natural occurring energy to harness our own energies and skills toward achieving our desires, working on bettering ourselves. For that reason, quantitative thinking must be the first principle that enables us to benefit from our natural state of existence. So we must then seek spirituality as our naturally occurring energy and use it to find our place and purpose in the universe, to find meaning in our lives. Doctrines, scriptures, and the ideology of religion are not about finding oneself; they are about worshipping others and giving them power over you.

Even if we hypothetically accept the idea of Jesus Christ for a moment, a critical reading of the scriptures shows us that Christ was an activist and that he never asked to be worshipped as a god. The fantasy story of Christ tells us that he stood with real people, the poor, the suffering, the ill and rejected in society. Christ stood against injustice, and he was an advocate. So if you are a believer in "Christ," then you must make better efforts when reading the scriptures to find out who Christ really was and what was the true purpose of these stories, and not get caught up in the religious dogma of it all. Scripture has been tainted by the self-serving control mechanisms of WSC.

Therefore, an objective reading of Christ's story tells us that he was not about hierarchical structures; he taught amongst the common folk, associated with prostitutes. He was not about fancy robes and symbols to worship, not about restrictive traditions such as dressing up for Sunday church services to display wealth. Therefore, WSC has nothing to do with the moral objectives these Bible stores were meant to deliver.

Nevertheless, the human condition's need for spirituality has been taken over by the lies of religious doctrines, and our authentic and spiritual selves have been hijacked for the shameless advancement of wealth, power, and privilege through white supremacy culture. WSC has deviously positioned itself well as an elegant spirituality, with rules that must be followed in order to get into heaven; but it is a form of control and exploitation. White supremacy culture could not have worked so well without the mind-control functionality of religion in place, which, of course, is powered by fear and damnation. WSC purposefully stifles individualism; individualism runs counter to religion, because religion is threatened by the free-thinking, rational mind.

It is obvious why laws were tied to religious doctrines; it gave them power and credibility through the institution of the church. The crafters of laws used religion as a justification to maintain the hierarchical structures in place in society to their benefit. WSC has used the image of Christ (a white man, with blond hair and blue eyes) as the superior standard for life for all humanity, and the brilliance of it was that it figured out how to get both Black and White people to buy into it. The ideology, institution, and authority of the church have been skillfully interwoven into the psyche of the Black Caribbean person. This, in turn, has allowed white supremacy to execute its power strategy with the *help* of brainwashed Black people. During the era of slavery and colonialism, Black people had no choice, for they were held by force; but in modern times, there are no excuses to be made. The acceptance of WSC is a choice!

GOD AND RELIGION were used to underpin slavery, and slavery, as we have discussed already, was fundamentally about economics, and white supremacy ideology became a key factor in the winning equation of white supremacy. So by knowing the truth about white supremacy, you can come to live in consciousness and make decisions based on what is real about the world. The big WSC lie continues in Christian churches today—particularly in the white evangelical Christian world, where Christianity more and more is associated with white nationalism and race.

The rise of Donald Trump is evidence of white nationalism cloaked in Christianity, when in fact WSC is nothing more than a political cover for a white supremacist racial and cultural agenda. False Christian Trump supporters, in their willful ignorance and hateful souls, have constructed a deluded narrative about the universe. In that narrative, it is whites' divine right to be the superior race in the world, and they weaponize and hide behind their bogus evangelical veneer like cowards in order to perpetuate this state of affairs. In the modern knowledge-based economy, they are increasingly becoming the most superfluous of people in the economy; automation and artificial intelligence have left these more rural and uneducated folk vulnerable and desperate. But instead of trying to educate and upskill, they resort to racism, seeking to blame others rather than take personal responsibility for themselves.

Nevertheless, blaming others has never really worked in the long term, so this white nationalist nonsense distracts them from the things they must do to survive in the new digital economy; the longer they take to recognize this reality, the greater the probability of their demise. As said throughout this book and as the nature of things goes, if you are not creating value in the world, then you have no value. So they should take heed of Darwinism, because if they cannot adapt to a changing world, they will eventually become extinct in that world.

The ignorance of this group is mind-boggling. They foolishly continue to militate against their own interests—against programs such as the Affordable Care Act, for example. Even though poor, uneducated whites are the most in need of the ACA, they absurdly fight against it, mainly because of their racial prejudice against the first Black President. In the end, they will continue to be the big losers, not unlike their supposed saviour, Donald Trump.

TAKE THE TIME and listen to the Reverend Jacqueline Lewis, Senior Pastor of the Middle Collegiate Church in New York City. Rev. Lewis has a 900-member multi-ethnic congregation, where she openly declares that in her place of worship there is no room for hate, bigotry, or anti-Semitism. She goes on to say about her church:

> *"There is the sense that every one of us is created in the image of God, so if we are, then God is also a Brown curvy Black woman with dreadlocks, and I love being in her image."*

Rev. Lewis is a pastor, but she is also an activist authentically working like Christ, who was an activist too, as discussed earlier. So like Christ, she does not judge, and everyone is welcome in her church, unlike racist white evangelical churches. Various populations are well represented in her church, including Black, White, Latino, Asian, gay, straight, bisexual, transgender, Native American, and wealthy congregants; everyone is included. WSC's core function is to divide, so it is up to those who understand the advocacy in the stories about Jesus—to act accordingly, and to call out the "white church" for what it is: a racist, white supremacist institution.

Christ was an activist, but WSC is a religious perversion of the stories, representing all that is bad in the world. So like Rev. Lewis is doing and in the words of Mahatma Gandh, "I like your Christ, but not your Christianity." Christ was also a revolutionary activist, and he changed things at great risk to himself, as the *story* goes. "Those of us who say we're Christian and do not think we're supposed to be activists, political, need to go back to your Bible and read those stories of Jesus and watch his hanging around with those with leprosy, hanging out with tax collectors, living on the edge and welcoming people to the table," says Rev. Lewis. Standing up for the vulnerable, the disadvantaged, and the disenfranchised is Christ-like, which is the opposite of what the white evangelical church is about.

WSC has been consistently attached to injustice: chattel slavery, reconstruction, Jim Crow, KKK, and the Republican Party in its present form. Things are simply recalibrated or repackaged differently over time to align with an evolving world. Nonetheless, in the final analysis, hate is hate and stupidity is stupidity—and the Republican Party fits that label perfectly. "The thing that has not changed is that persistent myth of white supremacy. That takes form in the Christian church where white supremacy masquerades as faith," says Rev. Lewis. All of that then gets built into our broader society, which fuels the virus of racism.

AT ITS CORE, *applied intelligence* is about having a discipline in place, a routine or operating system in which one can cultivate critical thinking within an analytical framework. It is easy to set a goal but harder to execute it, so *applied intelligence* provides the framework and mechanism within which to get things done. Also, without strategy and discipline in place, it is easy to fall into or be distracted by randomness, intuition, and emotion, which lead to errors in judgement and eventual failure. In his best-selling book *Atomic Habits,* author James Clear explains how having a "system" is essential to success. Clear shows how organization and systems have more to do with success than goal-setting alone. The system can assist the entrepreneur with defining a realistic vision working within a scientific framework, and determining how to increase the probability of making their dreams become reality, as long as intelligence forms the basis of their decision-making. At the very least, the applied intelligence process can be useful to people, and that is its prime objective: helping people.

"Goals can provide direction and even push you forward in the short-term, but eventually a well-designed system will always win. Having a system is what matters. Committing to the process is what makes the difference." – James Clear

Barbados is a prime example of white supremacy succeeding. Many in Barbados take pride in being called "Little Britain." WSC culture has done a number on Bajan culture! Barbadians' distortion of reality continues to amaze the intelligent observer. They happily continue to accept pennies on the tourism dollar while the 3.8% white population continue to dominate the economy and hoard and consume all of the island's wealth. But Barbadian society continues to celebrate white supremacy culture over a strong, Black, middle-class driven economy. While Barbados is fond of promoting a wonderful tourism product, the reality remains that the country's economy is revelling in servitude—trapped in a low-income, low-skilled existence, one of suffering while facilitating wealth for Whites. It seems that Barbados cannot see itself without being dominated by the British. Do they like it?

VICTIMHOOD

A software engineer and entrepreneur friend of mine, Andrew Bromfield, recently posted an interesting comment on LinkedIn

495

about the **"*Victimhood*"** mentality that many Black people harbour, and I believe it is worthy of being repeated here.

A victim mindset makes you believe that your position can only be improved by those who victimize you. Until then you are stuck.

However, once you ditch that mindset and become determined to succeed despite any obstacle, you will find that many are willing to support, respect, and promote you.

#Determination, #confidence, #resilience, and differentiating #capabilities are attractive qualities that will lead you to meet those who admire and possess them as well.

The world's a big place; seek out those who are genuinely attracted to your #grit and you will see how many doors open.

Have the courage to connect with those you admire and accept connections from those who admire you. It will pay off, trust me!
Do not limit yourself and do not hesitate; life moves quickly!

Many Black people in the Caribbean still adhere to the self-imposed culture of suffering, and this has contributed to the suppression of conscious aspirations. An inferiority complex lurks in their subconscious, preventing the impetus for growth and wealth creation. Self-doubt becomes more dominant, and the culture of suffering continues to reinforce itself. We can no longer blame the colonizers for our predicament, can no longer blame trauma; we have to deal with our problems. Whether we created them or not, they are still our problems to solve.

The Caribbean as a society is still incredibly young, when viewed in the context of world history. Therefore, we have a great deal more ahead of us to achieve; but if we choose to think small and let our fears govern our decision-making, we will never be able to harness our potential. Longevity in the universe is inherently based on sustainability, and sustainability is based on a productive economic existence—i.e., value creation.

WITH CLIMATE CHANGE, the scientific reality is that the entire Caribbean region could very well be underwater in the next hundred years or so, according to science. So what are we going to do about it now? What are we going to do to protect our future generations? Will we be that generation that stood idly by and did nothing?

Over the past 25 years, Caribbean economies have moved backwards when compared to other nations and to the technology levels necessary to push prosperity forward. The region has remained complicit in its own marginalization in modern times, clinging to dependence and the victimhood complex. Racism is not the problem; fragility is! And fragility killed our primal self-preservation instincts for the sophistication and innovation to thrive in the universe. People have become accustomed to promoting suffering and the romanticization of racism, which manifests itself and pushes our young people into believing that they are inherently and forever disadvantaged because of their race. Yes, we know that racism exists; tell us something that we do not know. However, if you let your emotions take over, racism will overtake you, and you will not be able to think clearly about reality or about the things you must do to get what you want out of life. The Black identity must transform itself into the image of power; we play to win and not merely to defend.

Blacks must decouple the duplicity of Christianity and understand how whites use narratives to blind us from seeing the universe as a place of opportunity and not suffering. However, Black populations continuously fall for the suffering narrative through our

497

ai

blind devotion to religion, not understanding that Christianity is a tool utilized against us in an economic conflict-driven world. This is a war, and competitors use all the tools and methods they can devise in order to win; that is the nature of things. We can never succeed, then, if we do not understand the war we are waging, a war that is filled with constant battles along the way, and winning some battles keeps us in the war. Not winning any battles keeps us in a constant losing position that creates an identity of losing and victimhood, leading us to stray to finding solutions based on fear and fragility, which only makes our situations and existence worse.

TEN PRACTICAL STEPS TO CHANGE

1. **Blackness and Wealth**: Do not cast poverty as a sign of righteousness. You need to succeed in order to secure your family's prosperity, happiness, and to give back to your community. This is required to lay the foundation for intergenerational wealth and opportunity. Our mindset must be ferocious in the hunt to mark and conquer new domains. Blackness must be identified with power, intelligence, and discipline in the pursuit of advancement, shedding the unproductive nature of the culture of suffering, because we ultimately become who we think we are in accordance with the way we behave.

2. **Getting Over Past Traumas**: Our history must not be allowed to hold us back or used as an excuse not to be bold and aggressive, to be willing to take risks. We must shed the victim-culture habits embedded deep within our psyche and form new courageous habits. Remember, the world is a jungle; conflict is inherent, and the laws of nature will always prevail. Every morning on the plains of Africa, when the gazelle wakes up, it knows it must outrun the fastest lion or be eaten. At the same time, when the lion wakes up, it knows

498

it must run faster and be more cunning than the slowest gazelle, or it will starve. This is nature!

3. **Do not let Religion Dictate the Culture of Ambition**: Christianity does not tell anyone not to seek wealth; wealth is necessary for family and community to prosper. Wealth compounds opportunity and prosperity creates security, which is fundamental to the human condition.

4. **Education**: (including financial education) is key to your communities' success; data shows that the more years of schooling you have, the greater probability of long-term sustainable wealth creation.

5. **Look After Each Other**: By improving your own life, you can meaningfully contribute to improving the lives of others, and the systems in which they live. Strong lions take care of their pride and territory. Share your wealth, invest in your community, and become leaders. Compassion and empathy for others in your community is essential. The idea of wealth is not simply to accumulate it, but to *share* it within the community. Individual success managed virtuously creates derivative exponential growth opportunities for others. The more you invest, the more it comes back to you.

6. **Always Practice *applied intelligence***: Apply scientific and sound thinking methods to build fact-based solutions to solve complex business and social problems. Build strategies; if possible, partner with other capable individuals within your community first; and always have a purpose for your business goals. You must seek to understand human systems and interconnectedness, so the better you understand the universe the more successful you will be in it. If you do not know how the system works, the chances are that the system is using you.

7. **Be Antifragile**: Make this second nature. Life has its challenges; our people have survived on slave ships and the

brutality of the institution of slavery. So do not complain about discrimination holding you back today, for there is no comparison between what we face and what our ancestors endured. It is time to get the job done and stop behaving like victims. If victimhood remains our mindset, we will remain stuck while the world passes us by. Figure out how to survive and then how to thrive, with no excuses and no retreat.

8. **Build Your Network Outside Your Community as Well;** money has no preference, and most of the major opportunities often reside outside of your community. So make good connections and build a strong network. Your value is very much determined by the number of quality connections you have. The world is a big place; explore it and conquer opportunities elsewhere. Be adventurous! Your frequencies will attract other like-minded individuals who want to do business with you. Money is a central motivator, and doing business comes down to relationship building; be genuine, network and get into the wealth system, and keep building those lasting and prosperous relationships.

9. **Be keenly aware of history;** everything today has already happened at one time or another. Be well-read, a student of history, and build your knowledge of the universe. Lifelong learning is critical to adaptation, survival, and thriving in new worlds.

10. **Always ask yourself,** *what is in it for me?* Always **do the math** involved in the opportunities presented to you and think quantitatively. Be analytical, follow and apply disciplined systems for decision-making, search for patterns, and do your best to limit emotion and intuition when making important decisions. Always remember that economics is not a morality play, its a power play!

ONCE AGAIN, we must examine the need to distinguish spirituality from religious doctrine. Those of us who can intelligently use the power of spirituality to satisfy the needs of the human condition, rather than depend on the *ideology of hope* embedded in those doctrines, stand the best chance of achieving happiness. Happiness is not the absence of adversity. Happiness is understanding that no one escapes adversity; what is important is how you manage it. Do not be fooled by religion. Utilize your emotional intelligence and exercise leadership over your own emotions and consciousness; find energy, enthusiasm, and purpose from your internal spirituality. Spirituality, not religion, is your true internal energy resource. Your authentic self-powers your mind and soul to act upon your individualism; knowing thyself is the first principle of knowing where you want to go.

Emotions are central to human existence, as we are emotional and sensitive animals; but we have also been given intelligence and reason as humans. Therefore, intelligence must be utilized and not be overtaken by emotion. We must apply the sophistication of intelligence to our human condition in order to achieve enlightenment and to stay out of the darkness. Finding and expressing your individuality is the most important thing you can do for yourself. Mastering of self, the mind, is the most powerful form of existence in the universe.

Hope leaves you to settle for the life you have rather than the life you want, and to exist in the perpetual state of stagnation and fear. This state of being robs you of your individualism and self-expression—of who you truly are. The sooner you cleanse yourself of the falsehood of hope and suffering, the better a chance you will have of living out your individual existence.

Many try to use Christian-based philosophy to try to rationalize hope and suffering as virtuous, but that is merely part of the WSC lie. The lies and atrocities attributable to WSC disqualify it from any philosophical legitimacy and moral authority. Freeing oneself from the falsehood of hope is energizing because it gives you the power to control your own life. Christian hope is highly restrictive, based on fear and control; it also produces anxiety. Hope limits the human spirit.

In the physical world, nothing changes unless some type of force or energy is applied to it, unless movement and activity occur—motion, friction, and collisions. There is no hope embedded in physics, and for that matter, there is no hope in the metaphysical world, either. Concrete things influence each other—actions and reactions, not hope. Physics can help us understand the natural universe, both cognitive and physical; and the universe is chemistry and biology too. A general knowledge of science teaches us that quantum orbital motion involves the quantum mechanical motion of rigid particles (such as electrons) and for a motion to happen, energy must be involved. Mass always needs force to set it in motion. Quantum mechanics is essentially about explaining how space and time are occupied and relate to events in nature. The objective of physics is to find out what is true or is not true. There is no room for hope here; hope only fills the space with nothingness.

Religious philosophy is ultimately useless because it does not involve building on any firm ground, merely succumbing to illusion. All philosophy must be grounded in some truth and virtue; WSC is not grounded in any objective truths, only lies.

Princeton University Professor Cornel West has been honest when speaking about hope in his book *Hope on a Tightrope*. West says that "real hope is grounded in a particularly messy struggle, and it can be betrayed by naïve projections of a better future that ignore the necessity of doing the real work" (West 2008, p. 5). So without real work and real things taking place, nothing can happen. Christian hope is a falsehood, a sedative for the masses. The physical world is real; hope does not exist.

Therefore, separating the intellectual mind from the primal emotional mind is critical to the progress of the Caribbean people. Some scholars have argued that the legitimacy of hope hinges on the good it does for society. However, they provide no evidence that this is the case; it is simply biased Christian ideology, which is fundamentally hopeless.

Scholar Anne Jeffrey, in her writings for the John Templeton Foundation, tries to create legitimacy for hope by positing that hope is compatible with faith, essentially arguing that if you cannot see the value of hope, then you do not believe in Christianity. But that is exactly my point about "buying the farm first" being a prerequisite of Christianity. It leaves no room for individual thinking! She goes on to argue that faith represents certainty in the unknown, effectively asking us to believe in the unknown rather than the known, to believe in stories rather than science. From my reading, it seems that Jeffery is arguing for the suspension of intellect and distracting yourself from the reality of life and the very laws of nature—for believing in a delusional construct of reality that does not exist.

Faith can only be effective if it is supported by the utility and application of spirituality. Spirituality is real because it has energy and purpose, usefulness and benefit. It provides you with internal strength and directional pull—with inspiration and resilience to pursue the life you want to live.

According to Jeffrey's reasoning, intellectual confidence is supplied by faith that gives rise to the Christian virtue of hope. This is pure nonsense, Dark Ages stuff—the suspension of intellect. There is no virtue in hope; it is a falsehood sold to those who choose willful ignorance or are vulnerable due to despair and fragility. Virtue has no correlation with hope; hope is fragile, whereas spirituality gives you resilience. Free will is virtuous! Virtue is about action, while hope is about inaction—about wishful thinking. Christian hope requires you to endure suffering in order to achieve virtue; why? This is wrong. Hope is only a false and empty promise under the condition of accepting a made-up "God" first, and above all else. So before hope or prayer can work for you, you must buy the farm by accepting Christian dogma. It is a very slick scheme indeed. Hope is adherence to the divine; but there exists nothing supernatural, only the laws of nature.

Chapter 21

Purpose & Wealth

"Wealth is the ability to fully experience life."
Henry David Thoreau

The overriding theme of this book has been the application of quantitative thinking and actions, through a disciplined system of *applied intelligence*. This is a necessity for a renaissance in thinking toward achieving socioeconomic self-determination—to experience life fully! And although the objective is to live a prosperous and happy life, happiness is never a given, never guaranteed; happiness requires real work and perseverance.

So why is the pursuit of wealth so important for happiness? Because the pursuit of wealth leads to security, which is a requirement for the human condition to satisfy the soul. In short, you need money in order to live happily in the universe; there can be no doubt about that. Nevertheless, there is a fall-off, so this is why spirituality is a necessary ingredient to authentic happiness.

Research shows life satisfaction levelling off as income increases. Recent research by Matthew Killingsworth of the University of California, Berkeley, also finds that the more happiness you want, the more expensive it gets. However, at the same time, they found that money is not nearly as important as other factors. Nobel Prize-winning economist Daniel Kahneman and Angus Deaton, both of Princeton University, found that happiness, as measured by people's perception of their own emotional well-being, levels off when income reaches about $90,000. The next dollar a person makes will cheer him/her slightly less than the last one did. The average difference in life satisfaction between two people earning $40,000 and $80,000 is about the same as that between two earning $80,000 and $160,000. Hence, the combined research, from Killingsworth and Kahneman and Deaton, found that health, spirituality, employment, and family are all most important for true happiness. In other words—for those who still need to be told—there is more to life than money. But money is still core to one's existence and security and happiness, nonetheless.

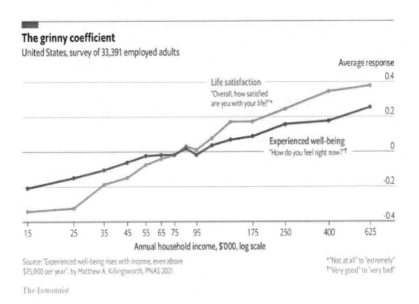

The grinny coefficient
United States, survey of 33,391 employed adults

Average response

Life satisfaction
"Overall, how satisfied
are you with your life?"*

Experienced well-being
"How do you feel right now?"†

0.4

0.2

0

-0.2

-0.4

15   25   35   45 55 65 75   95   175   250   400   625

Annual household income, $'000, log scale

Source: "Experienced well-being rises with income, even above
$75,000 per year", by Matthew A. Killingsworth, PNAS 2021

*"Not at all" to "extremely"
†"Very good" to "very bad"

The Economist

The lesson is that wealth accumulation is important, but only if it does not happen at the expense of other measures of well-being; therefore, having a "prosperous" future depends on balance.

A Douglas Blackwell report titled *Lifestyle & Investment* highlights that our deeply ingrained beliefs about money are shifting. This movement changes our attitudes towards what it means to be wealthy: instead of accumulating money for what it can buy, more of us want to use money to live the best life possible with what we have.

The traditional path to saving and investing has been to focus on the future (retirement) and to rely solely on numbers and return on investment (ROI). The emphasis now is "return on lifestyle" (ROL). Money does not exist for its own sake. Money exists as a utility that we use to improve our lives. How your returns compare to any index, fund, investment category, or another person are less consequential than whether you are meeting your own lifestyle goals. So money can buy happiness; you simply have to know how to spend it.

Is leaving a family legacy of wealth and happiness important to you? Is social responsibility and impact investing important to your legacy? In order to enjoy an inspired life purpose, you need to understand where all your money is coming from and where all of it is going—and why.

Inspired living puts quality before quantity by managing your assets in a way that improves your life and provides peace of mind. And from an investing perspective, money quickly loses its value for the purpose of generating happiness if the investment requires significant time, effort, and constant capital injections. It is contrary to the purpose of money to give up your prime lifestyle enjoyment years, to wait decades to enjoy a life that is not guaranteed.

The purposeful pursuit of wealth is a major component of self-preservation; it activates and fuels the human condition to drive for maximum security. It opens us up to fully living—growth, risks, fear, love and loss, happiness, resilience, perseverance, achievement, endurance, a sense of community and tribe, and a sense of belonging and purpose in our lives. But again, it should be balanced out by finding spirituality and your authentic happiness!

Most people in the Caribbean guide their children to grow up and obtain an education for the purpose of achieving higher incomes; this is universal, and we all understand that higher education leads to better job opportunities. However, for Caribbean people, this mindset must be shifted and accentuated. We must augment our thinking and our pursuit of education relative to the evolving world—the future of work, to be competitive as a society.

The history of civilization has taught us that power is derived from wealth. As Einstein said, we must rise to a higher dimension of thinking if we want to achieve better. Individual thinking frees us from falling into a permanent state of mediocrity, blending in with the herd and stifling our individualism. Seeking individuality is a virtuous existence because it takes courage to step *out of line* and express your full self. Our experiences so far have been mainly through others, expressing themselves by the creation and use of their power in the universe.

White supremacy's objective is to suppress our individualism and our entrepreneurship—an effort that, if successful, also suppresses our wealth creation potential. There can be no excuses, no rationalization as to why we cannot compete with the rest of the world. Mediocrity is a choice, and for Black people, mediocrity is the subconscious acceptance of white superiority and Black inferiority.

Therefore, happiness is the full expression of individualism and the separation from the herd mentality. This self-expression establishes your own culture and economic ambitions, which is central to asserting individualism. Seeking wealth and power purposefully is most natural, so we must feel good about trying to achieve it. We must bolster our spirituality with intellectualism and logic so as to drive our self-interests forward. Breaking free of the colonial mindset once and for all requires focused work, thinking, and actions. It requires the self-generation of your spiritual energy, finally freeing your mind to design your own future.

The universe reigns supreme, always and everywhere, and it does not care about you or know who you are. Subconscious adherence to—and behaviour in line with—white supremacy culture amounts to acceptance of Black inferiority! Many a Caribbean psyche still seeks the colonial masters' pat on the back, and some will even betray their own people simply to reach the proverbial "big house."

Aspiring or trying to live up to those still-lingering standards of bygone eras still lingers in many Caribbean people's minds.

Seeking entrepreneurship and wealth is natural in the world; it is the *sophistication of self-preservation*. Seeking wealth through the disciplined framework of *applied intelligence,* however, is intellectually sound, based on an understanding of how to advance effectively and efficiently. Wealth is power; power enables politics; and politics enables justice through public policy. So to create intergenerational opportunities and carve out your privilege, you must first devise a plan to create wealth. Wealth ensures your self-preservation and security. There is no other way, so do not waste your time or stray from reality; both will be difficult to retrieve.

WEALTH IS THE CREATOR OF POWER, so power does not happen on its own; power acquisition requires a purpose and methodology, a strategy, and tactics. A structured framework can help to develop wealth creation strategies. Therefore, achieving wealth in Caribbean society requires the exercise of *applied intelligence.*

Everything must be seen with a quantitative eye; the world functions through economic conflict for those scarce resources. The quantitative exploitation of people, land, and natural resources is how the world works. For example, if we go back to the 17th century, when Barbados was the richest colony in the British Empire, Barbados also represented the planned slave-society, the first anywhere in the world. So planning and strategy execution are central to success in any endeavour. Having a blueprint is simply sound practice. The strategy document for slavery was called the *"Barbados Slave Code,"* which was used to institutionalize brutality, mental abuse, and the subjugation of a people—to beat and dehumanize Black people into submission.

The Black populations of the Caribbean must seek our own path to create wealth and manifest our power in the universe. At the same time, however, we must recognize that there are forces still ranged against us that constantly seek to prevent our rise. Therefore, we must be strategic and ruthless about the gains we seek.

For Afro-Caribbean people, the adoption of quantitative thinking is of maximum necessity—not only for survival in the real world, but to have a chance to thrive in it as well. Accordingly, the construct of *applied intelligence* also provides the framework to optimize *emotional intelligence*. We should not pretend that emotion is not a factor or that we can eliminate it; rather, we should include and optimize its use to work best for us.

We cannot afford to waste precious time engaging in useless, patronizing, charity-tinted "development" theories. Economics is about transacting with value, and if we cannot offer anything of economic value, then we have nothing with which to transact. These are the basic first principles of self-preservation, and if we cannot grasp them then our prospects over the long term will be dim.

If we continue to rely on storytelling, on subconscious adherence to theoretical nonsense, then we will remain willfully and intellectually lazy and fragile, while our global competitors show robustness.

Our history as a Caribbean population is minuscule; 400 years is a blink of an eye relative to the thousands of years of our species' existence. So thinking in "Long-time," our society has more good years in front of us than we do behind us. The rise of a wonderful and prosperous Caribbean civilization can be in our future, but we have to make it happen ourselves.

What happened to the ancient "glorious" Greco-Roman civilizations? Greece and Italy today are at the bottom rungs of the European community. What about the great Mongol Empire, the most significant and long-lasting empire in history (1206 until 1368) that helped usher in the modern world? It, too, eventually came to an end. Empires rise and fall, and there is nothing standing in the way of creating a great Caribbean society if we put our minds to it. All things in the universe are created by the mind; that is what makes the world turn. So no goal is unattainable if the mind can envision it and then effectively execute a plan to make it manifest. It is time to begin envisioning the rise of a Caribbean Renaissance.

Logic and mathematical thinking must guide our consciousness. The Caribbean remains irrelevant and insignificant in the global economy, and in its present state, there is no evidence that the region has a bright economic future. No one is coming to save us; no one is coming to push us; no one is coming to build a digital transformation strategy for us. No one is coming—NO ONE!

We must flip the script and begin helping ourselves with a vision of the future that we determine ourselves, focusing instead on developing within the reality of the universe. We need to use logic to channel our energy and spirituality towards devising strategy and tactics. Understand that seeking wealth is a requirement for security; wealth creates power, and power—the power to survive and thrive in the universe—is required in order to get things done. Understand the utility of wealth, how its utility drives our primal human ambitions forward; understand, too, how our individuality develops our cultural and societal relevance. This is how we make our place in the universe. If we want our Black Lives to Matter, then we need to create wealth and power so that they will matter. We must create our value, because there can be no power without it; that is the hard but objective truth.

Throughout history, conformity has been a driver of immorality and wickedness. The madness of the crowd has combined with the false morality of Christian doctrines, which—as detailed earlier—have been used for mass murder and genocide. Consider, for example, the Christian Crusades, a long series of battles fought between 1096 and 1492 at the behest of medieval popes against a wide range of manufactured enemies of Christianity. Popes used the organized violence of the Crusades, to achieve the Church's political

ai

power goals—and act that strayed far from the teaching of Jesus Christ. The Christian religion is self-serving, serving its own economic, political, social, and cultural domination aspirations. Today, many white nationalists, anti-Muslim, anti-Black, anti-Jewish, right-wing racist groups call themselves "Crusaders," taking inspiration from the legacy of the Christian Crusades and white supremacy.

"The medieval crusades were a largely dreadful misdirection of religious enthusiasm towards painful and bloody ends. They were neither a glorious clash of civilizations nor a model for the world."

—Unknown

Conformity can be dangerous to your intellect and existence. Conformity culture does not encourage the asking of critical questions; it creates willful ignorance—that is why Facebook is so successful. Facebook's cognitive algorithms are a mind control and conformity mechanism to create mass stupidity, so that Facebook can continue to make more money from the willfully ignorant. Facebook thrives because people stop thinking for themselves and neglect to read books. They are driven by the quest to win "Likes" instead. They are never skeptical and cannot think critically. As Einstein once said; *Two things are infinite: the universe and human stupidity; and I am not sure about the universe.*

The de-intellectualization of the Black mind is like a plague, one that brings great risk to the survival of Caribbean populations. Sound thinking is a requirement to survive and thrive in the universe, so if we continue to be stupefied by social media, avoid reading books, and fail to do proper analysis, then— as Einstein tells us—our stupidity will prevail over us. One of the underlying themes of this book is the stoic theme that *it is always up to you.* From ancient times to the present day, this fundamental truth still rings true. Accordingly, knowledge is the most virtuous pursuit in the universe! Knowledge-seeking is the finder of truth. Today, knowledge acquisition is more important than ever before, because we live in a highly advanced and technologically driven world. Lifelong learning is fundamental to positive growth outcomes. However, nothing is ever a given, and nothing will be given to you; you must seek knowledge in order to learn and advance yourself.

Chapter 22

Talk and Ideology

The word "development," from the Eurocentric perspective, simply means the recalibration and modification of traditional white supremacy control structures of the West, towards the now reclassified "developing world." It is merely the clever transition from the direct controls and governance of the colonial era to indirect control methods today. In short, this new system maintains control in a less obvious and more sophisticated way. So after independence, we saw the rush of new Western advisors, technocrats, and academics replacing the colonial bureaucrats, and multinational corporations began to move in and take over even more. This was a clever transition under the guise of "development" and Western liberalization, of course, so the inherent and enduring hierarchical structures of white supremacy remained and simply readjusted to modern times.

Black thinkers such as Walter Rodney and Frantz Fanon produced great introspective works identifying the impact of colonialism on the humanity of Black Caribbean people. However, the Black leaders of today must not have done any of those readings, because it is as if the region has gone backwards in the 21st century. Many still have the mental slavery colonial mindset, unable or unwilling to remove the implanted white supremacy doctrines from their psyches. Consider, for example, Barbados's current Prime Minister, Mia Mottley, who portrays herself as a progressive. Since she took office in 2018, what economically measurable or quantifiable thing has she accomplished that can be meaningfully measured to show a solid economic future ahead? Unlike in the aforementioned "Asian Tiger" countries—Singapore

514

especially—there is no bold strategy anywhere to be found in Barbados. There is nothing but a great deal of talk and ideology that does nothing to change economic reality for Black Barbadians anytime soon. The only thing "achieved" so far has been the ceremonial gesture of replacing the Queen as the head of state and transitioning to a "Republic." Pomp and circumstance are always a good distraction from the painful existing reality; and as for having Rihanna and the wobbly then-Prince Charles in attendance…well, a good party makes people forget about their real problems, I suppose.

Absolutely nothing economically changed for Barbados as a result of it becoming a Republic. The Bajan economy continues to be dominated by a tiny white minority population, and Black politicians are still pleased with themselves for trading away the wealth of the nation in exchange for personal political status. If the region remains mired in such delusion, unable to understand that power flows from economics, not politics, then the region will not move forward to any level of sustainable prosperity. If leaders cannot grasp the elementary first principles of self-preservation and growth realities, then how can they be trusted to create economic security, wealth, and prosperity for their people?

Again, continuous symbolic gestures engulfed in nothingness create nothingness. How do these symbolic events change the economics of the people? What impact do they have on trade and commerce, on building export-driven economies? How do they build capacity for the decade ahead? How do they deal with digital transformation? How does it raise incomes and standards of living and contribute to the necessary rise of the middle class? "I think everybody is more concerned with their dollar today and what that means for tomorrow, especially with prices of things going up," said Laurie Callender, 43, an information technology specialist in Barbados, who was interviewed on TV media about Barbados becoming a republic. "People are more talking about that, in my opinion," she went on to say. So nice ceremonies do nothing to address real people's problems.

THE FOCUS must be on a bold shift away from the current low-tech, low-income, low-skilled, tourism and commodity-based economy profiles in the region. We must shift to a high-value-added product economy to move up the wealth curve. Maintaining commodity-only economies only reinforces past dependencies. Caribbean countries cannot build wealth through a system in which the prices of the resources they sell are controlled and set by the people to whom they are being sold. How does that make any sense?

Caribbean leadership must support and implement policies that promote innovation, resilience, science and technology, education, food security, and healthcare. We must first disrupt and transform ourselves in every possible way before we can make any meaningful change to our economies. Prosperity flows through an educated and high-skilled economy; so, education must be treated as a basic human right, because it is critically necessary for the survival of our species. In the new economy, math and science, technology, and knowledge-building is more important than at any other time in history.

Today, it is easy to see why the United States is failing, a major part of its population—generally concentrated in the Midwest and the South—is significantly behind when it comes to education for new economy skills. Now that most of the low-skilled manufacturing jobs are essentially gone, the general population is largely unskilled and unprepared for the future of work. Backlash in the form of white nationalism is the outlet for those folks who are becoming part of the great *useless class*. This is predictable in white supremacy culture; instead of taking responsibility, they simply blame others for their plight. Similarly, it is the Caribbean people's responsibility to take care of themselves and prepare for the future of work, and not resort to excuse-making and victimhood.

*The online education market is expected to reach $350 billion by 2025 as flexible learning technologies scale up. Online education enables learners to access resources from any location, at any time, at their own pace and can be tailored to their interests. Huge potential lies with these technologies. Training can be easily scaled-up if the relevant infrastructure is in place,* which was highlighted at the Next Einstein Form (NEF.org,) the largest science and innovation gathering on the African continent. Therefore, the Caribbean must shed the antiquated and analog British system of education, which the British no longer even use themselves. We must increasingly think and act quickly and transition to the world of online learning. We cannot rely exclusively on textbooks any longer. We need to be aligned with the digital world and access information digitally and in real time. Our learning curve must be practical and in stride with the evolving 21st century. The new-economy education focus must be long-term and inclusive; innovative and aggressive, with the objective being to win. We must encourage and reward performance, and feed future leaders with the required knowledge.

Government must fully understand the transformational magnitude of the knowledge-based economy, its prosperity differential, and be proactive in moving purposefully through this decade of transformation. Educational curriculum content must be designed based on where the world is going and not on where it has been. The use of data and AI in online education platforms is a vital tool for accelerating learning towards the future of work and prosperity. Optimally, a total focus on education that is aligned with new-economy growth is paramount for Caribbean prosperity.

As mentioned throughout this book, agriculture coupled with technology represents the single greatest opportunity for sustained prosperity in the Caribbean. Agriculture exists, but it is the application of technology to agriculture production that will monetize it and create profit and prosperity from it.

Global digital payment systems embedded in e-commerce digital platforms are making it easier each day for entrepreneurs to sell directly to consumers anywhere in the world, so there is really nothing standing in our way. Digital technology cuts out numerous middlemen, which leaves more profit in the hands of local entrepreneurs, which passes down to families and communities, spurring increased overall economic activity organically. AgTech is not only a siloed sector opportunity; it represents an enormous transformational growth opportunity for the region, and we must pursue it without delay.

There is no quantum equation that can model the universe and provide us with all the answers; there is no operating manual on how to succeed in the universe. From a quantitative perspective, the awesomeness of the universe is that it cannot ever be captured, contained, or even fully explained. The universe is always expanding—and so, too, is its related matter, variables, and dynamics. We do not know where or how it began, nor whether or how it will ever end. The universe is continuous and unpredictable; and most of all, the universe is math, and its calculations are governed by the laws of nature. So leave your intuition and feelings at the door, for the universe does not know who you are, nor does it care about you. Reality, nature, reigns supreme in this world. Therefore, the *sophistication*

of self-preservation is required to navigate it, along with an ***applied intelligence*** framework, if you want to win in the world.

Regardless of the changing times, self-interest remains steadfastly embedded in our humanity. Self-interest, individual gain, is the bedrock force of our human progression. It plays a core functional role in harnessing our efficiency and productivity—it is how we create our value. The critical understanding of the laws of nature, both the physical and the cognitive, is the core imperative that has driven successful civilizations over time. So an understanding of the nature of the universe is central to any individual or group looking to navigate their way successfully through the rough seas of life. If, however, we fail to understand the workings of the universe and its intrinsic functionality, then how can we find our footing in it? We will always be behind the prosperity curve, never a part of it.

So in our metaphysical existence as Caribbean people of African descent, the shaping of our success comes down to pursuing what we want most out of life. We must make things happen for ourselves. But exactly what is required to make things happen? A Renaissance in thinking is what is necessary. How you think is the first step to a future by design.

The thing to do next is to find ambition and vision, choose a disciplined strategy, and set your plan in motion. As Black people at some point, enough must be enough, and if not now, then when? We simply cannot continue this miserable existence at the bottom rungs of the universe. Nor can we keep blaming racism indefinitely, engaging in useless and distracting emotion-led wokeness, making ourselves feel good while leaving our heads underused. We must begin to look inwards before setting a strategy that can be executed outwardly. We must look to ourselves to lead ourselves, build resilience, and be antifragile for a change.

And believing in Bible stories has not been helpful to Black populations. We must stand up to the reality of our existence, have the intestinal fortitude to change behaviour, and deliver for ourselves.

IN THE BOOK "Guns, Germs, and Steel," author Jared Diamond analyzes a "cold-blooded fact of life" in his comparison between two countries: the Netherlands, and the African country of Zambia. Diamond observes that if an extraterrestrial visitor were to come to Earth and examine the Netherlands, in comparison to Zambia, they would surely conclude that Zambia, not the Netherlands, is the wealthy country. The extraterrestrial would say that the Netherlands has long winters and short summers and can only grow limited crops once per year, and for a very short period. They would also observe that the Netherlands lacks valuable mineral resources; it is low and flat and must import oil and natural gas to generate most of its energy. One-third of the Netherlands lies below sea level, facing the constant risk of flooding. So the extraterrestrial would surely see those traits of the Netherlands' as disadvantages.

Then the extraterrestrial turns to Zambia, which lies in southern Africa, and is very impressed by Zambia's enormous advantages. First, Zambia has no need to buy oil to generate energy, since all of its energy comes from hydroelectric power generated by huge dams across the Zambezi River. Those dams generate so much power that Zambia has a significant surplus of electricity to sell to its neighbouring countries. Unlike the Netherlands, Zambia is very rich in minerals like copper. Zambia has a warm and hospitable climate, and its farmers can grow multiple crops year-round, unlike the Netherlands. Zambia's tribes do not fight with each other; the country is relatively stable and peaceful. Zambians are hardworking and value education. So it would be easy to see how the extraterrestrial would conclude that Zambia is the rich country, and the Netherlands, lacking all those natural advantages, is the poor one.

However, as I am sure you have already guessed by now, the extraterrestrial would be very wrong about things. The average income of the Netherlands (at the time Diamond was writing) was 33 times higher than the average income in Zambia. At that time, the average income then was about US$48,940.00 per year in the Netherlands, compared to only about US$1,500 per year in Zambia. Today it is $3,776.00, compared to the poor country of the Netherlands, which is around $90 000.00.

So with all those natural advantages listed for Zambia, which allowed the Extraterrestrial to rate it as rich, how possibly has Zambia found itself in such a negative position? Diamond points out that the attributes associated with national wealth come down to democratic institutions and good leadership—"i.e., the laws, codes of behaviour, and operating principles of societies, governments, and economists." This is fundamentally correct, and it is further supported by significant evidence in the seminal book *Why Nations Fail* by Daron Acemoglu and James A. Robinson. In a nutshell, *Why Nations Fail* delves into the reasons why economic inequality is so common in the world today and identifies that poor decisions of those in political power and the elite are the main reason for unfairness, rather than culture, geography, climate, or any other factor.

In other words, people make decisions, and decisions matter! It comes down to what you do; it always does. Mindset, execution, and management are paramount. If leaders, officials, and the people are not doing what must be done to win within the prevailing realities and context of the universe, then they will lose. If incompetence and corruption reign, then you will only get out what you put in—garbage in, garbage out. What else would you expect? Once again, stop blaming the colonizer, the white man, etc.; we are all of a free mind, and nothing is ever predetermined.

Only you have the power to work towards the existence you want—not USAID, the UN, or the World Bank, charitably tinted developmental agencies or government programs, nor reliance on philanthropy. It is only us in the end; no one is coming to save us.

Here is another telling reality—leaving the resources of a country for other countries like China to exploit is ultimately a decision that leaders and their people make. Colonialism 2.0 cannot happen if you do not willingly participate in it. People simply sit on the veranda complaining while letting white supremacy culture run their lives. And now China is taking over. History is repeating; colonialism 2.0 is alive and well in Zambia and in Africa at large, and in the Caribbean as well.

Chinese colonialism 2.0 is strategically engaged in a well-designed and orchestrated debt trap strategy. Zambia, again, is in substantial debt to China and cannot service it; so China has boldly seized critical Zambian public assets for payment, breaking all the rules of national sovereignty. The same thing has happened in Jamaica and is creeping into the rest of the Caribbean. The debt trap strategy is designed to give massive loans to vulnerable countries that China knows can never repay. The objective for China is to use mounting debt to capture valuable public assets and natural resources to fuel its economic and geopolitical expansion plans.

The Guardian wrote on 11 December 2019: *"China steps in as Zambia runs out of loan options… Southern Africa's third-largest economy is a textbook example of the increasing debt facing a fast-growing continent."*

A Zambian rapper known as "Pil A" posted a track (see on YouTube under PiL A…China lyrics) with lyrics describing the feelings of many Zambians towards what the Chinese are doing in Zambia, and all over Africa for that matter: *"They put on smart suits and fly to China to sell our country. The roads belong to China. The hotels are for the Chinese. The chicken farms are Chinese. Even the brickworks are Chinese."*

This is exactly what is happening now in the Caribbean, but there seems to be no calypso or reggae songs being sung to warn the populace of what is going on. Everyone is operating on "island time."

So as in Africa, Caribbean politicians and the connected elites have no shame, the level of corruption and greed, buffoonery, and total lack of consideration of their people's needs is a disgrace. So please, do not blame China or the white man. Blame yourselves. Unless people change their mindset, wake up and stand up for themselves, and cease settling for a powerless and irrelevant existence, we will remain at the very bottom rungs of the global economy, bewildered and mired in irrelevance. Our suffering will only intensify as technology creates a greater divide between the North and South—the haves and the have-nots.

Once again, the reality of the universe is about using the sophistication of self-preservation, most of all through entrepreneurship, to create value and security for self, society, and country. Caribbean leadership must create policies that promote innovation, resilience, science, and technology, education, national food security and healthcare. But we must first disrupt our thinking and align ourselves with the realities of the universe. Stop complaining and playing the victim all the time! The universe is not listening, nor does it care. Get off the veranda and change your own lives before you seek to mess with the socioeconomic situation.

In 2020, for example, the global spice market was valued at about US$12 billion, according to a report from advanceconsulting.nl, titled *Spice Sector in Ethiopia*. In brief, the report was highlighting the business opportunity in the sector, and the expectation that it would continue to rise as high as approximately US$15 billion by 2025. Of note: exceptional growth in "Garlic, Ginger, Turmeric, Cumin, Cinnamon, Pepper, and other similar spices" is expected, according to the report. But Grenada, the reputed "Isle of Spice," has no existing plans to capitalize on this opportunity. Even a share of this global spice market would be worth billions to Grenada, bigger than its entire GDP! So the resources and opportunities are there, but the mindset is not. Grenada's leaders do not even have the technology or an enterprise-led high-growth strategy on its mind. So how could they even think about national wealth creation? In 2022, the idea that an island known for its spice resources has no idea how to capitalize on and monetize those resources is disheartening—but it is indicative of the inherent mindset, growth, and prosperity problem that the region faces.

A 2021 research report titled "Warning Signs Flashing…the Future of the Caribbean Agriculture Industry" by Douglas Blackwell Inc. highlights that "the demand for food, particularly personalized clean healthy food, is growing exponentially." The report also finds that technology is allowing many more players into the agricultural space, regardless of climate, through the leveraging of technology such as greenhouse growing systems. This is the booming AgTech sector, which is pumping out hundreds of billions of dollars of value annually around the world. For example, the Netherlands and Israel do not have the advantaged environments—particularly Israel, a tiny desert nation. But they have still managed to excel at agriculture-based food production, regardless of not having those natural advantages of climate and land that the Caribbean islands enjoy.

The report goes on to say that the Netherlands has been able to build a world-class agri-food sector, and despite being 1/185th the size of Australia, it generates 810 times more export earnings per hectare and nearly three times more agri-food export earnings. For both countries, all of this has been made possible through the intense application and utilization of technology, particularly inside greenhouse-growing applications. So you can make all the excuses you want about the legacy of colonialism; you cannot say anything about Israel, for it has only existed since 1948. Israel continues to succeed because it plans and rigorously commits to the type of existence its people want. The Israelis are realists, with a real-world strategy for getting things done! They adhere to that strategy with resolve and cleverness in navigating their way through the realities of the universe. The Caribbean, on the other hand, has nothing planned or anything to which it can commit; it continues to waste time talking and squandering its natural resources and competitive advantages. Change cannot happen unless you change your mindset first! And all things are possible from any individual, any country, and any region in the world, regardless of the environment.

Honesty and adherence to the laws of nature is the only path to success in an economic conflict-driven world. Build toward a culture of sophistication, intelligence, and high performance, with self-interest and value creation driving the pursuit of wealth, power, and influence, in the real world. The central problem we are looking at here is how Black populations of the Caribbean and its diaspora can break out from the bottom rungs of the global economy...how not to continue to fall for incoherent and ineffective ideas with no basis in reality...and how to stop succumbing to reactionary, emotionally driven solutions, often romanticized and not based on the reality of how the world works. The feel-good things are easy, but the reality is hard; nevertheless, we only exist in reality, and that can never be evaded.

We never go to the root of the problem, which is our thinking; we simply talk around it *ad nauseam*. We are simply creating a highly distracting cultural identity of always aiming low and being led by fear. We are always doing "Black" events to be seen and heard—but in reality, it is simply lamenting the misery of our existence, it breathes mediocrity, time-wasting, and avoidance of what actually must be done.

After George Floyd, we saw the phenomenon of the rise of Black non-profit organizations, instead of investing in entrepreneurship. It is simply more avoidance and distraction. Black people never do what needs to be done. Investing is how wealth is created, and from wealth, political power flows. Instead, we chicken out and bask in fragility, creating charitable ecosystems instead of entrepreneurial ones. In what universe have non-profits ever created profit?

Furthermore, these things hamper Black entrepreneurs in the real world from getting capital from the mainstream, because mainstream investors see all of this complaining, and they begin to believe that Black entrepreneurs cannot cut it in the real world. No one wants to invest in fragility.

In the end, we must be willing to tell the truth about ourselves, this is the first step to progress. We must understand that without risk, there can never be a reward, and you must have your skin in the game; otherwise, you are merely another distractive talker. Every successful race of people, every group, society, or country in history—had to invest in themselves to establish themselves; to create wealth and power to thrive in the universe. If you are not prepared to do that, then step off and stop talking. Please, enough is enough!

What would the Extraterrestrial think of us?

RELIGION SOOTHES the soul while robbing it of spiritual power. Over the journey from *Homo erectus* to *Homo sapiens*, human religions became the basis of all societies, developing first from supernatural explanations to religious doctrines later. From hunter-gatherer tribes to sedentary ones, all societies were built on rituals and adherence to some kind of "higher power." As time went on and Homo sapiens filled out the universe, rituals increasingly became the underlying force of societies and their culture. As more sedentary societies emerged, the need to create order, security, and group identity became more fortified in society. So supernatural explanations and traditions became more convenient as useful tools to govern societies. Tribal leaders and high priests gained more authority and legitimacy because they provided good storytelling explanations. This was the evolutionary progress of doctrinal religion. Religious structures emerged—buildings, temples, mosques, and churches, all becoming universal and laying the foundation for religious institutions to gain credibility and authority in societies. Laws were formed under religious institutions that used fear and morality to underpin it all.

Religious doctrines were written by the elites, and of course, they would write those rules in their own favour. In the end, religion became the basis for societies, and status and hierarchical leadership and authority structures formed and became the norm. Divine powers: the nobility, kings, lords, the Pope, the Catholic Church, and the elites, developed a self-serving system that *they* claimed was ordained by God. Religion became a useful tool for the control and manipulation of the masses. Leaders and Kings used their divine moral authority to wield power how they liked.

THERE IS NO REAL starting point to identify the emergence of WSC, but let us use the emergence of the Crusades as that point. They began during the reign of Pope Urban II (Latin: Urbanus II; c. 1035 – 29 July 1099) otherwise known as Odo of Châtillon or Otho de Lagery, who was the head of the Catholic Church and ruler of the Papal States from 12 March 1088 to his death. He is best known for initiating the Crusades. The Crusades were based on power and had nothing to do with anything legitimate or moral; they was simply about seeking power. The Pope had the power and authority to command "through God," and so he did. The Pope said that the Crusades' purpose was to free the Holy City of Jerusalem from the "infidels" and ensure access for the "pilgrims." In short, the Pope solidified the power of the Catholic Church by waging war and genocide. Power, corruption, brutality, ego, hubris, and lies—that is what the Crusades were about. These Crusades lasted for centuries, using murder and thievery as a route to riches and power. Thus began a Christian tradition of waging war in the name of God.

Each Crusade made up its own self-serving and false justifications but finding and extracting riches—gold, silver, precious stones, land, property, etc.—was always the real motive for the Crusades; it was all about profit, wealth, power, and privilege. The facts show that the Crusades used "Christianity-religion" as the primary motivator and justifier in seeking power and cultural supremacy. This power-hungry religion and belief in white superiority stems in large part from Christianity and the Crusades. From the First Crusade, in which the Crusaders massacred Muslims until "it was said, the streets ran red with blood" to the Battle of Nicopolis in 1396, during the "'last'" Crusade, in which an army of French and Hungarian knights was massacred—the Christian religion was the driving force behind it all.

527

THE LEGACY OF THE CRUSADES led to the emergence of military and religious orders. Knights had the job of protecting pilgrims as they travelled and enriched themselves along the way. The Crusades were very expensive and required increased taxation to fund them, so wars needed more innovative means of financing. Therefore, individual donors, merchants, and bankers developed to fund wars.

Europeans began to romanticize "Crusaders" and portray their soldiers and Knights as Christian heroes and noble warriors—recall the hymn "Onward, Christian Soldiers"—essentially using religion to justify war and genocide. The Crusades became important, viewed as heroes, blessed by God—superior in all ways as Christian warriors and defenders of the superior religion and race of people. These notions of superiority over the many centuries emboldened and hardened the European superiority mindset. This created a bold thirst for conquest: imperialism, slavery, and colonialism were all derived from a belief that whites had a divine right to dominate others.

THE IDEOLOGY OF RELIGION allows leaders to use religion to create belief systems that favour them, establishing hierarchical rule by an elite class using their "God-given-right" to rule others. WSC took away power from ordinary people and placed it entirely in the hands of a privileged few.

With that task accomplished, wealth-creation ecosystems were able to emerge unchallenged through the creation of the aristocracy. Suffering through Christianity became the culture for the masses while great wealth was reserved for the aristocrats. The acceptance of privilege, status, and rank for one group of people based on birth became the norm in a society underpinned by WSC ideology. The many rituals of birth, death, marriage, crime, and punishment all craftily evoked God for self-justification. Therefore, "religious ideology was the precursor to institutionalized religion, which buttressed the [king's] authority" (Guns, Germs, and Steel, p. 266). Christianity legitimized an elite class of people and maintained the privilege of that class, enabling it to rule intergenerationally. In simple terms, restrictive hierarchical structures were reinforced and legitimized by religious ideology.

We are now in the 21ˢᵗ century, and in the digital era, we are no longer basking in the darkness. Nevertheless, the stubborn big lie of WSC persists and unless we stop believing in it, it will continue to dominate us. With all the information and enlightenment that is available today, ignorance still is the choice of many. You are the one who chooses to exist in the comfort of delusion. You are the one who chooses to live with the avoidance of truth. You choose to be a victim; you choose suffering and weakness—it is always up to you.

Never be led by fear and rigid ideology; it merely prevents you from thinking and acting in your own best interests, unable to live a true and fulfilling life. The truth is liberating precisely because its is true, and it does set you free—to live the life you want and not the life others tell you to live. Truth is your free will, and individualism allows you to live free.

The human condition requires emotional support, satisfaction, and comfort, but good living requires intellect. So letting emotion override all else and adhering to ideology and Bible stories is counterproductive to living a successful life. Be guided by bottom-up common-sense thinking, not top-down religious doctrines created by others to dominate you. Individualism is the key to happiness because you are doing what YOU want to do! Also, you need not have an answer for everything in order to live in this world. We do not need a biblical storybook to tell right from wrong; we are capable enough as humans to decipher morality for ourselves. Spirituality, then, supports the human spirit in many aspects of our lives, with self-worth, courage, passion, creativity, and with the forging of purpose. Religion or spirituality? Conformity or individualism? Prosperity or poverty? Suffering or happiness? it is up to you in the end.

WITHOUT STRONG ROOTS, no tree can withstand the elements, and it will not be able to blossom. The elegance and beauty of a tree grows from the inside out. As with a tree, those internal forces of your human spirit must begin with having strong spiritual roots. Knowing yourself, being honest with yourself, and seeking truth instead of Bible stories to fortify your life is how internal happiness happens—which then blooms beautifully. Black people must wake up from religious slumber if they want to ever bloom in this world. Unfortunately, the constant stifling of our internal engineering—of our spirituality, free will, and individualism—traps us in the abyss, never creating opportunities for ourselves to build a great civilization. Religion is intrinsic to the basis of conflict in the world, to war, hate, and poverty; so why would we cling to something so destructive? The journey toward quantitative thinking, individualism and enlightenment must take place urgently for Caribbean peoples to take part in the prosperity of the 21st century.

History tells us that the Age of Enlightenment that took place 300 years ago (1685 – 1815), also known as the Age of Reason, was an intellectual and cultural movement that emphasized reason over superstition, science over blind faith. So white people determined how the universe works a long time ago and have been playing the Christianity-based suffering card for hundreds of years against others in order to benefit themselves. Black people have not yet deciphered the game of life; we are held suspended in the darkness of emotion and religion, not transitioning in any meaningful way to

530

intellectualism and science as the basis of our existence. Wealth and power are necessary in this world, so a 21st-century renaissance in thinking is desperately required; without it, our people and society will not survive.

In the darkness, you shall stay. For those who choose not to step into the light, ignorance and suffering become the identity of those not embracing knowledge.

Religion was designed to make you serve the interests of others; that is why it requires obedience. But spirituality serves your personal development needs—your free will. Religion has nothing to do with virtue and everything to do with control and restriction. Religion is dogmatic; it fears the bright light of truth, of science, and it calls for a devotion to ignorance. But spirituality builds resilience, because it focuses on what is true in the universe, and it harnesses your internal energy towards what you want to achieve. Religion creates problems, because its doctrines are based on ideology, which is based on fantasy; it can never square the circle of nature. Therefore, it only exists in a constant state of controlled hallucination, convincing people of the existence of things that are not real.

And so, reality is the only true thing, and if you go against reality, you are going against nature. Individuals who live in consciousness become aware of their surroundings and are better able to navigate their environment to their benefit. Individuality gives you logic and strength, the foundation for better mental well-being, and confidence in the pursuit of your path. The individuality of your free will and spirituality builds resilience, anti-fragility, and self-confidence. You are self-assured by your internal forces of the mind, logic, and intellect, and your primal instincts of self-preservation are sharpened and enhanced by your precise understanding of nature. Afflictions of anxiety, stress, and general negativity can no longer exist in this positive zone; one becomes fully aligned with nature. And it is there that you are a powerful! When you have purpose and cause, when you exist in the positive zone, it is difficult for anxiety and negativity to penetrate your purpose. With adherence to logic and intellect, reason over faith, and intelligent decision-making, you become stronger. Your internal forces, your spirituality, becomes your superpower in life—an unstoppable force in nature.

The most prudent thing that Black Caribbean people can do now is to enter the 21st century fully. This begins by extricating ourselves from the religious culture that has dominated our belief systems for far too long now. We must stop embracing the counterintuitive nature of suffering. Suffering is not the natural state of our human existence; it is simply a fiction imposed on you by those looking to control you. Seeking personal gain and prosperity, and mastering self-preservation, is what is natural and what leads to happiness.

Do what is in your interest first before you consider the interests of others. Identify and be aware of your adversaries, those in your world whose interests do not align with yours. Most importantly, be conscious of WSC, for that is truly the root of all your unnecessary suffering and misery. Find sustenance through your spiritual energy. Your body has electricity, which is real in nature; so use it to energize your mind and to take actions to develop a winning mindset. Whether you believe in "God" or simply a higher power does not matter. The only thing that matters is your adherence to reality and how you effectively utilize your internal forces and spirituality within the confines of nature.

IT IS HIGH TIME FOR US TO STOP BEING GULLIBLE. Religion has nothing to do with morality; heaven and hell are delusional distortions of reality for control of the human mind through fear. The construct of religion was created to be used by those who seek to profit from the labour of those who lack access to knowledge and learning. Religion is ultimately about economics; it functions as a utility for those who understand that controlling access to knowledge and the factors of production is how you acquire and control wealth. Therefore, from the slave-plantation system to the present day, the church is among the biggest factors in the suppression of intergenerational wealth creation and opportunities for Black populations. However, the brilliance of it all is that even in modern times, they have been able to do it directly through the Black mind itself. Black people have willingly allowed themselves to be held back by buying into white supremacy culture. Of course, it does not have to be that way; it is reversible if we can begin to apply intelligence as a steadfast routine of thought and behaviour in our daily lives.

My extended family on my father's side are all dark-skinned people, and my mother's family is of mixed race, all coming out of the plantation system in Grenada. (I only use skin colour here to provide context relative to the colonial era, when light skin and dark skin determined opportunity and outcomes in Caribbean cultures.) My dark-skinned paternal grandparents had always portrayed education, entrepreneurship, self-reliance, and personal responsibility as the underpinnings for success. Never wait or rely on others, they taught me; do for yourself, irrespective of the environment you are in.

Therefore, the expectations of achievement of my father's dark-skinned family were established early on through the first principles of self-preservation, which, again, is first to survive before you can thrive in the universe. Education was the strategy for my grandparents; they understood the reality of their existence and their surroundings, so they knew that being dark-skinned was a disadvantage in the world. Rather than wallow in self-pity, complaining about how unfair the world was, blaming others for their misfortune and making excuses, they got on with their children's education and advancement. In turn, their children pursued education and understood that high performance was an expectation in the Douglas family, that there was no room for the self-inflicted wound of victimhood. Education and knowledge acquisition became the basis for the pursuit of a better life. This foundation has contributed greatly to family culture and identity, perseverance and performance, intergenerationally.

My grandparents were also "religious" people; they were pioneers in the formation of the Seventh-Day Adventist Church in Grenada. However, like their enslaved ancestors before them, they were also wise about the utility of religion, using its spiritual components but steering clear of its dogma—white supremacy slant. For example, they used the Sabbath as a time of rest and reflection, regeneration—the body and mind needed downtime, rejuvenation and remotivation to take on the challenges ahead. So they "read the bible" from the inside out for their own inner engineering, strength, and guidance. It was not an external process from the "top-down" based on worshipping any construct of a "God" or "White-Jesus," nor for the sake of adherence to societal expectations—*for show*. The "church" was a utility, utilized effectively, for routine and discipline to get the best out of their families existence in the universe. Friday and Saturday Worship was used as a resource to build emotional strength, resilience, discipline, steadiness, antifragility, and the navigation of the rough waters in life.

The **intellectually** understood that the Sabbath day was made for their benefit (see Mark 2:27). The purpose of the Sabbath is to give us a certain day of the week on which to direct our thoughts and actions toward bolstering one's internal resilience and mental well-being.

Therefore, whether my grandparents knew it or not, they never bought the farm of WSC. Rather, they took what they needed from the concept of religion, namely spirituality and purpose, to support their interests and agenda. I remember both my grandparents fondly—my grandfather, calm and wise, and my grandmother, smiling and always greeting me with a big hug. They always made me feel special and beloved, and in my short period of time with them I can still remember, in photographic frame like quality, my interactions and conversations with them. I felt special, like the most important grandchild of them all, I mattered! This is what they embedded in my subconscious mind, and I stored that and bring it to consciousness when needed. This essentially made me *antifragile*. I was fortified by love and steely determination, so how could the universe ever hurt me?

It was mine for the taking. I might have been born on a tiny island in the Caribbean, but when I came to Canada at six years old, I was already ready for the world. The main message here is that we must understand nature and reality, intellectually! The principles of self-preservation are central to growth, and spirituality, not religion, is the most effective driver of life.

Today, all of these so-called programs to try to help Blacks, to help us succeed and find purpose are all well and good—but from where I stand, everything begins with self. Artificial methods do not have a history of any meaningful success. My grandparents were able to make use of the essence of religion, but applying intelligence in support of their dreams for their children. This was the most important achievement of their lives; it was their legacy—and it will be my most important achievement as well, if I can be as strong and as wise as my grandparents.

In the end, understanding the universe does not require any special type of education, intellectual capacity, or anything else. It simply requires a willingness to keep an open mind and live in consciousness, using reason and common sense to harness intellectual capacity. We must understand the metaphysical world and where power originates. Free your mind from the trickery of ideology and seek real information and knowledge, not stories. Free your mind and the rest will follow. Nevertheless, as Sigmund Freud once said:

"People do not really want freedom, because freedom involves responsibility, and most people are frightened of responsibility."

Freedom is a choice you make—and it is the right choice, if you want to amount to anything in life.

Achieving success and happiness requires hard work; it is never a given, nor is it never owed to you. Decide what you want and work hard and intelligently to get it. Accepting mediocrity and suffering instead of prosperity and happiness is a decision you will need to make at some point in your life.

My grandparents demonstrated that intellectual capacity and the strength and determination of the human spirit are fundamental to laying a foundation for intergenerational opportunity. In the end, they used the idea of religion but the utility of spirituality!

CHAPTER 23

The Required Disruption Culture

For any kind of socioeconomic and political change to take place, a catalyst is usually required, and some form of disruption must occur. It begins with the disruption of one's own mind. Disruption first begins in the mind by questioning the current situation and identifying the opportunities and desire for change. For Black Caribbean populations, the important thing is the here and now; we have spent enough time dwelling on our past trauma. It is time to focus on the present. We are not participating in the global economy and creating wealth through entrepreneurship, and without that, there can be no prosperity. We must disrupt the status quo and make changes to ourselves for ourselves.

Why is the Caribbean in such a perennial state of subpar performance relative to the global economy? Why do we always allow others to lead and claim all of the wealth while we remain poor and even become poorer? Why do we continually accept being at the bottom rungs of the socioeconomic ladder? Why the servitude and inferiority mentality? Why do we continue to live in fear, refusing to take entrepreneurial risks, and why do we never support our own people's ventures, like other cultures do? Why do we not live in consciousness and think strategically about agendas that include investment for transformation, wealth, power, and intergenerational opportunities? If we are not first willing to disrupt ourselves, we stand no chance of achieving prosperity.

Change requires disruption! Change is a bottom-up process that can only come from within—not from hot-air academics saying nothing in the "development" discourse. The pursuit of a *Caribbean*

Renaissance in thinking must stem from several core characteristics that can help with disruption. The first is that the Caribbean people must come to terms with their overwhelming subconscious existence, and their subconscious attachment to the big lie of white supremacy and Black inferiority, tied to Christianity. Unless we make a conscious effort to understand the nature of things, the framing and objectives of white supremacy culture, it will be difficult for us to make our mark effectively and have any influence and power in the world. Unless we first disrupting our mindset, we will not be able to take on our competitors with disruptive entrepreneurship.

Confronting those very hard truths is essential, and those truths will set you free. Truth must always correspond to facts. It is never about what you feel; identify and ignore fanciful storytelling and focus on the supportive data; that is where the truth lies. We can no longer subsist on the arbitrary tradition, superstition, fear, that underpin religion. We must become more sophisticated, and we must take a hard turn towards intellectual decision-making, logic, and common sense. Find the courage and self-control to act strategically and aggressively. The trendy emotional "woke" culture works against us, because in the "woke" mindset, we are not making decisions based on facts and the laws of nature; we make them based on emotion, which is not helpful in a power-driven world. System 1 (S1) is never the right system through which to make major long-term impactful decisions; it usually leads to failure. This dereliction and abandonment of critical thinking have caused the deterioration of our intellectual capacity, making us susceptible to fantastic stories instead of facts and logic.

Secondly, we must establish robust independent thinking based on science and not on the white supremacy culture. This fear-based thinking only leaves us in a state of fragility. So shed the victim complex. If you dwell on the past trauma of slavery and colonialism, racism, etc., or on the idea that you are owed reparations, then your thinking is faulty. No one owes you anything, and no one is coming to save you! The universe is characterized by competition and conflict; that is life, and we must deal with it. Black Caribbean people and the region's diaspora are losing—wasting time simply talking and talking, relying on the government and other actors to create wealth for them. This is the height of fragility! We cannot afford to continue hiding behind non-profit endeavours instead of seeking out and investing in Black entrepreneurs in technology, where true equity and wealth are created.

Constantly seeking out charity-based development based on academic theories instead of entrepreneurship is cowardly and futile. How do you expect to better yourself economically without wealth? Appealing to hearts and minds has never worked and never will; that is not how the real world works. Power is what works, and if you do not have it, you will never understand its *power*.

As I write, what is taking place with the invasion of Ukraine and with the treatment of Black students is a testament to the reality of power. Black people are seen as lacking power, and so we are treated with no respect and lack value and influence in the world. So we need to stop with the outrage and shock when we see Africans being mistreated and kicked off of trains while fleeing the war in Ukraine. Once again, the world is about the value you carve out and how to use that value as power and influence to get what you need in the universe. If you have no power, you will have no influence and you will be treated accordingly; that is the nature of things!

By contrast, consider the power of Israel, which sent its own planes to evacuate its students and other citizens from Ukraine during the invasion. And when Russian Foreign Minister, Sergey Lavrov, made a ridiculous remark about Nazism, Vladimir Putin was forced to apologize to Israel. A tiny Middle Eastern desert state wields so much power in the universe because it has created economic value for itself—**and political power flows from economic power, period!** This is how the real world works; understand it or suffer from it.

So we return to the question of mindset and the need for self-disruption: thinking long-term and building through the core first principles of growth. The key is to understand the systemic environment, the hierarchical structures within which you operate. If you do not play a meaningful role in that universe, then you are irrelevant to it. You do not matter, and nobody cares; other countries consider you a charity case. To be taken seriously, you must act seriously and make meaningful gains. Perception is reality; if we do not even perceive ourselves as serious players in the world then how can we expect others to do so?

The third point to underscore is *renaissance thinking*, which includes conscious and coherent thought and leadership, and a real commitment to disruption with a long-term benefit-seeking approach. Let us be honest: today's Caribbean political leadership is a clown show. Worse yet, we are allowing politicians to run our economy and make investment decisions by putting their self-interest ahead of the national interest. So what do we expect? Stale, incompetent rethread politicians and bureaucrats, greedy and corrupt, falling for anything and everything, selling out their people and desperately scrounging for scraps from white society's table—how can the investment world take the region seriously with this type of behaviour? So when countries like China come knocking, these leaders cannot help themselves.

THE DISRUPTIVE MINDSET brings enormous clarity of purpose, logic, and energy to the task of understanding how the world works and how to change things and create value for oneself. When members of any given society seek to be disruptive, change becomes an unstoppable force. So then, if an entire society decides to disrupt itself and change its collective minds, change becomes inevitable. It is important to grasp that the natural world never

540

changes, ever! It is how people strategically behave in the world; the use of their imagination and what they do next is how one gets what one wants. Major changes in thinking and beliefs that have endured for centuries have been able to change in many other societies over time, so why cannot we?

Successful change requires a "why" and a strategy as to how you are going to get it done. You cannot build upon wishful thinking. You must do the quantitative work to find the benefits of change and do the math to see how you can benefit from that change economically. Self-determination can only occur if you are consciously willing to express your individualism over your own dominion. Change is a bottom-up process; have you ever seen a house built from the roof down? Then why do we continue to go against logic and basic common sense, being suckers for top-down academic and development nonsense? The only things to which we must adhere to are the laws of nature and stay keenly focused on what is true and what is not true in the universe. All life grows from the bottom-up; top-down approaches go against nature, and I have NEVER seen anyone succeed while going against nature.

Climate and Change

An examination of the history of civilization over the last 12,000 years tells us that a stable climate is essential for any civilization to develop and sustain itself. So environmental factors have always played a role in the rise and fall of civilizations. The shift to farmable agricultural lands from inhospitable climates contributed to the sustainability of various human civilizations. Natural hazards like drought, floods, severe weather patterns, hurricanes, and tsunamis threaten sedentary existences. Drought has contributed to the fall of civilizations repeatedly, such as the Mayan civilization and even the mighty Mongol Empire, which thrived on the steppes of Eurasia between 1206 and 1368. During that time, the Mongol Empire expanded to cover most of Eurasia thanks to its innovation, advancing technology, commerce, governance, and of course, massive hordes of nomadic warriors. The steppes formed a belt of grassland that extended some 5,000 miles (8,000 km) from Hungary in the west through Ukraine and Central Asia to Manchuria in the east. Change in that climate significantly contributed to the fall of the Mongol Empire, the largest land empire in history. Therefore, nature remains the most powerful force in the universe, and you cannot get around dealing with nature for your human survival; our ability to thrive is dependent on the natural environment.

The general research on declining civilizations suggests that it takes civilizations about 200 years or so to decline fully, from an environmental perspective. This gradual effect keeps people complacent, and not motivated to act with urgency in the present. Our inability to look beyond the horizon and the inherent short-sightedness of not thinking in the long term can become fatal to populations. For the Caribbean especially, it will lead to certain extinction. So the risk to our species of a changing climate is real and growing! The Caribbean's geography, — a chain of small islands compared to countries with large landmasses in North America and Eurasia—means that advancing and unchecked climate change can put these small island territories underwater sooner than most people realize.

Going forward, SIS of the Caribbean will be among the first to experience dramatic destruction if their leaders do not begin to engage in long-term thinking. SIS will begin to sink into the Caribbean Sea, and there will also likely be a period of severe weather patterns even before that, making the region virtually uninhabitable. Therefore, a scenario in which Caribbean people begin to become climate change refugees, even as soon as mere years from now, is a scientifically discernible reality. It is a simple matter of climate math.

The world is warming, and the greenhouse effect, whereby heat from the sun becomes trapped in Earth's atmosphere, is essentially what causes climate change. This development is great for growing plants, but it is not so beneficial to human beings. So as climate change heats up the planet, it will claim land as well; and along with the increased uninhabitability of the territory, abandonment and forced migration will become inevitable. "Caribbean climate change refugees" will be a term in history one day.

Forced migration due to climate change will create a new atmosphere for conflict among and discrimination against Black Caribbean people. We know the story: the West does not want more migrants or refugees, so we are going to face a major humanitarian crisis in the future. So as climate change persists, many in the Caribbean might eventually have to emigrate to North America or elsewhere. This is a blueprint for conflict, discrimination, and despair. "It is especially alarming, then, that the world is entering into an unprecedented period of human migration, in large part due to climate change" (pg. 76, Walter, F. Barbara, *How Civil Wars Start*). The World Bank predicts that by 2050, over 140 million "climate migrants" will be fleeing around the world, so you can rest assured that the SIS of the Caribbean will be part of that.

The reality facing the Caribbean today is that eventually, climate change will lead to a significant number of natural disasters, and living in these tiny territories will be more than problematic. If Caribbean nations do not begin to prepare, their citizens will be forced to migrate around the world and be subjected to the pain and suffering of discrimination and outright rejection. Closed borders! Refugee camps! Western governments will begin to craft immigration policies specifically for Caribbean migration, turning them back at airports. Similar things happened during World War II, when shiploads of European Jews fleeing Nazi persecution were turned back, even from nations like Canada. Unimaginable, you say? Well, it is not imagination; it is reality, for history repeats itself—particularly when you are not paying attention. A more recent example is the case of migrant/refugees' crisis happening over the last decade and intensifying in the last few years or so, taking place in Europe.

Where we see people from Africa and the Middle East migrating to Europe and being frequently turned away, many tragic stories of humans drowning at sea. And the ones fortunate enough to make it, only to face discrimination by resurgent populist/white nationalists political parties across Europe, that seem to increasingly becoming main stream. Therefore, the extinction of the *Caribbean species* is a future reality, dictated by science—and if we do not deal with it in the present by getting our collective economic act together, we are simply sowing the seeds of a future demise.

THE CARIBBEAN AND the South Pacific islands will suffer the most! Based on the science, both are at the greatest risk of territorial extinction due to climate change. Large landmasses like Canada, however, will not be sinking into the ocean anytime soon. On my last visit to my place of birth, Grenada, while walking along Grand Anse beach, it was clear that this wonderful sandy beach had lost probably 25 feet or more over the past 40 years or so. And a friend's hotel on that beach will get water coming into the beach suites when heavy sea surges/storms come. Under an accelerating climate change scenario, however, SIS like Grenada could end up underwater in less than a hundred years.

The sea-level rise and extreme weather events will cause intensifying erosion, and worsened storm surges will threaten communities; critical infrastructure will be at risk and livelihoods will be destroyed. Georgetown, Guyana, for example, is listed as #8 on the list of cities around the world that could be underwater as soon as 2030, according to a report from timeout.com titled ***Cities that Could be Underwater by 2030***. The report also stated that some 90%

of Guyana's population lives on the coast; therefore, the country will need substantial sea wall bolstering if "Georgetown's central areas are to avoid massive damage."

Some highlighted points from the report:

- "Studies have shown that climate change could make storms more intense, particularly in the Caribbean and the western Pacific."
- "Current rates of sea-level rise are expected to continue for at least 100 years, so scientists project that coastlines will continue to be bombarded for generations to come. And it likely will not be just small, uninhabited islands that face an existential threat."
- "Scientists say the islands that disappeared in Hawaii, Japan and the Arctic are warnings of what could happen too much larger islands—and even continental coastlines around the world."

An NBC News report: ***Three Islands Disappeared—Past Year—Climate Change to Blame;*** shows the link between climate change and sea-level rise is well understood in science. Burning fossil fuels emits carbon dioxide, a greenhouse gas that traps heat in the atmosphere. As global surface temperatures increase, the planet's glaciers and ice sheets melt, raising sea levels.

- "On many islands—even ones that are not low-lying—the majority of critical infrastructure is right at the shoreline, whether it is ports, airports, primary roads, power plants or water treatment plants." "Most of these things are very close to the coast."

- Extreme weather's "knockout blow": "In a changing climate, particularly one where the sea level is rising, I think intense storms of that kind will be a bigger knockout blow."

This is the stark reality for the future of the Caribbean, and putting our collective heads in the warm sand will not make it go away. So what are we going to do about it? The science speaks loudly and clearly; are we going to continue ignoring it? Are we going to default to a dependency culture again and hope that others will come and save us? I hope we are not merely going to *pray* about it. Are we going to continue accepting money from China to "help" with climate projects, only to become trapped in the Chinese debt trap? Are you prepared to see the Chinese flag flown across the Caribbean one day? Are you prepared to see Chinese naval ships dock and remain in Caribbean ports one day soon? If you choose to not pay attention to the lessons of history, you are bound to repeat them. History always has winners and losers.

Accordingly, Georgetown, Guyana must build sophisticated sea walls to hold off the rising waters, and to fortify critical industry and infrastructure near the coasts, the low-lying vulnerable levels in the town. Building sea walls and sophisticated engineering requires money—a great deal of it. Materials, technology, and engineering will not be cheap, so without a high-performing and profitable export-oriented economy, vulnerable territories will not be able to raise the capital required to pay for the work. It would be wishful thinking, if not downright delusional, to believe or to depend on others coming to help you. We must "build the wall" ourselves because Mexico is certainly not going to pay for it.

There may be a need to redesign entire low-lying cities based on innovative and creative urban planning models; settlements may need to be relocated. We will need to prepare for the destruction of farmlands, so food security will become a critical issue. Therefore, increasingly, technology will become the most important consideration for our survival in the future. Greenhouse-growing systems technology will have to replace traditional farming given how critical food security and export-led growth are to the future viability of the region.

The fact is, everything will have to change if the Caribbean territory and populations want to exist 100 years from now. This will require cash in order to ensure survival. So driving towards a high value-added export-driven economy today is the only way to create enough equity to amass the necessary cash to ensure survival. We must also eschew our past focus on tourism and embrace the natural competitive advantage given to us by geography, and leverage agriculture and a zero-emissions-based export economy. That is where the cash is.

Ultimately, we must remain aware of the awesome power of nature; it might render even our best innovation and engineering solutions useless if sea levels rise above those walls. But we cannot afford to do nothing. Therefore, if island territories like the Caribbean and the South Pacific will become uninhabitable and eventually be submerged under the sea, then we must begin planning now to ensure that we have thriving economies that are able to generate the necessary wealth and put money in the pockets of our citizens. So if that day comes, and populations must emigrate, they can at least do so with wealth and dignity. The fact is that your immigration status will be much better if you are coming to another country with value and cash with which to establish yourself there.

According to the research organization "Global Americans," research foundation; approximately 70% of Caribbean populations live in coastal areas. Therefore, as climate inaction persists and sea levels continue to rise, these major urban areas will become flooded, wreaking havoc on SIS infrastructure and, of course, affecting entire populations. Santo Domingo will be the second-most-affected city in Latin America by rising global sea levels, according to Global Americans. Salt-water erosion, and coastal flooding, and will be one of the five cities most affected at a global scale. If that is the case, then can you imagine what will happen to tiny Caribbean islands? Tourism cannot exist without beaches, and science says that these are highly likely scenarios in the future.

OTHER COUNTRIES in the world will be welcoming to people who can add value to their economies, so again, your economic value potential may determine your survival outcomes. Countries simply want the most educated and skilled, and those with the financial resources to add value to their economies' GDPs not burden it. They too have their self-preservation needs. With wealth and skills, you will be welcomed; without them, you will not. The historical experiences of other Black and Brown people coming as refugees have not been good, to say the least; so, a potential scenario for Caribbean immigration in the case of climate disaster must be one where Blacks are welcomed for their resources. Other than that, the results will not be pleasant. So the only thing that you can do now is not procrastinate or stand frozen in fear like a deer caught in the headlights—you will get run over! Therefore, our survival depends on *self-disruption*. If we do not take a long-term risk mitigation view, we will end up as sitting ducks, taking our future as a viable species out of our hands.

There is an undeniable and desperate need to move the Caribbean psyche to one of reliance on information and objective truths and away from passivity and inaction. Applying *applied intelligence* to create the future must happen for us to survive. The only path forward is an authentic bottom-up growth strategy governed by the laws of nature. Civilizations must adapt to new environments and new challenges to survive and thrive in the world; this will never change, so we either do it or not. It cannot get any simpler than that.

Crisis creates opportunity, so the climate crisis is also an opportunity to reimagine society and to be creative, innovative, and entrepreneurial—the sophistication of self-preservation at its best. The climate crisis represents a generational and transcendent opportunity to disrupt our subpar existence and build toward a high-performance economy. The *applied intelligence* methodology and the use of data science, artificial intelligence, and machine learning applications can help the Caribbean people with fact-based discovery and industrial engineering, to uncover those purposeful opportunities that can create future value for our societies. The history of humanity tells us that those civilizations that have thrived and that have continued to do so in the modern era have been the ones that have been able to adapt effectively to a changing world.

Technological and economic applications must be applied to find lasting solutions. Entrepreneurship executed in the capitalist framework is how societal problems have always been solved. Entrepreneurs/enterprises have always solved the most pressing challenges that societies have faced. We need the urgency of the entrepreneurship culture to lead development and intelligent government policymaking to facilitate entrepreneurial and export-led growth. We need effective policymaking that can facilitate thriving capital markets throughout the region, fostering growth and letting global investors know that the region is serious. Our future is now. We need to craft a risk-taking environment and toss out the dependency culture. Such a mindset has led great civilizations to prosperity throughout history, so there is no reason why it cannot be done if we put our collective minds to it.

CHAPTER 24

The Way Forward

To find the optimal way forward, we must first return to first principles, therefore, the illustration below is meant to be a helpful thinking remainder, a guide along the way, as you think your way forward—always being the *Scientist.*

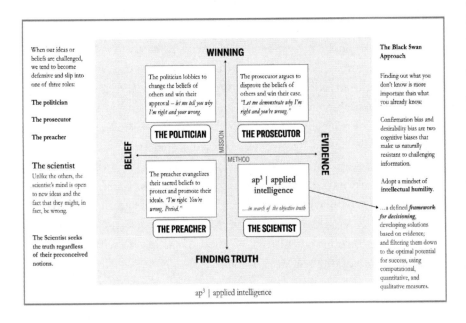

ap³ | applied intelligence

Here are some real and coherent ideas that must be pursued to move towards the advancement of a wealth and power-creating culture.

- *Firstly, solutions require gathering expertise,* as well as capable leadership in multiple areas: scientists, specialized policymakers, business leaders, entrepreneurs, philanthropists, social activists, and informed and motivated populations. There must be a combined purpose and cause.
- *Today, climate solutions are everywhere,* but most lack focused application in the pursuit of a real and sustainable solution for the Caribbean economy. Most critical climate solutions have been top-town and initiated by "development" agencies, not the essential bottom-up economic growth and evolution initiated by regional entrepreneurs. There is also a lack of supportive investment policies to drive local economies forward—a lack of capable and courageous policy leadership towards the 21st-century new globalized economy.
- *Solutions must be boldly defined* and approached based on technology and innovation to spur things along. Bold, courageous, and transformative thinking and actions and a tremendous sense of urgency are needed!
- *Real self-generated strategic action plans* must be devised, drawing from all the accessible knowledge fully available in the universe. Success can only come from within and must be firmly entrenched in the global capitalist system. There is no alternative means through which to achieve prosperity and happiness; only through entrepreneurship, enterprise, and profit can we reap wealth, power, and privilege.
- *The strategic objective* must be executed with speed and scale through *applied intelligence*. Leave emotion and intuition at the door and focus on **engineering your future!**

The following areas below must be among the core building blocks toward an optimal **zero-emissions economy**. Specific areas of research and innovation within those identified areas must be intensified and aligned with the following identified areas:

- **Agriculture & Technology AgTech** – this above all, must be the **#1** pursuit for Caribbean sustainable prosperity. As explained throughout this book, agriculture and the environment are the region's most optimal competitive advantages. If we cannot feed and nourish ourselves, how can we generate energy and build a prosperous society? So we must build our survival through food and nutritional security, which can only be accomplished by building a high-value-added, low-cost, high-profit, 21st century, export-driven economy!

  Secondly, we must transform food production from traditional farming, which is inefficient and unprofitable, susceptible to climate and the elements, to the efficiency and much-enhanced profitability of greenhouse technology-driven farming. Here, too, our geography becomes our competitive operational advantage for us; sun and wind create a *free energy resource* that will make our agricultural products highly competitive internationally. Renewable technology augments those natural energy sources and allows for leadership in zero-emissions business operations. It simply makes no sense to pay for the expensive dirty fuel oil that works to destroy our environment, when all it takes is some investment, innovation and determination to cleanly electrify small island states, ensuring our physical survival and building a foundation for a sustainable green growth economy.

- **Electric Transportation** – vehicles are significant emitters of fossil fuel emissions. So common sense tells us that switching from gasoline fuel transportation engines to electric ones is practical and logical. There is absolutely no reason why we cannot make that transition relatively quickly. The rest of the world is moving aggressively toward Electric Vehicles (EVs), so what are we waiting for? National incentives and policies specific to EVs must be put into place now!! Tax credits and rebates from the government must be funded by global climate action funds and agencies. Policies and incentives can change consumer behaviour, but no gas bill is incentive enough.

- **Activities** will spur more entrepreneurial activity, which will drive disruption, change, and a new economy. If Caribbean policymakers can get together seriously and craft a new bold policy that dictates that *by the end of the decade, all cars imported into the region must be EVs,* things will change in a hurry. You either adapt and change or be left behind. This will also drive massive business activity in infrastructure investment, funded by foreign entities, including software development. In reality, partnerships with major EV makers for charging stations is only the beginning, the big auto makers will make what-ever investment necessary to build global market share.

- **Decentralized Electricity/Zero-emissions Economy** – the reduction of CO^2 emissions to reduce the greenhouse effect is a real step towards ensuring the survival of the Caribbean's physical territory a mere 50 to 100 years from now. Secondly, if you no longer have a utility bill, that money stays in your pocket and eventually goes back into the local economy. Policies must be in place for new building construction (both commercial and residential), renovations, retrofits, and upgrades to a **zero-emissions economy standard**. This will spur new entrepreneurship, services, technology applications, software development, and economic activity that we cannot even imagine in the present.

Policies must be goal-oriented and clear. Efficiency goals and government audits to monitor the achievement of those goals must be enforced on buildings; incentives must be put in place for those physical changes to be completed effectively. We must use global capital markets and create financially profitable investments to create a green investment market, for **capital is what drives markets and economies.**

Without a doubt, intelligent policy-making will be essential to bring a future zero-emissions economy into being, so Caribbean governments must get their collective act together and strengthen institutions to work efficiently in the interest of the *people's economy.* Government must facilitate and offer legitimate incentives for foreign investment into local R&D—in the renewable energy and AgTech spaces, for starters. Local universities and colleges in the region must also get involved in securing the future! The University of the West Indies, St. George's University, and T.A. Marryshow Community College for AgTech; must participate in R&D for profitable enterprise development—research that focuses on advancing the new economy. Focused R&D will lead to breakthrough discovery technologies, creating efficiencies and profitability throughout the broader economies of the region.

This requires significant equity funding for start-ups, M&A, and transitioning incumbent companies and industries to the platform economy. We need serious strategies driven by *applied intelligence* to develop attractive capital markets. If clear and effective investment strategies with quantifiable return scenarios are effectively devised, the investments will come!

For example, PIMCO, the world's largest fixed-income investor, has an ESG (Environmental, Social, and Governance) investing initiative that involves promoting Sustainable Bond Investing to help lead the global recovery. From PIMCO's strategy titled *Key Takaways from ESG Investing:*

The bonds that serve as investments and sources of capital, and the human bonds that endure across communities, between nations, and among industries and investors. These are the bonds from which the world is building a more sustainable future

The COVID-19 pandemic has accelerated 21st-century technology-driven transformation. As more equitable societies build a more equitable global economy and community, the more people who can participate in the global economy, the more the global economy can grow—and the more the Caribbean can participate up the value chain, the wealthier it will become.

Profit helps with self-preservation, so seek profit. Make it a moral choice if you feel the need to do so; but whatever the case, go after it, for it is a matter of survival. Again, the "father of capitalism," Adam Smith, had it right: ***self-interest inherently involves a common interest.***

PIMCO believes that there is enough global entrepreneurial brainpower out there to put money behind it; so Caribbean leadership and entrepreneurship must create a strategy to go out and "get the bag," so to speak. The transformation to a zero-emissions economy via sustainable bond investing is happening now, and asset managers are seeking out real and scalable opportunities around the world, particularly in infrastructure projects in emerging markets. So what is stopping us? As discussed, climate change presents a big opportunity for Caribbean growth if we can play our cards right; it provides us with the opportunity to build a great transformative civilization. A zero-emissions economy of epic proportions can be achieved in the 21st century for Caribbean people of African descent; if they think quantitatively and act through *applied intelligence*, the future can be bright!

AFTER ALL IS SAID AND DONE, we had better make sure that there has been a lot more done than said. Our future prosperity and authentic happiness depend on executing the first principles of self-preservation. Every civilization that has ever thrived has had to find investment to fuel its growth. Even the smartest people, the best knowledge, and brightest ideas in the world will not make the world turn without **cash!** Entrepreneurs change the world, so we need more entrepreneurs in the region, supported by foreign capital. There is no other way.

Steve Jobs once said: *"The misfits, the rebels, the trouble-makers...the ones who see things differently...They push the human race forward, and while some may see them as the crazy ones, we see genius, because the ones who are crazy enough to think they can change the world, are the ones who do."*

Focusing on entrepreneurship-led growth pushes the necessary disruption levers, breaking the legacy of dependency culture and timidity. We need to make a quantum leap forward and play to win; the world waits for no one. A new dimension of thinking through *applied intelligence* is needed. We cannot make it with the same thinking that created the problem in the first place. There is no time for the weak-minded; we need lions, hunters, and cultivators. We need to execute with speed and precision; time is against us, because the rest of the world is moving rapidly ahead of us.

The book ***Speed & Scale: An Action Plan for solving Our Climate Crisis Now*** by author and billionaire venture capitalist John Doerr points out that, by the author's calculation, reaching net zero globally will require as much as US$1.7 trillion each year—and we will need to go full throttle for twenty years or more. Doerr lists 5 classes of funding, from a climate change mitigation opportunity perspective, that must be achieved for success, and into which the Caribbean region must find an entry in order to participate and benefit:

556

0.1   Financial Incentives
Increased global government subsidies and support for clean energy from $128 billion to $600 billion.

Does the Caribbean have a plan to tap into this global cash?

0.2   Government R& D
Increase public-sector funding of energy R&D from $7.8 billion to $40 billion a year in the U.S.; other countries should aim to triple current funding.

Does Caribbean leadership have a strategy to adopt the mechanisms required to raise money in global capital markets so as to fund critical build-back-better public sector investment?

0.3   Venture Capitalist
Expand investment of capital into private companies from $13.6 billion to $50 billion per year.

What is the plan here? This is an important domain to get right.

04   Project Financing
Increase zero-emissions project financing from $300 billion to $1 trillion per year.

There are vast sums of money available here, but we need real bottom-up enterprise equity projects that reflect the new economy in order to tap into it.

0.5   Philanthropic Investing

ai

Increased philanthropic dollars from \$10 billion to \$30 billion per year.

> We must treat philanthropic capital like venture capital, and put it into the hands of entrepreneurs so that it will not be squandered by the likes of politicians, government officials and academics who do not function in the real world.

Each year, billions of dollars find their way to funding all types of opportunities all over the world. Today, the core economic sectors getting most of the funding are AgTech, clean tech, and biotech, so we ought to join in those sectors. Receiving "loans" from China and thus falling right into the Chinese debt trap due to politicians' incompetence and depravity leads to long-term suffering for the Caribbean people. Other dubious programs like the Citizenship-by-Investment, which essentially is payment for a Caribbean nations passport, have led to nothing more than attracting suspicious characters and even outright criminals to our Caribbean shores. We need real mainstream growth mechanisms that aligns with the new globalized world, and produces real, impactful and measurable economic growth; not programs that produce negativity and pushes development further back.

Some more keys from Doerr, pg. 270:

- **Be ruthless in identifying the key risks up front and removing them.** Both entrepreneurs and investors must confront technological and market risks together, or the partnerships will not work. Find and exploit more opportunities through industrial engineering processes that can be applied to fact-based discoveries.
- **You are always raising money.** The message is simple: Be great fundraisers—be better than great. Recruit a range of investors in your funding rounds, especially those who can

558

write the big cheques. Also, seek out corporate partners; they are invaluable and can help enormously.

- **Performance matters**. Consumers will not pay more for a lower-quality product, even if it has eco-friendly branding. People pay for quality, and self-interest reigns supreme; so produce the best product you can at the lowest reasonable cost base.

- **Own the relationship with the customer**. The companies that do best sustain relationships with clients and listen to the clients' feedback, not their own.

- **Incumbents will fight back**. Do not expect industry incumbents (global or regional) to sit idly by; expect a difficult fight for survival. Some may roll over and die, but most will battle tooth and nail. This also provides you with an opportunity to learn and adjust in real-time and how to effectively fire back with death blows.

Nations that lead themselves through an enterprising culture have been able to survive and thrive exponentially over the long term. History has shown that entrepreneurship is the sophisticated accent of self-preservation. The use of primal instincts is first simply to survive, then to elevate to thinking quantitatively and making decisions in one's self-interest, to thrive over the long term. Therefore, supporting entrepreneurship means supporting survival. Investment in entrepreneurship pays back substantial long-term growth dividends to entire societies; it is the essence of self-manifestation of prosperity and happiness.

Now, in moving to conclude the last chapter and closing out this book, I have no brilliant endings. I only mean to say that the optimization of the *sophistication-of-self-preservation,* underwritten by ***applied intelligence*** is the most reliable driver of good and sustainable socioeconomic outcomes in the world, and that the pursuit of wealth and power is the most natural and essential. Control of the mind through conscious decision-making, with a disciplined operating framework or system, is highly necessary. However, without first having a strong understanding of the universe, it is difficult to make the most of it. Self-interest is paramount and is necessary and good for us. Suffering is **unnecessary** and should never be sought.

Constructive delusion leads to misery and failure, so stick to *reality* and avoid listening to stories. The universe takes no prisoners. You must manage your cognitive self for the outcomes you want most. You cannot change nature, but you can learn to play it in your favour. The survival and growth of our Caribbean society requires individual commitments to optimism, such an attitude spreads, and like a rising tide, optimism can lift all boats. Optimism provides you with the energy and courage you need to get through all the challenges, trials, and tribulations of life. So take a very optimistic view of technology, for it is the key to your future wealth and prosperity. Do not give in to the darkness of white supremacy, and always set a course towards the light of prosperity. The history of humanity is filled with inequality, violence, injustice, pain, and suffering, but there is also great pleasure and abundance to life; focus on that part!

Optimists think and behave differently, which is why they succeed over the constant veranda complainers. Optimists always seek knowledge to improve their circumstances; they invest in themselves, in others, and in sound, forward-looking ideas. The world keeps evolving; technology advances, more efficiencies are created, and new opportunities for wealth creation surround us each day. So be prepared when opportunity knocks! Do not wait on others; work as hard and as smart as you can to position yourself to capture opportunities and secure your family. Then contribute to your community and leave a legacy of building foundations for intergenerational wealth and opportunity. Attitude is everything, and imagination is vital. Work on your quantitative mind, on your mathematical thinking, because nature, the universe, all comes down to math in the end.

In the new economy, we are forced to think more quickly and more precisely—*applied intelligence* provides you with a vehicle to drive fast but with precision, while being accompanied by an intellectual framework to optimize decision-making. Fiercely protect your individualism and never fall for the madness of the crowd, especially the denseness of the religious herd.

Do not waste valuable time and energy with all the superfluous people you will encounter out there, because the world is filled with ignorance. Focus intelligently on what is important—on what is true rather than what is not true. Persistence beats resistance every time, so be persistent and timely. Conscious awareness is a skill that must be developed. Work on it! Things will never be perfectly smooth; the world exists in conflict and volatility, so find the opportunities within the volatility; search for the hidden symmetries. To make it through life successfully, you must first adhere to the reality of the universe, and learn to release your inner primal nature, your instincts of survival, which have served humans well for thousands of years. But at the same time, we must also learn to master those instincts with consciousness, quantitative intelligence, sophistication, and controlled aggression. Exercise you sophistication-of-self-preservation, which is entrepreneurship! We must have the view of an eagle, soaring over the terrain with brilliance while maintaining our individuality, and spirituality (IS), which "IS" our main superpower! Avoid the many distractions; our time and place in the universe are infinitesimal, so do not waste it living in delusion, or sitting on the veranda complaining. We must serve the moral obligation you have to your Caribbean community. Future generations are dependent on us. Think and act with *applied intelligence* because survival is the first rule to longevity. Our thinking can either lead us to one of two paths — to happiness or suffering; and that is what life comes down to in the end. Our journey in life then ranges between our experiences between these two paths, and all the events, trials, and tribulations we experience lead us to one or the other.

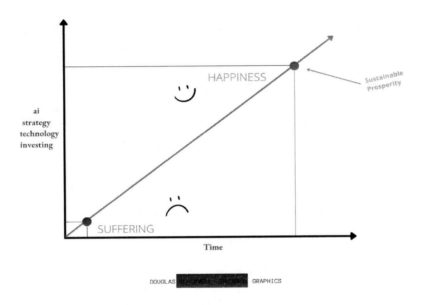

Therefore, the beginning of the end of suffering starts with the application of *applied intelligence* in our lives, an intelligent framework for decision-making, critical towards our prosperity in the 21st century.

Epilogue

There is no more time and energy to be spent on conferences and endless, time-wasting consultations. The time for action is now, and that action must be led by us. I recently watched a speech from Ghana's President, Nana Akufo-Addo, on December 18, 2022, at the U.S. Africa Leaders Summit, where he bluntly urged Africa to "stop begging" (YouTube: "Ghana's President, Nana Akufo-Addo, on December 18, 2022, at the U.S. Africa Leaders Summit.")

The President's message is easily relatable to the Caribbean's political leadership and to its people. The region has developed into a culture of economic dependency, sucking at the teat of white supremacy culture, always acquiescing to foreign entities—which becomes counterproductive, amounting to mental malnutrition. The region must wean itself off of this type of existence. "Begging" the West, as President Akufo-Addo put it, in the hope of being recognized and earning global respect is never going to work. It only serves to reinforce negative stereotypes and negative perceptions of the region as a whole.

President Akufo-Addo is right on target, and whether you want to hear it or not, "If we stop being beggars and spend African money inside the continent, Africa will not need to ask for respect from anyone; we will get the respect we deserve. If we make it prosperous as it should be, respect will follow." Similarly, where the Caribbean is concerned, the main theme of this book has been about applying intelligence to build our economic capacity. So again, everything ultimately comes down to economics, and prosperity develops and flows from the bottom up.

Caribbean states along with their diaspora must invest intelligently and relentlessly in the region—in innovation, knowledge-based ecosystems, and technology-related enterprise investments. Without investing in entrepreneurship, digital transformation, R&D, and more, there can be no positive growth outcomes. The pursuit of self-determination functions based on what we do, not based on what we say. Talk is cheap, and complaining only takes you right out of the game; so we need to get on with doing what we must to thrive in the 21st century.

When you listen to President Akufo-Addo's speech, it is easy to substitute "the Caribbean" for "Africa," because the message about development and growth applies perfectly to the Caribbean region. And with both having the experience of slavery to colonialism and neocolonialism, the message is quintessential.

His message also sends the underlying message that first and foremost, Caribbean people must understand that they are not Grenadians, Jamaicans, St. Lucians etc. We are all Caribbean people of African descent. The more we continue with the tribal mindset of being Barbadian or Trinidadian, for example, the more we simply pull ourselves apart. This mentality only weakens our resolve and builds division and fragility into our culture, rendering us unable to organize as a common community.

As a tiny territory of scattered individual states, there is no way that we can build enough capacity to be relevant in the global economy. Separated, we are too small to matter—the math is the math. Even the strongest individual lion cannot survive alone on the plains against a pack of aggressive hyenas. There is strength in numbers, especially when that strength is focused, strategic, and geared towards winning.

If we consolidate into a single market and economic union with a focus on building a knowledge-based economy as the top priority, we can be competitive enough to matter. Remaining attached to primitive tribal associations only assures and perpetuates our position at the bottom rungs of the global economy. Only through a practical economic union backed by a common currency, pegged to the U.S. dollar, underpinned by technology and intelligent ecosystems, can we ever have a chance to compete globally.

Let history be our guide in looking at the world today. Intelligent nations are forming trade alliances everywhere, whether it be small regional alliances or large ones like the NAFTA/USMCA trade agreements. The EU, of course, has existed for decades. Transnational economic agreements are forming, e.g., the Asia-Pacific Agreement for Trans-Pacific Partnership (CPTPP). The Government of Canada's trade promotion website states that "the Asia-Pacific is now the world's leading region of economic growth, offering big opportunities for trade and expansion. Canadian businesses can get ahead of the global competition by using the Comprehensive and Progressive Agreement for Trans-Pacific Partnership (CPTPP)—a free trade agreement between Canada and 10 other countries in the Asia-Pacific: Australia, Brunei, Chile, Japan, Malaysia, Mexico, New Zealand, Peru, Singapore and Vietnam." If wealthy countries like Canada are making trade arrangements with others like Asia, then they are certainly not making any deals with the Caribbean. Therefore, how do we expect to compete in a hyper-competitive and globalized world if we have no facilitated trade agreements, deals, or partnerships in place?

In the end, it is up to us to think big and construct end-to-end, fit-for-purpose solutions that we can own and integrate into our development agenda, strategically building the necessary capacity stacks in order to win. We need to be practical and combine data, technology, world-class business expertise and sophisticated deal-making to solve our complex problems. We must create our value in this universe; otherwise, we will have no value, becoming devalued by the universe and slipping quietly into the abyss of irrelevance.

All societies with an understanding of globalization and 21st-century transformation are assiduously forming global partnerships to grow their economies and to secure and sustain their nations' wealth and power. Yet the Caribbean has not even begun to think this way! There still exists no meaningful strategic framework with a workable vision for the future, only talk that disappears into nothingness as soon as it leaves the lips. The sheer level and lack of leadership and basic insight simply push the region further behind the global wealth curve, which has become totally out of sight at this point. Caribbean leaders continue to display shameful and harmful behaviour contrary to the economic security of their people, and future generations will suffer for it. In simple terms, if you are not making any gains, you are losing. Leaders continue not to connect the regional economy meaningfully to global supply chains, and larger Caribbean economies like Jamaica continue with the same old shortsighted behaviour and playbook. Jamaica's condition is characterized by reliance on IMF austerity packages, sinking deeper into the vicious Chinese debt trap; it is a country riddled with violent crime, corruption, self-destruction and squandering opportunities.

Caribbean policymakers have no strategy and no plan, while the region sits at the precipice of irrelevance, courting a negative inverse relationship to global transformation. While the rest of the world leverages the knowledge-based economy, augmenting development through intelligent technologies, Caribbean leaders continue to waste taxpayers' money with useless conferences for overpaid elites to enjoy the sound of their own voice. Never coming up with any measurable or productive results that can be applied to real peoples' lives.

Those in the diaspora who are hopefully no longer on "island time" have a moral obligation to show some leadership and help the region. As we have discussed in this book, the science of climate change tells us that the survival of the Caribbean territory is not guaranteed.

The scientific reality is that many of the islands will be uninhabitable and underwater in the future. Therefore, how will we prepare for these eventual probabilities? It will certainly require money for engineering to slow down the physical degradation of climate change; but eventually, nature will prevail. Thus, a mass migration problem for Caribbean people will ultimately materialize, and without wealth to settle our families elsewhere in the world, the future term "Caribbean Refugees" becomes closer to a future reality. We must adhere to the science and examine the history of climate change and mass migration over thousands of years. That includes the recent UN climate change projection that over 400 million displaced people around the world can be expected by 2050 due to the climate change fallout. There will certainly be a Caribbean component of those populations. We no longer enjoy the luxury of being able to bury our collective heads in the warm Caribbean beach sand, contrary to science and facts.

Let us again take inspiration from Ghana's President Akufo-Addo, who went on to note that African societies themselves bear the responsibility to make their countries attractive destinations for capital, etc. Similarly, the responsibility is ours to make the Caribbean an attractive place for people to live, and to persuade others around the world to see it as a place of opportunity. Therefore, we must change our mindset and envision a Caribbean opposite to the overriding common narrative in which it is currently mired. We must abandon the belief that we must leave the region for a better life abroad; we must flip the script and see a future sophisticated Caribbean, where high-skilled people from around the world want to come to invest, work, and make lives for themselves. We must see and promote the region as the ultimate triple threat: a great knowledge-based economy with ample opportunities and an extraordinary standard of living. So if we change our mindset, our perspectives will change, and we will begin to see the world and our place in it very differently. Our frequency in the universe will reach others, and perceptions about the region will change naturally. If we begin to think as winners, we will ultimately become winners, as long as we understand clearly that winning requires hard and smart work, and that only our minds can set our boundaries.

Our goal must be to become the most highly educated and skilled workforce on the planet. Our young people's education must be immediately transformed to align with the future of work, supported by data science and artificial intelligence in augmenting knowledge utility. Education must be relevant to the times and be accessible and updated in real time. Speed and precision are vital.

The impact of a sophisticated and successful Caribbean will shine brightly on the image of the region and its diaspora, because nothing succeeds like success. Success will increase trade activity; more good deals will be made, and more capital will be raised for investment. So we must stop the veranda complaining about inequality and fairness; have not we noticed that it falls on deaf ears? The universe neither knows nor cares about us or our misfortune or oppression. Get over it. We are not special to the universe—no form of matter is—and we exist for only a minuscule period, a nanosecond even, compared to the span of world history. "Our lives are so brief, compared with the slow unwinding of history," said Alexander Solzhenitsyn. *The Gulag Archipelago*, Part 5, Chapter 1. We must help ourselves first and foremost; that is the first principle of self-preservation, whereby you must first survive before you can thrive. No one is coming to save us; this is fundamental in nature, and it is about time for us to recognize that nature is the only place in which we exist. There is no alternative utopia, no heaven or hell; there is only nature and us. We are mere carbon in the end.

Part of the rationale for applied intelligence is to renew enthusiasm and spirit for a new thinking methodology, to produce an ambitious, profitable, and powerful region. We must change the Caribbean narrative from the characterization of always being behind, being late, operating on "island time." It is time to change that old narrative and characterization, and become known as being ahead of the times. The diaspora must step up and help to make the Caribbean a place for business investment and not merely tourism, since tourism cannot drive a middle-class economy. It must center on technology and innovation, high-growth sectors like AgTech, Fintech, Biotech, and the zero-emissions economy. The Caribbean diaspora must become partners in a shared vision and work with the region to build it into a reality. We want capital flowing from north to south to invest in transformative technology infrastructure and enterprise opportunities, keeping the wealth in the region to be compounded and expanded intergenerationally. That is how the wealthy countries did it; there is no other way to create wealth for nations, regardless of the purposefully self-serving misdirection narrative the past colonizers continue to spew. It is time to think for ourselves!

The second half of the 20th century saw Caribbean nations achieve independence, but until now, they have not been able to follow up with any acceptable level of sustained prosperity. The first half of the 21st century must see us ascend to a technologically advanced, wealthy, and powerful regional economic bloc. We cannot afford to let this 21st-century opportunity pass us by! If so, more than a century of acute poverty and suffering will be our self-created outcome, a self-inflicted wound. This must be the Caribbean Century, and we must get it right through the practical application of applied intelligence!

Respect is not something that is given; respect is earned, and if we want it, we must go out and earn it. "If we work at it, if we stop being beggars," then the Caribbean people will not need to ask for respect from anyone. Rather, what we do will speak loudly and powerfully enough for all to see and hear. The influence will automatically come, and respect and dignity will be earned and thus well deserved.

In the final analysis, the matter is simple: If we want global investors to take us seriously, then we first must take ourselves seriously, with a bold and dynamic strategy leading the way followed by intelligent actions. We must be self-starters and begin racking up some modest victories. Winning creates confidence and things start moving in your favour. Enough with the *ad nauseam* talk shops; we know what we need to do, and it is high time that we simply do it! If you are hesitant, then get out of the way; we do not need timidity, fragility, or any weak links on the ascending climb. We need strength, determination, and perseverance. We have run out of excuses for our lack of performance. Let us change that, design our future, and write our own story; control the narrative and let us find the courage and political will to lead ourselves to power and prosperity in the 21st century!

applied intelligence

Credits

Not in any order.

Stoic Wisdom: Ancient Lessons for Modern Resilience, Nancy Sherman

Infinite Powers: How Calculus Reveals the Secrets of the Universe, Steven Strogatz

Sapiens: A Brief History of Humankind, Yuval Noah Hatari

How Europe Underdeveloped Africa, Walter Rodney

Starry Messenger: Cosmic Perspective on Civilization, Neil deGrasse Tyson

Living With Co-occurring Addiction and Mental Health Disorders, Mark McGovern, Ph.D

The Nature of Economics, Jane Jacobs

The Wealth of Nations, Adam Smith

god is not Great: How Religion Poisons Everything, Christopher Hitchens

The Anti-Politics Machine: "Development," Depoliticization, and Bureaucratic Power in Lesotho, James Ferguson

Leading Change, John P. Kotter

Speed & Scale: An Action Plan for Solving Our Climate Crisis Now, John Doerr

Woke Racism: How A New Religion Has Betrayed Black America, John McWhorter

Fear Of A Black Universe: An Outsider's Guide To The Future Of Physics; Stephen Alexander

Why Nations Fail: The Origins Of Power, Prosperity, and Poverty, Daron Acemoglu, James A. Robinson

Range: Why Generalists Triumph In A Specialized World, David Epstein

Noise: A Flaw in Human Judgment, Daniel Kahneman

Think Fast and Slow, Daniel Kahneman

Team of Rivals: The Political Genius of Abraham Lincoln, Doris Kearns Goodwin

Thus Spoke Zarathustra, Friedrich Nietzsche

The Art of Thinking Clearly, Rolf Dobelli

The Black Swan: The Impact of the Highly Improbable, Nassim Nicholas Taleb

Skin In The Game: Hidden Asymmetries in Daily Life, Nassim Nicholas Taleb

The Swerve: How the World Became Modern, Stephen Greenblatt

21 Lessons for the 21st Century, Yuval Noah Harari

Guns, Germs, and Steel: The Fates of Human Societies, Jared Diamond

applied intelligence

The Horde: How The Mongols Changed The Modern World, Marie Favereau

Prisoners of Geography, Tim Marshall

Primal Leadership: Realizing The Power of Emotional Intelligence, Daniel Goleman

Superhubs: How The Financial Elite & Their Networks Rule Our World, Sandra Navidi

How Civil Wars Start, Barbara F. Walter

The Lemonade Life: How To Fuel Success, Create Happiness, and Conquer Anything, Zack Friedman

Trailblazer: The Power of Business As the Greatest Platform For Change, Marc Benioff

Inner Engineering: A Yogi's Guide to Joy, Sadhguru

Atomic Habits, James Clear

Blue Ocean Strategy: How to Create Uncontested Market Space and Make the Competition Irrelevant, W. Chan and Renee Mauborgne

Notes

Prologue 1

1. "Marcus Aurelius quotes," writer Steven Gambardella, PhD, Medium.com.

2. Cassie Kozyrkov, the Chief Decision Scientist at Google, *Fooled by statistical significance: do not let poets lie to you,* points out in her article how statistics can fool you.

3. ADAM SMITH'S WORK, *The Wealth of Nations*, published in 1776, remains the most comprehensive treatment of the nature of economics and political economy ever written.

4. *Guns, Germs, and Steel,* by author Jared Diamond, pg. 36, 37

5. Toni Morrison, Portland State University, 1975, speeches and TV interviews

6. Sapiens, Yuval Noah Harari, 2014

7. Quote from Dr Debra Thompson, Prof. McGill University, and I've had several discussions with her on race topics.

Prologue 2

8. *Beyond Good and Evil (1886)*, Nietzsche argues that the prevailing morality law is based on   an artificial creation and not natural laws; the European Christian moral system is harmful to humanity.

9. Generally relied on Nietzsche's general philosophy to underpin the arguments about Christianity.

10. From the Book, *The Swerve*, Greenblatt, 2011; here relied on his work about the Greek philosopher Lucretius, over 2000 years ago explained the universe to us: *"An infinite number of atoms move randomly through space and time, colliding, intertwining, and forming complex formations and*

structures known as matter."

11. *The Swerve: How The World Became Modern* by Harvard Professor Stephen Greenblatt, heavily relied on his entire book in this section to deal with Christianity in framing my arguments.

12. Chris Bryant, The Guardian, his writings, and discussions on British aristocracy.

13. Reading the classic philosophers—the ancient Stoics, *Stoic Wisdom*, Nancy Sherman, the
book is a review of all the ancient stoic's writings.

14. Franz Fanon, *The Wretched of the Earth*, 1961, 1963 in English, explains the Black human
Condition.

Chapter 1: The Nature of Economics

15. Thing Theory of development, Jacobs pg, 44, *The Nature of Economics*.

16. The Tetlock study, conducted by psychologist Philip Tetlock, is about the business of political and economic "experts" wreaking havoc in people's lives.

17. Talib, The Black Swan pg. 151, discussion on why experts and particularly economists are often wrong.

18. *Range: Why Generalists Triumph In A Specialized World*, author David Epstein demonstrates that the most efficient path to success in any domain is often away from reliance on specialists.

19. Dr Lisa Feldman Barret has a theory about how emotions happen, the *Theory of Constructed Emotions. How* past experiences control our present emotional reactions.

20. *Thinking, Fast & Slow,* Kahneman, 2011, talks about two systems of thought; the first is System 1 (SI) which is quick and spontaneous, but often inaccurate, and System 2 (S2) is slow and methodical and looks for facts when engaging memory.

21. Calculus has been relied on here in putting together the applied intelligence concepts.

22. *INFINITE POWERS, How CALCULUS Reveals the Secrets of the Universe,* Professor Steven Strogatz, 2020.

Chapter 2: Beyond Theories
23. Nassim Nicholas TALEB, *The Black Swan,* special interests, and self-serving institutions.

24. Isaac Newton and Galileo relied on their math and science to explain the universe.

25. The Mongol Empire and how they ushered in the modern world through its expansion and dominance of Eurasia between about 1206 to 1368. *The Horde,* pg. 14, 39., Marie Favereau 2021.

26. Historian Yuval Noah Harari points out, *Homo Sapiens* are built as they are, ruled by their nature, and at the core, you cannot change *human nature.* Sapiens, 2014.

27. *SUPERHUBS, Sandra Navidi,* 2017*,* our ignorance about the world will work against us, showing that the world is run by the most powerful, those elite few in global finance.

28. Navidi: *technologization, financialization and globalization.*

Chapter 3: applied intelligence

29. Douglas Blackwell Inc. Research, 2022, douglasblackwell.net, *Data Science, progression towards AI and Machine Learning*

30. *Nature Always Prevails – The Curious Case of Long-Term Capital Management (LTCM);* Perry C. Douglas, Medium.com

31. Dr Stephon Alexander, *Fear of a Black Universe,* 2021, processes need to be underpinned with logic and coherence and be "empirically warrantable."

32. applied intelligence ap3 equation, proprietary equation to Douglas Blackwell Inc.
33. *The Six Steps Approach to Data Intelligence,* Douglas Blackwell Inc., Research, 2021.

Chapter 4: The Value of applied intelligence

34. The Flow of applied intelligence, illustration @ Douglas Blackwell, 2022.

35. Angellist Venture research, charts.

36. *"SEC Concept Release,"* the report called for broad-based early-stage venture capital indexing.

37. *Blue Ocean Strategy,* Chan and Mauborgne, 2005. BOS is based on a study of 150 strategic moves (spanning more than 100 years and 30 industries), BOS development models show that lasting success comes not from battling competitors but from creating "blue oceans"– untapped new market spaces ripe for growth.

38. FIVE ROARING WAVES, Douglas Blackwell Strategy.

Chapter 5: Individuals and Societies

39. *Antifragility* was first introduced to me via Stephen Dubner, author of Freakonomics, and my many readings of Nicholas Nassim Talib's books and talks about *antifragility.*

40. Dr Timnit Gebru, researcher and co-founder of Black-in-AI, discussion on "ethical AI."

41. General readings of philosopher Immanuel Kant, on "judgment and inference."

Chapter 6: The Decade of Transition

42. 5th Industrial Revolution (5IR) terminology can be traced coming out of the World Economic Forum over the last 5yrs, Davos, Switzerland, by founder, German Engineer, and economist Klaus

Schwab. Meaning: The Fifth Industrial Revolution, or 5IR, encompasses the notion of harmonious
human–machine collaborations, with a specific focus on the well-being of the multiple stakeholders (i.e., society, companies, employees, customers).

43. *Maximum Utility* is an artificial construct from mathematics called a *utility*; *applied intelligence* | ap3 uses it as a utility for a numerical value used to represent the amount of benefit that is achieved
through the implementation of an idea.

44. *Visual of how algorithm decision-making works,* image @ Douglas Blackwell Images.

Chapter 7: Quantitative Thinking & the Racism Disorder
45. *Discourse on Method,* 1637, René Descartes philosopher and Mathematician, reliance on his work to frame my quantitative thinking work.

46. In addressing the self-inflicted **DISORDER OF RACISM**, relied on the book *Living with Co-occurring Addiction and Mental Health Disorders,* author Mark McGovern, Ph.D, to frame and
create a basis of discussion to underpin the argument.

47. Here, I rely heavily on the Nobel Prize, Pulitzer Prize, and Presidential Medal of Freedom-winning author Toni Morrison. It is her basic thought on the concept of "race" that helps me expand on the idea of the "disorder of racism."

48. For data analysis, the following book was used, the fifth edition of the book *Diagnostic and*
Statistical Manual of Mental Disorders; by the American Psychiatric Association.

49. Mental Health America (MHA), *analysis of racism and mental health.*

50. *Buckingham Palace official resigns over 'unacceptable' comments to Black charity founder,* By Max Foster and Joshua Berlinger, CNN Updated 9:32 AM EST, Wed November 30, 2022.

51. Daniel Kahneman, *Thinking, Fast and Slow,* S2 over S1 is the most effective way to think.

52. HUMAN INTELLIGENCE WIT ARTIFICIAL INTELLIGENCE, illustrative example @ Douglas Blackwell Strategies.

Chapter 8: The REAL Truth Behind European Wealth Creation

53. Yuval Noah Harari, *21 Lessons for the 21st Century,* 2018, …questioning liberalism by observing that the once-dominant white Anglo-Saxon nations (i.e., Britain and the United States) are currently experiencing a period of "disillusionment" about liberal ideals.
54. "Make America Great Again" and "Brexit," white nationalist movements.

55. Criticism of Niall Ferguson, white supremacy culture, reviewing his book, *Empire: How Britain Made the Modern World.*

56. April 2021, British Prime Minister Boris Johnson said via British TV/media that systemic racism does not exist in the modern U.K.

57. Pickleball is a new sport that athletes have been investing in.

Chapter 9: Economics | Decision Making

58. Iceberg image @ Douglas Blackwell Inc.

59. Engage in well-known Freudian theories and link them to S1 thinking.

60. This chapter relies on work done by Dr Renée Richardson Gosline of MIT's Sloan School of Management, where she is the principal research scientist at the Initiative on The Digital Economy. The intersection between behavioural economics and technology and its implications for cognitive bias. Her concept of "The Outsourced Mind."

61. The Sophistication of Self-Preservation |SSP theme and concept incorporates *The Outsourced Mind* into the ap3 equation.

62. Dr Richardson Gosline has termed the phrase *Homo Techologicus,* which means that our minds are co-creating with technology.

63. The examination of Sandals 2012 deal and the aftermath, the Government of Grenada's deal-making—tax wavers etc.

64. United Nations World Tourism Organization [UNWTO], 2019

65. World Travel and Tourism Council [WTTC], 2019

66. *Caribbean Island Tourism: Pathway to Continued Colonial Servitude,* Etudes Caribbeennes, *2015* Alfred Wong summarizes the problem with tourism.

Chapter 10: Food, Money & Power

67. FY2020 stood at $1.1 billion, with 133 deals, ASEAN

68. Pitchbook. VC-backed agritech, Pitchbook Research, 2021 Annual Agtech Report.

69. "BlackNorth Initiative," ttps://blacknorth.ca.

70. *Is the biggest greenhouse in the U.S. the future of farming?* by Liz Kang (video by Dan Tham, CNN Updated 3:19 AM ET, Wed October 6, 2021),

71. REPORT (November 2020) from the Caribbean Export Development Agency about organic beauty products, aged rum, and hot pepper sauce.

72. Grace Kennedy Foods (GKF) annual report 2020, https://www.gracekennedy.com/wp-content/uploads/GKAR2020-2 3_04_2021_compressed.pdf

73. Bloomberg Intelligence, 2020, titled, "Plant-Based Foods Poised for Explosive Growth."
74. *Report; Establishing an Organic Certification System in the Caribbean*, 2004.
75. Organic Growers and Consumers Association (OGCA)

76. Research by Douglas Blackwell Inc., 2021, titled *CARICOM, agriculture and the Digital Age,* lays out how the Caribbean can best position itself in the massive global organic market and build global market share.

77. *Certified Caribbean Organic*, 2021, Douglas Blackwell Research.

Chapter 11: Understanding The Economics of Racism

78.   Kwame Nkrumah, ***Neo-Colonialism: The Last Stage of Imperialism,*** first published in 1965. Nkrumah defined the independence transition as nothing more than neo-colonialism.

79.   "Understandingslavery.com," a chronological account of how slavery, colonialism, and imperialism are inherently linked.

80.   *The first Black Slave Society…anywhere in the world,* Sir Hilary Beckles, BBC documentary.
81.   THE BARBADOS SLAVE CODE of 1661.

82.   A deep knowledge of Sir Hilary Beckles's writings, conversations etc., has been used widely in this chapter.

83.   The Latin American debt crisis of the 1980s was used to illustrate the power relationship between North and South. World Bank and IMF intervention.

84.   ISI (Industrial Substitution Industrialization) 1974 to 1985, Brazil engaged ISI as a growth strategy.

85.   The Brady Plan was then implemented in 1989; it was a debt securitization plan to secure private bank lenders.

86.   1980's Foreign Debt, the Brazilian experience; https://www.bresserpereira.org.br/index.php/economics/1980-s-foreign-debt/10253-6649

87.   Canadian International Development Agency (CIDA.) https://www.international.gc.ca/world-monde/funding-financement/funding_development_projects-financement_projets_developpement.aspx?lang=eng

88. Inter-American Development Bank (IAD,) Expression of Interest Document.

89. OECS | Organization of Eastern Caribbean States.

Chapter 12: Do Not Blame China

90. "Asian Tigers": the Four Asian Tigers are the developed East Asian economies of Hong Kong, Singapore, South Korea, and Taiwan.

91. The Chinese Belt and Road Initiative (BRI), https://www.cfr.org/backgrounder/chinas-massive-belt-and-road-initiative

92. Caribbean Investigative Journal Network (CIJN,) 2019, article titled *China's Opaque Caribbean Trail: Dreams, Deal, and Debt;* *https://www.cijn.org/chinas-opaque-caribbean-trail-dreams-deals-and-debt/*

93. VICE documentary on YouTube titled *"Undercover In Guyana: Exposing Chinese Business in South America,"* https://www.youtube.com/watch?v=sOOFSJqBYTY.

Chapter 13: The Power Transition

94. The International RenewableEnergy Agency (IRENA,) is an intergovernmental organization mandated to facilitate cooperation, advance knowledge, and promote the adoption and sustainable use of renewable energy.

95. CARICOM, https://caricom.org/.

96. *Recover Better with Sustainable Energy Guide* the UN Secretary-General for Sustainable Energy. Highlights key policies that Caribbean governments should adopt to ensure a successful energy

transition.

97. St. George's University (SGU) in Grenada https://www.sgu.edu/ is owned by a Canadian private equity investor, Atlas Partners https://www.altas.com.

98. ZEGE, Douglas Blackwell report on EV market opportunity in the Caribbean region.

Chapter 14: Caribentricity

99. The analysis supported by *Mental Slavery,* 2000, by author Barbara Fletchman Smith, provides a critical cultural psychoanalysis of the enduring and complex effects of slavery.

100. Douglas Blackwell's analysis, titled *Genesis Green Growth, G3, 2020.*
101. *Grenada Tourism: Why are we killing the goose?*, Now Grenada, 2020.

102. A New Paradigm: Locally Inclusive Hospitality (LIH;) LIH is a proprietary tourism business strategy developed by Douglas Blackwell Inc.

103. *Independent Boutique Hotel and Villa Rentals (IBHV,)* Douglas Blackwell Inc. enterprise modelling.

Chapter 15: The Fierce Change of the Digital Now

104. *"AI and the Rise of the Creative Class—the Demise of the Useless Class."*, 2020, Perry C. Douglas, Medium.com.

105. The Art of War, the ancient Chinese General Sun Tzu says: Amid crisis, there is an opportunity. 106. *21 Lessons for the 21st Century"* and *"Sapiens,"* historian Yuval Noah Harari.
107. *Content Creators (C²)*; developed by Douglas Blackwell.

108. McKinsey & Co. McKinsey Global Institute (MGI,) 2019, presented a report titled *Twenty-five years of digitization: Ten insights into how to play it right.*
109. Porter, Operational Effectiveness (OE,) Harvard Professor Michael E. Porter.

110. Blue Ocean Strategy, BOS was developed by Professors W. Chan Kim and Renée Mauborgne, INSEAD business school, Fontainebleau, France and based on a study of 150 strategic moves (spanning more than 100 years and 30 industries).

Chapter 16: Emerging Markets & Industrial Engineering

111. Pitchbook's online publication *Private Equity News and Trends*, https://pitchbook.com/news/private-equity.

112. McKinsey's 2019 *Global Private Markets Review.*

113. Investopedia, emerging markets definition; https://www.investopedia.com/terms/e/emergingmarketeconomy.asp

114. The term "industrial engineering" is defined by Douglas Blackwell's enterprise strategies and explanation illustrations @

Douglas Blackwell.

115.   ENTERPRISE   SINGAPORE,
https://www.enterprisesg.gov.sg/about-us/overview

Chapter 17: Knowledge is the New Money

116. Skill-for-value-metric, those who occupy the top of the skill ladder are essentially at the top of the economic food chain, so to speak. They become the most-sought-after, best-paid workers. image @Michael Simmons.

117. Data Watch article, Sept 30th, 2021; titled: "Japan races to hire 270,000 artificial intelligence engineers," puts the urgency of digital transformation into perspective.

118. The illustration below shows, before digitization (BD) and after digitization (AD;) Accelerated Intelligence, Michael Simmons.

Chapter 18: In Long-Time

119. 5th Industrial Revolution (5IR)—The Sequences of the five Industrial Revolutions, info derived from World Economic Forum, Illustration by Douglas Blackwell.

120. A Phenomenal Journey Towards 5IR, Illustration by Douglas Blackwell.

121. Carbon dioxide in the atmosphere over the past century due to global industrialization has led to a "global greening," please see the following publication: *Carbon Dioxide Benefits the World: See for Yourself* @ CO2Coalition.org.

122. Vertical Greenhouse Technology Farming Systems, 2022, Douglas Blackwell strategy report, titled, *Greenhouse Technology Farming Systems*.

123. AgFunder's latest Farm Tech Investment Report; ASEAN agrifood tech start-up investing; AgTech through the effective use of greenhouse technology systems, FoodTech and AgTech data reveal a mega-economic opportunity in high-value farm-based food production.

124. LONG TIME terminology, Douglas Blackwell strategies, *theories-narrative-hype-time, data, and market-time, 10x Time* illustration at @ Michael Simmons.

125. Figure 4, *Estimated Impact of Technology Platforms on Economic Productivity;* ARK Investment Management LLC, 2019.

126. Successful S-Curve of Growth and Strategic Inflection Point; illustration @ Douglas Blackwell.

Chapter 19: Success is a Mindset

127. At the beginning of this chapter, the book *Why Nations Fail* is relied on to form the basis of understanding how inequality happens.

128. Illustration @Pew Research Center's Form on Religious & Public Life, *Size of Major Religious Groups,* 2010.

129. Perry C. Douglas, *Amazing Grace*, Revisited, 2022, medium.com.

Chapter 20: You Simply Cannot Get Around It…

130. Analysis of Donald Trump on white nationals, taken from general review through media-- white supremacist racial and cultural agenda.

131. Reverend Jacqueline Lewis, Senior Pastor of the Middle Collegiate Church in New York City. Rev. Lewis has a 900-member multi-ethnic congregation; Christ was an activist, authentically Christianity.

132. *Victimhood*, Andrew Bromfield, 2022, his LinkedIn page, the mentality that many Black people harbour.

133. TEN PRACTICAL STEPS TO CHANGE, these are steps to success/winning in the real world.

Chapter 21: Purpose & Wealth

134. Research by Matthew Killingsworth of the University of California, taken from the work of Nobel Prize-winning economist Daniel Kahneman and Angus Deaton, both of Princeton University, found that happiness, as measured by people's perception of their own emotional well-being, levels off when income reaches approximately $90,000.

135. The Economist, 2021, *The grinny coefficient,* having a "prosperous" future depends on balance. Graph illustration @ Killingsworth.

136. Douglas Blackwell's report, 2022, titled *Lifestyle & Investment | "return on lifestyle"* (ROL;) highlights that our deeply ingrained beliefs about money are shifting.

Chapter 22: Talk and Ideology

137. Next Einstein Form (NEF.org,) is the largest science and innovation gathering on the African continent.

138. Storytelling about the "extraterrestrial visitor;" see article by Perry C. Douglas, The Extraterrestrial Visitor, 2022, medium.com.

139. 2021 research report titled "Warning Signs Flashing…the Future of the Caribbean Agriculture Industry" by Douglas Blackwell Inc., 2022.

Chapter 23: The Required Disruption Culture

140. The "Climate and Change" section uses fallen empires in history, to show how climate change has a lot to do with how empires fall.; The Mongol Empire, which thrived on the steppes of Eurasia between 1206 and 1368 is used as the prime example.

141. Based on science, the Caribbean region is at great risk of territorial extinction due to a warming planet/climate change: https://www.timeout.com/things-to-do/cities-that-could-be-underwater-by-2030

142. *Three Islands Disappeared in the Past Year; is Climate Change to Blame?*, https://www.nbcnews.com/mach/science/three-islands-disappeared-past-year-climate-change-blame-ncna1015316

Chapter 24: The Way Forward

143. *Always being the Scientist, illustration* @ ai -applied intelligence, Douglas Blackwell Images.

144. The list of 0.5 relied upon the book *Speed & Scale: An Action Plan for Solving Our Climate Crisis Now*, by author and billionaire venture capitalist John Doerr.

145. Happiness/Suffering illustration @ Douglas Blackwell images.

Manufactured by Amazon.ca
Acheson, AB

13831462R00324